Connected Mathematics™

UNIT	STRAND
Variables and Patterns *Introducing Algebra*	**Algebra**
Stretching and Shrinking *Similarity*	**Geometry**
Comparing and Scaling *Ratio, Proportion, and Percent*	**Number and Operations**
Accentuate the Negative *Integers*	**Number and Operations**
Moving Straight Ahead *Linear Relationships*	**Algebra**
Filling and Wrapping *Three-Dimensional Measurement*	**Measurement**
What Do you Expect? *Probability and Expected Value*	**Data Analysis and Probability**
Data Around Us *Number Sense*	**Number and Operations**

Glenda Lappan James T. Fey
William M. Fitzgerald Susan N. Friel
Elizabeth Difanis Phillips

Prentice
Hall

Glenview, Illinois
Needham, Massachusetts
Upper Saddle River, New Jersey

Connected Mathematics™ was developed at Michigan State University with the support of National Science Foundation Grant No. MDR 9150217.

This project was supported, in part, by the
National Science Foundation
Opinions expressed are those of the authors and not necessarily those of the Foundation

The Michigan State University authors and administration have agreed that all MSU royalties arising from this publication will be devoted to purposes supported by the Department of Mathematics and the MSU Mathematics Education Enrichment Fund.

ISBN 0-13-067735-3
2 3 4 5 6 7 8 9 10   05 04 03 02

The Connected Mathematics Project Staff

Project Directors

James T. Fey
University of Maryland

William M. Fitzgerald
Michigan State University

Susan N. Friel
University of North Carolina at Chapel Hill

Glenda Lappan
Michigan State University

Elizabeth Difanis Phillips
Michigan State University

Project Manager

Kathy Burgis
Michigan State University

Technical Coordinator

Judith Martus Miller
Michigan State University

Curriculum Development Consultants

David Ben-Chaim
Weizmann Institute

Alex Friedlander
Weizmann Institute

Eleanor Geiger
University of Maryland

Jane Mitchell
University of North Carolina at Chapel Hill

Anthony D. Rickard
Alma College

Collaborating Teachers/Writers

Mary K. Bouck
Portland, Michigan

Jacqueline Stewart
Okemos, Michigan

Graduate Assistants

Scott J. Baldridge
Michigan State University

Angie S. Eshelman
Michigan State University

M. Faaiz Gierdien
Michigan State University

Jane M. Keiser
Indiana University

Angela S. Krebs
Michigan State University

James M. Larson
Michigan State University

Ronald Preston
Indiana University

Tat Ming Sze
Michigan State University

Sarah Theule-Lubienski
Michigan State University

Jeffrey J. Wanko
Michigan State University

Evaluation Team

Mark Hoover
Michigan State University

Diane V. Lambdin
Indiana University

Sandra K. Wilcox
Michigan State University

Judith S. Zawojewski
National-Louis University

Teacher/Assessment Team

Kathy Booth
Waverly, Michigan

Anita Clark
Marshall, Michigan

Julie Faulkner
Traverse City, Michigan

Theodore Gardella
Bloomfield Hills, Michigan

Yvonne Grant
Portland, Michigan

Linda R. Lobue
Vista, California

Suzanne McGrath
Chula Vista, California

Nancy McIntyre
Troy, Michigan

Mary Beth Schmitt
Traverse City, Michigan

Linda Walker
Tallahassee, Florida

Software Developer

Richard Burgis
East Lansing, Michigan

Development Center Directors

Nicholas Branca
San Diego State University

Dianne Briars
Pittsburgh Public Schools

Frances R. Curcio
New York University

Perry Lanier
Michigan State University

J. Michael Shaughnessy
Portland State University

Charles Vonder Embse
Central Michigan University

Special thanks to the students and teachers at these pilot schools!

Baker Demonstration School
Evanston, Illinois

Bertha Vos Elementary School
Traverse City, Michigan

Blair Elementary School
Traverse City, Michigan

Bloomfield Hills Middle School
Bloomfield Hills, Michigan

Brownell Elementary School
Flint, Michigan

Catlin Gabel School
Portland, Oregon

Cherry Knoll Elementary School
Traverse City, Michigan

Cobb Middle School
Tallahassee, Florida

Courtade Elementary School
Traverse City, Michigan

Duke School for Children
Durham, North Carolina

DeVeaux Junior High School
Toledo, Ohio

East Junior High School
Traverse City, Michigan

Eastern Elementary School
Traverse City, Michigan

Eastlake Elementary School
Chula Vista, California

Eastwood Elementary School
Sturgis, Michigan

Elizabeth City Middle School
Elizabeth City, North Carolina

Franklinton Elementary School
Franklinton, North Carolina

Frick International Studies Academy
Pittsburgh, Pennsylvania

Gundry Elementary School
Flint, Michigan

Hawkins Elementary School
Toledo, Ohio

Hilltop Middle School
Chula Vista, California

Holmes Middle School
Flint, Michigan

Interlochen Elementary School
Traverse City, Michigan

Los Altos Elementary School
San Diego, California

Louis Armstrong Middle School
East Elmhurst, New York

McTigue Junior High School
Toledo, Ohio

National City Middle School
National City, California

Norris Elementary School
Traverse City, Michigan

Northeast Middle School
Minneapolis, Minnesota

Oak Park Elementary School
Traverse City, Michigan

Old Mission Elementary School
Traverse City, Michigan

Old Orchard Elementary School
Toledo, Ohio

Portland Middle School
Portland, Michigan

Reizenstein Middle School
Pittsburgh, Pennsylvania

Sabin Elementary School
Traverse City, Michigan

Shepherd Middle School
Shepherd, Michigan

Sturgis Middle School
Sturgis, Michigan

Terrell Lane Middle School
Louisburg, North Carolina

Tierra del Sol Middle School
Lakeside, California

Traverse Heights Elementary School
Traverse City, Michigan

University Preparatory Academy
Seattle, Washington

Washington Middle School
Vista, California

Waverly East Intermediate School
Lansing, Michigan

Waverly Middle School
Lansing, Michigan

West Junior High School
Traverse City, Michigan

Willow Hill Elementary School
Traverse City, Michigan

Variables and Patterns

Introducing Algebra

Mathematical Highlights	4
Investigation 1: Variables and Coordinate Graphs	5
1.1 Preparing for a Bicycle Tour	5
1.2 Making Graphs	7
Applications—Connections—Extensions	10
Mathematical Reflections	17
Investigation 2: Graphing Change	18
2.1 Day 1: Philadelphia to Atlantic City	18
2.2 Day 2: Atlantic City to Lewes	20
2.3 Day 3: Lewes to Chincoteague Island	22
2.4 Day 4: Chincoteague Island to Norfolk	23
2.5 Day 5: Norfolk to Williamsburg	24
Applications—Connections—Extensions	26
Mathematical Reflections	35
Investigation 3: Analyzing Graphs and Tables	36
3.1 Renting Bicycles	37
3.2 Finding Customers	38
3.3 Predicting Profit	39
3.4 Paying Bills and Counting Profits	40
Applications—Connections—Extensions	42
Mathematical Reflections	48
Investigation 4: Patterns and Rules	49
4.1 Heading Home	50
4.2 Changing Speeds	51
4.3 Calculating Costs and Profits	52
Applications—Connections—Extensions	54
Mathematical Reflections	60
Investigation 5: Using a Graphing Calculator	61
5.1 Graphing on a Calulator	61
5.2 Making Tables on a Calculator	63
Applications—Connections—Extensions	64
Mathematical Reflections	68
Looking Back and Looking Ahead: Unit Reflections	69
Glossary	71
Index	73

Stretching and Shrinking
Similarity

Mathematical Highlights   4

Investigation 1: Enlarging Figures   5
   1.1 Stretching a Figure   5
   Applications—Connections—Extensions   9
   Mathematical Reflections   13

Investigation 2: Similar Figures   14
   2.1 Drawing Wumps   15
   2.2 Nosing Around   18
   2.3 Making Wump Hats   21
   Applications—Connections—Extensions   22
   Mathematical Reflections   27

Investigation 3: Patterns of Similar Figures   28
   3.1 Identifying Similar Figures   28
   3.2 Building with Rep-tiles   29
   3.3 Subdividing to Find Rep-tiles   31
   Applications—Connections—Extensions   33
   Mathematical Reflections   40

Investigation 4: Using Similarity   41
   4.1 Using Similarity to Solve a Mystery   41
   4.2 Scaling Up   43
   4.3 Making Copies   44
   4.4 Using Map Scales   45
   Applications—Connections—Extensions   47
   Mathematical Reflections   58

Investigation 5: Similar Triangles   59
   5.1 Using Shadows to Find Heights   59
   5.2 Using Mirrors to Find Heights   61
   5.3 Using Similar Triangles to Find Distances   63
   Applications—Connections—Extensions   64
   Mathematical Reflections   74

Investigation 6: Stretching and Shrinking with a Computer   75
   6.1 Drawing Similar Figures with a Computer   75
   6.2 Stretching and Shrinking Flags   79
   Applications—Connections—Extensions   81
   Mathematical Reflections   84

The Unit Project   85

Looking Back and Looking Ahead: Unit Reflections   86

Glossary   88

Index   91

Comparing and Scaling

Ratio, Proportion, and Percent

Mathematical Highlights 4

Investigation 1: Making Comparisons 5
   1.1 Writing Ads 5
   1.2 Targeting an Audience 7
   1.3 Getting the Message Across 8
   Applications—Connections—Extensions 10
   Mathematical Reflections 15

Investigation 2: Comparing by Finding Percents 16
   2.1 Comparing Leisure Activities 17
   2.2 Comparing Your Class to the Nation 18
   Applications—Connections—Extensions 20
   Mathematical Reflections 25

Investigation 3: Comparing by Using Ratios 26
   3.1 Mixing Juice 27
   3.2 Helping the Cook 29
   3.3 Sharing Pizza 30
   Applications—Connections—Extensions 31
   Mathematical Reflections 36

Investigation 4: Comparing by Finding Rates 37
   4.1 Comparing Fuel Economy 38
   4.2 Using Unit Rates 40
   4.3 Solving Problems with Rates 42
   4.4 Buying Beads 43
   Applications—Connections—Extensions 44
   Mathematical Reflections 51

Investigation 5: Estimating Populations and Population Densities 52
   5.1 Estimating the Size of a Crowd 52
   5.2 Estimating a Deer Population 54
   5.3 Finding Population Densities 55
   5.4 Comparing the Dakotas 57
   5.5 Predicting Traffic Jams 58
   Applications—Connections—Extensions 59
   Mathematical Reflections 64

Investigation 6: Choosing Strategies 65
   6.1 Scaling Up or Down 65
   6.2 Using Rules of Thumb 67
   6.3 Selecting Delegates 68
   Applications—Connections—Extensions 73
   Mathematical Reflections 81

The Unit Project 82

Looking Back and Looking Ahead: Unit Reflections 84

Glossary 87

Index 89

Accentuate the Negative

Integers

Mathematical Highlights	4
Investigation 1: Extending the Number Line	5
1.1 Playing MathMania	6
1.2 Winning the Game	8
1.3 Measuring Temperature	9
Applications—Connections—Extensions	12
Mathematical Reflections	17
Investigation 2: Adding Integers	18
2.1 Adding on a Number Line	19
2.2 Inventing a New Model	21
Applications—Connections—Extensions	26
Mathematical Reflections	33
Investigation 3: Subtracting Integers	34
3.1 Subtracting on a Chip Board	35
3.2 Subtracting on a Number Line	40
3.3 Exploring Patterns	43
3.4 "Undoing" with Addition and Subtraction	44
Applications—Connections—Extensions	46
Mathematical Reflections	52
Investigation 4: Multiplying and Dividing Integers	53
4.1 Rising and Falling Temperatures	53
4.2 Studying Multiplication Patterns	56
4.3 Playing the Integer Product Game	57
4.4 Dividing Integers	59
Applications—Connections—Extensions	60
Mathematical Reflections	66
Investigation 5: Coordinate Grids	67
5.1 Extending the Coordinate Grid	67
5.2 Breaking Even	71
5.3 Using a Calculator to Explore Lines	72
5.4 Exploring Window Settings	73
5.5 Revisiting Jean's Problem	75
Applications—Connections—Extensions	77
Mathematical Reflections	82
Looking Back and Looking Ahead: Unit Reflections	83
Glossary	86
Index	88

Moving Straight Ahead
Linear Relationships

Mathematical Highlights 4

Investigation 1: Predicting from Patterns 5
    1.1 Conducting an Experiment 5
    Applications—Connections—Extensions 9
    Mathematical Reflections 14

Investigation 2: Walking Rates 15
    2.1 Walking to the Yogurt Shop 17
    2.2 Changing the Walking Rate 18
    2.3 Walking for Charity 19
    2.4 Walking to Win 21
    2.5 Crossing the Line 22
    Applications—Connections—Extensions 24
    Mathematical Reflections 34

Investigation 3: Exploring Lines with a Graphing Calculator 35
    3.1 Getting to the Point 36
    3.2 Graphing Lines 37
    3.3 Finding Solutions 39
    3.4 Planning a Skating Party 41
    Applications—Connections—Extensions 44
    Mathematical Reflections 52

Investigation 4: Solving Equations 53
    4.1 Paying in Installments 53
    4.2 Using the Symbolic Method 54
    4.3 Analyzing Bones 57
    Applications—Connections—Extensions 59
    Mathematical Reflections 63

Investigation 5: Exploring Slope 64
    5.1 Climbing Stairs 64
    5.2 Finding the Slope of a Line 66
    5.3 Connecting Points 68
    Applications—Connections—Extensions 70
    Mathematical Reflections 79

Investigation 6: Writing an Equation for a Line 80
    6.1 Solving Alphonso's Puzzle 80
    6.2 Converting Temperatures 81
    6.3 Solving the Mystery of the Irish Elk 82
    Applications—Connections—Extensions 84
    Mathematical Reflections 91

Looking Back and Looking Ahead: Unit Reflections 92

Glossary 95

Index 100

Filling and Wrapping
Three-Dimensional Measurement

Mathematical Highlights   4

Investigation 1: Building Boxes   5
    1.1 Making Cubic Boxes   5
    1.2 Making Rectangular Boxes   7
    1.3 Flattening a Box   8
    1.4 Testing Flat Patterns   9
    Applications—Connections—Extensions   10
    Mathematical Reflections   14

Investigation 2: Designing Packages   15
    2.1 Packaging Blocks   16
    2.2 Saving Trees   17
    Applications—Connections—Extensions   19
    Mathematical Reflections   23

Investigation 3: Finding Volumes of Boxes   24
    3.1 Filling Rectangular Boxes   24
    3.2 Burying Garbage   26
    3.3 Filling Fancy Boxes   26
    Applications—Connections—Extensions   29
    Mathematical Reflections   36

Investigation 4: Cylinders   37
    4.1 Filling a Cylinder   38
    4.2 Making a Cylinder from a Flat Pattern   39
    4.3 Designing a New Juice Container   40
    Applications—Connections—Extensions   41
    Mathematical Reflections   45

Investigation 5: Cones and Spheres   46
    5.1 Comparing Spheres and Cylinders   47
    5.2 Comparing Cones and Cylinders   49
    5.3 Melting Ice Cream   50
    Applications—Connections—Extensions   51
    Mathematical Reflections   56

Investigation 6: Scaling Boxes   57
    6.1 Building a Bigger Box   58
    6.2 Scaling Up the Compost Box   59
    6.3 Looking at Similar Prisms   60
    Applications—Connections—Extensions   61
    Mathematical Reflections   67

Investigation 7: Finding Volumes of Irregular Objects   68
    7.1 Displacing Water   68
    Applications—Connections—Extensions   70
    Mathematical Reflections   72

The Unit Project   73

Looking Back and Looking Ahead: Unit Reflections   74

Glossary   77

Index   81

What Do You Expect?

Probability and Expected Value

Mathematical Highlights   **4**

Investigation 1: Evaluating Games of Chance   **5**
    1.1 What's in the Bucket?   **5**
    1.2 Matching Colors   **6**
    1.3 Making Purple   **8**
    1.4 Making Counting Trees   **10**
    Applications—Connections—Extensions   **13**
    Mathematical Reflections   **21**

Investigation 2: Analyzing Number-Cube Games   **22**
    2.1 Playing the Addition Game   **22**
    2.2 Playing the Multiplication Game   **23**
    Applications—Connections—Extensions   **24**
    Mathematical Reflections   **31**

Investigation 3: Probability and Area   **32**
    3.1 Cracking Level 1   **32**
    3.2 Cracking Level 2   **34**
    Applications—Connections—Extensions   **36**
    Mathematical Reflections   **40**

Investigation 4: Analyzing Two-Stage Games   **41**
    4.1 Choosing Paths   **41**
    4.2 Finding the Best Arrangement   **43**
    Applications—Connections—Extensions   **45**
    Mathematical Reflections   **49**

Investigation 5: Expected Value   **50**
    5.1 Shooting the One-and-One   **50**
    5.2 Finding Expected Value   **51**
    Applications—Connections—Extensions   **53**
    Mathematical Reflections   **58**

Investigation 6: Carnival Games   **59**
    6.1 Drawing Marbles   **59**
    6.2 Choosing the Best Game   **60**
    6.3 Taking a Computer Safari   **61**
    Applications—Connections—Extensions   **64**
    Mathematical Reflections   **68**

Investigation 7: Analyzing Sequences of Outcomes   **69**
    7.1 Counting Puppies   **69**
    7.2 Guessing Answers   **70**
    Applications—Connections—Extensions   **74**
    Mathematical Reflections   **78**

The Unit Project   **79**

Looking Back and Looking Ahead: Unit Reflections   **81**

Glossary   **84**

Index   **86**

Data Around Us

Number Sense

Mathematical Highlights	4
Investigation 1: Interpreting Disaster Reports	5
1.1 Comparing Disasters	5
1.2 Aiding Hurricane Victims	7
Applications—Connections—Extensions	9
Mathematical Reflections	11
Investigation 2: Measuring Oil Spills	12
2.1 Describing an Oil Spill	12
2.2 Finding Benchmarks for Units of Measure	14
2.3 Developing a Sense of Large Numbers	16
Applications—Connections—Extensions	19
Mathematical Reflections	22
Investigation 3: Comparing Large Numbers	23
3.1 Playing Dialing Digits	24
3.2 Getting Things in Order	25
3.3 Rounding Numbers	28
3.4 Comparing Hog Populations	29
Applications—Connections—Extensions	31
Mathematical Reflections	37
Investigation 4: How Many Is a Million?	38
4.1 Thinking Big	38
4.2 Thinking Even Bigger	39
4.3 Using Scientific Notation	41
Applications—Connections—Extensions	44
Mathematical Reflections	50
Investigation 5: Every Litter Bit Hurts	51
5.1 Going Hog Wild	51
5.2 Recycling Cans	52
5.3 Going Down the Drain	53
5.4 Making Mountains out of Molehills	54
Applications—Connections—Extensions	55
Mathematical Reflections	60
Investigation 6: On an Average Day	61
6.1 Recycling Cans	61
6.2 Making Comparisons in Two Ways	62
6.3 Comparing by Using Rates	63
Applications—Connections—Extensions	64
Mathematical Reflections	69
Looking Back and Looking Ahead: Unit Reflections	70
Glossary	73
Index	74

Connected Mathematics®

Variables and Patterns

Introducing Algebra

Student Edition

Glenda Lappan
James T. Fey
William M. Fitzgerald
Susan N. Friel
Elizabeth Difanis Phillips

Prentice
Hall

Glenview, Illinois
Needham, Massachusetts
Upper Saddle River, New Jersey

Connected Mathematics® was developed at Michigan State University with the support of National Science Foundation Grant No. MDR 9150217.

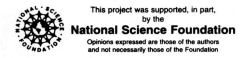

This project was supported, in part, by the
National Science Foundation
Opinions expressed are those of the authors and not necessarily those of the Foundation

The Michigan State University authors and administration have agreed that all MSU royalties arising from this publication will be devoted to purposes supported by the Department of Mathematics and the MSU Mathematics Education Enrichment Fund.

Photo Acknowledgements: 16 (Chicago) © Jean-Claude Lejeune/Stock, Boston; 16 (Melbourne) © Joe Carini/The Image Works; 18 © Rick Smolan/Stock, Boston; 22 © Fredrik Bodin/Stock, Boston; 23 © William Johnson/Stock, Boston; 24 © Larry Mulvehill/The Image Works; 32 © Duomo, Inc.; 36 © Joe McBride/Tony Stone Images; 42 © Addison Geary/Stock, Boston; 51 © E. Strenk/Superstock, Inc.; 57 © Topham/The Image Works

RAGBRAI is a registered trademark of the Des Moines Register and Tribune Co.
Turtle Math is a registered trademark of LCSI.

Contents

Mathematical Highlights   4

Investigation 1: Variables and Coordinate Graphs   5
    1.1 Preparing for a Bicycle Tour   5
    1.2 Making Graphs   7
    Applications—Connections—Extensions   10
    Mathematical Reflections   17

Investigation 2: Graphing Change   18
    2.1 Day 1: Philadelphia to Atlantic City   18
    2.2 Day 2: Atlantic City to Lewes   20
    2.3 Day 3: Lewes to Chincoteague Island   22
    2.4 Day 4: Chincoteague Island to Norfolk   23
    2.5 Day 5: Norfolk to Williamsburg   24
    Applications—Connections—Extensions   26
    Mathematical Reflections   35

Investigation 3: Analyzing Graphs and Tables   36
    3.1 Renting Bicycles   37
    3.2 Finding Customers   38
    3.3 Predicting Profit   39
    3.4 Paying Bills and Counting Profits   40
    Applications—Connections—Extensions   42
    Mathematical Reflections   48

Investigation 4: Patterns and Rules   49
    4.1 Heading Home   50
    4.2 Changing Speeds   51
    4.3 Calculating Costs and Profits   52
    Applications—Connections—Extensions   54
    Mathematical Reflections   60

Investigation 5: Using a Graphing Calculator   61
    5.1 Graphing on a Calulator   61
    5.2 Making Tables on a Calculator   63
    Applications—Connections—Extensions   64
    Mathematical Reflections   68

Looking Back and Looking Ahead: Unit Reflections   69

Glossary   71

Index   73

Variables and Patterns

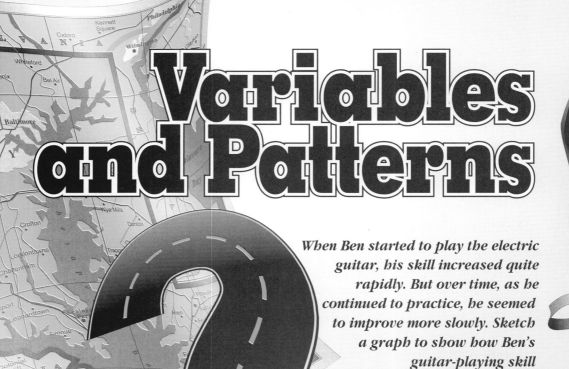

When Ben started to play the electric guitar, his skill increased quite rapidly. But over time, as he continued to practice, he seemed to improve more slowly. Sketch a graph to show how Ben's guitar-playing skill progressed over time from when he first started playing. What variables might affect the rate at which his playing improved?

List three things about yourself and the world that change. Explain how some of these changes might be related to each other. For example, your height changes as your age changes. How would you represent these changes in a table or graph?

Compare the rental fees of two companies. East Coast Trucks charges $4.25 for each mile a truck is driven. Philadelphia Truck Rental charges $200 for a week, or any part of a week, and an additional $2.00 for each mile a truck is driven. Which of these two companies offers a better rate? If you were renting a truck, what variables might influence your decision?

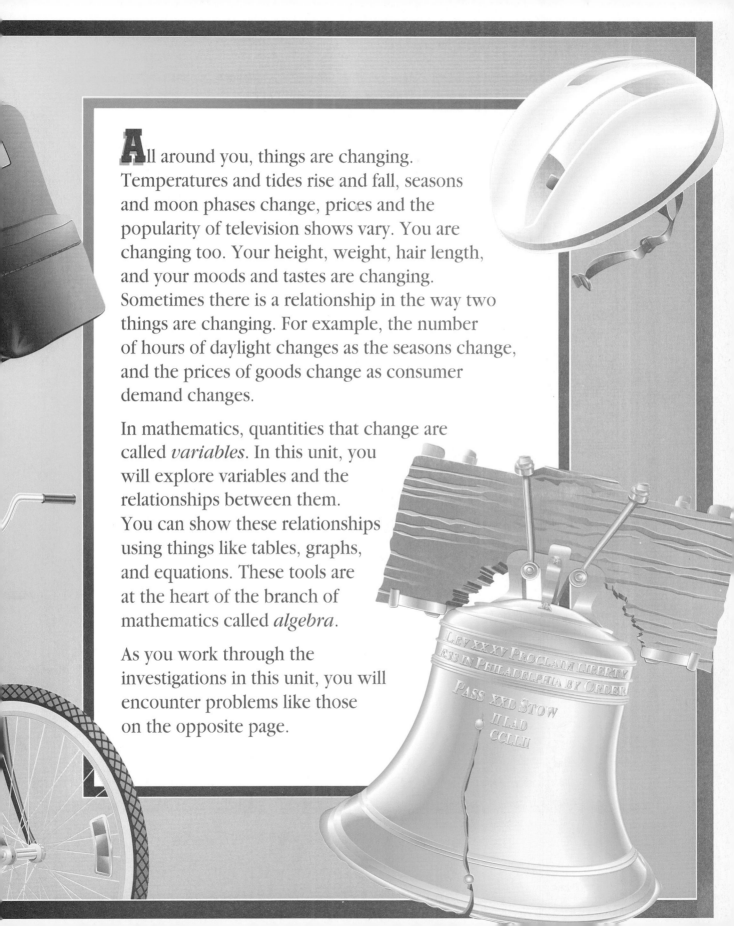

All around you, things are changing. Temperatures and tides rise and fall, seasons and moon phases change, prices and the popularity of television shows vary. You are changing too. Your height, weight, hair length, and your moods and tastes are changing. Sometimes there is a relationship in the way two things are changing. For example, the number of hours of daylight changes as the seasons change, and the prices of goods change as consumer demand changes.

In mathematics, quantities that change are called *variables*. In this unit, you will explore variables and the relationships between them. You can show these relationships using things like tables, graphs, and equations. These tools are at the heart of the branch of mathematics called *algebra*.

As you work through the investigations in this unit, you will encounter problems like those on the opposite page.

Mathematical Highlights

In *Variables and Patterns* you will explore some of the basic ideas of algebra. The unit should help you to

- Recognize problem situations in which two or more quantitative variables are related to each other;

- Find patterns that help in predicting the values of a dependent variable as values of other related independent variables change;

- Construct tables, graphs, and simple symbolic expressions that describe patterns of change in variables;

- Solve problems and make decisions about variables using information given in tables, graphs, and symbolic expressions; and

- Use a graphing calculator to make tables and graphs of relations between variables and to answer questions about those relations.

As you work on the problems of this unit, ask questions about problem situations that involve related quantities: *What are the variables in the problem? How are the variables in this problem related to each other? What patterns appear in the tables or graphs of relationships among variables? How can those patterns be used to make predictions and answer questions about the related variables?*

INVESTIGATION

Variables and Coordinate Graphs

The bicycle was invented in 1791. Today there are over 100 million bicycles in the United States. People of all ages use bicycles for transportation and sport. Many people spend their vacations taking organized bicycle tours.

Did you know?

RAGBRAI—which stands for Register's Annual Great Bicycle Ride Across Iowa—is a week-long cycling tour across the state of Iowa. It has been held every summer since 1973. Over 7000 riders dip their back bicycle wheels into the Missouri River along Iowa's western border, spend seven days biking through Iowa's countryside and towns (following a different route every year), and end the event by dipping their front bicycle wheels into the Mississippi River on the state's eastern border.

1.1 Preparing for a Bicycle Tour

The popularity of bicycle tours gave five college students—Sidney, Celia, Liz, Malcolm, and Theo—an idea for a summer business. They would operate bicycle tours for school and family groups. They chose a route from Philadelphia, Pennsylvania, to Williamsburg, Virginia, including a long stretch along the ocean beaches of New Jersey, Delaware, and Maryland. They decided to name their business Ocean and History Bike Tours.

While planning their bike tour, the five friends had to determine how far the touring group would be able to ride each day. To figure this out, they took test rides around their hometowns.

Think about this!

- How far do you think you could ride in a day?
- How do you think the speed of your ride would change during the course of the day?
- What conditions would affect the speed and distance you could ride?

To answer the questions above, you would need to take a test ride yourself. Although you can't ride your bike around the classroom, you can perform a simple experiment involving jumping jacks. This experiment should give you some idea of the patterns commonly seen in tests of endurance.

Problem 1.1

This experiment requires four people:
- a jumper (to do jumping jacks)
- a timer (to keep track of the time)
- a counter (to count jumping jacks)
- a recorder (to write down the number of jumping jacks)

As a group, decide who will do each task.

Prepare a table for recording the total number of jumping jacks after every 10 seconds, up to a total time of 2 minutes (120 seconds).

Time (seconds)	0	10	20	30	40	50	60	70	...
Total number of jumping jacks									

Here's how to do the experiment: When the timer says "go," the jumper begins doing jumping jacks. The counter counts the jumping jacks out loud. Every 10 seconds, the timer says "time" and the recorder records the total number of jumping jacks the jumper has done so far. Repeat the experiment four times so that everyone has a turn at each of the four tasks.

■ Problem 1.1 Follow-Up

Use your table of jumping jack data to answer these questions:

1. How did your jumping jack rate (the number of jumping jacks per second) change as time passed? How is this shown in your table?

2. What might this pattern suggest about how bike-riding speed would change over a day's time on the bicycle tour?

1.2 Making Graphs

In the jumping jack experiment, the number of jumping jacks and the time are variables. A **variable** is a quantity that changes or *varies*. You recorded your data for the variables in a table. Another way to display your data is in a coordinate graph. A **coordinate graph** is a way to show the relationship between two variables.

There are four steps to follow when you make a coordinate graph.

Step 1 *Select two variables.*

For example, for the experiment in Problem 1.1, the two variables are *time* and *number of jumping jacks*.

Step 2 *Select an axis to represent each variable.*

If time is one of the variables, you should usually put it on the *x*-axis (the horizontal axis). This helps you see the "story" that occurs over time as you read the graph from left to right. So, in a graph of the jumping jack data, time would go on the *x*-axis, and the number of jumping jacks would go on the *y*-axis (the vertical axis).

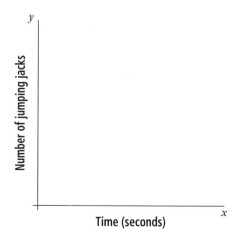

In many cases, you can determine which variable to assign to which axis by thinking about how the two variables are related. Does one variable *depend* on the other? If so, put the **dependent variable** on the *y*-axis and the **independent variable** on the *x*-axis. The number of jumping jacks depends on time. So, put number of jumping jacks (the dependent variable) on the *y*-axis and time (the independent variable) on the *x*-axis. You may have encountered the terms *dependent variable* and *independent variable* while doing experiments in your science classes.

Step 3 *Select a scale for each axis.*
For each axis, you need to determine the largest and smallest values you want to show on your graph and how you want to space the scale marks.

In the jumping jack experiment, the values for time are between 0 and 120 seconds, so in a graph of this data, you could label the *x*-axis (time) from 0 to 120. Since you collected data every 10 seconds, you could place marks at 10-second intervals.

The scale you use on the *y*-axis (number of jumping jacks) depends on the number of jumping jacks you did. For example, if you did 97 jumping jacks, you could label your scale from 0 to 100. Since it would be messy to put a mark for every jumping jack, you could put a mark for every 10 jumping jacks.

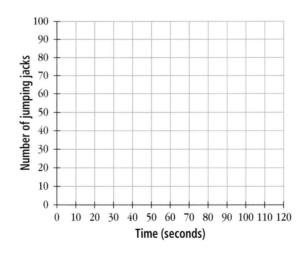

Step 4 *Plot the data points.*

For example, suppose that at 60 seconds, you had done 65 jumping jacks. To plot this information, start at 60 on the *x*-axis (time) and follow a line straight up. On the *y*-axis (number of jumping jacks), start at 65 and follow a line straight across. Make a point where the two lines intersect. This point indicates that in 60 seconds, you did 65 jumping jacks.

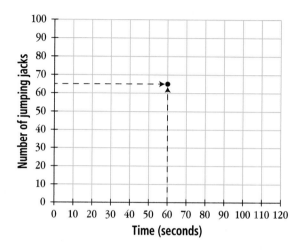

Problem 1.2

A. Make a graph of your jumping jack data.

B. What does your graph show about jumping jack rate as time passes? (Another way to say this is, What does your graph show about the *relationship* between the number of jumping jacks and time?)

■ Problem 1.2 Follow-Up

Is the relationship you found between the number of jumping jacks and time easier to see in the table or the graph? Explain your answer.

As you work on these ACE questions, use your calculator whenever you need it.

Applications

1. The convenience store across the street from Metropolis School has been keeping track of their popcorn sales. The table below shows the total number of bags sold beginning at 6:00 A.M. on a particular day.

a. Make a coordinate graph of these data. Which variable did you put on the *x*-axis? Why?

b. Describe how the number of bags of popcorn sold changed during the day. Explain why these changes may have occurred.

Time	Total bags sold
6:00 A.M.	0
7:00 A.M.	3
8:00 A.M.	15
9:00 A.M.	20
10:00 A.M.	26
11:00 A.M.	30
noon	45
1:00 P.M.	58
2:00 P.M.	58
3:00 P.M.	62
4:00 P.M.	74
5:00 P.M.	83
6:00 P.M.	88
7:00 P.M.	92

2. The graph below shows the numbers of cans of soft drink purchased each hour from a school's vending machine in one day (6 means the time from 5:00 to 6:00, 7 represents the time from 6:00 to 7:00, and so on).

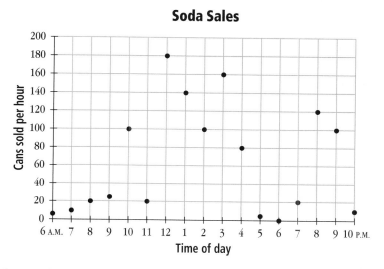

Soda Sales

a. The graph shows the relationship between two variables. What are the variables?

b. Describe how the number of cans sold changed during the day. Give an explanation for why these changes might have occured.

3. Below is a chart of the water depth in a harbor during a typical 24-hour day. The water level rises and falls with the tides.

Hours since midnight	0	1	2	3	4	5	6	7	8	9	10	11	12
Depth (meters)	10.1	10.6	11.5	13.2	14.5	15.5	16.2	15.4	14.6	12.9	11.4	10.3	10.0

Hours since midnight	13	14	15	16	17	18	19	20	21	22	23	24
Depth (meters)	10.4	11.4	13.1	14.5	15.4	16.0	15.6	14.3	13.0	11.6	10.7	10.2

a. When is the water deepest? What is the depth at that time?

b. When is the water shallowest? What is the depth at that time?

c. During what time interval does the water depth change most rapidly?

d. Make a coordinate graph of the data. Describe the overall pattern you see.

e. How did you determine what scale to use? Do you think everyone in your class used the same scale?

Connections

4. The mayor of Huntsville and her advisory board were trying to persuade a company to build a factory in the town. They told the company's owner that the population of Huntsville was growing very fast and would provide the factory with an abundant supply of skilled labor. A local environmental group protested, saying this company had a long history of air and water pollution. They tried to persuade the factory owner that the population was not increasing as fast as the mayor's group had indicated. The company hired their own investigator to research the situation. When the three parties met, each party presented a graph. The graphs are shown below and on the next page.

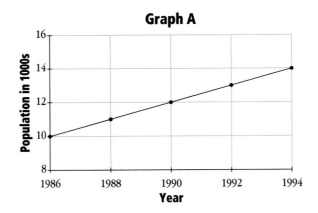

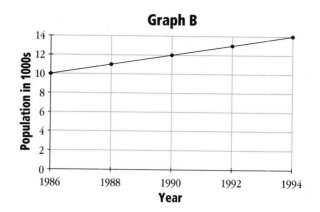

Graph B

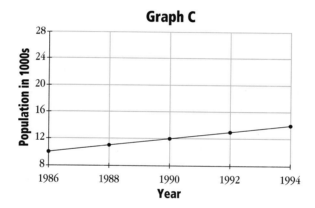

Graph C

a. Which graph do you think was presented by the mayor? The environmentalists? The company's investigator? Explain your reasoning.

b. Is it possible that all the graphs correctly represent the population growth in Huntsville? Why or why not?

c. Describe the relationship between time and population as shown in the graphs.

5. After doing the jumping jack experiment, Andrea and Ken compared their graphs. Because his points were higher, Ken said he did more jumping jacks than Andrea in the 120 seconds. Do you agree? Why or why not?

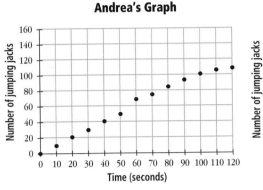

Andrea's Graph

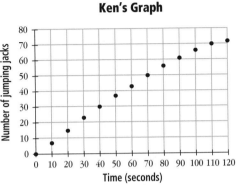

Ken's Graph

6. The operators of Ocean and History Bike Tours wanted to compare their plans with other bicycle tour companies. The bike tour they were planning would take five days, and they wondered if this might be too long or too short for people. Malcolm called 18 different companies and asked, "How many days is your most popular bike trip?" Here are the answers he received:

3, 6, 7, 5, 10, 7, 4, 2, 3, 3, 5, 14, 5, 7, 12, 4, 3, 6

a. Make a line plot of the data.

b. Find the range, median, mean, and mode of the data.

c. On the basis of this information, should Ocean and History Bike Tours change the length of the five-day trip? Explain your reasoning.

7. Which of the following graphs best represents the relationship between a person's age and height? Explain your choice. If you feel that none of the graphs shows this relationship, draw and explain your own graph.

a.

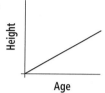

b.

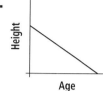

c.

d.

Extensions

8. The number of hours of daylight in a day changes throughout the year. We say that the days are "shorter" in winter and "longer" in summer. The following table shows the number of daylight hours in Chicago, Illinois, on a typical day during each month of the year (January is month 1, and so on).

Month	Daylight hours
1	10.0
2	10.2
3	11.7
4	13.1
5	14.3
6	15.0
7	14.5
8	13.8
9	12.5
10	11.0
11	10.5
12	10.0

a. Describe any relationships you see between the two variables.

b. On a grid, sketch a coordinate graph of the data. Put months on the *x*-axis and daylight hours on the *y*-axis. Do you see any patterns?

c. The seasons in the Southern Hemisphere are the opposite of the seasons in the Northern Hemisphere. When it is summer in North America, it is winter in Australia. Melbourne, Australia, is about the same distance south of the equator as Chicago is north of the equator. Sketch a graph showing the relationship you would expect to find between the month and the hours of daylight in Melbourne.

January in Chicago

January in Melbourne

d. Put the (month, daylight) values from your graph in part c into a table.

Mathematical Reflections

In this investigation, you learned about variables. You made tables and graphs to show how different variables are related. These questions will help you summarize what you have learned:

1 In this investigation, you conducted a jumping jack experiment, collected the data in a table, and made a coordinate graph of the data. Your table and graph showed the relationship between two variables. What were the two variables? How did one variable affect the other?

2 **a.** Name some things in the world around you that vary and that can be counted or measured. Name two variables that you think are related.

b. Explain how you could make a graph to show the relationship between the two related variables from part a. How would you decide which variable should be on the x-axis and which should be on the y-axis?

Think about your answers to these questions, discuss your ideas with other students and your teacher, and then write a summary of your findings in your journal.

Graphing Change

Sidney, Liz, Celia, Malcolm, and Theo found they could comfortably ride from 60 to 90 miles in one day. They used these findings, along with a map and campground information, to plan a five-day tour route. The students wondered how the route would actually work for cyclists. For example, rough winds coming off the ocean or lots of steep hills might make the trip too difficult for some riders.

The friends set off to test the proposed tour route. To make sure the trip would appeal to high school students, Sidney asked her 13-year-old brother, Tony, and her 15-year-old sister, Sarah, to come along. The five college students planned to collect data during certain parts of the trip and use their findings to write detailed reports. They could use their reports to improve their plans and to explain the trip to potential customers.

2.1 Day 1: Philadelphia to Atlantic City

The students began their bike tour near the Liberty Bell and Independence Hall in historic Philadelphia, Pennsylvania. Their goal for the first day was to reach Atlantic City, New Jersey. Sidney, Liz, Sarah, Celia, and Malcolm rode their bicycles. Theo and Tony followed along in a van with the camping gear and repair equipment. Tony recorded the distance reading on the van's trip odometer every half hour from 8:00 A.M. to 4:00 P.M. A map for the entire trip, and Tony's recordings from the first day, are given on the next page.

Time (hours)	Distance (miles)
0.0	0
0.5	9
1.0	19
1.5	26
2.0	28
2.5	38
3.0	47
3.5	47
4.0	47
4.5	54
5.0	59
5.5	67
6.0	73
6.5	78
7.0	80
7.5	86
8.0	89

Problem 2.1

Write a report summarizing the data Tony collected on day 1 of the tour. Describe the distance traveled compared to the time. Look for patterns of change in the data. Be sure to consider the following questions:

- How far did the riders travel in the day? How much time did it take them?

- During which time interval(s) did the riders make the most progress? The least progress?

- Did the riders go further during the first half or the second half of the day's ride?

■ Problem 2.1 Follow-Up

Describe any similarities between the jumping jack data you recorded in Problem 1.1 and the data Tony collected.

Day 2: Atlantic City to Lewes

On the second day of their bicycle trip, the group left Atlantic City and rode five hours south to Cape May, New Jersey. This time, Sidney and Sarah rode in the van. From Cape May, they took a ferry across the Delaware Bay to Lewes, Delaware. They camped that night in a state park along the ocean. Sarah recorded the following data about the distance traveled until they reached the ferry:

Time (hours)	Distance (miles)
0.0	0
0.5	8
1.0	15
1.5	19
2.0	25
2.5	27
3.0	34
3.5	40
4.0	40
4.5	40
5.0	45

Problem 2.2

A. Make a coordinate graph of the (time, distance) data given in the table.

B. Sidney wants to write a report describing day 2 of the tour. Using information from the table or the graph, what could she write about the day's travel? Be sure to consider the following questions:

- How far did the group travel in the day? How much time did it take them?
- During which time interval(s) did the riders make the most progress? The least progress?
- Did the riders go further in the first half or the second half of the day's ride?

C. By analyzing the table, how can you find the time intervals when the riders made the most progress? The least progress? How can you find these intervals by analyzing the graph?

D. Sidney wants to include either the table or the graph in her report. Which do you think she should include? Why?

■ Problem 2.2 Follow-Up

1. Look at the second point on your graph as you count from the left. We can describe this point with the *coordinate pair* (0.5, 8). The first number in a **coordinate pair** is the value for the *x*-coordinate, and the second number is the value for the *y*-coordinate. Give the coordinate pair for the third point on your graph. What information does this point give?

2. Connecting the points on a graph sometimes helps you see a pattern more clearly. You can connect the points in situations in which it makes sense to consider what is happening in the intervals *between* the points. The points on the graph of the data for day 2 can be connected because the riders were moving during each half-hour interval, so the distance was changing.
   a. Connect the points on your graph with straight line segments.
   b. How could you use the line segments to help you estimate the distance traveled after $\frac{3}{4}$ of an hour (0.75 hours)?

3. The straight line segment you drew from (4.5, 40) to (5.0, 45) gives you some idea of how the ride might have gone between the points. It shows you how the ride would have progressed if the riders had traveled at a steady rate for the entire half hour. The actual pace of the group, and of the individual riders, may have varied throughout the half hour. These paths show some possible ways the ride may have progressed:

Match each of these connecting paths with the following travel notes.
   a. Celia rode slowly at first and gradually increased her speed.
   b. Tony and Liz rode very quickly and reached the campsite early.
   c. Malcolm had to fix a flat tire, so he started late.
   d. Theo started off fast. After a while, he felt tired and slowed down.

Day 3: Lewes to Chincoteague Island

On day 3 of the tour, the students left Lewes, Delaware, and rode through Ocean City, Maryland, which has been a popular summer resort since the late 1800s. They decided to stop for the day on Chincoteague Island, which is famous for its annual pony auction.

Did you know?

Assateague Island, located next to Chincoteague Island, is home to herds of wild ponies. According to legend, the ancestors of these ponies swam ashore from a Spanish vessel that capsized near the island in the late 1500s. To survive in a harsh environment of beaches, sand dunes, and marshes, these sturdy ponies eat saltmarsh, seaweed, and even poison ivy!

To keep the population of ponies on the island under control, an auction is held every summer. During the famous "Pony Swim," the ponies that will be sold swim across a quarter mile of water to Chincoteague Island.

Celia collected data along the way and used it to make the graph below. Her graph shows the distance the riders were from Lewes as the day progressed. This graph is different from the graph made for Problem 2.2, which represented the *total* distance traveled as the day progressed.

Day 3 Progress

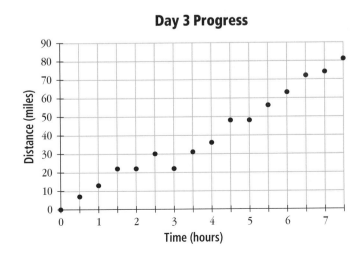

Problem 2.3

A. Would it make sense to connect the points on this graph? Explain.

B. Make a table of (time, distance) data from the information in the graph.

C. What do you think happened between hours 2 and 4? Between hours 1.5 and 2?

D. Which method of displaying the (time, distance) data helps you see the changes better, a table or a graph? Explain your choice.

■ Problem 2.3 Follow-Up

Use the graph to determine the total distance the riders traveled on day 3. Explain how you determined your answer.

2.4 Day 4: Chincoteague Island to Norfolk

On day 4, the group traveled from Chincoteague Island to Norfolk, Virginia. Norfolk is a major base for the United States Navy Atlantic Fleet. Malcolm and Sarah rode in the van. They forgot to record the distance traveled each half hour, but they did write some notes about the trip.

Malcolm and Sarah's Notes

- We started at 8:30 A.M. and rode into a strong wind until our midmorning break.
- About midmorning, the wind shifted to our backs.
- We stopped for lunch at a barbecue stand and rested for about an hour. By this time, we had traveled about halfway to Norfolk.
- At around 2:00 P.M., we stopped for a brief swim in the ocean.
- At around 3:30 P.M., we had reached the north end of the Chesapeake Bay Bridge and Tunnel. We stopped for a few minutes to watch the ships passing by. Since bikes are prohibited on the bridge, the riders put their bikes in the van, and we drove across the bridge.
- We took $7\frac{1}{2}$ hours to complete today's 80-mile trip.

Problem 2.4

A. Make a table of (time, distance) data that reasonably fits the information in Malcolm and Sarah's notes.

B. Sketch a coordinate graph that shows the same information.

■ Problem 2.4 Follow-Up

Explain how you used each of the six notes to help you make your table and graph.

2.5 Day 5: Norfolk to Williamsburg

The last stop on the Ocean and History Bike Tour was Williamsburg, Virginia. In America's colonial period, Williamsburg was the capital of Virginia. The buildings of that period have been restored so visitors can imagine what life was like there in the eighteenth century.

After the riders finished lunch, they decided to have a race. The winner would receive $50 from the tour company's first profits. Theo had an electronic speedometer on his bike. It recorded his *speed* every 10 minutes during the 90-minute race.

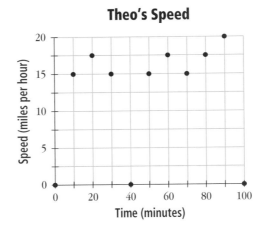

Theo's Speed

(Graph: vertical axis labeled "Speed (miles per hour)" ranging 0 to 20; horizontal axis labeled "Time (minutes)" ranging 0 to 100.)

■ 24 Variables and Patterns

Problem 2.5

A. What was Theo's fastest recorded speed, and when did it occur?

B. What was Theo's slowest recorded speed, and when did it occur?

C. Describe the changes in Theo's speed during the race.

D. The graph only shows Theo's speed at 10-minute intervals; it does not tell us what happened between 10-minute marks. The paths below show five possibilities of how Theo's speed may have changed during the first 10 minutes. Explain in writing what each connecting path would tell about Theo's speed.

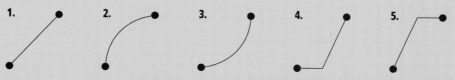

Problem 2.5 Follow-Up

1. Would it be possible for the path below to represent Theo's progress between 10-minute marks? Why or why not?

2. During which 10-minute period(s) of the race did Theo's speed change the most?

As you work on these ACE questions, use your calculator whenever you need it.

Applications

1. Here is a graph of temperature data collected on the students' trip from Atlantic City to Lewes.

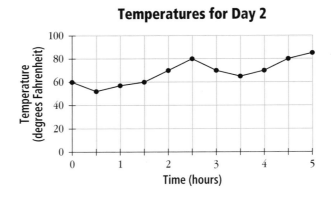

Temperatures for Day 2

a. This graph shows the relationship between two variables. What are they?

b. Make a table of data from this graph.

c. What is the difference between the day's lowest and highest temperature?

d. During which time interval(s) did the temperature rise the fastest? Fall the fastest?

e. Is it is easier to use the table or the graph to answer part c? Why?

f. Is it is easier to use the table or the graph to answer part d? Why?

g. On this graph, what information is given by the lines connecting the points? Is it necessarily accurate information? Explain your reasoning.

2. Katrina's parents kept a record of her growth from her birth until her eighteenth birthday. Their data is shown in the table below.

Age (years)	Height (inches)
birth	20
1	29
2	33.5
3	37
4	39.5
5	42
6	45.5
7	47
8	49
9	52
10	54
11	56.5
12	59
13	61
14	64
15	64
16	64
17	64.5
18	64.5

a. Make a coordinate graph of Katrina's height data.

b. During which time interval(s) did Katrina have her largest "growth spurt"?

c. During which time interval(s) did Katrina's height change the least?

d. Would it make sense to connect the points on the graph? Why or why not?

e. Is it easier to use the table or the graph to answer parts b and c?

3. Make a table and a graph of (time, temperature) data that fit the following information about a day on the road:

- We started riding at 8 A.M. The day was quite warm, with dark clouds in the sky.
- About midmorning the temperature dropped quickly to 63°F, and there was a thunderstorm for about an hour.
- After the storm, the sky cleared and there was a warm breeze.
- As the day went on, the sun steadily warmed the air. When we reached our campground at 4 P.M. it was 89°F.

4. Amanda is a student at Cartwright Middle School. She is learning how to make graphs. She made the two graphs below to show how her level of hunger and her feelings of happiness changed over the course of a day. She forgot to label the graphs.

a.

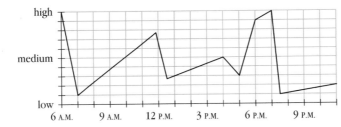

b.

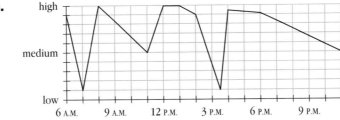

Here are written descriptions of how the two variables changed throughout the day. Use these descriptions to determine which graph shows the relationship between time and hunger and which graph shows the relationship between time and happiness. Explain your reasoning.

Hunger: Amanda woke up really hungry and ate a large breakfast. She was hungry again by her lunch period, which began at 11:45. After school, she had a snack before basketball practice, but she had a big appetite by the time she got home for dinner. Amanda was full after dinner and did not eat much before she went to bed.

Happiness: Amanda woke up in a good mood, but got mad because her older brother hogged the bathroom. She talked to a boy she likes on the morning bus. Amanda enjoyed her morning classes but started to get bored by lunch time. At lunch, she sat with her friends and had fun. She loves her computer class, which is right after lunch, but then didn't enjoy her other afternoon classes. After school, Amanda had a good time at basketball practice. She spent the evening washing her dog and doing other chores.

5. Here is a graph Celia drew on the bike trip.

   a. What does this graph show?

   b. Is this a reasonable pattern for the speed of a cyclist? Of the van? Of the wind? Explain each of your conclusions.

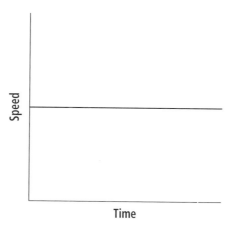

6. The graph below shows the results of a survey of people over age 25 who had completed different levels of education. The graph shows the median salary for people with each level of education.

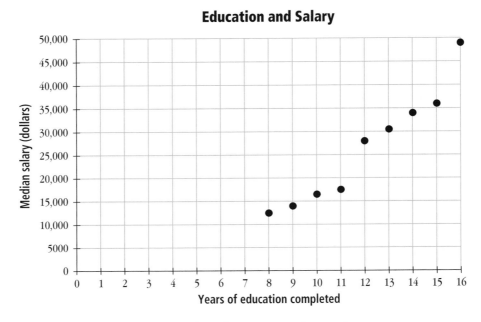

Education and Salary

a. Make a table that shows the information in the graph.

b. After how many years of education do salaries take a big jump? Why do you think this happens?

c. Do you find it easier to answer part b by looking at the graph or your table? Explain your reasoning.

7. When Ben first started to play the electric guitar, his skill increased quite rapidly. Over time, as Ben continued to practice, he seemed to improve more slowly.

a. Sketch a graph to show how Ben's guitar-playing skill progressed over time since he began to play.

b. Your graph shows the relationship between two variables. What are they?

c. What other variables might affect the rate at which Ben's playing improves?

8. Think of something in your life that varies with time, and make a graph to show how it might change as time passes. Some possibilities are the length of your hair, your height, your moods, or your feelings toward your friends.

Connections

9. This table shows the percent of American children in each age group who smoke.

Age	Percent
12	1.7
13	4.9
14	8.9
15	16.3
16	25.2
17	37.2

Source: National Household Survey on Drug Abuse (1991 figures)

a. Make a bar graph of this information.

b. Based on the data, estimate the percent of 18-year-olds who smoke. Explain your reasoning.

c. What relationship does there seem to be between smoking and age? Do you think this pattern continues beyond the teenage years? Explain your reasoning.

10. The following table shows the winners and the winning times for the women's Olympic 400-meter dash since 1964.

Marie-Jose Perec

Year	Name	Time (seconds)
1964	Celia Cuthbert, AUS	52.0
1968	Colette Besson, FRA	52.0
1972	Monika Zehrt, E. GER	51.08
1976	Irena Szewinska, POL	49.29
1980	Marita Koch, E. GER	48.88
1984	Valerie Brisco-Hooks, USA	48.83
1988	Olga Bryzguina, USSR	48.65
1992	Marie-Jose Perec, FRA	48.83

a. Make a coordinate graph of the (year, time) information given in the table. Be sure to choose a scale that allows you to see the differences between the winning times.

b. What patterns do you see in the table and graph? For example, do the winning times seem to be rising or falling? In which year was the best time earned?

Extensions

11. The school booster club sells sweatshirts.

    a. Which, if any, of the following graphs describes the relationship you expect between the price charged for each sweatshirt and the profit made? Explain your choice, or draw a new graph you think better describes this relationship. Explain your reasoning.

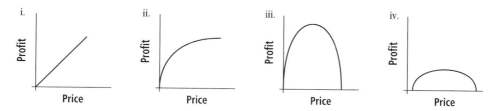

i. Profit / Price   ii. Profit / Price   iii. Profit / Price   iv. Profit / Price

    b. What variables can affect the club's profits?

12. The sketch below shows two bicycles—one with normal wheels, and one with wheels shaped like regular hexagons. Imagine that you put a reflector on the front wheel of each bike and then stood to the side to watch the reflector's path as the bike is ridden past you. Sketch this path:

    a. If the reflector is placed at the center of each front wheel.

    b. If the reflector is placed at the outer edge of each front wheel (near the tire).

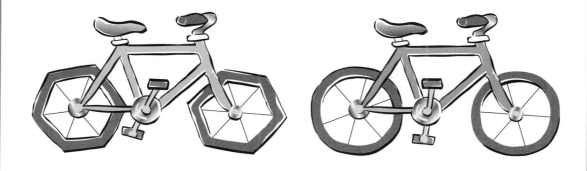

13. Chelsea can pedal her bike at a steady pace for long periods of time. Think about how her speed might change if she rode in a wind that fit the pattern shown on the graph below.

    a. Sketch a coordinate graph of how Chelsea's speed would change over time if the wind were at her back (a tailwind).

    b. Sketch a coordinate graph of how Chelsea's speed would change over time if she had to ride against the wind (a headwind).

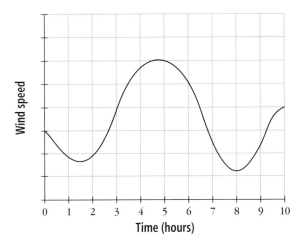

Mathematical Reflections

In this investigation, you analyzed data given in tables, graphs, and written reports. These questions will help you summarize what you have learned:

1 What are the advantages and disadvantages of a table?

2 What are the advantages and disadvantages of a graph?

3 What are the advantages and disadvantages of a written report?

Think about your answers to these questions, discuss your ideas with other students and your teacher, and then write a summary of your findings in your journal.

Analyzing Graphs and Tables

In this investigation, you will continue to use tables and graphs to compare information and make important decisions. Using tables, graphs, and words to represent relationships is an important part of algebra.

Coming up with the idea for Ocean and History Bike Tours was only the first step for the five friends in starting their business. They have other important plans to make as well. Many of these plans involve questions about money.

- What will it cost to operate the tours?
- How much should customers be charged?
- What profit will be left when all the bills are paid?

To answer these questions, the five business partners decided to do some research. They wanted to plan carefully so they would end up with a profit after they had paid all their expenses.

Think about this!

- With your classmates, make a list of the things the tour operators will have to provide for their customers. Estimate the cost of each item per customer.

- How much do you think customers would be willing to pay for the five-day tour?

- Based on your estimates of costs and possible income, will the partners earn a profit?

3.1 Renting Bicycles

The tour operators decided to rent bicycles for their customers rather than having customers bring their own bikes. They called two bike shops and asked for estimates of rental fees.

Rocky's Cycle Center sent a table of weekly rental fees for various numbers of bikes.

Number of bikes	5	10	15	20	25	30	35	40	45	50
Rental fee	$400	535	655	770	875	975	1070	1140	1180	1200

Adrian's Bike Shop sent a graph of their weekly rental fees. Since the rental fee depends on the number of bikes, they put the number of bikes on the *x*-axis.

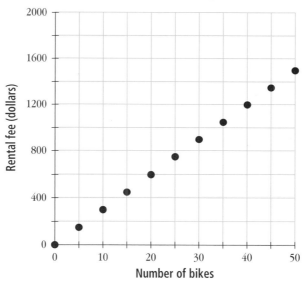

Adrian's Bike Shop Fees

Problem 3.1

A. Which bike shop should Ocean and History Bike Tours use? Explain your choice.

B. Explain how you used the information in the table and the graph to make your decision.

■ Problem 3.1 Follow-Up

1. In the graph from Adrian's Bike Shop, would it make sense to connect the points with a line? Why or why not?

2. How much do you think each company would charge to rent 32 bikes?

3. Recognizing patterns and using patterns to make predictions are important mathematical skills. Look for patterns in the table and graph on page 37. For each display, describe in words the pattern of change in the data.

4. Based on the patterns you found in part 3, how can you predict values that are not included in the table or graph?

3.2 Finding Customers

Sidney, Liz, Celia, Malcolm, and Theo had a route planned and a bike shop chosen. Now they needed customers. They had to figure out what price to charge so they could attract customers and make a profit.

To help set a price, the partners did some market research. They obtained a list of people who had taken other bicycle tours and asked 100 of them which of the following amounts they would be willing to pay for the Ocean and History Bike Tour: $150, $200, $250, $300, $350, $400, $450, $500, $550, $600. The results are shown in the table.

Tour price	Number who would be customers at this price
$150	76
200	74
250	71
300	65
350	59
400	49
450	38
500	26
550	14
600	0

Problem 3.2

A. If you were to make a graph of the data, which variable would you put on the *x*-axis? Which variable would you put on the *y*-axis? Explain your choices.

B. Make a coordinate graph of the data on grid paper.

C. Based on your graph, what price do you think the tour operators should charge? Explain your reasoning.

■ Problem 3.2 Follow-Up

1. The number of people who said they would take the tour depended on the price. How does the number of potential customers change as the price increases?

2. How is the change in the number of people who said they would go on the tour shown in the table? On the graph?

3.3 Predicting Profit

Based on the results of their survey, the tour operators decided to charge $350 per person for the tour. Of course, not all of this money would be profit. To estimate their profit, they had to consider the expenses involved in running the tour. Sidney estimated these expenses and calculated the expected profit for various numbers of customers. She made the graph below to present her predictions to her partners. Since the profit depends on the number of tour customers, she put the number of customers on the *x*-axis.

Estimated Tour Profits

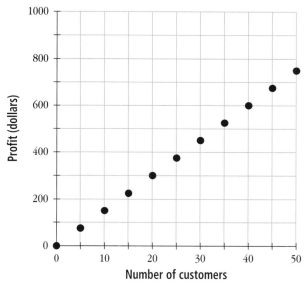

Problem 3.3

Study the graph on the previous page.

A. How much profit will be made if 10 customers go on the tour? 25 customers? 40 customers?

B. How many customers are needed for the partners to earn a $200 profit? A $500 profit? A $600 profit?

C. How does the profit change as the number of customers increases? How is this pattern shown in the graph?

D. If the tour operators reduced their expenses but kept the price at $350, how would this change the graph?

■ Problem 3.3 Follow-Up

In the profit graph, points at the intersection of two grid lines, such as (20, 300) and (40, 600), are easy to read. Use the "easy to read" points to figure out what the profit would be if only 1 customer went on the tour. How about 2 customers? 3 customers? 100 customers? Describe, in words, the estimated profit for any number of customers.

3.4 Paying Bills and Counting Profits

Sidney was nervous about the partners using her rough estimates to make important decisions. She decided to look more carefully at the company's expected costs and the resulting profit. She found that although the trip would bring in $350 from each rider, it would have operating costs of $30 for each person's bike rental, $125 for each person's food and camp costs, and $700 per tour to rent the van for the trip. Sidney put her estimated cost and income data in a table. Here is the start of her table:

Number of customers	Income	Bike rental	Food and camp costs	Van rental
1	$350	$30	$125	$700
2	700	60	250	700
3				
4				
5				
6				
7				
8				
9				
10				

Problem 3.4

A. Copy Sidney's table. Complete it to give information about income and estimated costs for up to 10 customers.

B. How does the income column change as the number of customers increases? Explain how you can use this relationship to calculate the income for any number of customers.

C. Add and complete a column for "Total cost" (including bike rental, food and camp costs, and van rental) to your table. How does the total cost change as the number of customers increases? Describe how you can calculate the total cost for any number of customers.

D. Add and complete a column for "Profit." What profit would be earned from a trip with 5 customers? 10 customers? 25 customers?

■ Problem 3.4 Follow-Up

1. What other patterns of change do you see in the table?

2. What is the least number of customers needed for the tour to make a profit?

3. What do you think is the least number of customers needed to make it worthwhile for the students to run the tour? Explain your answer.

As you work on these ACE questions, use your calculator whenever you need it.

Applications

1. This table shows the fees charged for campsites at one of the campgrounds on the Ocean and History Bike Tour:

Number of campsites	1	2	3	4	5	6	7	8
Total campground fee	$12.50	25.00	37.50	50.00	62.50	75.00	87.50	100.00

a. Make a coordinate graph of these data.

b. Would it make sense to connect the points on your graph? Why or why not?

c. Using the table, describe the pattern of change you find in the total campground fee as the number of campsites needed increases. How is this pattern shown in your graph?

2. A camping-supply store rents camping gear for $25 per person.

a. Using increments of 5 campers, make a table showing the total rental charge for 0 to 50 campers. Make a coordinate graph of these data.

b. Compare the pattern of change in your table and graph with patterns you found in the campground fee data in question 1. Describe the similarities and differences between the two sets of data.

3. The tour partners need to rent a truck to transport camping gear, clothes, and bicycle repair equipment. They checked prices at two truck rental companies.

a. East Coast Trucks charges $4.25 for each mile a truck is driven. Make a table of the charges for 0, 25, 50, 75, 100, 125, 150, 175, 200, 225, 250, 275, and 300 miles.

b. Philadelphia Truck Rental charges $200 for a week, or any part of a week, and an additional $2.00 for each mile a truck is driven. Make a table of the charges for renting a truck for five days and driving it 0, 25, 50, 75, 100, 125, 150, 175, 200, 225, 250, 275, and 300 miles.

c. On one coordinate grid, plot the charge plans for both rental companies. Use a different color to mark each company's plan.

d. Based on your work in parts a–c, which truck rental company do you think would be the best deal for the partners?

4. Dezi's family just bought a VCR. Dezi's mom asked him to research rental prices at local video stores. Source Video has a yearly membership package. The manager gave Dezi this table of prices:

Source Video Membership/Rental Packages

Number of videos rented	0	5	10	15	20	25	30
Total cost	$30	35	40	45	50	55	60

Extreme Video does not have a membership package. Dezi made the graph below to show how the cost at Extreme Video is related to the number of videos rented.

Video Rentals from Extreme Video

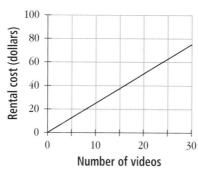

a. If both video stores have a good selection of movies, and Dezi's family plans to watch about two movies a month, which video store should they choose?

b. Write a paragraph explaining to Dezi how he could decide which video store to use.

c. For each store, describe the pattern of change relating the number of videos rented to the cost.

Connections

5. This summer Jamie is going to Washington, D.C., to march in a parade with his school band. He plans to set aside $25 at the end of each month to use for the trip. Which of the following graphs shows how Jamie's savings will build as time passes?

a.

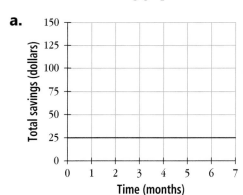

b.

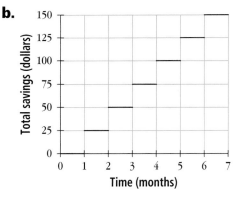

c.

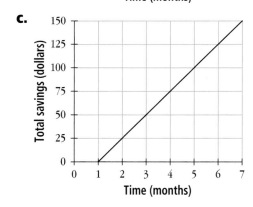

6. Jacy works at a department store on the weekends. This graph represents Jacy's parking expenses. Describe what the graph tells you about the costs for the parking garage Jacy uses.

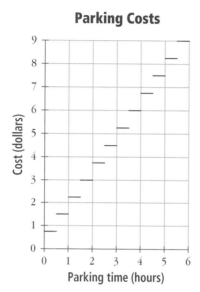

Parking Costs

7. Recall that the area of a rectangle is its length times its width.

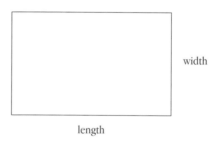

width

length

a. Make a table of the different whole-number values for the length and width of a rectangle with an area of 24 square meters.

b. Make a coordinate graph of your data from part a. Put length on the *x*-axis and width on the *y*-axis.

c. Describe what happens to the width as the length increases.

8. Recall that the perimeter of a rectangle is the sum of its side lengths.

a. Make a table of all the possible whole-number values for the length and width of a rectangle with a perimeter of 24 meters.

b. Make a coordinate graph of your data from part a. Put length on the x-axis and width on the y-axis.

c. Describe what happens to the width as the length increases.

d. Would it make sense to connect the points in this graph? Explain your reasoning.

9. Here are the box office earnings (in millions of dollars) for a popular movie after each of the first eight weeks following its release.

Weeks in theaters	1	2	3	4	5	6	7	8
Weekly earnings (millions of $)	16	22	18	12	7	4	3	1

a. Make a coordinate graph showing the weekly earnings after each week. Since a film's weekly earnings depend on the number of weeks it is in theaters, put the weeks in theaters on the x-axis and the weekly earnings on the y-axis.

b. Write a short description of the pattern of change in the data table and in your graph. Explain how the movie's weekly earnings changed as time passed, how this change is shown in the table and the graph, and why this change might have occured.

c. What were the *total earnings* of the movie in the eight weeks?

d. Make a coordinate graph showing the total earnings after each of the first eight weeks.

e. Write a short description of the pattern of change in your graph of total earnings. Explain how the movie's total earnings changed over time, how this change is shown in the table and the graph, and why this change might have occurred.

Extensions

10. You can use *Turtle Math* software to draw regular polygons. At each vertex of a polygon, the turtle must make a turn. The size of the turn is related to the number of sides in the polygon. To draw an equilateral triangle, for example, you have to make 120° turns at each vertex.

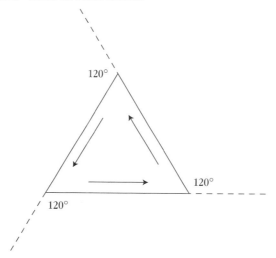

a. Copy and complete the following table, which shows how a turtle turn is related to the number of sides in a regular polygon.

Number of sides	3	4	5	6	7	8	9	10
Degrees in turn	120°							

b. Make a coordinate graph of the (sides, degrees) data.

c. What pattern of change do you see in the degrees the turtle must turn as the number of sides increases? How is that pattern shown in the table? In the graph?

Mathematical Reflections

In this investigation, you learned to use data presented in tables and graphs to help you describe patterns of change in two related variables. You used patterns of change to describe how to predict the value of one variable from the value of the other variable. These questions will help you summarize what you have learned:

1 Imagine a situation in which variable y depends on variable x (for example, y might be profit and x the number of items sold). If y increases as x increases, how would this be indicated in a table? In a graph?

2 If variable y decreases as variable x increases (for example, y might be the amount of money in your wallet on a trip and x the time you have been traveling), how would this be indicated in a table? In a graph?

3 In a coordinate graph of two related variables, when do the points lie in a straight line?

4 In a coordinate graph of two related variables, when is it appropriate to connect the points?

Think about your answers to these questions, discuss your ideas with other students and your teacher, and then write a summary of your findings in your journal.

Patterns and Rules

So far in this unit, you have studied many of the variables involved in the Ocean and History Bike Tours business. By using tables and graphs, you have investigated how these variables are related to one another. For example, you explored how the number of customers is related to profit and how the number of hours of riding is related to the distance covered. As you study how variables are related, you are learning about algebra.

Sometimes the relationship between two variables can be described with a simple **rule**. Such rules are very helpful in making predictions for values that are not included in a table or a graph of a set of data. In previous investigations, you described rules in words. In this investigation, you will use symbols to express rules. Here are some examples:

- If the tour operators charge $350 per customer, the rule for calculating the tour income can be expressed as:

$$\text{income} = 350 \times \text{number of customers}$$

  This rule gives the relationship between income and the number of customers: the income is 350 times the number of customers.

- The rule for calculating the circumference of a bicycle wheel (or any circle) can be written as:

$$\text{circumference} = \pi \times \text{diameter}$$

  You can use this rule to calculate the circumference of any circle, as long as you know its diameter.

Rules, like those above, that are expressed with mathematical symbols are sometimes referred to as **equations** or **formulas**.

A shorter way to write rules relating variables is to replace the word names for the variables with single letters. For example, in the rule for income, you could write *I* for *income* and *n* for the *number of customers.* The rule would then become:

$$I = 350 \times n$$

If you let *C* stand for *circumference* and *d* stand for *diameter,* you could write the rule for the circumference of a wheel as:

$$C = \pi \times d$$

You can shorten these rules even more. In algebra, when a number is multiplied by a variable, the multiplication sign is often omitted. So, you could write the above rules as:

$$I = 350n \qquad \text{and} \qquad C = \pi d$$

When you see a rule, such as $I = 350n$, with a number next to a letter, multiply. So, $I = 350n$ means $I = 350 \times n$ and $C = \pi d$ means $C = \pi \times d$.

4.1 Heading Home

When the Ocean and History Bike Tour reached Williamsburg, the tired riders packed their bikes and gear in the van and headed back toward Philadelphia. They traveled by interstate highway, and averaged a steady 55 miles per hour for the 310-mile trip home.

You have seen that making a table and a graph can help you understand how the time and the distance traveled are related.

Time (hours)	Distance (miles)
0	
1	
2	
3	
4	
5	
6	
7	
8	

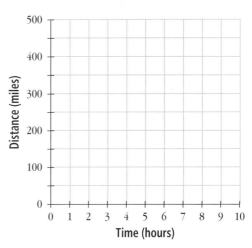

Problem 4.1

A. Copy and complete the table and graph on the previous page to show the relationship between distance and time if the students traveled at a rate of 55 miles per hour.

B. Use your table and graph to estimate the total distance traveled after

   1. 3 hours   **2.** $4\frac{1}{2}$ hours   **3.** $5\frac{1}{4}$ hours

C. If the students continued driving at a steady 55 miles per hour, how far would they go in

   1. 10 hours   **2.** $12\frac{1}{3}$ hours   **3.** 15 hours

D. Look for patterns in the table and graph that help you calculate the distance traveled for any given time. Write a rule, using words, that explains how to calculate the distance traveled for any given time.

E. Use symbols to write your rule from part D as an equation.

■ Problem 4.1 Follow-Up

1. How could you find the distance traveled after $3\frac{1}{4}$ hours by using the table? The graph? The equation?

2. Estimate how much time it took the students to reach each of the following cities on their route:

   a. Richmond, Virginia—about 55 miles from Williamsburg

   b. Baltimore, Maryland—about $\frac{3}{4}$ of the way from Williamsburg to Philadelphia

   c. Philadelphia, Pennsylvania—about 310 miles from Williamsburg

4.2 Changing Speeds

The speed limit on many sections of the interstate highway is 65 miles per hour. If the students had traveled at this speed for the whole trip, it would have taken them less time to get home. However, if they had stopped for rest and food breaks, they would have probably averaged a slower speed, such as 50 miles per hour.

Problem 4.2

A. Make tables of time and distance data, similar to the table you made for Problem 4.1, for travel at 50 miles per hour and 65 miles per hour.

Plot the data from both tables on one coordinate grid. Use a different color for each set of data. Using a third color, add data points for the times and distances traveled at 55 miles per hour (from Problem 4.1).

B. How are the tables for the three speeds similar? How are they different?

C. How are the graphs for the three speeds similar? How are they different?

D. 1. Look at the table and graph for 65 miles per hour. What pattern of change in the data helps you calculate the distance for any given time? In words, write a rule that explains how to calculate the distance traveled for any given time.

2. Use symbols to write your rule as an equation.

E. 1. Now write a rule, in words, that explains how to calculate the distance traveled for any given time when the speed is 50 miles per hour.

2. Use symbols to write your rule as an equation.

F. How are the rules for calculating distance for the three speeds similar? How are they different?

■ Problem 4.2 Follow-Up

1. After arriving in Philadelphia, Malcolm took the interstate home. He wrote the equation $d = 60t$ to represent his trip home. Explain this equation in words.
2. How long would it take to reach Philadelphia—310 miles from Williamsburg— traveling at 50 miles per hour? 60 miles per hour? 65 miles per hour?

4.3 Calculating Costs and Profits

Sidney started a table like the one on the next page to help the partners determine their profit for the tour. In Problem 3.4, you completed this table for up to 10 customers. You also wrote rules, in words, describing the patterns of change you found in the table.

Sidney wants to use symbols to write equations for these rules, so she can predict costs and profit for any number of customers. For example, in the introduction of this unit the equation for the rule for calculating income was given as $I = 350 \times n$, or $I = 350n$, where I represents the income in dollars for n customers.

Number of customers	Income	Bike rental	Food and camp costs	Van rental	Total cost	Profit
1	$350	$30	$125	$700	$855	⁻$505
2	700	60	250	700	1010	⁻310
3	1050	90	375	700	1165	⁻115
4	1400	120	500	700	1320	80
5	1750	150	625	700	1475	275
6	2100	180	750	700	1630	470
7	2450	210	875	700	1785	665
8	2800	240	1000	700	1940	860
9	3150	270	1125	700	2095	1055
10	3500	300	1250	700	2250	1250

Problem 4.3

A. Write an equation for the rule to calculate each of the following costs for any number, n, of customers.

1. bike rental   **2.** food and camp costs   **3.** van rental

B. Write an equation for the rule to determine the *total cost* for any number, n, of customers.

C. Write an equation for the rule to determine the *profit* for any number, n, of customers.

■ Problem 4.3 Follow-Up

1. Theo's father has a van he will let the students use at no charge. Which of these equations represents the total cost if they use his van?

    a. $C = 125 + 30$ **b.** $C = 125n + 30n$

    c. $C = 155$ **d.** $C = 155 + n$

2. If the partners require customers to supply their own bikes, which of these is the new equation for total cost? (Assume the students will rent a van.)

    a. $C = 125n + 700$ **b.** $C = 125 + 700 + n$

    c. $825n$ **d.** $C = 350n + 125n + 700$

3. If customers must supply their own bikes, which equations below represent the profit? (Assume the students will rent a van.)

    a. $P = 350 - (125 + 700 + n)$ **b.** $P = 350n - 125n + 700$

    c. $P = 350n - (125n + 700)$ **d.** $P = 350n - 125n - 700$

As you work on these ACE questions, use your calculator whenever you need it.

Applications

1. The El Paso Middle School girls' basketball team drove from El Paso to San Antonio for the Texas State Championship game. The trip was 560 miles. Their bus averaged 60 miles per hour on the trip.

a. Make a table and a graph of time and distance data for the basketball team's bus.

b. Estimate the distance traveled by the bus after each of the following times:

   i. 2 hours   **ii.** $2\frac{3}{4}$ hours   **iii.** $3\frac{1}{2}$ hours   **iv.** 7.25 hours

c. How are 2 hours and the distance traveled in 2 hours represented in the table? On the graph?

d. How are $2\frac{3}{4}$ hours and the distance traveled in $2\frac{3}{4}$ hours represented in the table? On the graph?

e. What rule relating time and distance could help you calculate the distance traveled for any given time on this trip?

f. The bus route passed through Sierra Blanca, Texas, which is 90 miles from El Paso. How long did it take the bus to get to Sierra Blanca?

g. The bus route also passed through Balmorhea, Texas, which is $\frac{1}{3}$ of the way from El Paso to San Antonio. How long did it take the bus to get to Balmorhea?

h. How long did it take the bus to complete its 560-mile trip to San Antonio?

2. The equation $d = 70t$ represents the distance, in miles, covered after traveling at 70 miles per hour for t hours.

    a. Make a table that shows the distance traveled, according to this equation, for every half hour between 0 hours and 4 hours.

    b. Sketch a graph that shows the distance traveled between 0 and 4 hours.

    c. If $t = 2.5$ hours, what is d?

    d. If $d = 210$ miles, what is t?

    e. You probably made your graph by plotting points. In this situation, would it make sense to connect these points with line segments?

In 3–6, use symbols to express the rule as an equation. Use single letters to stand for the variables. Identify what each letter represents.

3. The area of a rectangle is its length multiplied by its width.

4. The number of hot dogs needed for the picnic is two for each student.

5. Taxi fare is $2.00 plus $1.10 per mile.

6. The amount of material needed to make the curtains is $4\frac{3}{8}$ yards per window.

7. This table shows the relationship between the number of riders on a bike tour and the daily cost of providing box lunches.

Customers	1	2	3	4	5	6	7	8	9
Lunch cost	$4.25	8.50	12.75	17.00	21.25	25.50	29.75	34.00	38.25

    a. Write an equation for a rule relating lunch cost, L, and number of customers, n.

    b. Use your equation to find the lunch cost if 25 people are on the tour.

    c. How many people could eat lunch if the tour leader had $89.25?

Connections

In 8 and 9, use the following information: In previous units, you discovered that the circumference, radius, and diameter of a circle are related. These relationships involve a special number named with the Greek letter π. The exact value of π is an infinite decimal that begins 3.14159265358. The approximation 3.14 is commonly used. For any circle:

$$\text{circumference} = \pi \times \text{diameter}$$

Since the diameter of a circle is twice its radius, you can also write this as:

$$\text{circumference} = \pi \times 2 \times \text{radius}$$

8. The wheels on Kai's bike are 27 inches in diameter. His little sister, Masako, has a bike with wheels that are 20 inches in diameter. Sometimes Kai and Masako go out for evening bike rides around their neighborhood.

  a. How far will Kai go in one complete turn of his wheels?

  b. How far will Masako go in one complete turn of her wheels?

  c. How far will Kai go in 500 turns of his wheels?

  d. How far will Masako go in 500 turns of her wheels?

e. How many times will Kai's wheels have to turn to cover 100 feet? (Remember that there are 12 inches in 1 foot.)

f. How many times will Masako's wheels have to turn to cover 100 feet?

g. How many times will Kai's wheels have to turn to cover 1 mile? (Remember that there are 5280 feet in 1 mile.)

h. How many times will Masako's wheels have to turn in order to cover 1 mile?

9. The old-fashioned bicycle shown here is called a "penny farthing" bicycle. These bikes had front wheels as large as 5 feet in diameter! Suppose the front wheel of this bicycle has a diameter of 5 feet.

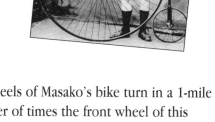

a. What is the radius of the front wheel?

b. How far will this bike travel in 100 turns of the front wheel?

c. How many times will the front wheel turn in a 3-mile trip?

d. Compare the number of times the wheels of Masako's bike turn in a 1-mile trip (see question 8h) with the number of times the front wheel of this penny farthing bike turns in a 3-mile trip. Why do the numbers compare this way?

10. Celia came up with the equation $d = 8t$ to represent the number of miles the bikers could travel in t hours at a speed of 8 miles per hour.

a. Make a table that shows the distance traveled every half hour, up to 5 hours, if the bikers ride at this constant speed for 5 hours.

b. How far would the bikers travel in 1 hour? 3 hours? 4.5 hours? 6 hours?

11. Sean just bought a new CD player and speakers from the Audio Source for $315. The store offered Sean an interest-free payment plan that allows him to pay in weekly installments of $25.

   a. How much will Sean still owe after one payment? After two payments? After three payments?

   b. Using n to stand for the number of payments and A for the amount still owed, write an equation for calculating A for any given value of n.

   c. Use your equation to make a table and a graph showing the relationship between n and A.

   d. As n increases by 1, how does A change? How is this change shown in the table? On the graph?

   e. How many payments will Sean have to make in all? How is this shown in the table? How is this shown on the graph?

Extensions

12. a. If you know the distance and the time you have traveled on a car trip, you can calculate the average speed of the trip. Find the average speed for each pair of distance and time values below.

Distance (miles)	Time (hours)	Average speed (miles per hour)
145	2	_____
110	2	_____
165	2.5	_____
300	5.25	_____
446	6.75	_____
528	8	_____
862	9.5	_____
723	10	_____

   b. Write an equation for calculating the average speed, s, for any distance, d, and time, t.

13. The trip from Ocean City, Maryland, to Chincoteague Island, Virginia, is about 40 miles.

    a. How long will the trip take if the riders average 6 miles per hour?

    b. How would the time for the trip change if the average speed increased? If the average speed decreased?

14. Maurice and Cheri made graphs of the equation $y = 4x + 20$ in their math class.

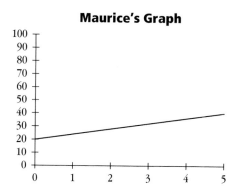

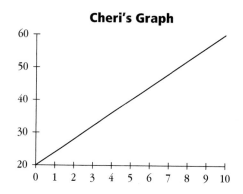

    a. Describe the similarities between the two graphs.

    b. Describe the differences between the two graphs.

    c. Can both of these graphs represent the same equation? Explain your reasoning.

Mathematical Reflections

In this investigation, you learned to use symbols to write equations for rules relating variables. These questions will help you summarize what you have learned:

1 The Larson family is traveling from Michigan to Florida at an average speed of 60 miles per hour. Write an equation for a rule you can you use to calculate the distance they have traveled after any given number of hours.

2 What are the advantages of having an equation to represent the Larson family's situation? What are the advantages to having a table? A graph?

Think about your answers to these questions, discuss your ideas with other students and your teacher, and then write a summary of your findings in your journal.

Using a Graphing Calculator

In the last investigation, you wrote equations to describe patterns and to show how variables are related. Such equations are used in mathematics, science, economics, and many other subject areas. So far, you have written equations that fit the patterns you observed in tables and graphs. Sometimes, you will need to create a table or graph that fits a given equation. In this investigation, you will use a tool called a *graphing calculator* to make graphs and tables that fit a given equation.

5.1 Graphing on a Calculator

The organizers of the Ocean and History Bike Tour need to bring spare parts in the van in case any of the customers have problems with their bikes. They think they will have enough tires if they bring two spare tires for each customer. Theo wrote this rule as the equation $t = 2c$, where t is the number of spare tires needed for c customers.

You can use a graphing calculator to make a graph of Theo's equation. To use a calculator to make graphs and tables, you need to type in an equation that uses the letters y and x to represent the variables. We write these equations so that x is the independent variable and y is the dependent variable. Rewriting Theo's equation using x and y, we get $y = 2x$, where y is the number of tires needed for x customers.

When you press the $\boxed{Y=}$ button, you get a screen like the one below. The calculator gives the "$y =$" part of the equation; you need to type in the rest. You can enter Theo's equation, $y = 2x$, by pressing $\boxed{2}$, followed by the letter $\boxed{X}$.

```
Y1=2X
Y2=
Y3=
Y4=
```

After you enter the equation, press GRAPH to see the graph. Here is the graph of $y = 2x$.

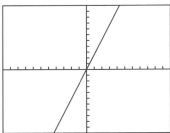

Problem 5.1

Experiment with your graphing calculator and the following equations. Graph one set of equations at a time. For each set, two of the graphs will be similar in some way, and one of the graphs will be different. Answer questions A and B for each set.

Set 1:	$y = 3x - 4$	$y = x^2$	$y = 3x + 2$
Set 2:	$y = 5$	$y = 3x$	$y = 1x$
Set 3:	$y = 2x + 3$	$y = 2x - 5$	$y = 0.5x + 2$
Set 4:	$y = 2x$	$y = 2 \div x$	$y = x + 5$

A. 1. Which two equations in the set have graphs that are similar?

2. In what ways are the two graphs similar?

3. In what ways are the equations for the two graphs similar?

B. 1. Which equation in the set has a graph that is different from the graphs of the other equations?

2. In what way is the graph different from the other graphs?

3. In what way is the equation different from the other equations?

■ Problem 5.1 Follow-Up

1. Use the equation $y = 2x$ to answer the following questions.
- **a.** If $x = 2$, what is y?
- **b.** If $x = \frac{2}{3}$, what is y?
- **c.** If $x = 3.25$, what is y?
- **d.** You can make a table to show pairs of numbers that fit an equation. Complete the following table for the equation $y = 2x$.

x	0	1	2	3	4	5	6
y							

2. Complete the following table for the equation $y = 2x + 3$.

x	0	1	2	3	4	5	6
y							

3. How is the table for $y = 2x + 3$ in question 2 similar to the table for $y = 2x$ in question 1?

5.2 Making Tables on a Calculator

Some graphing calculators can create tables of data for an equation. To use your calculator to create a table, first press $\boxed{Y=}$ and type in an equation. Then, press $\boxed{TABLE}$ to see the table for that equation. Here is part of the table for the equation $y = 2x$.

X	Y1
0	0
1	2
2	4
3	6
4	8
5	10
X=0	

Problem 5.2

A. 1. Use your calculator to make a table for the equation $y = 3x$.

2. Copy part of the calculator's table onto your paper.

3. Use your table to find y if $x = 5$.

B. 1. Use your calculator to make a table for the equation $y = 0.5x + 2$.

2. Copy part of the calculator's table onto your paper.

3. Use your table to find y if $x = 5$.

■ Problem 5.2 Follow-Up

1. Use your calculator to make a graph for the equation $y = 3x$. Describe the graph.

2. Use your calculator to make a graph for the equation $y = 0.5x + 2$. Describe the graph.

3. How do the graphs for questions 1 and 2 compare?

4. How would you make a graph for the equations $y = 3x$ and $y = 0.5x + 2$ without a graphing calculator?

As you work on these ACE questions, use your calculator whenever you need it.

Applications

1. Trevor entered an equation into his graphing calculator, and it displayed this table and graph.

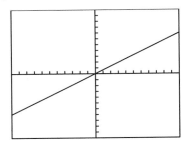

X	Y1
0	0
1	.5
2	1
3	1.5
4	2
5	2.5
X=0	

a. If $x = 5$, what is y?

b. How is this shown on the table? On the graph?

c. What equation did Trevor enter into his calculator?

2. Ziamara used her calculator to make a graph of the equation $y = 4x$. She noticed that the point (0, 0) was on the graph. Name three other points that are on the graph. Explain how you found these points.

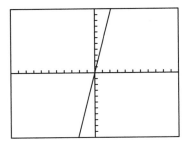

3. Each of the following tables shows how two variables are related. Find a pattern in each table. Use the pattern to complete the missing entries. Express the rule for the pattern as an equation, using the given letters as variable names.

a.

A	0	1	2	3		8	20	100
B	0	7	14	21	28			

b.

X	0	1	2	3	4	8	20	100
Y	6	7	8	9				

c.

X	0	1	2	3	4	8	20	100
Y	1	3	5	7				

d.

R	0	1	2	3	4	6	10	20
S	0	1	4	9	16			

Connections

4. You have seen that many of the costs for the Ocean and History Bike Tour depend on the number of customers. This table shows the relationship between the number of customers and the cost of the ferry ride from Cape May, New Jersey, to Lewes, Delaware.

Customers	1	2	3	4	5	6	7	8	9
Ferry cost	$2.50	5.00	7.50	10.00	12.50	15.00	17.50	20.00	22.50

a. Write an equation relating ferry cost, f, and number of customers, n.

b. Use your equation to find the cost if 35 people are on the tour.

c. How many people could cross on the ferry if the tour leader had $75?

5. Look back at question 4 on page 28 in Investigation 2. The first graph shows the relationship between Amanda's hunger and the time of day. Could you represent this relationship in a table? Could you represent this relationship with an equation? Explain your reasoning.

6. The rules for calculating area and perimeter for common polygons are often written with symbols. Using *A* for area, *P* for perimeter, *b* for base, *h* for height, *l* for length, and *w* for width, write equations for the rules for finding the area and perimeter of each figure below. These equations are usually called *formulas*.

a.

b.

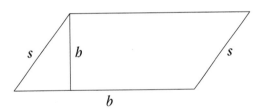

c.

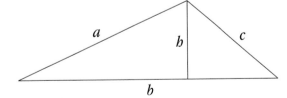

Extensions

7. When the tour partners had a 30-mile race on the last day, they gave the two young riders, Tony and Sarah, a half-hour head start. For this first half hour, Tony and Sarah rode at a steady pace of 12 miles per hour. After their half-hour head start, they kept up a fairly steady pace of about 10 miles per hour. When the others started riding, they went at a fairly steady pace of about 15 miles per hour.

    a. Make a table and a graph showing the relationship between distance and time for each group of riders.

    b. Will the older riders catch up with Tony and Sarah before the end of the 30-mile race? Explain your answer using both the tables and the graphs.

    c. Use d for distance traveled (in miles) and t for riding time (in hours) from when the second group started riding to write equations showing the relationship between these two variables for

        i. Tony and Sarah   **ii.** The other riders

Mathematical Reflections

In this investigation, you learned how to use a graphing calculator to make graphs and tables from equations. These questions will help you summarize what you have learned:

1 Write a letter to a friend explaining how to use a graphing calculator to make graphs and tables. Use a specific example to illustrate your explanation.

2 The number of tents the tour organizers need is $\frac{1}{2}$ times the number of customers.

a. Write an equation for a rule you can use to calculate the number of tents for any number of customers.

b. Does your equation give you enough information to make a table and a graph? Why or why not?

3 Think of a situation for which you can make a graph and a table, but not an equation.

Think about your answers to these questions, discuss your ideas with other students and your teacher, and then write a summary of your findings in your journal.

Looking Back and Looking Ahead

Unit Reflections

Working on the problems of this unit, you explored some of the big ideas in algebra. You learned how to identify *variables*, quantities that change in value as time passes or in response to change in other quantities. You learned how to collect and display data in *tables* and *coordinate graphs*, how to look for patterns relating *independent* and *dependent variables*, and how to express those patterns in words and in *equations* or *formulas*. Most important of all, you learned how to study tables, graphs, and equations to answer questions about variables.

Using Your Algebraic Reasoning—To test your understanding and skill in use of algebraic ideas and techniques, consider an example of how algebra is involved in a business that we all use or depend on—the shipping of packages from town to town, across the country, and around the world.

1 *When you take a package to the post office or to a package-shipping company, one big concern is the cost for shipping and insuring the package.*

a. List at least three variables that will affect the cost of shipping a package.

b. For each variable you list, explain its effect on the shipping cost.

2 *Suppose that a service offers to ship any package weighing at most two pounds to any place in the United States in two days or less for a price that depends on distance. The total charge is a $5 handling fee plus $0.01 for each mile that the package is carried.*

a. Copy and complete the table of sample shipping charges for such packages:

Distance in miles	100	200	300	400	500	1000	1500	2000
Shipping Cost								

Describe the pattern by which shipping cost increases as shipping distance increases.

b. Use grid paper to make a graph showing shipping charges for any distance between 0 and 2000 miles. Use appropriate labels and scales on the axes.

c. Write an equation or formula that gives the relation between distance, d, in miles and shipping cost, C, in dollars for this special rate.

d. Use a graphing calculator and the rule in part c to check your answers to part a and part b.

e. Use one or more of the tools you have—rule, table, graph, equation, and calculator—to answer these questions about shipping cost.

   i. What is the cost for shipping a package 450 miles?

   ii. How far can you ship a two-pound package at a cost of $35 or less?

Explaining Your Reasoning—When you use mathematical calculations to solve a problem or make a decision, you should be able to justify each step in your reasoning. Answer these questions about your work on Problems 1 and 2.

1. How did you arrive at the entries in the table of shipping costs for distances from 100 to 2000 miles?

2. How did you choose labels and scales for axes on the graph of shipping cost and distance? Did you plot only data pairs falling on grid points or did you connect those points with a smooth graph? Explain your choice of graphing strategy.

3. How could you convince someone that you have the right formula relating distance and shipping cost?

4. Why did you use the table, graph, equation, or rule in words to answer the questions of Problem 2e?

5. If you were asked to write a report describing the relationship between shipping distance and cost, what might be gained by including the table? The graph? The formula? What are the limitations of each type of display in showing the relationship?

The algebra ideas and techniques you've used in this unit will be applied and extended in many future algebra units of *Connected Mathematics* such as *Moving Straight Ahead*, *Thinking with Mathematical Models*, and *Say It with Symbols*. Understanding variables and patterns is essential to your future "mathematical life" in school and in work—to solve problems in architecture, medicine, economics, computing, engineering, and statistics.

Glossary

change To become different. For example, temperatures rise and fall, prices increase and decrease, and so on. In mathematics, quantities that change are called *variables.*

coordinate graph A graphical representation of pairs of related numerical values that shows the relationship between two variables. It relates the independent variable (shown on the *x*-axis) and the dependent variable (shown on the *y*-axis).

coordinate pair An ordered pair of numbers used to locate a point on a coordinate grid. The first number in a coordinate pair is the value for the *x*-coordinate, and the second number is the value for the *y*-coordinate.

dependent variable One of the two variables in a relationship. Its value depends upon or is determined by the other variable called the independent variable. For example, the cost of a long distance phone call (dependent variable) depends on how long you talk (independent variable).

equation, formula A rule containing variables that represents a mathematical relationship. An example is the formula for finding the area of a circle: $A = \pi r^2$.

independent variable One of the two variables in a relationship. Its value determines the value of the other variable called the dependent variable. If you organize a bike tour, for example, the number of people who register to go (independent variable) determines the cost for renting bikes (dependent variable).

pattern A change that occurs in an predictable way. For example, the squares on a checkerboard form a pattern in which the colors of the squares alternate between red and black. The sequence of square numbers: 1, 4, 9, 16, . . . forms a pattern in which the numbers increase by the next odd number. That is, 4 is 3 more than 1, 9 is 5 more than 4, 16 is 7 more than 9, and so on.

relationship An association between two or more variables. If one of the variables changes, the other variable may also change, and the change may be predictable.

rule A summary of a predictable relationship that tells how to find the value of a variable. It is a pattern which is consistent enough to be written down, made into an equation, graphed, or made into a table. For example, this rule relates time, rate, and distance: distance is equal to rate times time, or $d = rt$.

scale A labeling scheme used on each of the axes on a coordinate grid.

symbolic form Anything written or expressed through the use of symbols. For example, letters and numbers are often used instead of words to represent mathematical rules.

table A list of values for two or more variables that shows the relationship between them. Tables often represent data made from observations, from experiments, or from a series of arithmetic operations. A table may show a pattern of change between two variables that can be used to predict values for other entries in the table.

variable A quantity that can change. Letters are often used as symbols to represent variables in rules or equations that describe patterns.

x-axis The number line that is horizontal on a coordinate grid.

y-axis The number line that is vertical on a coordinate grid.

Index

Algebra, 3
   variable relationships and, 49
Assateague Island, 22
Axes, on a coordinate graph, 7–8

Change
   ACE, 26–34, 42–47
   graphing, 18–25, 36–41
   recording on a table, 18–25, 36–41
   verbal description of, 18–25, 36–41
Continuous relationship, 18–25, 36–41
Coordinate graph
   ACE, 10–17, 26–34, 42–47
   making, 7–9
   to show change, 18–25, 36–41
Coordinate pair, 21
Coordinate point, plotting, 9

Data
   ACE, 10–17, 26–34, 42–47
   experimental, 6–9
   on a graph, 4, 7–16, 18–25, 36–41
   on a table, 4, 18–25, 36–41
   verbal description of, 4, 18–25, 36–41
Dependent variable, 8
Discrete relationship, 18–25, 36–41

Equation, 4 *See also* **Formula**
   ACE, 54–59, 64–67
   for cost, 52–53
   to describe a pattern, 4, 49–53
   for distance, 50–51
   graphing, 61–63
   for income, 52
   for profit, 52–53
   to relate variables, 49–53
   for a rule, 49–53
   for speed, 51–52
   table for, 63
   table of variables for, 4, 49–53
   writing, 49–53
Experiment, jumping jack, 6–9

Formula, 4 *See also* **Equation**
   ACE, 54–59
   circumference of a circle, 49–50
   rules and, 49–53

Graph
   ACE, 10–17, 26–34, 42–47, 54–59, 64–67
   from an equation, 61–63
   coordinate, 7–9
   on a graphing calculator, 61–63
   patterns and, 49–53
   predicting from, 36–40
   for recording change, 18–25, 36–41
   rules and, 49–53
   selecting a scale for, 8
Graphing calculator
   ACE, 64–67
   graphing on, 4, 61–63
   making tables on, 4, 63

Independent variable, 8
Investigation
   Analyzing Graphs and Tables, 36–48
   Graphing Change, 18–35
   Patterns and Rules, 49–60
   Using a Graphing Calculator, 61–68
   Variables and Coordinate Graphs, 5–17

Journal, 17, 35, 48, 60, 68

Logo, drawing regular polygons with, 47
Looking Back and Looking Ahead:
    Unit Reflections, 69–70

Mathematical Highlights, 4
Mathematical Reflections, 17, 35, 48,
    60, 68

Pattern, 7
    ACE, 42–47, 54–59
    predicting from, 7, 38, 41
    relating variables, 49–53
    rules and, 49–53
Polygon, drawing regular, 47
Prediction
    from a graph, 4, 36–40
    from a pattern, 7, 38, 41
    from a table, 40–41
    using rules, 49–53

Range of values, 8
Relationship, 9
    ACE, 26–34, 42–47, 54–59
    continuous, 18–25, 36–41
    discrete, 18–25, 36–41
    graphic description of, 18–25, 36–41
    money and number, 36–41, 52–53
    time and distance, 18–24, 50–51
    time and speed, 24–25, 51–52
    verbal description of, 18–25, 36–41
Rule, 49
    ACE, 54–59
    equation for, 49–53

patterns and, 49–53

Scale, selecting, 8

Table, 6
    ACE, 10–17, 26–34, 42–47, 54–59,
        64–67
    from an equation, 63
    on a graphing calculator, 63
    to organize data, 6–9
    predicting from, 40–41
    recording change on, 18–25, 36–41
    rules and, 49–53
Turtle Math, drawing regular polygons,
    47

Variable, 3, 7
    ACE, 10–17, 42–47, 54–59
    dependent, 8
    expressing relationships with, 18–25,
        36–41
    independent, 7
    relating with equations, 49–53
    representation on a coordinate grid,
        7–9
Verbal description
    ACE, 7–16, 26–34, 42–47, 54–59
    of a relationship, 18–25, 36–41,
        49–53

x-**axis**, 7–8
x-**coordinate**, 21

y-**axis**, 7–8
y-**coordinate**, 21

Connected  Mathematics®

Similarity

Student Edition

Glenda Lappan
James T. Fey
William M. Fitzgerald
Susan N. Friel
Elizabeth Difanis Phillips

Prentice
Hall

Glenview, Illinois
Needham, Massachusetts
Upper Saddle River, New Jersey

Connected Mathematics® was developed at Michigan State University with the support of National Science Foundation Grant No. MDR 9150217.

This project was supported, in part, by the
National Science Foundation
Opinions expressed are those of the authors and not necessarily those of the Foundation

The Michigan State University authors and administration have agreed that all MSU royalties arising from this publication will be devoted to purposes supported by the Department of Mathematics and the MSU Mathematics Education Enrichment Fund.

Photo Acknowledgements: 14 © Superstock, Inc.; 21 © Barbara Alper/Stock, Boston; 25 © G. Ricatto/Superstock, Inc.; 30 © Mark M. Boulton/Photo Researchers, Inc.; 37 © Nita Winter/The Image Works; 45 © Peter Menzel/Stock, Boston; 55 © J. Mahoney/The Image Works; 70 © Ira Kirschenbaum/Stock, Boston; 72 © N. Rowan/The Image Works

Turtle Math is a registered trademark of LCSI.

Contents

Mathematical Highlights — 4

Investigation 1: Enlarging Figures — 5
    1.1 Stretching a Figure — 5
    Applications—Connections—Extensions — 9
    Mathematical Reflections — 13

Investigation 2: Similar Figures — 14
    2.1 Drawing Wumps — 15
    2.2 Nosing Around — 18
    2.3 Making Wump Hats — 21
    Applications—Connections—Extensions — 22
    Mathematical Reflections — 27

Investigation 3: Patterns of Similar Figures — 28
    3.1 Identifying Similar Figures — 28
    3.2 Building with Rep-tiles — 29
    3.3 Subdividing to Find Rep-tiles — 31
    Applications—Connections—Extensions — 33
    Mathematical Reflections — 40

Investigation 4: Using Similarity — 41
    4.1 Using Similarity to Solve a Mystery — 41
    4.2 Scaling Up — 43
    4.3 Making Copies — 44
    4.4 Using Map Scales — 45
    Applications—Connections—Extensions — 47
    Mathematical Reflections — 58

Investigation 5: Similar Triangles — 59
    5.1 Using Shadows to Find Heights — 59
    5.2 Using Mirrors to Find Heights — 61
    5.3 Using Similar Triangles to Find Distances — 63
    Applications—Connections—Extensions — 64
    Mathematical Reflections — 74

Investigation 6: Stretching and Shrinking with a Computer — 75
    6.1 Drawing Similar Figures with a Computer — 75
    6.2 Stretching and Shrinking Flags — 79
    Applications—Connections—Extensions — 81
    Mathematical Reflections — 84

The Unit Project — 85

Looking Back and Looking Ahead: Unit Reflections — 86

Glossary — 88

Index — 91

Stretching and Shrinking

Many stores, particularly those that stay open late into the night, have surveillance cameras. One night the local Dusk to Dawn convenience store was robbed. The surveillance camera had taken several photographs during the robbery. By inspecting a picture of the robber standing in front of the cash register, police were able to determine the robber's height. How did they do it?

Draw a triangle on a sheet of paper. Can you divide the triangle into identical smaller triangles that are the same shape as the original triangle?

How tall is your school building? How high is the top of a basketball backboard? How can you find the height of something tall without measuring it?

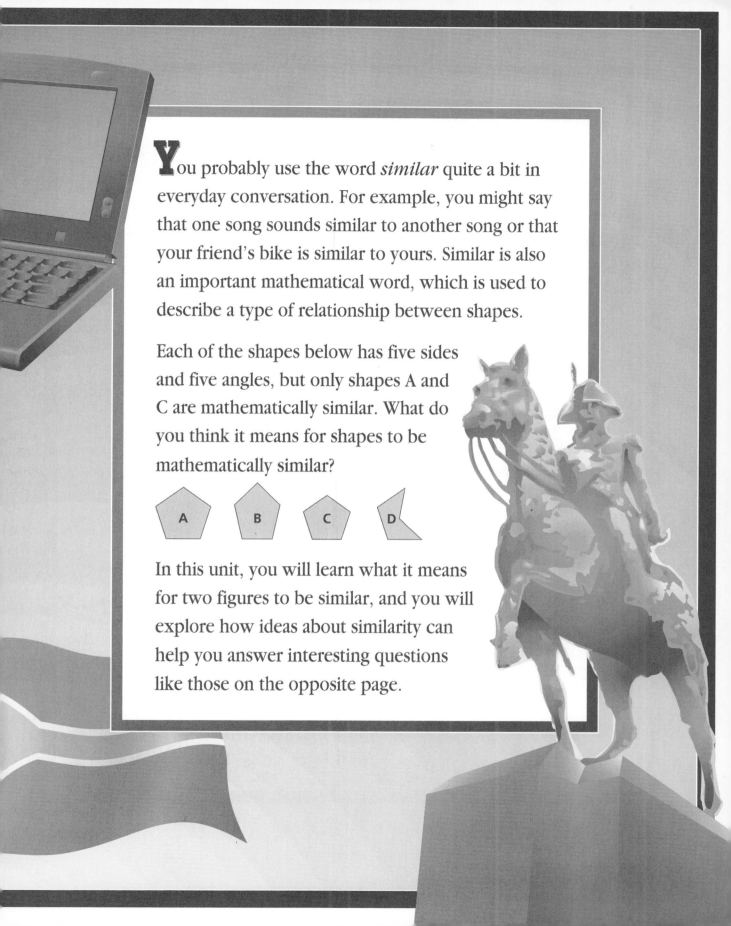

You probably use the word *similar* quite a bit in everyday conversation. For example, you might say that one song sounds similar to another song or that your friend's bike is similar to yours. Similar is also an important mathematical word, which is used to describe a type of relationship between shapes.

Each of the shapes below has five sides and five angles, but only shapes A and C are mathematically similar. What do you think it means for shapes to be mathematically similar?

In this unit, you will learn what it means for two figures to be similar, and you will explore how ideas about similarity can help you answer interesting questions like those on the opposite page.

In *Stretching and Shrinking* you will explore the geometry concept of similarity. The unit should help you to:

● Recognize similar figures visually and identify that figures are similar by comparing sides and angles;

● Understand and use the equivalence of ratios of sides to examine similar figures and find unknown lengths;

● Understand the relationship between measures of lengths in figures and the scale factor relating two similar figures;

● Use the scale factor between figures to scale a figure up or down and to predict the lengths of corresponding edges and areas; and

● Use the concept of similarity to solve everyday problems.

As you work the problems in this unit, make it a habit to ask yourself questions about situations that involve similar figures: *What is the same and what is different about two similar figures? What determines whether two shapes are similar? When figures are similar, how are the lengths, areas, and scale factor related?*

Enlarging Figures

In this investigation, you will use rubber bands to make enlargements of drawings. Although this is not a precise way to enlarge drawings, it's fun—and you can see some interesting relationships between a figure and its enlarged image.

Think about this!

As you work on this investigation, think about these questions:

- When a figure is enlarged, which of its features remain the same?
- When a figure is enlarged, which of its features change?

1.1 Stretching a Figure

Michelle, Daphne, and Mukesh are the officers of their school's Mystery Book Club. Mukesh designed a flyer inviting new members to attend the club's next meeting.

Do you love a Good Mystery?

Then come to the next meeting of the Mystery Book Club.
Tuesday, November 2
at 3:30 P.M. in room 222

Daphne thought it would be a good idea to make a large poster announcing the meeting. She wanted to use the detective figure from the flyer, but at a larger size. Michelle showed her a clever way to enlarge the figure by using rubber bands.

Instructions for stretching a figure

1. Make a "two-band stretcher" by tying the ends of two identical rubber bands together. Bands about 3 inches long work well.

2. Tape the sheet with the picture you want to enlarge to your desk next to a blank sheet of paper. If you are right-handed, put the figure on the left. If you are left-handed, put it on the right.

Right-handed Setup   Left-handed Setup

3. With your finger, hold down one end of the stretcher on point *P*. Point *P* is called the *anchor point*.

4. Put a pencil in the other end of the stretcher. Stretch the rubber bands with your pencil until the knot is on the outline of your picture.

5. Guide the knot around the original picture, while your pencil traces out a new picture. (Don't allow any slack in the rubber bands.) This new drawing is the **image** of the original drawing.

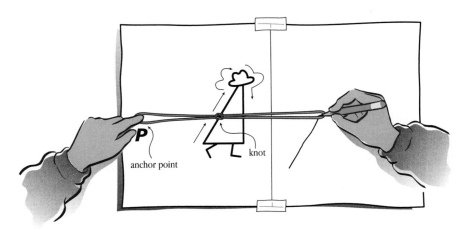

A. Use the method described on the previous page to enlarge the figures on Labsheets 1.1 and 1.2.

B. *Compare* is an important word in mathematics. When you **compare** two figures, you look at what is the *same* and what is *different* about them. Compare each original figure to the enlarged image you made. Make a detailed list about what is the same and what is different about them. Be sure to consider

- the lengths of the line segments
- the areas
- the angles (for figures with angles)
- the general shape of the figure

Explain each comparison you make in detail. For example, rather than just saying that two lengths are different, tell exactly which lengths you are comparing and explain how they differ.

■ Problem 1.1 Follow-Up

Michelle used her stretcher to enlarge triangle *ABC*. She labeled the vertices of the image *A′*, *B′*, and *C′* (read, "A prime, B prime, and C prime") to show that they *correspond* to the vertices *A*, *B*, and *C* of triangle *ABC*.

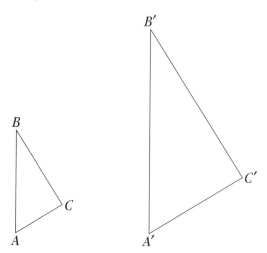

In mathematics, we use the word **corresponding** to describe how parts of a figure are related to parts of an enlargement or reduction of the figure. In the triangles above, ∠*BAC* and ∠*B′A′C′* are corresponding angles, and side *AB* and side *A′B′* are corresponding sides.

1. Name each pair of corresponding sides and each pair of corresponding angles in triangles ABC and $A'B'C'$.

2. **a.** Copy triangle ABC onto a sheet of paper. Choose an anchor point, and enlarge the triangle with your stretcher.

   b. Predict what would happen if you moved the anchor point up or down and further away from triangle ABC and then used your stretcher to enlarge it. Test your prediction by choosing a new anchor point and enlarging the triangle. Is your prediction correct?

   c. Predict what would happen if you moved the anchor point up or down and closer to triangle ABC and then used your stretcher to enlarge it. Test your prediction. Is it correct?

As you work on these ACE questions, use your calculator whenever you need it.

Applications

1. Triangle *PQR* is an enlargement of triangle *STU*. Name all the pairs of corresponding sides and all the pairs of corresponding angles between the triangles.

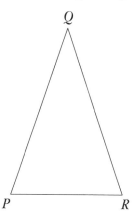

2. Copy square *WXYZ* and anchor point *P* onto a sheet of paper. Enlarge the square with your two-band stretcher. Label the image *W′X′Y′Z′* so that vertex *W′* corresponds to vertex *W*, vertex *X′* corresponds to vertex *X*, and so on.

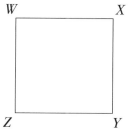

a. How does the length of side *W′X′* compare to the length of side *WX*?

b. How does the perimeter of square *WXYZ* compare to the perimeter of square *W′X′Y′Z′*?

c. How many copies of square *WXYZ* can fit inside square *W′X′Y′Z′*? (In other words, how do their areas compare?)

3. Copy parallelogram *ABCD* and anchor point *P* onto a sheet of paper. Enlarge the parallelogram with your two-band stretcher. Label the image *A′B′C′D′* so that vertex *A′* corresponds to vertex *A*, vertex *B′* corresponds to vertex *B*, and so on.

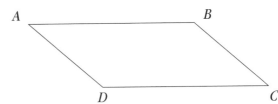

   P

a. How do the side lengths of parallelogram *A′B′C′D′* compare to the side lengths of parallelogram *ABCD*?

b. How many copies of parallelogram *ABCD* can fit inside parallelogram *A′B′C′D′*? (In other words, how do their areas compare?)

Connections

4. Copy circle *C* and anchor point *P* onto a sheet of paper. Make an enlargement of the circle using your two-band stretcher.

P

a. How do the diameters of the circles compare?

b. How do the areas of the circles compare? Explain your reasoning.

Extensions

5. Circle A' is an enlargement of a smaller circle A made by using a two-band stretcher. Circle A is not shown.

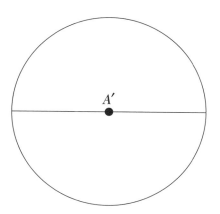

   a. How does the diameter of circle A' compare to the diameter of circle A?

   b. How does the area of circle A' compare to the area of circle A?

6. **a.** Suppose each of the small circles below has a diameter of 8 centimeters, and the large circle has a diameter of 16 centimeters. What is the combined area of the two small circles?

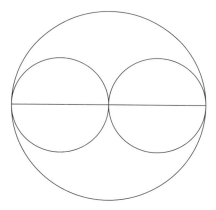

   b. What is the area inside the large circle and above the two small circles?

7. Make a three-band stretcher by tying three identical rubber bands together. Use this stretcher to enlarge the drawing on Labsheet 1.1.

a. How does the shape of the image compare to the shape of the original figure?

b. How do the lengths of the line segments in the two figures compare?

c. How do the areas of the two figures compare?

Mathematical Reflections

In this investigation, you learned how to use a stretcher to enlarge figures. These questions will help you summarize what you have learned:

1 Suppose you used your two-band stretcher to enlarge the rectangle below.

    a. How would the side lengths of the enlarged rectangle compare to the side lengths of the original rectangle?

    b. How would the perimeter of the enlarged rectangle compare to the perimeter of the original rectangle?

    c. How would the area of the enlarged rectangle compare to the area of the original rectangle?

2 How does the location of the anchor point affect the image drawn with a stretcher?

Think about your answers to these questions, discuss your ideas with other students and your teacher, and then write a summary of your findings in your journal.

Similar Figures

Zack and Marta wanted to design a computer game that involved several animated characters. Marta asked her uncle Carlos, a programmer for a video game company, about computer animation. Carlos explained that the computer screen can be thought of as a grid made up of thousands of tiny points called *pixels.* To animate figures, you need to enter the coordinates of key points on the figure. The computer uses these points to draw the figure in different positions.

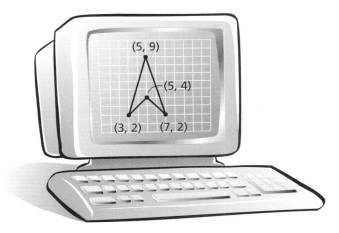

Marta told her uncle that sometimes the figures in their game would need to change size. Her uncle explained that a computer can make figures larger and smaller if you give it a rule for finding the key points in the new figure from key points in the original figure.

2.1 Drawing Wumps

Zack and Marta's computer game involves a family called the Wumps. The members of the Wump family are various sizes, but they all have the same shape. Mug Wump is the game's main character. By enlarging or reducing Mug, a player can transform him into other Wump family members.

Zack and Marta experimented on paper with enlarging and reducing figures on a coordinate grid. First, Zack drew Mug Wump on dot paper. Then, he labeled the key points from *A* to *Z* and from *AA* to *FF* and listed the coordinates for each point. Marta described the rules that would transform Mug into different sizes to create other members of the Wump family.

Lurking among the members of the Wump family are some impostors who, at first glance, look like the Wumps but are actually quite different.

A. Use the instructions below to draw Mug Wump on the dot paper grid on Labsheet 2.1B. Describe Mug's shape.

B. Use Labsheet 2.1A and two more copies of Labsheet 2.1B to make Bug, Lug, Thug, and Zug. After drawing the characters, compare them to Mug. Which characters are the impostors?

C. Compare Mug to the other characters. What things are the same about Mug and Zug? Mug and Lug? Mug and Bug? Mug and Thug? What things are different? Think about the general shape, the lengths of sides, and the angles of each figure.

Instructions for drawing Wumps

1. To draw Mug, use the sets of coordinate pairs given in the chart on the next page. Plot the points from the "Mug Wump" column on Labsheet 2.1B. Connect the points with line segments as follows:

- For Set 1, connect the points in order, and then connect the last point to the first point.
- For Set 2, connect the points in order (don't connect the last point to the first point).
- For Set 3, connect the points in order, and then connect the last point to the first point.
- For Set 4, make a dot at each point (don't connect the dots).

2. To draw Zug, Lug, Bug, and Thug, use the given rule to find the coordinates of each point. For example, the rule for finding the points for Zug is $(2x, 2y)$. This means that you multiply each of Mug's coordinates by 2. Point A on Mug is $(2, 0)$, so the corresponding point A on Zug is $(4, 0)$. Point B on Mug is $(2, 4)$, so the corresponding point B on Zug is $(4, 8)$.

3. Plot the points for Zug, Lug, Bug, and Thug, and connect them according to the directions in step 2.

Rule	Mug Wump (x, y)	Zug $(2x, 2y)$	Lug $(3x, y)$	Bug $(3x, 3y)$	Thug $(x, 3y)$
Point	Set 1	Set 1	Set 1	Set 1	Set 1
A	(2, 0)	(4, 0)			
B	(2, 4)	(4, 8)			
C	(0, 4)				
D	(0, 5)				
E	(2, 5)				
F	(0, 8)				
G	(0, 12)				
H	(1, 15)				
I	(2, 12)				
J	(5, 12)				
K	(6, 15)				
L	(7, 12)				
M	(7, 8)				
N	(5, 5)				
O	(7, 5)				
P	(7, 4)				
Q	(5, 4)				
R	(5, 0)				
S	(4, 0)				
T	(4, 3)				
U	(3, 3)				
V	(3, 0) (connect V to A)				
	Set 2 (start over)	Set 2	Set 2	Set 2	Set 2
W	(1, 8)				
X	(2, 7)				
Y	(5, 7)				
Z	(6, 8)				
	Set 3 (start over)	Set 3	Set 3	Set 3	Set 3
AA	(3, 8)				
BB	(4, 8)				
CC	(4, 10)				
DD	(3, 10) (connect DD to AA)				
	Set 4 (start over)	Set 4	Set 4	Set 4	Set 4
EE	(2, 11) (make a dot)				
FF	(5, 11) (make a dot)				

1. In mathematics, we say that figures like Mug and Zug (but not Mug and Lug) are **similar.** What do you think it means for two figures to be mathematically similar?

2. The members of the Wump family are all similar. How do their corresponding sides compare? How do their corresponding angles compare?

2.2 Nosing Around

All the members of the Wump family have the same angle measures. Is having the same angle measures enough to make two figures similar? All rectangles have four right angles. Are all rectangles similar? What about these two rectangles?

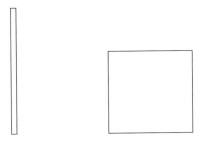

These rectangles are not similar, because they don't have the same shape—one is tall and skinny, and the other looks like a square. To be similar, it is not enough for figures to have the same angle measures.

In this problem, you will investigate rectangles more closely to try to figure out what else is necessary for two rectangles to be similar. You will compare side lengths, angle measures, and perimeters.

One way to compare two quantities is to form a **ratio**. For example, Mug Wump's nose is 1 unit wide and 2 units long. To compare the width to the length, we can use the ratio *1 to 2,* which can also be written as the fraction $\frac{1}{2}$.

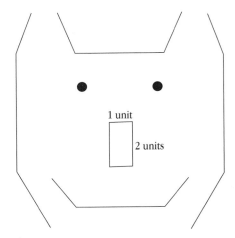

Problem 2.2

Copy the chart below. The Wumps in the chart are numbered according to their size. Mug is Wump 1. Since the segments that make up Zug are twice as long as the segments that make up Mug, Zug is Wump 2. Since the segments that make up Bug are three times as long as the segments that make up Mug, Bug is Wump 3. Since Lug and Thug are not similar to the Wumps, they are at the bottom of the chart.

A. Look carefully at the noses of Mug, Zug, Bug, Lug, and Thug. In your table, record the dimensions, the ratio of width to length ($\frac{width}{length}$), and the perimeter of each nose.

B. Look at the data you recorded for Mug, Zug, and Bug. What patterns do you see? Explain how the values in each column change as the Wumps get bigger. Look for relationships between the values in the different columns.

C. The rule for making Wump 4 is $(4x, 4y)$. The rule for making Wump 5 is $(5x, 5y)$. Add data to the chart for Wumps 4 and 5. Do their noses fit the patterns you noticed in part B?

D. Use the patterns you found to add data for Wumps 10, 20, and 100 to the chart. Explain your reasoning.

E. Do Lug's nose and Thug's nose seem to fit the patterns you found for the Wumps? If not, what makes them different?

The Wump Noses (Plus Lug and Thug)

Wump	Width of nose	Length of nose	$\frac{Width}{Length}$	Perimeter
Wump 1 (Mug)	1	2	$\frac{1}{2}$	
Wump 2 (Zug)	2			
Wump 3 (Bug)	3			
Wump 4				
Wump 5				
$\vdots$				
Wump 10				
Wump 20				
Wump 100				
Lug				
Thug				

■ Problem 2.2 Follow-Up

To find the length, width, and perimeter of Zug's nose, we can multiply the length, width, and perimeter of Mug's nose by 2. The number 2 is called the *scale factor* from Mug's nose to Zug's nose. The **scale factor** is the number that we multiply the dimensions of an original figure by to get the dimensions of an enlarged or reduced figure.

The scale factor from Mug to Bug is 3. You can multiply the side lengths of Mug's nose by 3 to find the side lengths of Bug's nose. We can also say that the side lengths and the perimeters *grow by a scale factor of 3*.

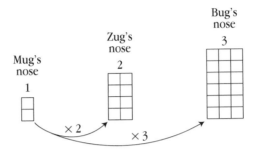

1. Is there a scale factor from Mug's nose to Wump 4's nose? Why or why not?

2. Is there a scale factor from Mug's nose to Thug's nose? Why or why not?

3. The dimensions of Bug's nose are 3 × 6. Suppose this nose is enlarged by a scale factor of 3.
   a. What are the dimensions of the new nose?
   b. What is the perimeter of the new nose?

4. a. What is the scale factor from Wump 2 to Wump 10?
   b. What is the scale factor from Wump 10 to Wump 2?

Making Wump Hats

Zack and Marta experimented with multiplying each of Mug's coordinates by different whole numbers to create other similar figures. Marta wondered how multiplying the coordinates by a decimal, or adding numbers to or subtracting numbers from each coordinate, would affect Mug's shape. When she asked her uncle about this, he gave her the coordinates for a new shape—a hat for Mug to wear—and some rules to try on the shape.

Point	Hat 1 (x, y)	Hat 2 $(x + 2, y + 2)$	Hat 3 $(x + 3, y - 1)$	Hat 4 $(2x, y + 2)$	Hat 5 $(2x, 3y)$	Hat 6 $(0.5x, 0.5y)$
A	(0, 4)	(2, 6)	(3, 3)	(0, 6)	(0, 12)	(0, 2)
B	(0, 1)					
C	(6, 1)					
D	(4, 2)					
E	(4, 4)					
F	(3, 5)					
G	(1, 5)					
H	(0, 4)					

Problem 2.3

Use the table and dot paper grids on Labsheets 2.3A and 2.3B.

- To make Mug's hat, plot points *A–H* from the Hat 1 column on the grid labeled Hat 1, connecting the points as you go.

- For Hats 2–6, use the rules in the table to fill in the coordinates for each column. Then, plot each hat on the appropriate grid, connecting the points as you go.

■ Problem 2.3 Follow-Up

1. What rule would make a hat with line segments $\frac{1}{3}$ the length of Hat 1's line segments?
2. What happens to a figure on a coordinate grid when you add to or subtract from its coordinates?
3. What rule would make a hat the same size as Hat 1 but moved up 2 units on the grid?
4. What rule would make a hat with line segments twice as long as Hat 1's line segments and moved 8 units to the right?

As you work on these ACE questions, use your calculator whenever you need it.

Applications

1. The triangles below are similar.

    a. Name the pairs of corresponding sides.

    b. Name the pairs of corresponding angles.

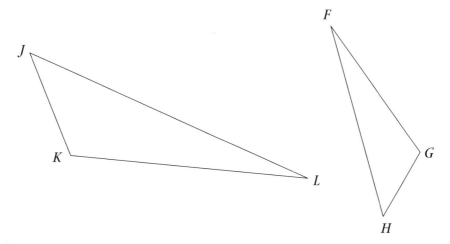

2. Mug's grandparents, Chug and Hug, are the fourth and fifth members of the Wump family (in the table for Problem 2.2, Chug is Wump 4 and Hug is Wump 5). How do the side lengths and angle measures of Mug's grandparents compare to the side lengths and angle measures of Mug? You may use the table from Problem 2.2 to help you answer this question.

3. If you used the rule $(6x, 6y)$ to transform Mug into a new figure, how would the angles of the new figure compare to Mug's angles? How would the side lengths of the new figure compare to Mug's side lengths?

4. If you used the rule $(0.5x, 0.5y)$ to transform Mug into a new figure, how would the angles of the new figure compare to Mug's angles? How would the side lengths of the new figure compare to Mug's side lengths?

5. If you used the rule $(3x + 1, 3y - 4)$ to transform Mug into a new figure, how would the angles of the new figure compare to Mug's angles? How would the side lengths of the new figure compare to Mug's side lengths? How would the location of the new figure compare to Mug's location?

6. a. Draw a triangle ABC with vertices A $(0, 0)$, B $(3, 0)$, and C $(0, 4)$.

b. Draw a triangle $A'B'C'$ by applying the rule $(2.5x, 2.5y)$ to the vertices of triangle ABC.

c. How do the lengths of the sides of triangle $A'B'C'$ compare to the lengths of the corresponding sides of triangle ABC?

d. How do the measures of the angles of triangle $A'B'C'$ compare to the measures of the corresponding angles of triangle ABC?

e. Are triangles ABC and $A'B'C'$ similar? Explain.

7. a. Draw a triangle XYZ with vertices X $(5, 8)$, Y $(0, 5)$, and Z $(10, 2)$.

b. Apply a rule to triangle XYZ to get a similar triangle, $X'Y'Z'$, with a scale factor of 1. What rule did you use? How do the lengths of the sides of triangle $X'Y'Z'$ compare to the lengths of the corresponding sides of triangle XYZ?

c. Apply a rule to triangle XYZ to get a similar triangle, $X''Y''Z''$, with a scale factor of $\frac{1}{5}$. What rule did you use? How do the lengths of the sides of triangle $X''Y''Z''$ compare to the lengths of the corresponding sides of triangle XYZ?

8. a. Use triangle ABC from question 6 and the rule $(3x, y)$ to draw a new triangle.

b. How do the measures of the angles of the new triangle compare to the measures of the corresponding angles of triangle ABC?

c. Are the two triangles similar? Explain.

9. a. Copy rectangle *ABCD* onto a piece of grid paper.

   b. Make a similar rectangle by applying a scale factor of 1.5 to rectangle *ABCD*. Label the new rectangle *A'B'C'D'*.

   c. Make another similar rectangle by applying a scale factor of 0.25 to rectangle *ABCD*. Label the new rectangle *A"B"C"D"*.

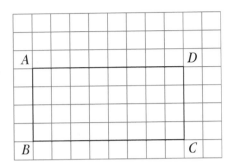

   d. Tell how the lengths of the sides of each new rectangle compare to the lengths of the corresponding sides of rectangle *ABCD*.

   e. Are rectangles *A'B'C'D'* and *A"B"C"D"* similar to each other? If so, what is the scale factor from rectangle *A'B'C'D'* to rectangle *A"B"C"D"*? What is the scale factor from rectangle *A"B"C"D"* to rectangle *A'B'C'D'*?

   f. If you make a rectangle by adding 3 units to each side of rectangle *ABCD*, will it be similar to rectangle *ABCD*? Explain your reasoning.

10. Redraw Hat 1 (from Problem 2.3). Draw a new hat by applying the rule $(2x + 1, 2y + 2)$ to Hat 1. How does the new hat compare to Hat 1? Are they similar? Explain your reasoning.

Connections

11. a. On centimeter grid paper, draw a rectangle with an area of 14 square centimeters. Label it *ABCD*.

   b. Use a rule to transform rectangle *ABCD* into a rectangle that is twice as long and twice as wide. Label the rectangle *A'B'C'D'*. What rule did you use to make rectangle *A'B'C'D'*?

   c. What is the perimeter of rectangle *A'B'C'D'*? How does it compare to the perimeter of rectangle *ABCD*?

12. You can think of a map as a reduced copy of a real country, state, or city. A map is similar to the place it represents. Below is a map of South Africa. The scale for the map is 1 centimeter = 240 kilometers. This means that 1 centimeter on the map represents 240 kilometers in the real world. Using this scale and a ruler, estimate these distances:

Cape Town, South Africa

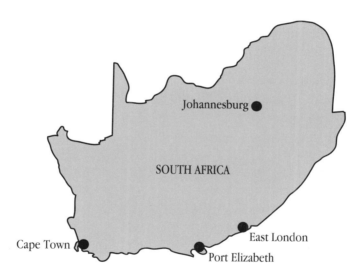

a. Cape Town to Port Elizabeth

b. Johannesburg to East London

Extensions

13. Select a drawing of a comic strip character from a newspaper or magazine. Draw a grid over the figure, or tape a transparent grid on top of the figure. Identify key points on the figure and then enlarge the figure by applying the rule $(2x, 2y)$ to the points.

14. Point A has coordinates $(2, 4)$, point B has coordinates $(6, 1)$, and point C has coordinates $(1, 1)$.

    a. A rule is appled to A, B, and C to get A', B', and C'. Point A' is at $(7, 3)$ and point B' is at $(11, 0)$. Where is point C' located?

    b. A different rule is applied to A, B, and C to get A'', B'', and C''. Point A'' is at $(4, 7)$ and point B'' is at $(12, 1)$. Where is point C'' located?

    c. A different rule is applied to A, B, and C to get A''', B''', and C'''. Point A''' is at $(6, 7)$ and point B''' is at $(10, 1)$. Where is point C''' located?

Mathematical Reflections

In this investigation, you made a character named Mug Wump on a coordinate grid. Then, you used rules—such as (2*x*, 2*y*) and (2*x*, *y*)—to transform Mug into other characters. Some of the characters you made were similar to Mug Wump, and some weren't. These questions will help you summarize what you have learned:

1 How did you decide which characters were similar to Mug Wump?

2 What types of rules produced figures similar to Mug Wump? What types of rules did not? Explain your answers.

3 If two figures are similar, describe the relationships between their

a. general shapes

b. angle measures

c. side lengths

Think about your answers to these questions, discuss your ideas with other students and your teacher, and then write a summary of your findings in your journal.

Patterns of Similar Figures

In the last investigation, you met the Wump family. You found that Mug, Bug, and Zug are similar—they have exactly the same shape. You also discovered that, to make a figure that is similar to a given figure, you keep the same angles and multiply each length of the original figure by the same number. For example, to go from Mug to Zug, you use the same angles and multiply each length by 2. To make a smaller member of the Wump family, you could shrink Mug by keeping the same angles and multiplying each length by a number less than 1, such as 0.5.

3.1 Identifying Similar Figures

How good are you at spotting changes in a figure's shape? Can you look at two figures and decide whether they are similar? In the last investigation, you learned some mathematical ideas about what makes figures similar. Here, you will use your visual perception to predict which figures might be similar, and then use mathematics to check your predictions.

Problem 3.1

Examine the four sets of polygons on Labsheet 3.1. Two shapes in each set are similar, and the other is an impostor.

In each set, which polygons are similar? Explain your answers. You may cut out the polygons if it helps you think about the question.

■ Problem 3.1 Follow-Up

1. For each pair of similar figures on Labsheet 3.1, tell what number the side lengths of the small figure must be multiplied by to get the side lengths of the large figure. (You learned that this number is the scale factor from the small figure to the large figure.)

2. For each pair of similar figures on Labsheet 3.1, tell what number the side lengths of the large figure must be multiplied by to get the side lengths of the small figure. (This number is the scale factor from the large figure to the small figure.)

3. How are the scale factors in parts 1 and 2 related?

Rectangle set

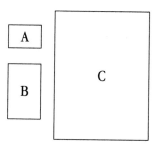

Parallelogram set

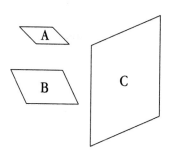

Decagon set

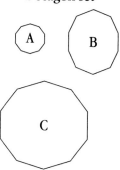

Star set

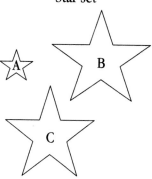

3.2 Building with Rep-tiles

A **rep-tile** is a shape whose copies can be put together to make a larger, similar shape. The small triangle below is a rep-tile. The two large triangles are formed from copies of this rep-tile. Can you explain why each large triangle is similar to the small triangle?

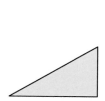
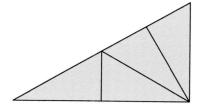
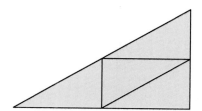

This reptile is *not* a rep-tile.

In this problem, your challenge is to figure out which of the shapes below are rep-tiles.

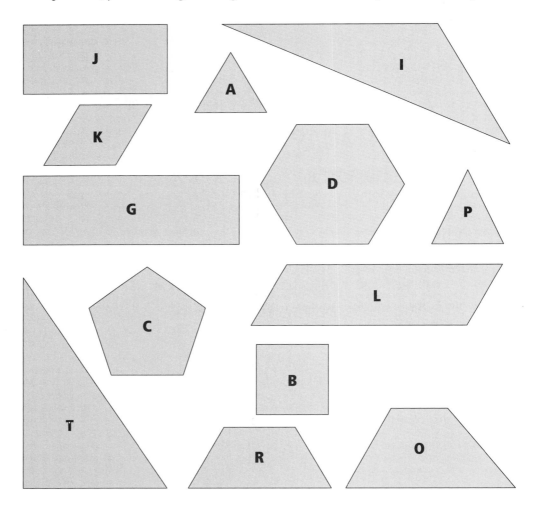

Problem 3.2

Use the shapes shown on page 30 from your ShapeSet™, or cut out copies of the shapes from Labsheet 3.2.

A. Start with four copies of one of the shapes. Try to find a way to put the four copies together—with no overlap and no holes—to make a larger, similar shape. If you are successful, make a sketch showing how the four shapes (rep-tiles) fit together, and give the scale factor from the original shape to the new shape. Repeat this process with each shape.

B. For each rep-tile you found in part A, try to find a different way to arrange the copies to get a similar shape. Sketch each new arrangement. How does the scale factor for each new arrangement compare to the scale factor for the first arrangement?

C. Start with one of the rep-tiles you found in part A. Try to add copies of the rep-tile to this shape to make the next-largest similar shape. If you are successful, make a sketch showing how the copies fit together. Repeat this process with each rep-tile you found in part A.

■ Problem 3.2 Follow-Up

1. Examine your work from Problem 3.2 carefully. What is the relationship between the scale factor and the number of copies of an original shape needed to make a larger, similar shape?

2. Is the number of copies of an original shape used to make a new shape related to the side lengths or the area of the new shape?

3.3 Subdividing to Find Rep-tiles

In Problem 3.2, you arranged rep-tiles to form larger, similar shapes. In this problem, you reverse the process. You start with a large shape and try to divide it into smaller, congruent shapes that are similar to the original shape. (Two shapes are *congruent* if they are exactly the same size and shape.) An example is shown at right.

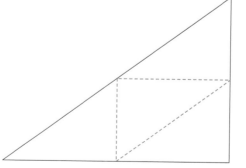

Problem 3.3

The shapes below appear on Labsheet 3.3. Try to find a way to divide each shape into four congruent, smaller shapes that are similar to the original shape. For each shape, give the scale factor from the smaller shape to the original shape.

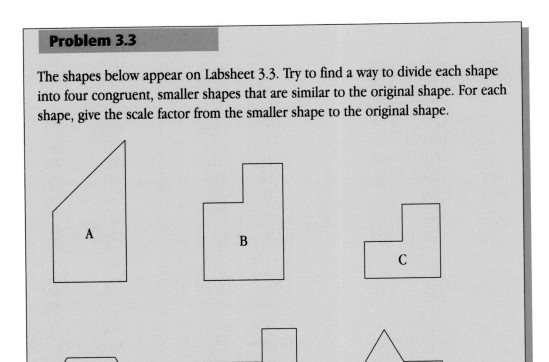

If you have trouble dividing a shape, experiment by cutting out copies of the shape and putting them together as you did in Problem 3.2.

■ Problem 3.3 Follow-Up

1. Choose one of the shapes on Labsheet 3.3. Divide each small figure within the shape in the same way you divided the original shape. How many of these new shapes does it take to cover the original shape?

2. For the shape you subdivided in question 1, what is the scale factor from the smallest shape to the original shape?

3. How does the scale factor from question 2 relate to the number of the smallest shapes it takes to cover the original shape? What is the relationship between the scale factor and the areas of the large and small figures?

As you work on these ACE questions, use your calculator whenever you need it.

Applications

1. The sides that form the right angle of a right triangle are called the *legs* of the triangle. This right triangle has legs of length 2 centimeters and 3 centimeters. Draw three triangles that are similar to this triangle.

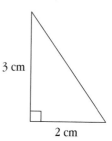

3 cm

2 cm

In 2–5, a pair of similar triangles is given. Find the missing measurement.

2.

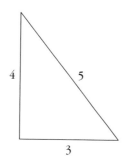

4   5

3

2   a

1.5

$a = ?$

3.

8.75   10.5

7

2.5 b

2

$b = ?$

4.

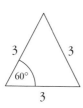

3   3

60°

3

4   4

c

4

$c = ?$

5.

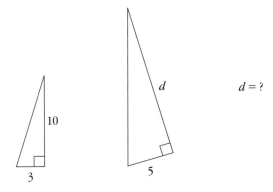

$d = ?$

In 6 and 7, decide which polygon is similar to polygon A. Explain your answer. To check your answer, you may want to trace the figures onto another sheet of paper and cut them out.

6.

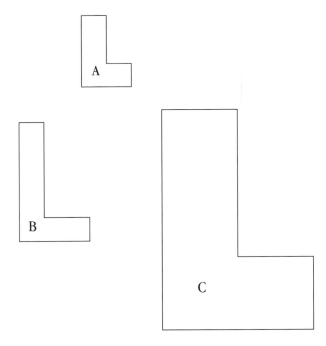

7.

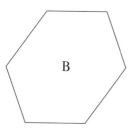

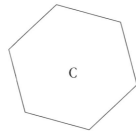

In 8–10, make a copy of the shape. Then, find a way to divide it into four identical, smaller shapes that are each similar to the original shape.

8.

9.

10.

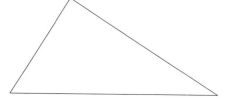

Connections

In 11–14, use this information: The Rosavilla School District wants to build a new middle school building. They asked architects to make scale drawings of some possible layouts for the building. After much discussion, the district narrowed the possibilities to these two:

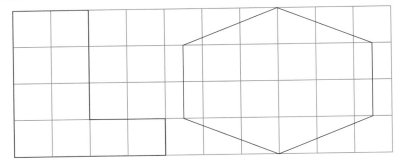

Scale
1 cm = 40 m

11. **a.** What is the area of the L-shaped scale drawing?

   b. What is the area of the hexagonal scale drawing?

12. **a.** What would be the area of the L-shaped building?

   b. What would be the area of the hexagonal building?

13. The school board likes the L-shaped layout but wants a building with more space. If they increase the L-shaped model by a scale factor of 2, how would the area of the scale drawing change? How would the area of the building change?

14. After more discussion, the architects made a detailed drawing of the final plans for the building and the school grounds using the scale 1 centimeter = 5 meters.

   a. In the drawing, the fence around the football field is 75 centimeters long. How long will the fence around the actual field be?

   b. In the drawing, the gymnasium floor has an area of $7\frac{1}{2}$ square centimeters. How much floor covering will be needed to build the gym?

c. The music teacher is excited about her new music room! It will be a rectangular room that is 20 meters long and has a floor area of 300 square meters. What are the dimensions of the music room in the scale drawing?

Extensions

15. A **midpoint** is a point that divides a line segment into two equal parts. Each part is one half the length of the original line segment. Draw a figure on grid paper by following these steps:

Step 1 Draw an 8-by-8 square.
Step 2 Mark the midpoint of each side.
Step 3 Connect the midpoints in order with four line segments to form a new figure. (The line segments should not intersect inside the square.)
Step 4 Repeat steps 2 and 3 three more times, each time working with the newest figure.

a. What kind of figure is formed when the midpoints of the sides of a square are connected?

b. Find the area of the original square.

c. Find the area of the new figure that is formed at each step.

d. How do the areas change between successive figures? Look at your drawing. Why does your answer make sense?

e. Are there any similar figures in your drawing? Explain.

16. Rectangle A is similar to rectangle B and also similar to rectangle C. Can you conclude that rectangle B is similar to rectangle C? Explain your answer. Use drawings and examples to illustrate your answer.

17. Are all squares similar? Explain your answer.

18. **a.** Which shapes below are similar? How do you know?

b. State a scale factor for each pair of similar shapes you found in part a. Be specific about the direction of the scale factor. For example, if you found that A and B are similar, state whether the scale factor you give is from A to B or from B to A.

c. For each pair of similar shapes you found, predict how the two areas compare.

19. **a.** Which shapes below are similar? How do you know?

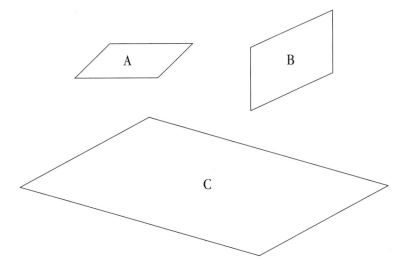

b. State a scale factor for each pair of similar shapes you found in part a. Be specific about the direction of the scale factor. For example, if you found that A and B are similar, state whether the scale factor you give is from A to B or from B to A.

c. For each pair of similar shapes you found, predict how the two areas compare.

20. a. Copy the large shape below, and subdivide it into nine copies of the small shape.

b. What is the scale factor from the small shape to the large shape?

c. How does the area of the large shape compare to the area of the small shape?

d. If two shapes are similar, how can you use the scale factor from the smaller shape to the larger shape to predict how the areas of the shapes compare?

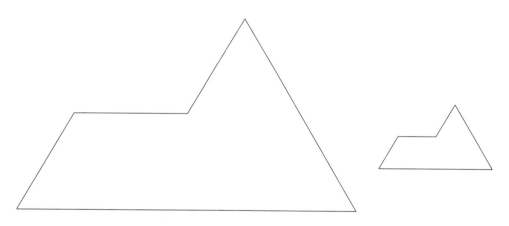

Mathematical Reflections

In this investigation, you determined whether shapes were similar by comparing corresponding parts. You also explored rep-tiles, shapes whose copies can be put together to make larger, similar shapes. These questions will help you summarize what you have learned:

1 How can you decide whether two figures are similar?

2 What does a scale factor between two similar figures tell you?

3 Explain how you can find a scale factor between two similar figures. Use an example to explain your thinking.

4 Explain how you can use the scale factor to determine how the area of an enlarged figure compares to the area of the original figure.

Think about your answers to these questions, discuss your ideas with other students and your teacher, and then write a summary of your findings in your journal.

INVESTIGATION

Using Similarity

By now, you should have a good understanding of what it means for two figures to be similar. In the last investigation, you created similar figures by putting identical smaller figures together and by dividing a figure into identical smaller figures. You learned that the *scale factor* is the number that a figure's side lengths must be multiplied by to get the side lengths of a similar figure. By finding the number of figures it took to cover a larger, similar figure, you discovered the relationship between the scale factor and the areas of two similar figures. In this investigation, you will use all of your new knowledge to solve some interesting problems.

4.1 Using Similarity to Solve a Mystery

Many stores, particularly those that stay open late into the night, have surveillance cameras. One night the local Dusk to Dawn convenience store was robbed. The surveillance camera had taken several photographs during the robbery. By inspecting a picture of the robber standing in front of the cash register, police were able to determine the robber's height. How did they do it?

Did you know?

Measurement is used in investigatory and police work all the time. For example, some stores that have surveillance cameras mark a spot on the wall 6 feet from the floor so that, when a person is filmed standing near the wall, it is easier to estimate that person's height. Investigators take measurements of skid marks at the scene of auto accidents to help them determine the speed of the vehicles involved. Photographs and molds may be made of footprints at a crime scene to help determine the type of shoe and the weight of the person who made the prints. And measurements of holes and damage made by bullets can help investigators determine the type of gun that shot the bullet and the direction from which it was shot.

Problem 4.1

The teacher's guides for Connected Mathematics measure $8\frac{1}{2}$" by 11". Below is a photograph of a middle school teacher holding a teacher's guide.

A. Use the photograph to figure out how tall the teacher is. Explain your procedure.

B. How do you think the police determined the robber's height?

■ Problem 4.1 Follow-Up

1. Estimate the height of the door in the photograph.

2. Do you think your estimate in question 1 is an underestimate or an overestimate? Why?

Scaling Up

The concept of similarity has many practical applications. For example, designers often make a model of an object and then scale it up or down to make the real object. What kinds of models are likely to be smaller than the real objects? What kinds of models are likely to be larger than the real objects?

Problem 4.2

Raphael is closing his bookstore. He wants to place a full-page advertisement in the newspaper to announce his going-out-of-business sale. A full-page ad is 13" by 22", which allows for a white border around the ad.

Raphael used his computer to make an $8\frac{1}{2}$" by 11" model of the advertisement, but he wants the newspaper ad department to enlarge it to full-page size. Is this possible? Explain your reasoning.

■ Problem 4.2 Follow-Up

What would you suggest Raphael say to the ad department about making a full-page, similar ad from his model?

4.3 Making Copies

When you use a copy machine to enlarge or reduce a document, you are dealing with similarity. On most copy machines, you indicate how much you want to enlarge or reduce something by entering a percent.

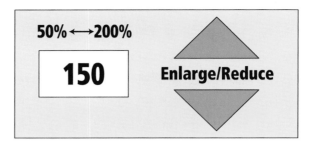

Problem 4.3

Raphael wants to make posters for his sale by enlarging his $8\frac{1}{2}$" by 11" ad. Raphael thinks big posters will get more attention, so he wants to enlarge his ad as much as possible.

The copy machines at the copy shop have cartridges for three paper sizes: $8\frac{1}{2}$" by 11", 11" by 14", and 11" by 17". The machines allow users to enlarge or reduce documents by specifying a percent between 50% and 200%. For example, to enlarge a document by a scale factor of 1.5, a user would enter 150%. This tells the machine to enlarge the document to 150% of its current size.

A. Can Raphael make a poster that is similar to his original ad on any of the three paper sizes—without having to trim off part of the paper? Why or why not?

B. If you were Raphael, what paper size would you use to make a larger, similar poster on the copy machine? What scale factor—expressed as a percent—would you enter into the machine?

■ Problem 4.3 Follow-Up

1. How would you use the copy machines described in the problem to reduce a drawing to 25% of its original size? Remember, the copy machines only accept values between 50% and 200%.

2. How would you use the copy machines to reduce a drawing to $12\frac{1}{2}$% of its original size?

3. How would you use the copy machines to reduce a drawing to 36% of its original size?

4.4 Using Map Scales

We use maps to help us find our way in unfamiliar places, to plan vacations, and to learn about other parts of the world. Maps are like scale drawings: they show a large area of land at a reduced size. To get a sense of the size of the place a map represents, you must know to what scale the map was drawn.

Arches National Park in Utah

Here is a map of the state of Utah. You can use the scale on the map to calculate distances.

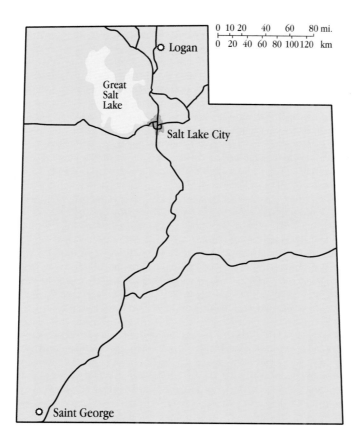

Problem 4.4

A. How can you use the scale on the map to calculate the scale factor between the map and the real state? What is the scale factor?

B. How many miles of fencing would it take to surround the state of Utah?

C. Use the scale to estimate the area of Utah. Explain your work.

D. If you drove at a steady speed of 55 miles per hour, about how long would it take you to travel from Logan to Saint George?

■ Problem 4.4 Follow-Up

The total land and water area of the United States is about 3,717,522 square miles. What percent of this total area is the area of Utah?

As you work on these ACE questions, use your calculator whenever you need it.

Applications

1. Find all the pairs of similar rectangles in the set below. For each pair you find, give the scale factor from one of the rectangles to the other.

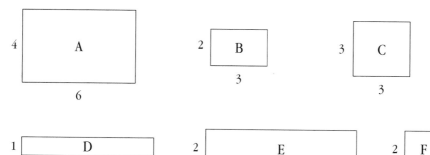

2. The rectangles below are similar.

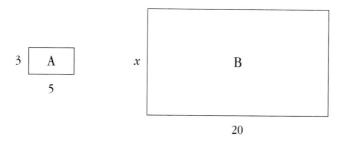

a. What is the value of x?

b. What is the scale factor from rectangle A to rectangle B?

c. Find the area of each rectangle.

d. What is the relationship of the area of rectangle A to the area of rectangle B?

3. The rectangles below are similar.

x 1
8   4

    a. What is the value of x?

    b. What is the scale factor from rectangle C to rectangle D?

    c. Find the area of each rectangle.

    d. What is the relationship of the area of rectangle C to the area of rectangle D?

4. The rectangles below are similar.

    a. What is the value of x?

    b. What is the scale factor from rectangle E to rectangle F?

    c. Find the area of each rectangle.

    d. What is the relationship of the area of rectangle E to the area of rectangle F?

5. The rectangles below are similar.

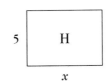

    a. What is the value of x?

    b. What is the scale factor from rectangle G to rectangle H?

    c. Find the area of each rectangle.

    d. What is the relationship of the area of rectangle G to the area of rectangle H?

6. Sort the rectangles below into sets of similar rectangles. Describe the method you use.

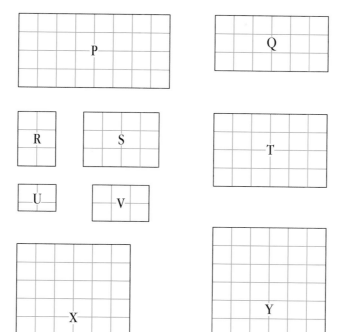

7. Ms. Auito wants to buy new carpeting for her bedroom. The bedroom floor is a rectangle, 9 feet by 12 feet. Carpeting is sold by the square yard.

a. How much carpeting does Ms. Auito need to buy?

b. If the carpeting costs $22 per square yard, how much will the carpet for the bedroom cost?

8. Ms. Auito (from question 7) really liked the carpet she bought for her bedroom, and she would like to buy the same carpet for her large library. The floor of her library is similar to the floor of her 9-foot-by-12-foot bedroom. The scale factor from the bedroom to the library is 2.5.

   a. What are the dimensions of the library?

   b. How much carpeting does Ms. Auito need for the library?

   c. How much will the carpet for the library cost?

9. Here is a drawing of Duke. The scale factor from Duke to the drawing is $12\frac{1}{2}\%$.

   a. How long is Duke from his nose to the tip of his tail?

   b. To build a doghouse for Duke, you would need to know his height so you could make a doorway to accommodate him. How tall is Duke?

   c. The local copy center has a machine that will print on poster-size paper. You can enlarge or reduce a document by specifying a setting between 50% and 200%. How could you use the machine to make a life-size picture of Duke?

10. Samantha drew triangle *ABC* on a grid, then applied a rule to make the triangle on the right.

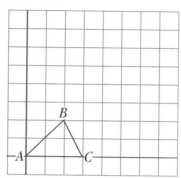 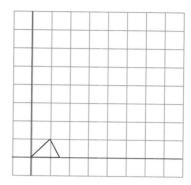

a. What rule did Samantha apply to make the new triangle?

b. Is the new triangle similar to triangle *ABC?* Explain. If the triangles are similar, give the scale factor from triangle *ABC* to the new triangle.

11. Samantha drew triangle *JKL* on a grid, then applied a rule to make the triangle on the right.

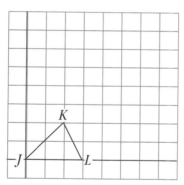 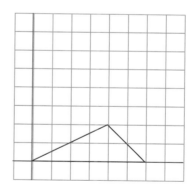

a. What rule did Samantha apply to make the new triangle?

b. Is the new triangle similar to triangle *JKL?* Explain. If the triangles are similar, give the scale factor from triangle *JKL* to the new triangle.

12. Samantha drew triangle *XYZ* on a grid, then applied a rule to make the triangle on the right.

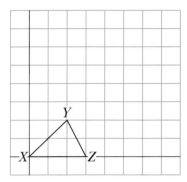 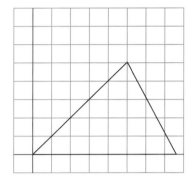

a. What rule did Samantha apply to make the new triangle?

b. Is the new triangle similar to triangle *XYZ?* Explain. If the triangles are similar, give the scale factor from triangle *XYZ* to the new triangle.

13. Examine the figures below.

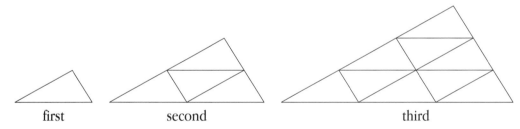

first   second   third

a. If the pattern continues, how many copies of the smallest triangle (the triangle labeled "first") will be in the fourth figure? The fifth figure? The tenth figure? Explain your reasoning.

b. Which of the larger figures is the first figure similar to? For any similar figures you find, give the scale factor from the first figure to the larger figure.

14. A rectangle has a perimeter of 20 centimeters and an area of 24 square centimeters.

    a. Sketch the rectangle on centimeter grid paper.

    b. Find the perimeter and area of the rectangle that is made by enlarging the rectangle you drew by a scale factor of 3.

    c. Find the perimeter and area of the rectangle that is made by enlarging the original rectangle by a scale factor of 10.

    d. Find the perimeter and area of the rectangle that is made by enlarging the original rectangle by a scale factor of $\frac{1}{2}$.

15. Rectangles B and C are similar to rectangle A.

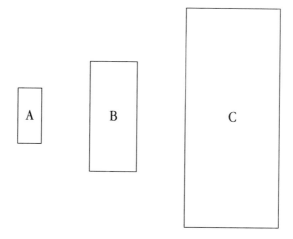

    a. What is the scale factor from rectangle A to rectangle B?

    b. What is the scale factor from rectangle A to rectangle C?

    c. How many rectangle A's would it take to cover rectangle B?

    d. How many rectangle A's would it take to cover rectangle C?

    e. What is the scale factor from rectangle C to rectangle A?

    f. What is the scale factor from rectangle C to rectangle B?

Connections

In 16–19, tell whether the triangles are similar. If they are, give a scale factor.

16.

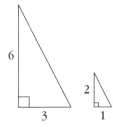

17.

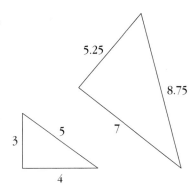

18.

19.

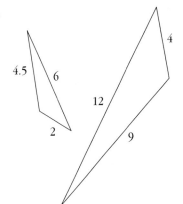

20. a. For each pair of similar triangles in questions 16–19, find the ratio of a side length of the larger triangle to the corresponding side length of the smaller triangle.

b. How does the ratio of a side length of a larger triangle to the corresponding side length of a smaller, similar triangle relate to the scale factor from the smaller triangle to the larger triangle?

21. On May 3, 1994, Nelson Mandela became the president of South Africa.

Nelson Mandela

A new flag was created as a symbol of unity. Here is a drawing of the new flag:

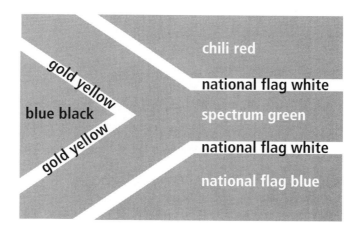

a. What is the area of the blue-black triangle in this drawing? ("Blue-black" is a shade of black.) Take whatever measurements you need to find the area.

b. What is the area of the chili-red section? Explain your reasoning.

c. Estimate the area of the spectrum-green section. Explain your reasoning.

22. Betsine Rosela would like to make a real flag from the drawing in question 21. She has decided that the scale factor from the drawing to her real flag will be 10.

    a. How much blue-black material will Betsine need?

    b. How much chili-red material will she need?

    c. How much spectrum-green material will she need?

    d. How much national-flag-blue material will she need?

23. An antique shop has a large dollhouse that is a model of a real house. The scale factor from the dollhouse to the real house is 12.

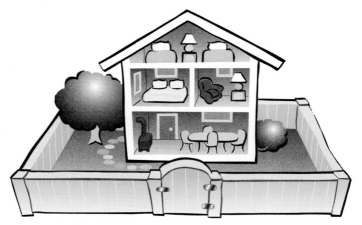

    a. If there is $6\frac{2}{3}$ meters of fencing around the dollhouse, how long is the fence around the real house?

    b. If the area of the living-room floor in the dollhouse is $\frac{1}{4}$ of a square meter, how much carpeting will be needed to cover the living-room floor in the real house?

    c. If it takes $\frac{1}{20}$ of a can of paint to paint the outside of the dollhouse, how many cans would it take to paint the exterior of the real house?

    d. What is the scale factor from the real house to the dollhouse?

    e. If there are four windows on the front of the dollhouse, how many windows are on the front of the real house?

24. On grid paper, draw two triangles that are not similar, if possible. Explain how you know the triangles are not similar. If it is impossible to draw two such triangles, explain why.

25. On grid paper, draw two rectangles that are not similar, if possible. Explain how you know the rectangles are not similar. If it is impossible to draw two such rectangles, explain why.

26. On grid paper, draw two squares that are not similar, if possible. Explain how you know the squares are not similar. If it is impossible to draw two such squares, explain why.

27. On grid paper, draw two rectangles that are not similar but that have equal corresponding angles, if possible. Explain how you know the rectangles are not similar. If it is impossible to draw two such rectangles, explain why.

28. On grid paper, draw two triangles that are not similar but that have equal corresponding angles, if possible. Explain how you know the triangles are not similar. If it is impossible to draw two such triangles, explain why.

Extensions

29. **a.** Enlarge the drawing of the flag in question 21 by a scale factor of 3. Color your enlarged flag as closely as possible to the indicated colors.

b. What is the area of the blue-black section in your flag? The chili-red section? The spectrum-green section? Explain how you found your answers.

30. What happens if you enlarge a drawing by a scale factor of 1? Explain your answer. As part of your explanation, draw a picture of a figure and its enlargement by a scale factor of 1.

31. What is the relationship between the areas of two similar figures that are related by a scale factor of 1?

Mathematical Reflections

In this investigation, you used scale factors and their relationships to side lengths and areas in similar figures to solve real-world problems. These questions will help you summarize what you have learned:

1 How can you decide whether two figures are similar?

2 What does a scale factor between two similar figures tell you about the relationships between the length and area measures of the figures?

3 If the scale factor from a small figure to a large figure is given as a percent, how can you find the side lengths of the large figure from the side lengths of the small figure?

4 Decide whether each pair of rectangles below is similar. If the rectangles are similar, give the scale factor from the rectangle on the left to the rectangle on the right. If they aren't, explain why.

a.

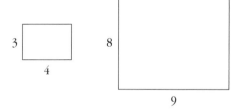

b.

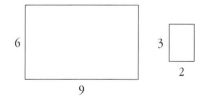

Think about your answers to these questions, discuss your ideas with other students and your teacher, and then write a summary of your findings in your journal.

Similar Triangles

How tall is your school building? You could find the answer to this question by climbing a ladder and measuring the building with a tape measure, but there are easier—and less dangerous!—ways to find the height of a building. In this investigation, you will see how you can use what you know about similar triangles to estimate heights and distances that are difficult or impossible to measure directly.

5.1 Using Shadows to Find Heights

If an object is outdoors, you can use shadows to help estimate its height. The diagram below illustrates how the method works.

On a sunny day, an object casts a shadow. If you hold a meterstick perpendicular to the ground, it will also cast a shadow. The diagram below shows two triangles. One is formed by an object, its shadow, and an imaginary line. The other is formed by a meterstick, its shadow, and an imaginary line. These two triangles are similar.

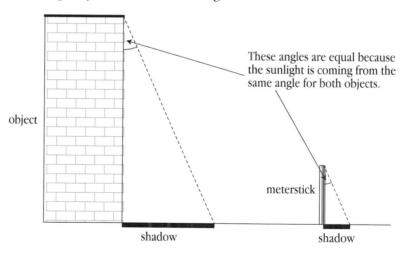

These angles are equal because the sunlight is coming from the same angle for both objects.

object

meterstick

shadow

shadow

To find the height of the object, you can measure the lengths of the two shadows and apply what you know about similar triangles.

Think about this!

Examine the diagram of the shadow method on the previous page. Can you explain why each angle of the large triangle is equal to the corresponding angle of the small triangle?

Problem 5.1

Mr. Anwar's class is using the shadow method to estimate the height of their school building. They have made the following measurements and sketch:

Length of the meterstick = 1 m
Length of the meterstick's shadow = 0.2 m
Length of the building's shadow = 7 m

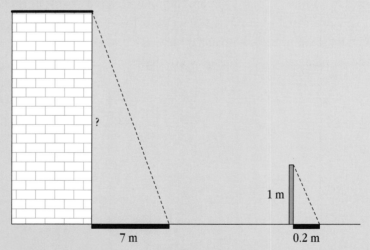

7 m   1 m   0.2 m

A. Use what you know about similar triangles to find the building's height from the given measurements. Explain your work.

B. With your class, choose a building or other tall object. Work with your group to estimate the object's height using the shadow method. In your answer, include the measurements your group made, and explain in words and drawings how you used these measurements to find the object's height.

Problem 5.1 Follow-Up

Work with your teacher to pool the results from all the groups. Make a line plot of the data. What does your line plot tell you about the object's height? Save the line plot to use in Problem 5.2.

5.2 Using Mirrors to Find Heights

The shadow method is useful for estimating heights, but it only works outdoors and on a sunny day. In this problem, you will use a mirror to help estimate heights. The mirror method works both indoors and outdoors. All you need is a level spot near the object whose height you want to estimate.

The mirror method is illustrated below. Place a mirror on a level spot at a convenient distance from the object. Back up from the mirror until you can see the top of the object in the center of the mirror. The two triangles shown in the diagram are similar.

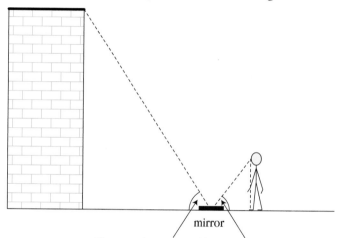

mirror

These angles are equal because light reflects off of a mirror at the same angle at which it hits the mirror.

To find the object's height, you need to measure three distances and then apply what you know about similar triangles.

Think about this!

Examine the diagram of the mirror method. Can you explain why each angle of the large triangle is equal to the corresponding angle of the small triangle?

Problem 5.2

Jim and Qin-Zhong, students in Mr. Anwar's class, are using the mirror method to estimate the height of their school building. They have made the following measurements and sketch:

Height from the ground to Jim's eyes = 150 cm
Distance from the middle of the mirror to Jim = 100 cm
Distance from the middle of the mirror to the building = 600 cm

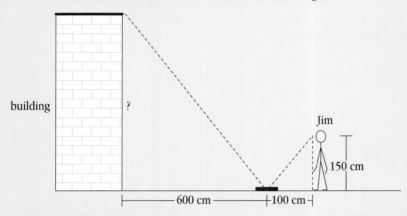

A. Use what you know about similar triangles to find the building's height from the given measurements. Explain your work.

B. With your group, use the mirror method to estimate the height of the same object or building you worked with in Problem 5.1. In your answer, include all the measurements your group made, and explain in words and drawings how you used the measurements to find the object's height.

C. How does the height estimate you made using the shadow method compare with the height estimate you made using the mirror method? Do you think your estimates for the object's height are reasonable? Why or why not?

Problem 5.2 Follow-Up

1. Work with your teacher to pool the results from all the groups. Make a line plot of the data.
2. Compare the line plot of the estimates you made using the mirror method to the line plot of the estimates you made using the shadow method (from Problem 5.1 Follow-Up). Which method seems to give more consistent results?

5.3 Using Similar Triangles to Find Distances

Mr. Anwar's class went to Bevort Pond for a picnic. Darnell, Angie, and Trevor wanted to find the distance across the pond. Darnell and Angie suggested that Trevor swim across with the end of a tape measure in his mouth. Trevor declined—the water was very cold! They decided to try to use what they had learned about similar triangles to find the distance across the pond. They drew a diagram and started making the necessary measurements.

Problem 5.3

Here is the diagram Darnell, Angie, and Trevor made, including their measurements.

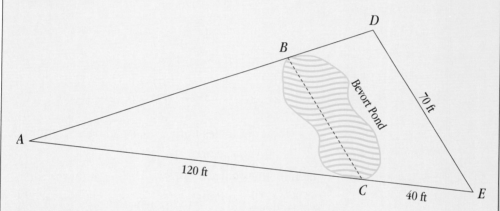

A. Name the two similar triangles in the diagram.

B. What is the scale factor from the large triangle to the small triangle?

C. What is the distance across the pond (measured along the dotted line)?

D. On your school grounds or in your neighborhood, find a pond or some other feature, such as a park, a playground, or a wooded area. Use the ideas in this problem to estimate the distance across the feature. Explain your work carefully.

Problem 5.3 Follow-Up

Is the large triangle Darnell, Angie, and Trevor measured the only one that will work to find the distance across the pond? If you think other triangles could be used, make a drawing of Bevort Pond showing another triangle that could be measured to determine the distance across the pond. If you think no other triangles would work, explain why not.

As you work on these ACE questions, use your calculator whenever you need it.

Applications

1. The triangles below are similar.

    a. Name all pairs of corresponding sides.

    b. Name all pairs of corresponding angles.

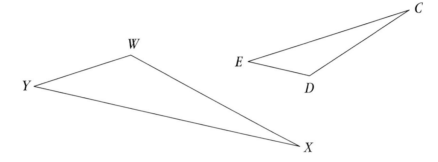

2. **a.** In the figure below, identify the similar triangles.

    b. Name all pairs of corresponding sides for the similar triangles you found.

    c. Name all pairs of corresponding angles for the similar triangles you found.

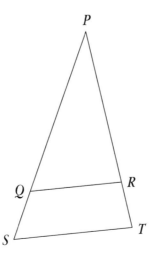

3. Daphne used the shadow method to estimate the height of the basketball backboard on the school playground. Here are the measurements she recorded. Use them to find the distance from the ground to the top of the backboard.

Length of meterstick = 1 m   Length of meterstick's shadow = $\frac{1}{2}$ m

Length of backboard's shadow = $\frac{3}{2}$ m

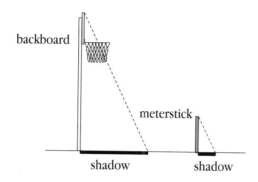

backboard

meterstick

shadow   shadow

4. Darius used the shadow method to estimate the height of the flagpole in front of the city library. Here are the measurements he recorded. Use them to find the height of the flagpole.

Length of meterstick = 1 m   Length of meterstick's shadow = 5 cm

Length of flagpole's shadow = 38 cm

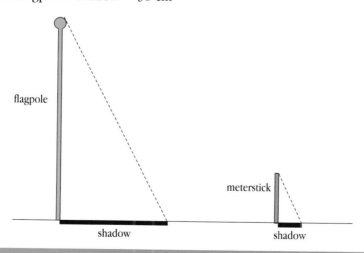

flagpole

meterstick

shadow   shadow

5. The principal asked Hank to demonstrate what he was learning in math class. Hank decided to use the mirror method to estimate the principal's height. Here are the measurements Hank recorded. Use them to find the principal's height.

Height from the ground to Hank's eyes = 1.5 m
Distance from the center of the mirror to Hank = 3 m
Distance from the center of the mirror to the principal = 3.7 m

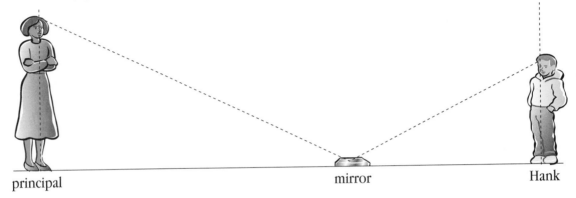

principal   mirror   Hank

6. Stacia and Byron used the mirror method to estimate the height of their math classroom. Below are the measurements and sketch they made. Use them to find the height of the classroom.

Height from the ground to Stacia's eyes = 1.5 m
Distance from the center of the mirror to Stacia = 1 m
Distance from the center of the mirror to the classroom wall = 2.4 m

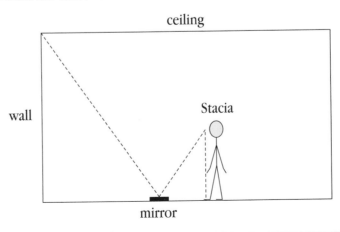

7. A stick 2 meters long casts a shadow 0.5 meters long. At the same time, the Washington Monument casts a shadow 42.25 meters long. How tall is the Washington Monument?

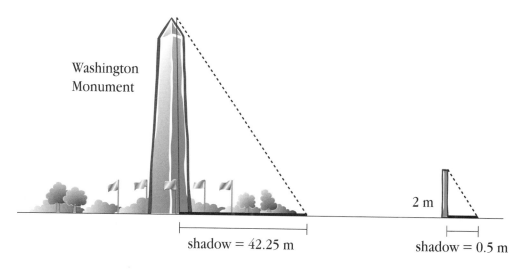

Washington Monument

2 m

shadow = 42.25 m

shadow = 0.5 m

8. Joan used a mirror to estimate the height of a flagpole. Below are the measurements she recorded. What is the height of the flagpole?

Height from the ground to Joan's eyes = 5 feet
Distance from the center of the mirror to Joan = 2 feet
Distance from the center of the mirror to the flagpole = 9 feet

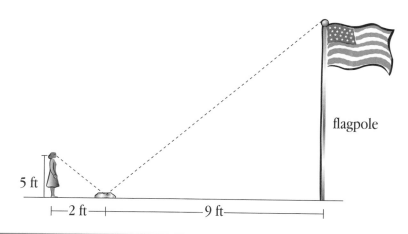

flagpole

5 ft

2 ft

9 ft

9. What is the distance across the gravel pit shown in the drawing?

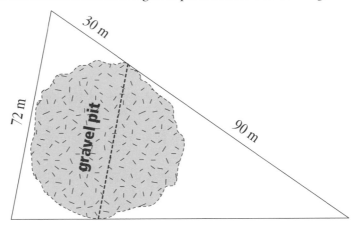

Connections

10. Look carefully at the figure below.

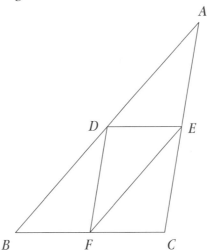

a. Which line segments look parallel?

b. Segment *DE* connects the midpoints of segments *AB* and *AC*. How does the length of segment *BC* compare to the length of segment *DE?* Explain.

11. Look carefully at the figure below.

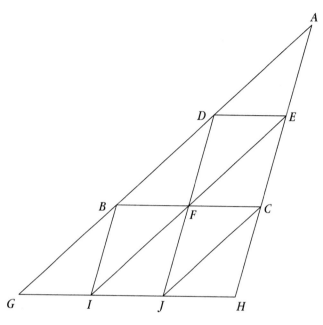

a. Which line segments look parallel?

b. How does this figure relate to the figure in question 10?

c. How does the length of segment *DE* compare to the length of segment *BC* and segment *GH?*

d. How are line segments *CJ*, *EI*, and *AG* related?

e. How are line segments *BI*, *DJ*, and *AH* related?

Extensions

12. Use the mirror method, the shadow method, or another method involving similar triangles to find the height of a telephone pole, a light pole, or a statue in your town. Report your results, and explain your method.

13. Tang plans to make some repairs on the roof of a building. He needs a ladder to reach the roof, but he's not sure how long the ladder should be. He thinks he has found a way to use similar triangles to find the height of the building. He stands 9 meters from the building and holds a 30-centimeter ruler in front of his eyes. The ruler is 45 centimeters from his eyes. He can just see the top and bottom of the building as he looks above and below the ruler.

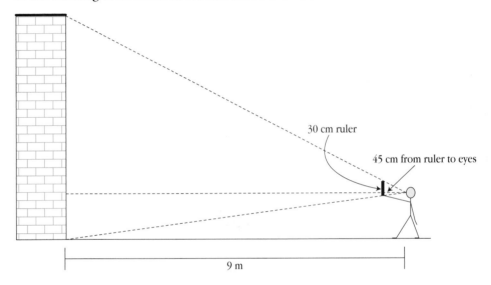

30 cm ruler

45 cm from ruler to eyes

9 m

a. Do you see any similar triangles in the diagram that can help Tang figure out how tall the building is? Explain.

b. How tall is the building? Explain your reasoning.

14. In an *annular eclipse,* the Moon moves between the Earth and Sun, blocking part of the Sun's light for a few minutes. The Moon does not entirely cover the Sun; instead, a ring of light appears around the shadow of the Moon. In about 240 B.C., Aristarchus used eclipses to help correctly calculate the distances between the Earth, Moon, and Sun.

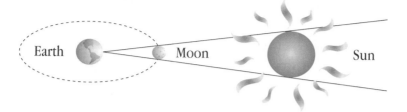

On May 10, 1994, there was an annular eclipse. Marquez's class decided to make some measurements they could use to calculate the distance from the Earth to the Moon. They constructed a viewing box like the one shown below.

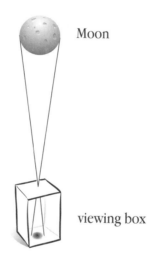

During the eclipse, the image of the Moon almost completely covered the Sun. The Moon's shadow and the ring of light surrounding it appeared on the bottom of the viewing box. The Moon's image was 1 meter from the hole and had a diameter of 0.9 centimeter. The class read in their science book that the actual diameter of the Moon is about 3500 kilometers. Use this data to find the distance to the Moon at the time of the eclipse.

15. a. Some evening when you see a full moon, go outside with a friend and use a coin to exactly block the image of the moon. How far from your eyes do you have to hold the coin? Can you hold the coin yourself, or does your friend have to hold it for you?

b. The diameter of the Moon is about 2160 miles, and the distance from the Earth to the Moon is about 238,000 miles. Use these numbers, the diameter of your coin, and the concept of similar triangles to compute the distance you would have to hold the coin from your eye to just block the Moon. How does the distance you computed compare to the distance you measured in your experiment?

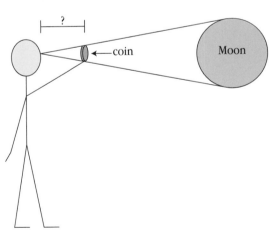

16. Parallel lines *BD* and *EG* below are cut by line *AH*. Eight angles are formed by the lines—four around point *C* and four around point *F*.

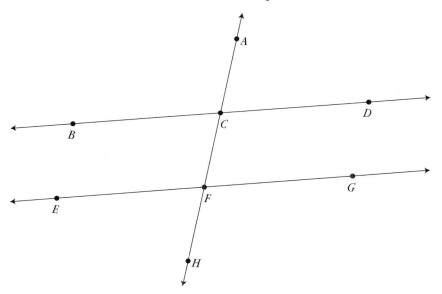

a. Find every angle that appears to be congruent to ∠*ACD*.

b. Find every angle that appears to be congruent to ∠*EFC*.

Mathematical Reflections

In this investigation, you used what you know about similar triangles to find heights of buildings and to estimate other inaccessible distances. These questions will help you summarize what you have learned:

1. Explain at least two ways you can use similar triangles to measure things in the real world. Illustrate your ideas with an example.

2. What properties of similar triangles are useful for estimating distances and heights?

3. If you take any two similar triangles and place the small triangle on top of the large triangle so that a pair of corresponding angles match, what can you say about the sides of the two triangles opposite these corresponding angles?

Think about your answers to these questions, discuss your ideas with other students and your teacher, and then write a summary of your findings in your journal.

Stretching and Shrinking with a Computer

In this investigation, you will use a computer program called *Turtle Math* to enlarge and reduce figures. You may already know how to use *Turtle Math* to draw figures. In this investigation, you will draw figures and then use tools to stretch and shrink them.

6.1 Drawing Similar Figures with a Computer

The problems in this investigation use only two commands: `fd` (forward) and `rt` (right turn).

When you begin a new *Turtle Math* session, you will see a turtle facing upward in the center of the Drawing window.

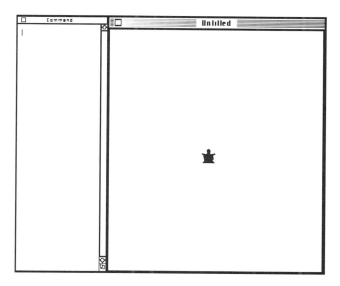

You tell the turtle how to move by typing commands in the Command window. Try telling the turtle to move forward: type fd, followed by a space, followed by a number. The number tells the turtle how many steps to take.

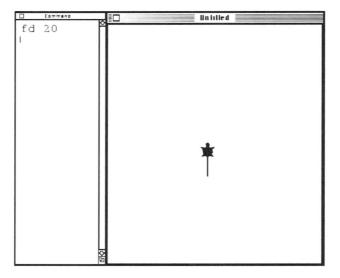

As the turtle moves, it leaves a track on the screen. Type another fd command to make the turtle go farther.

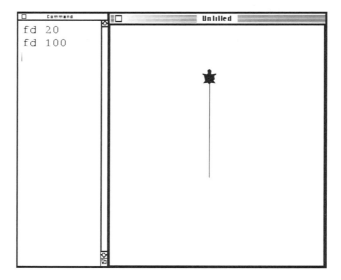

Now try making the turtle change direction: type the `rt` command, followed by a space, followed by a number. The number tells the turtle how many degrees to the right (clockwise) to turn.

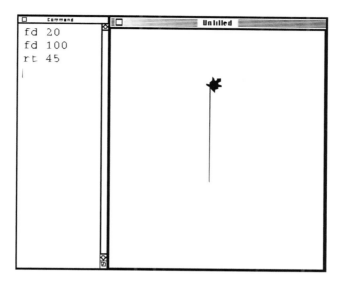

Notice that the turtle does not leave a track when you type a `rt` command. The `rt` command only tells the turtle to face a new direction. To continue drawing the track, type another `fd` command.

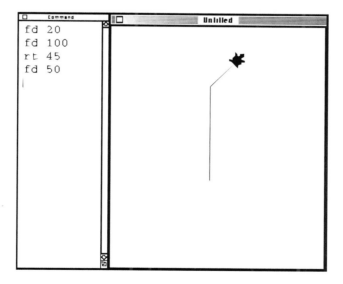

A selection of tools appears at the top of the *Turtle Math* screen. In this problem, you will use the Scale tool and the Change Shape tool. These tools let you change the size and shape of a figure.

Scale   Change Shape

Problem 6.1

Choose one of the figures below. Make the figure by typing the commands in the Command window.

Equilateral triangle	Rectangle	Right trapezoid
fd 60	fd 30	fd 52
rt 120	rt 90	rt 90
fd 60	fd 70	fd 30
rt 120	rt 90	rt 60
fd 60	fd 30	fd 60
	rt 90	rt 120
	fd 70	fd 60

After you've drawn the figure, save a copy of it on your computer. To save the drawing, select Save My Work from the File menu. Type a name for your drawing and then click on Save. After you've saved a copy of your drawing, experiment with using the Scale tool and Change Shape tool on your figure. Anytime you want to return to the original figure, just choose Open My Work from the File menu and select the name you chose for your drawing.

A. Which features of the original figure change when you use the Scale tool? Which features of the original figure change when you use the Change Shape tool? Be sure to discuss numbers of sides, side lengths, and angle measures.

B. Which features of the original figure stay the same when you use the Scale tool? Which features of the original figure stay the same when you use the Change Shape tool?

■ **Problem 6.1 Follow-Up**

Can either of the tools you investigated be used to create similar figures? To justify your answer, make sketches of what you see on the computer screen including side lengths and angle measures.

6.2 Stretching and Shrinking Flags

You have already studied how scale factors are related to lengths and areas of similar figures. *Turtle Math* is an excellent tool for investigating this concept further.

Problem 6.2

The set of commands below will draw a flag. Type in the commands exactly as they are shown; don't use any shortcuts. When you are finished, save a copy of your flag by using Save My Work from the File menu.

```
fd 80
rt 90
fd 50
rt 90
fd 30
rt 90
fd 50
```

Use the Scale tool to make enlargements and reductions of the flag. Make a chart like the one below, and fill in the missing information.

Scale factor	Sketch of figure	Height of flagpole	Length of flag	Width of flag	Area of flag
1	50 / 30 / 80	80 steps	50 steps	30 steps	1500 square steps
2					
0.5					
−1					

■ Problem 6.2 Follow-Up

1. What happens to the flag when it is changed by a negative scale factor? Explain why you think this happens.

2. Which scale factors make a flag that is the same size as the original?

3. Which scale factors make a flag that is smaller than the original?

4. Which scale factors make a flag that is larger than the original?

As you work on these ACE questions, use your calculator whenever you need it.

Applications

1. Tonya wrote this *Turtle Math* program to draw a star.

```
rt 18
fd 80
rt 144
fd 80
rt 144
fd 80
rt 144
fd 80
rt 144
fd 80
```

a. Change Tonya's program to draw a star that is similar to Tonya's but a different size.

b. What is the scale factor from Tonya's star to the star your program draws?

Connections

2. Squares A and B were made using *Turtle Math.* The Grid tool was used to display a coordinate grid. You can use the grid to measure the size of each square in numbers of turtle steps.

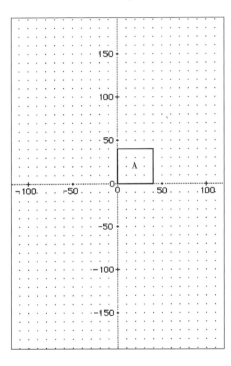 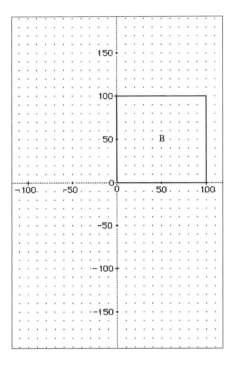

a. What is the scale factor from square A to square B?

b. What is the scale factor from square B to square A?

Extensions

3. The drawing below shows the Drawing window, with a grid, before any commands are entered.

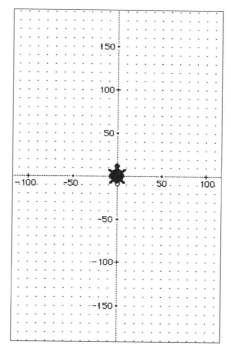

a. Jeff entered the commands below. Make a sketch that shows the turtle's new position.

```
fd -20
fd -35
fd 15
fd -70
fd 160
```

b. Jeff erased the commands to return the turtle to its starting point. Then, he entered each command *twice*. Make a sketch that shows the turtle's new position.

Mathematical Reflections

In this unit, you have explored what the word *similar* means in mathematics. These questions will help you summarize what you have learned:

1 If two figures are similar, what characteristics of the figures are the same?

2 If two figures are similar, what characteristics of the figures may be different?

3 What does a scale factor tell you about two similar figures?

Think about your answers to these questions, discuss your ideas with other students and your teacher, and then write a summary of your findings in your journal.

All-Similar Shapes

Throughout this unit, you have worked with problems that helped you understand what it means for two shapes to be similar. You have learned that not all rectangles are similar. For example, an $8\frac{1}{2}$ by 11-inch sheet of paper is rectangular, and so is a business size envelope, but the envelope is long and narrow—not the same shape as the sheet of paper.

A group of students decided to look at rectangles that are square. They found that no matter what size square they drew, every square was similar to shape B in the ShapeSet and to all other squares. They concluded that *all squares are similar!* They decided to call a square an All-Similar shape.

The students wondered whether there were any other All-Similar shapes like the square. That is, are there any other groups of shapes called by the same name that are similar to all other shapes called by that name? Use your ShapeSet to investigate this question.

1. Make a list of the names of all the different types of shapes in the ShapeSet—squares, rectangles, triangles, equilateral triangles, circles, and regular hexagons.

2. For each type of shape, list the shapes (using their letter names) that belong in that group.

3. Sort the different types of shapes into two groups: All-Similar shapes (such as squares) and shapes that are not All-Similar (such as rectangles).

4. Describe the ways in which All-Similar shapes are alike.

Unit Reflections

Working on the problems in this unit helped you to understand the concept of *similarity* as it is applied to geometric shapes. You learned how to create similar shapes and how to determine whether two shapes are similar. You also discovered the relationships between the areas and perimeters of similar shapes and investigated applications using properties of similar shapes.

Using Your Understanding of Similarity— To test your understanding of similarity consider the following problems that ask you to recognize similar shapes and deduce their properties.

1 *The square has been subdivided into six triangles and four parallelograms. Some pairs of triangles and some pairs of parallelograms are similar.*

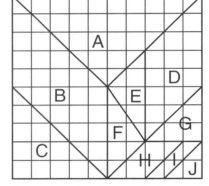

a. List two pairs of similar triangles in the figure. For each pair, give a scale factor that describes the size relationship of the two triangles.

b. Pick one pair of similar triangles and explain how their perimeters are related and how their areas are related.

c. List several pairs of triangles in the figure that are *not similar.*

d. List all pairs of similar parallelograms in the figure. For each pair, give a scale factor that describes the size relationship between the two parallelograms.

e. Pick two similar parallelograms and explain how their perimeters are related and how their areas are related.

f. List several pairs of parallelograms in the figure that are *not similar*.

2 *Suppose that a triangle is drawn on a coordinate grid.*

   a. Which of the following rules will transform the given triangle into a similar triangle?

     i. $(3x, 3y)$ **ii.** $(x + 3, y + 2)$ **iii.** $(2x, 4x)$

     iv. $(2x, 2y + 1)$ **v.** $(1.5x, 1.5y)$

   b. For each of the rules in part a that will produce a shape similar to the original triangle, give the scale factor from the original triangle to its image.

3 *The seventh-grade class photograph at Tierra del Sol Middle School measures 12 cm by 20 cm. The class officers want to enlarge the photo to fit on a large poster.*

   a. Can the original photo be enlarged to 60 cm by 90 cm?

   b. Can the original photo be enlarged to 42 cm by 70 cm?

Explaining Your Reasoning—To answer the questions in Problems 1–3, you had to use several basic properties of similar figures. You should be able to justify the answers you gave by applying those basic principles of similarity.

   1. What condition(s) must be satisfied for two polygons to be called similar? What questions do you ask yourself when deciding whether two shapes are similar?

   2. Suppose shape A is similar to shape B and the scale factor from A to B is a number k.

     a. How will the perimeters of the two figures be related?

     b. How will the areas of the two figures be related?

   3. If two triangles are similar, what do you know about

     a. the measures of sides in the two figures?

     b. the measures of angles in the two figures?

   4. Which of the following statements about similarity are true and which are false?

     a. Any two equilateral triangles are similar.

     b. Any two rectangles are similar.

     c. Any two squares are similar.

     d. Any two isosceles triangles are similar.

You will study and use ideas of similarity in several future *Connected Mathematics* units, especially when it is important to compare sizes and shapes of geometric figures. Basic principles of similarity are also used in a variety of practical and scientific problems when enlarging or shrinking of images is needed as in photography and photocopying.

compare When we compare objects, we examine them to determine how they are alike and how they are different. We compare when we classify objects by size, color, weight, or shape. We compare when we decide that two figures have the same shape or that they are not similar.

congruent figures Figures that have corresponding angles of the same measure and corresponding sides of the same length.

coordinate graphing Making a graph using pairs of numbers (x, y)—called the x- and y-coordinates—to locate positions on a coordinate plane. The x-coordinate tells how far to move right or left (horizontally) from the origin, and the y-coordinate tells how far to move up or down (vertically). The combination of the two moves locates a unique point in the plane. For example, the pair of numbers $(3, {}^{-}0.5)$ indicates the point 3 units to the right of the origin and 0.5 units down.

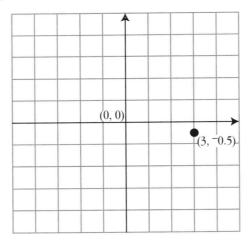

corresponding Corresponding sides or angles have the same relative position in similar figures. In this pair of similar shapes, side AB corresponds to side $A'B'$, and $\angle BCD$ corresponds to $\angle B'C'D'$.

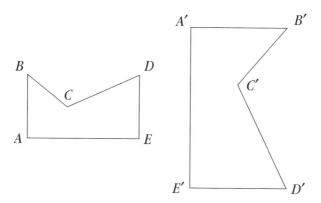

image The figure that results from some transformation of a figure. It is often of interest to consider what is the same and what is different between a figure and its image.

ratio A ratio is a comparison of two quantities that tells the scale between them. Here are some examples of uses of ratios:

- In the similar figures above, suppose $AB = 2$ and $A'B' = 3$. Then the ratio of the length of AB to the length of $A'B'$ is $\frac{2}{3}$. The ratio of the length of $A'B'$ to the length of AB is $\frac{3}{2}$.

- If a small figure is enlarged by a scale factor of 2, the ratio of the small figure's area to the large figure's area will be $\frac{1}{4}$. The ratio of the large figure's area to the small figure's area will be $\frac{4}{1}$ or 4.

scale factor The number used to multiply the coordinates of a figure to stretch or shrink it. If the scale factor is 3, all the lengths in the image are three times the corresponding lengths in the original. If the scale factor is $\frac{2}{3}$, the image has lengths $\frac{2}{3}$ those of the original. The scale factor can be found by forming the ratio, or quotient, of the length of a side of the image to the length of the corresponding side in the original. The scale factor can be given as a fraction, a decimal, or a percent. If the scale factor is larger than 1, the image is larger than the original figure. If the scale factor is positive but less than 1, the image is smaller than the original figure. If the scale factor is 1, the original and the image are congruent. On a coordinate grid, it can be seen that scale factors less than 0 flip the figure over the x and y axes in addition to stretching or shrinking it. Scale factors between 0 and $^-1$ shrink the original; scale factors less than $^-1$ stretch the original, and a scale factor of $^-1$ produces an image congruent to the original but at a different place in the plane.

similar figures Figures with the same shape. Two figures are mathematically similar if and only if their corresponding angles are equal and the ratios of all pairs of corresponding sides are equal. The ratio $\frac{\text{image side length}}{\text{original side length}}$ is the scale by which all sides of the original figure "stretch" or "shrink" into the corresponding sides of the image figure.

Index

Angle measure, of similar figures, 7–8, 18

Area
scale factor and, 28–32
of similar figures, 4, 7

Compare, meaning of, 7
Congruent shapes, 31
Coordinate grid, similar figures on, 4, 14–21
Corresponding parts of similar figures, 7–8, 14–21

Draw program, 15

Enlarging, 4
ACE, 9–12, 22–26, 47–57, 81–83
using algebraic rules, 18–21
using percent, 44
using a rubber band stretcher, 5–8
using scale factor, 20, 28–32, 41–46
using Turtle Math, 75–80
Equivalent ratios, 18–20
indirect measurement and, 59–63
Estimation
distance using scale, 45–46
length using similar triangles, 4, 59–63

Graphics program, 15

Image, 6
Indirect measurement
ACE, 63–73
using similar triangles, 59–63
Investigation
Enlarging Figures, 5–13
Patterns of Similar Figures, 28–40
Similar Figures, 14–27
Similar Triangles, 59–74
Stretching and Shrinking with a Computer, 75–84
Using Similarity, 41–58

Journal, 13, 27, 40, 58, 74, 84

Labeling, similar figures, 7–8
Looking Back and Looking Ahead: Unit Reflections, 86–87

Mathematical Highlights, 4
Mathematical Reflections, 13, 27, 40, 58, 74, 84
Measurement
indirect using similar triangles, 59–63
use in police work, 41
Midpoint, 37

Paint program, 15
Pattern, similar figures and, 28–32

Percent, scale factor and, 44
Perimeter, similar figures and, 18–20
Pixel, 14, 15

Ratio, 18
    scale factor and, 20
    similar figures and, 18–20
Reducing, 4
    ACE, 22–26, 33–39, 47–57, 81–83
    using percent, 44
    using scale factor, 20, 28–32, 44–46
    using Turtle Math, 75–80

Scale, 20
    map, 45–46
    similarity and, 41–46
    Turtle Math command, 78–80
Scale factor, 4, 20, 41
    ACE, 22–26, 33–39, 47–57
    area and, 28–32
    determining, 28–32
    for finding distance, 45–46
    percent and, 44
    similar figures and, 18–20, 41–46
Similar figures, 4, 18
    ACE, 9–12, 22–26, 33–39, 47–57,
    64–73
    angle measures and, 7–8, 18

areas of, 4, 7
comparing, 4, 7
corresponding parts of, 7–8, 14–21
drawing, 5–8
estimating with, 59–63
identifying, 14–18
labeling, 7–8
perimeter and, 18–20
scale factor and, 20, 28–32, 41–46
with Turtle Math, 75–80
Similarity, 4, 5–8, 14–18
    ACE, 9–12, 22–26, 33–39, 47–57,
    64–73
    algebraic rules and, 18–21
    indirect measurement and, 59–63
    ratio and, 18–20
    scale and, 28–32, 41–46

Transformation See also Enlarging;
  Reducing
    ACE, 22–26
    distorted, 15–21
    using algebraic rules, 15–21
Triangles, estimating length with
  similar, 59–63
Turtle Math
    ACE, 81–83
    similar figures and, 4, 75–80

Connected  Mathematics®

Comparing and Scaling

Ratio, Proportion, and Percent

Student Edition

Glenda Lappan
James T. Fey
William M. Fitzgerald
Susan N. Friel
Elizabeth Difanis Phillips

Prentice
Hall

Glenview, Illinois
Needham, Massachusetts
Upper Saddle River, New Jersey

Connected Mathematics® was developed at Michigan State University with the support of National Science Foundation Grant No. MDR 9150217.

This project was supported, in part,
by the
National Science Foundation
Opinions expressed are those of the authors
and not necessarily those of the Foundation

The Michigan State University authors and administration have agreed that all MSU royalties arising from this publication will be devoted to purposes supported by the Department of Mathematics and the MSU Mathematics Education Enrichment Fund.

Contents

Mathematical Highlights   4

Investigation 1: Making Comparisons   5
    1.1 Writing Ads   5
    1.2 Targeting an Audience   7
    1.3 Getting the Message Across   8
    Applications—Connections—Extensions   10
    Mathematical Reflections   15

Investigation 2: Comparing by Finding Percents   16
    2.1 Comparing Leisure Activities   17
    2.2 Comparing Your Class to the Nation   18
    Applications—Connections—Extensions   20
    Mathematical Reflections   25

Investigation 3: Comparing by Using Ratios   26
    3.1 Mixing Juice   27
    3.2 Helping the Cook   29
    3.3 Sharing Pizza   30
    Applications—Connections—Extensions   31
    Mathematical Reflections   36

Investigation 4: Comparing by Finding Rates   37
    4.1 Comparing Fuel Economy   38
    4.2 Using Unit Rates   40
    4.3 Solving Problems with Rates   42
    4.4 Buying Beads   43
    Applications—Connections—Extensions   44
    Mathematical Reflections   51

Investigation 5: Estimating Populations and Population Densities   52
    5.1 Estimating the Size of a Crowd   52
    5.2 Estimating a Deer Population   54
    5.3 Finding Population Densities   55
    5.4 Comparing the Dakotas   57
    5.5 Predicting Traffic Jams   58
    Applications—Connections—Extensions   59
    Mathematical Reflections   64

Investigation 6: Choosing Strategies   65
    6.1 Scaling Up or Down   65
    6.2 Using Rules of Thumb   67
    6.3 Selecting Delegates   68
    Applications—Connections—Extensions   73
    Mathematical Reflections   81

The Unit Project   82

Looking Back and Looking Ahead: Unit Reflections   84

Glossary   87

Index   89

Comparing and Scaling

Arvind and Mariah are testing four different orange juice recipes to see which tastes best. Mix A has 2 cups of orange juice concentrate and 3 cups of water; mix B has 1 cup of concentrate and 4 cups of water; mix C has 4 cups of concentrate and 8 cups of water; and mix D has 3 cups of concentrate and 5 cups of water. Which mix will taste the most "orangey"?

Madeline's car went 580 miles with 19 gallons of gas. Luis's car went 452 miles with 15.5 gallons of gas. Which car got better gas mileage?

South Dakota has a population of 721,000 and a land area of 75,896 square miles. North Dakota has a population of 638,000 and a land area of 68,994 square miles. Which of these states is more densely populated?

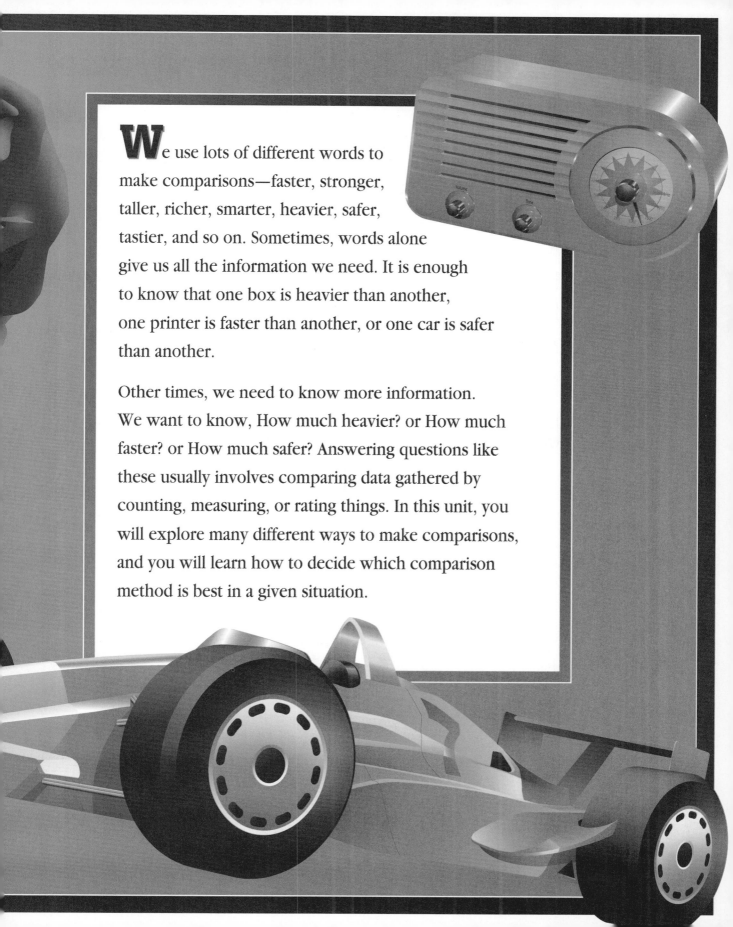

We use lots of different words to make comparisons—faster, stronger, taller, richer, smarter, heavier, safer, tastier, and so on. Sometimes, words alone give us all the information we need. It is enough to know that one box is heavier than another, one printer is faster than another, or one car is safer than another.

Other times, we need to know more information. We want to know, How much heavier? or How much faster? or How much safer? Answering questions like these usually involves comparing data gathered by counting, measuring, or rating things. In this unit, you will explore many different ways to make comparisons, and you will learn how to decide which comparison method is best in a given situation.

Mathematical Highlights

In *Comparing and Scaling* you will explore ways of making comparisons among quantities and ways of reasoning about quantities. The unit should help you to

- Understand and use the everyday language that asks comparison questions, such as "Which car has the best fuel economy?" and "What percent of girls play basketball?";

- Decide when the most informative comparison is the difference between two quantities, and when it is the ratio between a pair of quantities;

- Find equivalent ratios to make accurate and insightful comparisons;

- Scale a ratio up or down so that a larger or smaller object or population has the same relative characteristics as the original;

- Set up and solve proportions that arise in applications;

- Look for patterns in rate tables usable for making predictions beyond the table;

- Connect unit rates with the rule describing the situation and the constant growth in a table with a straight-line graph; and

- Solve problems which involve making comparisons and reasoning with rates, ratios and proportions.

As you work on the problems in this unit, ask yourself questions about situations that involve making comparisons and reasoning with rates, ratios and proportions: *What quantities are in the problem? How are they related? Am I being asked to make a comparison? If so, what computations will be the most useful to perform to make a comparison? Can the relationships be expressed as differences, rates, ratios, or proportions? What models or diagrams might be useful in solving the problem?*

INVESTIGATION 1

Making Comparisons

It's easy to decide which of two numbers is larger or smaller. However, it's not as easy to decide on the best way to explain *how much* larger or smaller one number is than another—especially when one or both of the numbers are fractions. In this unit, you will learn several ways to compare numbers.

1.1 Writing Ads

In their advertisements, companies often refer to surveys to show that people prefer their product over a competitor's product. An ad for Bolda Cola starts like this:

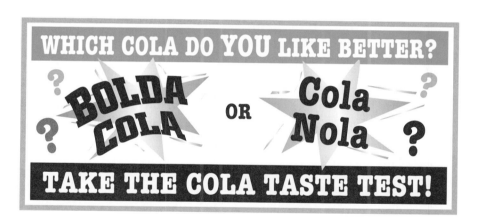

To complete the ad, Bolda Cola wants to report the results of their taste tests. A copywriter from the advertising department has proposed four possible concluding statements.

In taste tests, people who preferred **BOLDA COLA** outnumbered those preferring **Cola Nola** by a ratio of **17,139 to 11,426.**

In taste tests, **5713** more people preferred **BOLDA COLA** to **Cola Nola**.

In taste tests, **60%** prefer **BOLDA COLA** to **Cola Nola**.

Problem 1.1

A. Describe what you think each of the four statements means. Explain how each shows a comparison. Be sure to tell *what* is being compared and *how* it is being compared.

B. Is it possible that all four advertising claims are based on the same survey data? Explain your answer.

C. Which comparison do you think is the most accurate way to report the survey data? Why?

D. Which comparison do you think would be the most effective advertisement for Bolda Cola? Why?

■ **Problem 1.1 Follow-Up**

Write two more statements comparing the popularity of the two colas. Explain each statement you write.

1.2 Targeting an Audience

Many middle and high school students work delivering papers, mowing lawns, or baby-sitting. Students who have money of their own to spend are a common target audience for radio and television ads. Information about the amount of time students spend watching television or listening to the radio influences how companies who want to sell products to them spend their advertising dollars. Advertisers want to know which type of media will best get their message across.

Problem 1.2

A survey of 100 students at Neilson Middle School found that 60 students prefer watching television in the evening and 40 prefer listening to the radio.

A. Read the statements below about how Neilson students prefer to spend their evenings. Tell whether each statement accurately reports the results of the survey. Explain your answers.

1. 6 out of 10 students prefer television to radio.

2. Students prefer radio to television by a ratio of 4 to 6.

3. Students who prefer television outnumber those who prefer radio by 20.

4. Students who prefer television outnumber those who prefer radio by a ratio of 3 to 2.

5. The number of students who prefer watching television is 1.5 times the number who prefer listening to radio.

6. 40% of the students prefer radio to television.

7. $\frac{3}{5}$ of the students prefer television to radio.

B. If you were writing a paper to convince local merchants that they would reach more students by advertising on the radio than on television, which statement from above would you use? Why?

C. Imagine that you are the advertising director for a television station in the town where Neilson is located. You have been asked to prepare a report for a meeting between your ad department and a large local skateboard manufacturer. Which accurate statement from above would you use to try to convince the manufacturer to advertise on your station? Why?

Conduct a quick survey in your class to find out how many students prefer watching television in the evening and how many prefer listening to the radio. Record the results in a table.

1. For each statement in part A on page 7, write a similar statement about your class data.

2. In what ways is your class data similar to the Neilson data? In what ways is your data different?

3. You may have heard people talk about an interest group *manipulating* data to promote their cause. This doesn't mean they used incorrect data, but that they made careful decisions about which data to use and how to represent the data to support their cause. How could you manipulate your class data to persuade local merchants to advertise on radio rather than on television?

1.3 Getting the Message Across

Camping is a popular activity in the United States. Every year, millions of families visit national, state, and local parks to enjoy the wonders of nature. While some of these visitors "rough it" in tents, many prefer cabins, trailers, and campers—bringing a few comforts of home to the wilderness.

The following table gives data on the popularity of camping for several age groups in the United States. It shows the number of people in each age group who go camping at least twice a year. The numbers in the table are projections based on data from a sample of 10,000 households.

Camping Data

	Ages 12–17	Ages 18–24	Ages 25–34
Total in the age group	21,304,000	26,650,000	41,808,000
Number who camp at least twice a year	5,336,000	4,767,000	10,000,000

Source: National Sporting Goods Association, as found in the *Statistical Abstract of the United States 1995*. Published by the Bureau of the Census, Washington, D.C., p. 260.

Problem 1.3

Suppose you were asked to write a news story about the popularity of camping in the United States based on the data in the table.

A. What headline would you use for your story? What would your first sentence be?

B. Write five statements you could use in your story to compare the popularity of camping among people in the three age groups. In each statement, be clear about which groups you are comparing. Your comparisons should be specific and based on mathematics.

■ Problem 1.3 Follow-Up

According to the data, what percent of people from age 12 to 34 go camping at least twice a year?

As you work on these ACE questions, use your calculator whenever you need it.

Applications

In 1–4, use the following information: Oksana surveyed her class to find out how students spend their time over a weekend. On Friday, she distributed a list of activities and asked her classmates to keep track of how many hours they spent from midnight on Friday to midnight on Sunday doing each activity. On Monday, she collected the data and found the mean number of hours the students spent in each category. She put her results in a table.

Weekend Activities

Activity	Average number of hours
Sleeping	18.4 hours
Eating	3.5 hours
Recreation	7.4 hours
Talking on the phone	0.6 hours
Watching television	3.7 hours
Doing chores or homework	4.7 hours
Other	9.7 hours

In 1–3, use Oksana's data to fill in the blanks to create an accurate statement.

1. In comparing time spent watching television to recreation time, students spent more time ＿＿＿＿＿＿＿ than ＿＿＿＿＿＿＿ by a ratio of ＿＿＿＿＿＿＿ to ＿＿＿＿＿＿＿.

2. The number of hours spent watching television is about ＿＿＿＿＿＿＿ times the number of hours spent doing chores or homework.

3. In comparing time spent eating and sleeping to time spent in recreation and watching television, ＿＿＿＿＿＿＿ percent of the weekend was spent ＿＿＿＿＿＿＿, and ＿＿＿＿＿＿＿ percent was spent ＿＿＿＿＿＿＿.

4. Make up a comparison like those in questions 1–3 about the data in Oksana's table. Tell why you think your comparison is interesting.

Connections

5. Below is a drawing of the spinner used in the Big Wheel game at the Waverly Middle School fun night. The chart shows the data from 236 spins of the Big Wheel.

Spin Results

Win	Lose
46	190

a. Use the data in the table to make a ratio comparison, a percent comparison, and a difference comparison.

b. Choose one of the methods of comparison from part a (ratios, percents, or differences). Think of a situation in which this method would be an effective way to report the spin results. Explain your reasoning.

c. Explain how you could find the probability of getting a win in one spin of the spinner without using the data in the chart.

d. Do the results in the table seem to agree with or contradict the probability statement you made in part c?

6. Copy the number line below. Add labels for 0.25, $\frac{6}{8}$, $1\frac{3}{4}$, and 1.3.

7. Write two fractions with different denominators so that one fraction is less than the other. Tell which fraction is larger.

8. Write a fraction and a decimal so that the fraction is greater than the decimal.

In 9–11, rewrite the pair of numbers, inserting < or > to make a true statement.

9. $\frac{4}{5}$ $\frac{11}{12}$ **10.** 2.5   0.259   **11.** $1\frac{3}{4}$ 1.5

Extensions

12. The first row of the table below shows the number of hours visitors spent in federal recreation areas in 1980 and 1990. Some of these federal recreation areas are managed by the National Forest Service. The second row of the table shows how many of the hours from the first row were spent in National Forest Service areas.

Hours Spent in Recreation Areas

	Visitor hours in 1980	Visitor hours in 1990
Federal recreation areas	6,367,000,000	7,567,000,000
National Forest Service areas	2,819,000,000	3,157,000,000

Source: 1980, the U.S. Heritage Conservation and Recreation Service; 1990, the U.S. National Park Service; as found in the *Statistical Abstract of the United States 1995*. Published by the Bureau of the Census, Washington, D.C., p. 251.

a. Write statements for each year, 1980 and 1990, comparing visitor hours in National Forest Service areas to visitor hours in all federal recreation areas.

b. Do the statements you wrote show visitor hours in National Forest Service areas growing or declining in comparison to visitor hours in federal recreation areas? Explain how you got your answer.

13. The table below shows the number of new books and new editions published in several subject areas in 1980 and 1990.

New Books and New Editions

Subject	Published in 1980	Published in 1990
Art	1691	1262
Education	1011	1039
Fiction	2835	5764
Juvenile	2859	5172
Literature	1686	2049
Total new books and new editions	42,377	46,738

Source: *Publishers Weekly,* as found in the *Statistical Abstract of the United States 1995.*
Published by the Bureau of the Census, Washington, D.C., p. 580.

a. Compare the change in the number of new books and new editions published in 1980 and 1990 in each subject area by computing differences.

b. For 1980, find the percent of all new books and new editions that were published in each subject area.

c. For 1990, find the percent of all new books and new editions that were published in each subject area.

d. Describe how the percent of books published in each subject area changed from 1980 to 1990.

e. Which method of comparison (differences or percents) would you choose if you were a librarian making a case for an increased budget for fiction books in your library? Explain your reasoning.

f. Which method of comparison would you choose if you were a reporter writing an article about trends in the book-publishing business over time? Explain your reasoning.

14. Write an advertisement that will be more effective than the one below.

Three thousand seven hundred fourteen out of four thousand nine hundred fifty-two dentists surveyed recommend sugarless gum to their patients who chew gum.

Sugarless Gum

Mathematical Reflections

In this investigation, you explored several ways of comparing numbers. Here are five methods for making comparisons, with examples:

Ratios:
: In taste tests, people who preferred Bolda Cola outnumbered those who preferred Cola Nola by a ratio of 3 to 2.

Differences:
: Students who prefer television outnumber those who prefer radio by 20.

Fractions:
: $\frac{3}{5}$ of cola drinkers prefer Bolda Cola to Cola Nola.

Percents:
: 28% of people aged 12–17 go camping.

Scaling:
: The number of students who prefer watching television is 1.5 times the number who prefer listening to the radio.

These questions will help you summarize what you have learned:

1 Give another example of each type of comparison listed above.

2 What information do you get from a ratio comparison that you don't get from a difference comparison?

Think about your answers to these questions, discuss your ideas with other students and your teacher, and then write a summary of your findings in your journal.

Comparing by Finding Percents

What do you like to do during your free time? Do you enjoy exercising or playing sports? A 1991 survey found that the five most popular sports activities in the United States are bicycle riding, camping, exercise walking, fishing, and swimming.

Think about this!

With your class, discuss the kinds of sports activities you like to participate in. Identify four or five activities that are different from those mentioned in the national survey. List these activities, along with the activities found in the national survey, on the board. Then, survey the class, asking each student which activities he or she participates in more than once a year. Tally the results for boys and girls separately. Save the data so that you can compare your class with the national survey in a later problem.

The problems in this investigation ask you to make comparisons about data. In particular, you are asked to think about ways to use percents to make comparisons.

Remember that percent means "out of 100." You can find a percent by first dividing to find a decimal. For example, the table below shows the number of males in the United States and the number of them who swim. To find the percent of males who swim, first divide the number of male swimmers by the total number of males to get a decimal. Then, round the decimal to the nearest hundredth and change the decimal to a percent.

Males in the U.S.	111,851,000
Males who swim	27,713,000

For this data, $27,713,000 \div 111,851,000 = 0.24776711$, which rounded to the nearest hundredth is 0.25. The decimal 0.25 is equivalent to 25%, so about 25% of males swim.

2.1 Comparing Leisure Activities

The table below gives data about participation in the five most popular sports activities in the United States—bicycle riding, camping, exercise walking, fishing, and swimming. The numbers are projections based on a 1993 survey of 10,000 households. The survey counted anyone 7 years old or older who participated in an activity more than once per year. Some people participated in more than one activity. The numbers in the "Total in group" row are the total number of people in the United States population in each group.

Participation in Sports Activities

Activity	Males	Females	Ages 12–17	Ages 55–64
Bicycle riding	24,562,000	23,357,000	8,794,000	2,030,000
Camping	23,165,000	19,533,000	5,336,000	2,355,000
Exercise walking	21,054,000	43,373,000	2,816,000	7,782,000
Fishing	30,449,000	14,885,000	4,945,000	3,156,000
Swimming	27,713,000	33,640,000	10,874,000	2,756,000
Total in group	**111,851,000**	**118,555,000**	**21,304,000**	**20,922,000**

Source: National Sporting Goods Association, as found in the *Statistical Abstract of the United States 1995.* Published by the Bureau of the Census, Washington, D.C., p. 260.

Problem 2.1

In the table above, look for interesting patterns in the data for males and females and in the data for the two age groups.

A. Why don't the numbers in the columns add to the given totals?

B. Write three statements that use percents to make comparisons about the numbers of male and female participants in the various activities. Explain how you found the percents.

C. Write three statements that use percents to make comparisons about the numbers of teenage and older-adult participants in the various activities.

D. Write three statements that make comparisons about the data without using percents.

1. Explain how you might decide when percents would be a good way to make a comparison and when other forms of comparison would be better. Use examples if they help explain your ideas.

2. Can you compare the participation of teenage boys in these activities to the participation of older-adult women by using the data in the table? Explain.

2.2 Comparing Your Class to the Nation

Statistics that are based on data from a small group of people, or from people who live in a particular area, may be quite different from statistics based on a national survey. For example, if there is a lake or another body of water in your area, fishing may be more popular in your class than in the nation as a whole.

In this problem, you will compare your class data with the data from the national survey. When the total numbers in two data sets are very different, representing the data values as percents of a total is a useful way to compare the data sets. Finding percents is a way of creating a common scale for two data sets by expressing all the data values as numbers "out of 100."

Did you know?

Here are some interesting percents:

• About 71% of the earth is covered by water.
• Females make up about 51.3% of the population of the United States.
• About 99% of all homes in the United States have at least one TV set, about 66% have at least two TV sets, and 65% get cable television.
• Of all the computers in the world, about 43% are in use in the United States, 22% in Europe, and 7% in Japan.
• More than 70% of the waste produced in the United States ends up in landfills.

Source: *1996 Information Please Almanac.* Ed. Otto Johnson. New York: Houghton Mifflin, 1995.

Problem 2.2

You conducted a class survey at the beginning of this investigation. Now, organize the results for bicycle riding, camping, exercise walking, fishing, and swimming into a table similar to the one on page 17. Your table should have separate columns for males and females.

A. Look back at the three statements you wrote in part B of Problem 2.1 comparing the numbers of male and female participants in the various activities. Now, make the same comparisons for boys and girls in your class.

B. Compare the statements about your class data to the statements about the national data.

C. Write three statements comparing sports activities of all students in your class to those of

    1. 12 to 17 year olds in the national survey

    2. 55 to 64 year olds in the national survey

■ Problem 2.2 Follow-Up

1. Write a paragraph telling how your class data is like the national data and how it is different. For any ways in which your class data appears to be different from the national data, give reasons why you think your class is different.

2. In your class survey, you added several activities to the five listed in the national survey. Write at least three statements comparing the numbers of boys and girls in your class who participate in these activities.

As you work on these ACE questions, use your calculator whenever you need it.

Applications

In 1–8, use the following information: A homeroom class of 32 eighth graders at Springbrook Middle School completed a survey about their participation in team sports. Each student was asked to list any sport he or she liked to play. The results for four of the most popular sports are given in this table.

Participation in Team Sports

Sport	Female	Male
Basketball	14	13
Track and field	7	13
Softball	10	8
Football	4	11
Total surveyed	**17**	**15**

1. What fraction of the class is female?

2. What percent of the class is female?

3. What percent of the class is male?

4. Write two statements comparing participation in basketball to participation in football.

5. In which sport does the greatest percent of the class participate?

6. In which sport does the greatest percent of the male students participate? Explain your answer.

7. In which sports is there a greater percent of female participation than male participation? Explain your answer.

8. If the percents of participation in these sports for all students at Springbrook are approximately the same as the percents for this class, about how many of the 368 female students in the school like to play softball?

In 9–15, use the table below, which shows the national data on exercise walking.

Participation in Exercise Walking

Activity	Males	Females	Ages 12–17	Ages 55–64
Exercise walking	21,054,000	43,373,000	2,816,000	7,782,000
Total in group	**111,851,000**	**118,555,000**	**21,304,000**	**20,922,000**

Source: National Sporting Goods Association, as found in the *Statistical Abstract of the United States 1995*. Published by the Bureau of the Census, Washington, D.C., p. 260.

9. What percent of the 55–64 age group walks for exercise?

10. What percent of the 12–17 age group walks for exercise?

11. What percent of males walks for exercise?

12. Write a statement comparing the number of males who walk for exercise to the number of females who walk for exercise.

13. Write a statement comparing the number of 12 to 17 year olds who walk for exercise to the number of 55 to 64 year olds who walk for exercise.

14. Look back at your class data. Describe how your class data on exercise walking is similar to the national data and how it is different.

15. Suppose your class data reflected the same percents as the national data. How many males and females in your class would exercise walk?

Connections

16. Below are floor plans for two college dorm rooms. One is for two students, and the other is for one student.

    a. Are the floors of the two rooms similar rectangles? Explain.

    b. For each room, what is the floor area?

    c. Which room gives each student the most space?

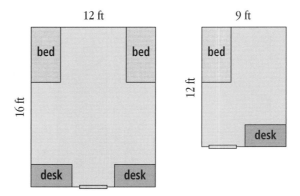

17. **a.** Plot the points (8, 6), (8, 22), and (24, 14) on grid paper. Connect them to form a triangle.

    b. Draw the triangle you get when you apply the rule $(0.5x,\ 0.5y)$ to the three points from part a.

    c. How are the triangles from parts a and b related?

    d. The area of the smaller triangle is what percent of the area of the larger triangle?

    e. The area of the larger triangle is what percent of the area of the smaller triangle?

18. In a–f, rewrite the sentence, replacing the question mark with a number that makes the sentence true.

a. $\frac{3}{4} < \frac{?}{12}$

b. $\frac{3}{4} = \frac{?}{12}$

c. $\frac{3}{4} > \frac{?}{12}$

d. $\frac{5}{9} < \frac{?}{15}$

e. $\frac{5}{9} = \frac{?}{15}$

f. $\frac{5}{9} > \frac{?}{15}$

g. Explain your strategies for solving these problems.

19. Write two fractions with different denominators and a sum of $\frac{4}{5}$.

20. Write two decimal numbers with three or fewer digits each and a sum of 12.36.

21. Write a decimal number and a fraction with a sum of 0.593.

22. A store is having a 30% off sale. How would you determine an item's sale price?

Extensions

In 23 and 24, look at the table of data about participation in sports activities on page 17.

23. Which sports activity has the greatest percent of participation by females? Which has the greatest percent of participation by males?

24. Which sports activity is most popular among the 12–17 age group? Explain.

25. Kent's department store is having a Super Saturday Sale during which every item is 25% off. When you walk in the door, a salesperson hands you a coupon for an additional 10% off the reduced price of any item. Your friend says, "Wow—if you buy something with your coupon, you will get 35% off the original price!" Is your friend correct? Why or why not?

26. At Kent's department store (from question 25), you decide to buy a T-shirt with an original price of $20. The sales clerk first uses your coupon to reduce the original price by 10% and then applies the 25% discount. Did you save more than you would have if the clerk had applied the 25% discount first and then used the 10% off coupon? Explain your answer.

Mathematical Reflections

In this investigation, you used percents to make comparisons. You compared data for males and females and for teenagers and older adults. You developed your skill in making comparisons and in deciding what kinds of comparisons make sense. These questions will help you summarize what you have learned:

1 Give an example of a situation in which it makes sense to use percents to make comparisons.

2 Using your example from part 1, show how to make a comparison using percents.

3 Explain why percents are useful for making comparisons.

4 Give an example of a situation in which you think another form of comparison is better than percents. Explain your reasoning.

5 Can you find a percent comparison from a ratio comparison? Explain how, or tell what additional information you would need.

Think about your answers to these questions, discuss your ideas with other students and your teacher, and then write a summary of your findings in your journal.

Comparing by Using Ratios

Another useful way to compare numbers is to form *ratios.* You looked at ratios informally in Investigation 1. In this investigation, you will learn to form and interpret ratios in order to make comparisons. Let's look at some examples of statements containing ratios.

In taste tests, people who preferred Bolda Cola outnumbered those who preferred Cola Nola by a ratio of 3 to 2.

The ratio of boys to girls in our class is 12 boys to 15 girls.

The ratio of boys to students in our class is 12 boys to 27 students.

The ratio of kittens to cats in our neighborhood is $\frac{1}{4}$.

The sign in the hotel lobby says 1 dollar Canadian: 0.85 dollars U.S.

A paint mixture calls for 5 parts blue paint to 2 parts yellow paint.

In these examples, ratios are written in three different ways: using the word "to," as in 5 to 8, using the ":" symbol, as in 5:8, and using fraction notation, as in $\frac{5}{8}$. All three forms—5 to 8, 5:8, and $\frac{5}{8}$—mean that for every five of the first item, there are eight of the second item.

Many real-world problems involve scaling a ratio up or down to find an *equivalent ratio.* This requires finding larger or smaller numbers with the same relationship as the numbers in the original ratio. For example, the ratios 2:3, 4:6, and 6:9 are all equivalent. Suppose a shade of purple paint is made using 2 parts red paint to 3 parts blue. You would get the same shade of purple whether you mixed 2 gallons of red paint to 3 gallons of blue paint, 4 gallons of red paint to 6 gallons of blue paint, or 6 gallons of red paint to 9 gallons of blue paint.

3.1 Mixing Juice

Every year, the seventh grade students at Langston Hughes School go on an outdoor-education camping trip. During the week-long trip, the students study nature and participate in recreational activities. Everyone pitches in to help with the cooking and cleanup.

Arvind and Mariah are in charge of making orange juice for all the campers. They make the juice by mixing water and orange juice concentrate. To find the mix that tastes best, Arvind and Mariah decided to test some recipes on a few of their friends.

Problem 3.1

Arvind and Mariah tested four juice mixes.

Mix A
2 cups concentrate
3 cups cold water

Mix B
1 cup concentrate
4 cups cold water

Mix C
4 cups concentrate
8 cups cold water

Mix D
3 cups concentrate
5 cups cold water

A. Which recipe will make juice that is the most "orangey"? Explain your answer.

B. Which recipe will make juice that is the least "orangey"? Explain your answer.

C. Assume that each camper will get $\frac{1}{2}$ cup of juice. For each recipe, how much concentrate and how much water are needed to make juice for 240 campers? Explain your anwer.

■ Problem 3.1 Follow-Up

1. How did you use ratios in solving Problem 3.1?

2. For each recipe, how much concentrate and how much water is needed to make 1 cup of juice?

Did you know?

Here are some interesting ratios:

- There are about 21 white vans on the road for every purple van.
- In 1994, about 493 music CDs were sold for every 10 albums sold.
- For the first 60 miles of depth, the temperature of the earth increases 1°F for every 100–200 feet.
- The ratio of people 5 to 17 years old in the United States to people 85 years of age or older is about 15 to 1.
- Cigarette smoking accounts for 3 out of 10 deaths due to cancer.

Source: *World Almanac and Book of Facts 1996.* Ed. Robert Famighetti. Mahwa, New Jersey: Funk and Wagnalls, 1995.

3.2 Helping the Cook

The camp cook must buy enough ingredients for all the meals he intends to prepare during the week. One of the cook's most popular meals is spaghetti. The spaghetti recipe he uses calls for canned tomatoes. The CannedStuff store has large cans of tomatoes on sale, five cans for $4.00. The cook says he can make sauce for five to six campers from each can of tomatoes.

Problem 3.2

Suppose you are assigned to help the cook order supplies.

A. How many cans of tomatoes would you advise the cook to buy to make spaghetti for the 240 campers? Explain your answer.

B. How much would these cans of tomatoes cost altogether?

■ Problem 3.2 Follow-Up

1. At the EatMore grocery store, you can buy seven cans of tomatoes for $6.00. The cans are the same size as the cans at CannedStuff. Are the tomatoes at EatMore a better buy than the tomatoes at CannedStuff? Explain your answer.

2. Gus was trying to figure out how to think about the EatMore price of seven cans of tomatoes for $6.00. He divided 7 by 6 and got 1.16666667. He then divided 6 by 7 and got 0.85714286. What does each of these numbers mean in the context of seven cans of tomatoes for $6.00?

3.3 Sharing Pizza

On the last day of camp, the cook served pizza. The camp dining room has two kinds of tables. A large table seats 10 people, and a small table seats 8 people. The cook tells the students who are serving dinner to put four pizzas on each large table and three pizzas on each small table.

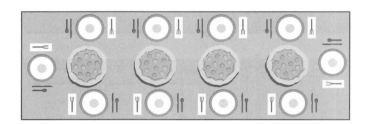

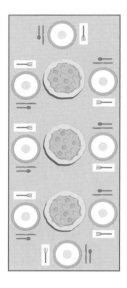

Problem 3.3

A. If the pizzas at a table are shared equally by everyone at the table, will a person sitting at a small table get the same amount of pizza as a person sitting at a large table? Explain your reasoning.

B. The ratio of large tables to small tables in the dining room is 8 to 5. There are exactly enough seats for the 240 campers. How many tables of each kind are there?

■ Problem 3.3 Follow-Up

1. How were ratios helpful in thinking about the problem?

2. How many pizzas will the cook need in order to put four on each large table and three on each small table?

As you work on these ACE questions, use your calculator whenever you need it.

Applications

1. At camp, Miriam learned how to use a pottery wheel. She can make 3 bowls in 2 hours. How long will it take her to make a set of 12 bowls?

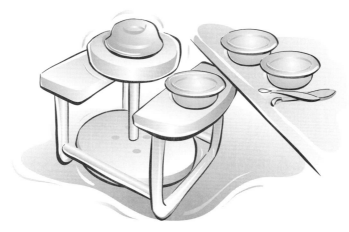

2. The camp cook's favorite recipe for salad dressing calls for 2 tablespoons of lemon juice and 6 tablespoons of olive oil. If the cook wants to make a large batch of salad dressing using 3 cups of oil, how much lemon juice will he need? (There are 16 tablespoons in 1 cup.)

3. You need to buy several dozen avocados to make guacamole dip for a party. At the co-op, you can buy 7 avocados for $6.00. At the Cheapy Food Mart, 5 avocados cost $4.50. At which store will you get the better buy?

4. Friendly Food Store has Cocoa Blast cereal on sale this week at a price of $8.25 for five boxes. Best Food Store is offering the same size box of Cocoa Blast at a price of $3.50 for two boxes. Which offer gives you the most cereal for your money?

5. In the ads for Bolda Cola from Investigation 1, one possible concluding statement says "by a ratio of 3 to 2" and another says "by a ratio of 17,139 to 11,426." These ratios are equivalent. Write four other statements containing ratios equivalent to these ratios.

6. At Louis Armstrong School, Ms. Turini's homeroom has 18 boys and 12 girls.

   a. What is the ratio of boys to girls in Ms. Turini's homeroom?

   b. What is the ratio of girls to boys?

   c. What is the ratio of boys to students in the class?

   d. What is the ratio of students in the class to boys?

7. Lakisha is attending a party at her favorite pizza parlor. Three tables are set up for the guests. After the pizzas are placed on the tables, the guests are asked to sit anywhere they choose. The small table has 5 seats and 2 pizzas, the medium table has 7 seats and 3 pizzas, and the large table has 12 seats and 5 pizzas. The pizzas at each table will be shared equally. Where should Lakisha sit if she is very hungry?

8. Elena works in the animal nursery at the county zoo. The baby monkeys eat a mixture of high-fiber nuggets and high-protein formula. Last month, Elena mixed 4 cups of nuggets and 6 cups of high-protein formula to make the food for each feeding. This month, the monkeys can eat more at each feeding.

   a. If Elena uses 8 cups of nuggets in the new mix, how much high-protein formula should she use?

   b. If Elena uses only 6 cups of nuggets, how much formula should she use?

   c. If Elena uses 7.5 cups of formula, how many cups of nuggets should she use?

In 9–11, use the apple juice recipes below.

Mix W
3 cups concentrate
4 cups cold water

Mix X
3 cup concentrate
5 cups cold water

Mix Y
6 cups concentrate
9 cups cold water

Mix Z
5 cups concentrate
8 cups cold water

9. a. If you made a single batch of mix W, what fraction of the batch would be concentrate? Answer the same question for mixes X, Y, and Z.

 b. Rewrite your answers to part a as percents.

10. Which recipe would make the most "appley" juice?

11. If you made only 1 cup of mix W, how much water and how much concentrate would you need? Answer the same question for mixes X, Y, and Z.

Connections

12. The diagram below illustrates the equivalence of two fractions. Find the missing numerator.

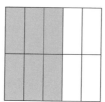 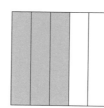

$$\frac{?}{10} = \frac{3}{5}$$

In 13–18, replace the question mark with a number to make a true statement.

13. $\frac{3}{15} = \frac{?}{30}$

14. $\frac{1}{2} = \frac{?}{20}$

15. $\frac{?}{20} = \frac{3}{5}$

16. $\frac{18}{30} = \frac{?}{15}$

17. $\frac{?}{15} = \frac{3}{5}$

18. $\frac{9}{15} = \frac{12}{?}$

19. Illustrate your answer to question 13 by drawing a picture like the one in question 12.

In 20–23, replace the question marks with numbers to make a true statement.

20. $\frac{6}{14} = \frac{?}{21} = \frac{?}{28}$

21. $\frac{?}{27} = \frac{8}{36} = \frac{?}{45}$

22. $\frac{?}{20} = \frac{?}{25} = \frac{6}{30}$

23. $\frac{?}{8} = \frac{15}{?} = \frac{24}{32}$

Extensions

24. Here is a drawing of Mr. Stickman.

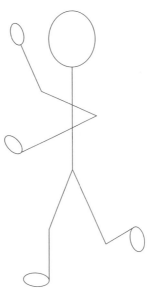

a. Draw a picture of Twiggy Stickman. She is $\frac{1}{2}$ as tall as Mr. Stickman.

b. Draw a picture of Branchy Stickman. He is $\frac{2}{3}$ as tall as Twiggy.

c. Branchy's height is what fraction of Mr. Stickman's height? Explain your reasoning.

d. Use some other form of comparison to rewrite the fraction comparisons in parts a, b, and c.

25. a. What fraction of this square is shaded?

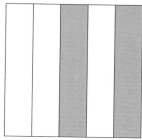

b. What fraction of this square is shaded?

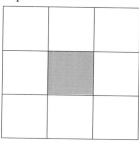

c. Draw a picture to show a fraction with a denominator of 10 that is equivalent to the fraction shaded in part a. Tell what fraction of your drawing is shaded.

d. Draw a picture to show a fraction with a denominator of 27 that is equivalent to the fraction shaded in part b. Tell what fraction of your drawing is shaded.

e. What percent of the square in part a is shaded?

f. What percent of the square in part b is shaded?

g. What is the ratio of the shaded area to the unshaded area in part a?

h. What is the ratio of the shaded area to the unshaded area in part b?

i. The squares in parts a and b are the same size. What is the ratio of the shaded part of the square in part a to the shaded part of the square in part b? Be careful—the answer is not 2 to 1.

Mathematical Reflections

In this investigation, you learned about ratios and about using ratios to make comparisons. These questions will help you summarize what you have learned:

1. Explain how to form a ratio and how ratios can be used to compare two numbers. Use examples to help explain your thinking.

2. What strategy can you use to compare two ratios? Be very specific. Your strategy should allow you to tell whether the two ratios are the same or different. Make up a problem that can be solved by using your strategy.

In Investigation 2, you used percents to make comparisons. In Investigation 3, you used ratios to make comparisons.

3. The percent of orange concentrate in a juice mix is 60%. What is the ratio of concentrate to water in the mix?

4. The ratio of concentrate to water in a juice mix is 3 to 5. What percent of the mix is concentrate?

Think about your answers to these questions, discuss your ideas with other students and your teacher, and then write a summary of your findings in your journal.

Comparing by Finding Rates

In this unit, you have been using percents and ratios to make comparisons. Now, look at these examples of a special kind of comparison you probably encounter frequently:

My mom's new car gets 45 miles per gallon on the expressway.

We need two sandwiches for each person at the picnic.

I earn $3.50 per hour baby-sitting for my neighbor.

Tomatoes are on sale five for $4.00.

The sign above the mystery meat in the cafeteria says 355 calories : 6 ounces.

James can run at a rate of 8.5 kilometers per hour.

Each statement above compares two *different* things: miles to gallons, sandwiches to people, dollars to hours, tomatoes to dollars, calories to ounces, and kilometers to hours. Comparisons of two different things, like those in the statements above, are called **rates.** They tell us the *rate* at which something happens.

You can scale a rate up or down to find an equivalent rate. For example, consider this problem:

Ms. Balog's car gets 45 miles to the gallon on the highway. How much gas will the car use if Ms. Balog drives it 180 miles on the interstate?

Here are two ways you might solve this problem:

Method 1
Divide 180 by 45 to find out how many groups of 45 there are in 180. The result is 4, which means the car will use 4 gallons of gas.

Method 2
Write a ratio and scale up to find the answer:

45 miles per gallon means	45 miles :	1 gallon
or	90 miles :	2 gallons
or	135 miles :	3 gallons
or	180 miles :	4 gallons

The car will use 4 gallons of gas.

4.1 Comparing Fuel Economy

After graduating from the University of Colorado, Luis and Madeline both got teaching jobs in Denver. They each bought a new car for commuting to work, and one afternoon they had a friendly argument about whose car was better. Luis claimed his car was more fuel-efficient. Madeline challenged him to prove his claim. Since they would both be traveling home for Thanksgiving, Luis suggested they use their trips to test the gas mileage of their cars.

Madeline and Luis are from different small towns in southern Colorado, but the routes from Denver to both towns follow I-25 for the first 190 miles to Trinidad.

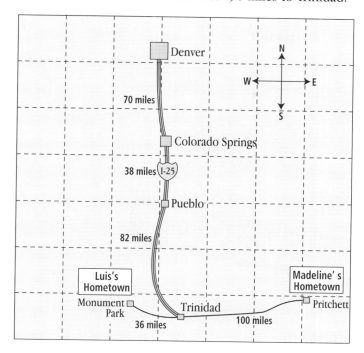

When the two friends returned from the holiday, they compared their fuel economy. Madeline's car used 19 gallons for the trip from Denver to Pritchett and back. Luis's car used only 15.5 gallons of gas for the trip from Denver to Monument Park and back. He said this proved his car was more fuel-efficient than Madeline's. Madeline disagreed.

Problem 4.1

Use the gasoline and mileage data to help settle Madeline and Luis's argument.

Which car do you think is more fuel-efficient on the highway? Explain how you decided and why you think you are correct.

■ Problem 4.1 Follow-Up

Would it make sense to use percents to settle this argument? If so, show how; if not, explain why.

4.2 Using Unit Rates

The advertisements below use rates to describe sale prices. How would you compare the value of the offers described in the two ads?

One way to compare rates like these is to do some division to find unit rates. **Unit rates** are rates in which one of the numbers is 1 unit. For example, 55 miles per hour is a unit rate because it tells the number of miles driven for every 1 hour, and 99¢ a pound is a unit rate because it tells the cost for every 1 pound.

Think about this!

Look back at the examples at the beginning of this investigation. Which of these statements are examples of unit rates?

You can compare the advertisements above by finding the *price per CD* (that is, the price for 1 CD) at each store. The price per CD is $5.99 at Music City and $5.71 at CD World.

Problem 4.2

When Madeline and Luis compared the fuel economy of their new cars, they found these rates:

Madeline's car went 580 miles with 19 gallons of gasoline.
Luis's car went 452 miles with 15.5 gallons of gasoline.

Use this information to answer the following questions.

A. For each car, find a unit rate describing the mileage. Which car got better gas mileage? In other words, which car went more miles per gallon of gas?

B. Complete a table like the one below, showing the fuel used and the miles covered by each car based on the unit rates you found in part A. We call this kind of table a *rate table*.

Gallons of gas	0	1	2	3	4	5	6	7	8
Miles in Madeline's car									
Miles in Luis's car									

C. Look at the patterns in your table. For each car, write an equation for a rule you can use to predict the miles driven (m) from the gallons of gas used (g).

D. Use the rules you wrote in part C to find the number of miles each car could cover if it used 9.5, 15.5, 19, 23.8, 100, 125, and 150 gallons of gasoline.

▪ Problem 4.2 Follow-Up

1. Use your data from B or D to sketch graphs of the (gallons, miles) data for each car.
2. How are your two graphs alike? How are they different?
3. What do you think makes the two graphs different?

Solving Problems with Rates

Suppose Sascha, a champion bicyclist, wants to see how far he can travel in an hour. He starts timing himself when he reaches a speed of 45 miles per hour. He maintains this speed for 10 minutes. Sascha starts to feel tired and slows down to 30 miles per hour for the next 5 minutes. He then reduces his speed to 25 miles per hour for the next 30 minutes. Finally, Sascha feels exhausted as he finishes the last 15 minutes at 15 miles per hour.

Problem 4.3

A. Make a graph showing Sascha's total distance traveled over time. Use 5-minute time intervals on the *x*-axis.

B. How far did Sascha travel in his 1-hour ride? Explain.

C. If you could maintain a steady speed of 13 miles per hour on a bike, how long would it take you to travel the same distance Sascha traveled in his 1-hour ride?

D. If you were racing Sascha, what constant (steady) speed would you have to maintain to tie him?

■ Problem 4.3 Follow-Up

Can you write a single equation that will allow you to predict Sascha's total distance at any time during his 1-hour ride? Why or why not?

Did you know?

The highest speed ever recorded on a pedal-powered bike was 152.284 miles per hour. John Howard performed this amazing feat on July 20, 1985, at Bonneville Salt Flats, Utah. He was able to reach this speed by following a car, which acted as a windshield for him and his bike.

Source: *Guinness Book of Records 1994*. Ed. Peter Matthews. New York: Bantam Books, 1994, p. 615.

4.4 Buying Beads

Stores often use rates in their advertisements. Rather than using unit rates, advertisements often give the cost for several items. For example, a grocery store might advertise five cans of tomatoes for $4.00. Such advertisements may entice customers to buy more. But, even though an ad gives the price for several items, you can usually buy fewer items at the same rate.

The owner of a crafts store believes that price displays like the one below get her customers' attention. However, when customers want amounts other than 10, 15, or 20 beads, figuring the bill is not easy.

Problem 4.4

Write an equation relating the cost (c) and the number of beads (x) for each type of bead:

Spheres: $c =$ _____

Cubes: $c =$ _____

Cylinders: $c =$ _____

■ Problem 4.4 Follow-Up

For each type of bead, you could find two unit rates. You could find the number of beads for each unit of cost (in other words, for each cent), and you could find the cost for each bead.

1. Which unit rate would be most useful if you were trying to figure out the number of beads you could buy with a certain amount of money?

2. Which unit rate would be most useful if you were trying to figure out how much money a certain number of beads costs?

As you work on these ACE questions, use your calculator whenever you need it.

Applications

1. The manager of Quality Dairy stores says it takes 1000 pounds of milk to make 100 pounds of cheddar cheese.

    a. Make a rate table showing the amount of milk needed to make 100 pounds to 1000 pounds of cheddar cheese in increments of 100 pounds (this means 100 pounds, 200 pounds, 300 pounds, and so on).

    b. Make a graph showing the relationship between pounds of milk and pounds of cheddar cheese. Think carefully about which variable should go on each axis.

    c. Find a unit rate relating pounds of milk to pounds of cheddar cheese. Use the rate you find to write an equation relating pounds of milk (m) to pounds of cheese (c).

    d. Give one advantage of each form of representation—the graph, the table, and the rule.

2. The Quality Dairy manager said it takes 700 pounds of milk to make 100 pounds of cottage cheese.

    a. Make a rate table showing the amount of milk needed to make 100 pounds to 1000 pounds of cottage cheese in increments of 100 pounds.

    b. Make a graph showing the relationship between pounds of milk and pounds of cottage cheese. Think carefully about which variable should go on each axis.

    c. Find a unit rate relating pounds of milk to pounds of cottage cheese. Use the rate you find to write an equation relating pounds of milk (m) to pounds of cottage cheese (c).

    d. Compare the graph in this question to the graph in question 1. Explain how they are alike and how they are different. What is the cause of the differences between the two graphs?

3. The world-champion milk producer in 1993 was a 6-year-old cow from Oxford, New Hampshire. The cow, Tullando Royalty Maxima, produced 58,952 pounds of milk in that year!

a. Look back at your answers to question 2. How much cottage cheese could be made from the milk that Maxima produced during 1993?

b. The average weight of a dairy cow is 1400 pounds. How many dairy cows would be needed to equal the weight of the cottage cheese made from Maxima's yearly production of milk?

c. One gallon of milk weighs about 8.6 pounds. Suppose a milk bucket holds about 3 gallons. About how many milk buckets would Maxima's *daily* production of milk fill?

d. One pound of milk fills about two glasses. About how many glasses of milk could you fill with Maxima's *daily* production of milk?

4. On their morning commutes to work, Golda travels 10 miles in about 15 minutes and Dale travels 23 miles in about 30 minutes. Who has the faster average speed?

5. Rolanda and Louise rode bikes at a steady pace along a narrow road with no traffic. Rolanda rode 8 miles in 32 minutes. Louise rode 2 miles in 10 minutes. Who was riding the fastest?

6. Fasiz and Kari were driving at the same speed along a bumpy country road. Fasiz drove 8 kilometers in 24 minutes. How far did Kari drive in 6 minutes?

7. Students at Langston Hughes School rode to camp on several buses. On the long dirt road leading to the camp, the buses covered only 6 miles in 10 minutes.

a. At this speed, how long would it take the buses to cover 18 miles?

b. At this speed, how far would the buses go in 15 minutes?

8. a. Mara's car can be driven 580 miles with 20 gallons of gasoline. Make a rate table showing the number of miles her car can be driven with 1, 2, 3, . . . , 10 gallons of gas.

b. Joel's car can be driven 450 miles with 15 gallons of gasoline. Make a rate table showing the number of miles his car can be driven with 1, 2, 3, . . . , 10 gallons of gas.

9. The local grocery store has videotapes on sale, $3.00 for 2 tapes. You have $20.

    a. How many tapes can you buy?

    b. If there is a 7% sales tax on the tapes, how many can you buy?

Connections

10. Franky's Fudge Factory provides customers with the following information about the calories in their fudge.

Caloric Content of Franky's Fudge

Grams of fudge	Calories
50	150
150	450
300	900
500	1500

    a. Fiona ate 75 grams of fudge. How many calories did she consume?

    b. Freddy consumed 1000 calories worth of fudge. How many grams of fudge did he eat?

    c. Describe a rule you can use to find the number of calories in any number of grams of Franky's fudge.

11. This table shows how to convert liters to quarts.

Liters	Quarts
1	1.06
4	4.24
5	5.30
9	9.54

    a. About how many liters are in 5.5 quarts?

    b. About how many quarts are in 5.5 liters?

    c. Write an equation that relates liters (L) and quarts (Q).

In 12–16, find a unit rate, and use it to write an equation relating the two variables.

12. 12 cents for 20 beads **13.** 8 cents for 10 nails

14. 450 miles on 15 gallons of gasoline

15. 3 cups of water for 2 cups of orange concentrate

16. $4.00 for 5 cans of soup

In 17 and 18, replace the question mark with a number to make a true sentence.

17. $\frac{4}{9} \times ? = 1\frac{1}{3}$ **18.** $? \times 2.25 = 90$

19. Write two fractions whose product is between 10 and 11.

20. Write two decimals whose product is between 1 and 2.

21. The table of data below shows the mean times that students in one seventh grade class spend on several activities during the weekend.

  a. The *stacked bar graph* on the next page was made using the data from the table. Explain how it was constructed.

  b. Suppose you are writing a report summarizing the class's data. You have space for either the table or the graph, but not both. What is one advantage of including the table? What is one advantage of including the stacked bar graph?

How We Spend Our Weekends

Category	Boys	Girls	All students
Sleeping	18.8 hours	18.2 hours	18.4 hours
Eating	4.0 hours	2.7 hours	3.5 hours
Recreation	7.8 hours	6.9 hours	7.4 hours
Talking on the phone	0.5 hours	0.7 hours	0.6 hours
Watching TV	4.2 hours	3.0 hours	3.7 hours
Doing chores, homework	3.6 hours	5.8 hours	4.7 hours
Other	9.1 hours	10.7 hours	9.7 hours

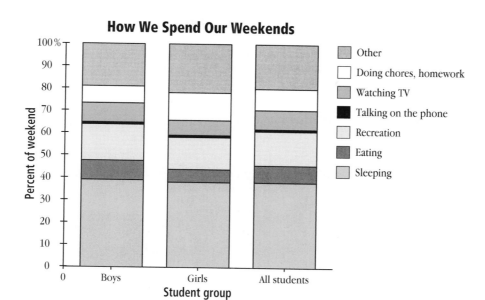

How We Spend Our Weekends

Legend:
- Other
- Doing chores, homework
- Watching TV
- Talking on the phone
- Recreation
- Eating
- Sleeping

Extensions

22. A cider mill has pressed a 240-liter vat of apple juice. The mill has many kinds of containers in which to pack juice.

a. The mill owner wants to package the entire vat of juice in containers of the same size. Complete this table to show the number of containers of each size needed to hold the entire vat of juice.

Volume of container (liters)	10	4	2	1	$\frac{1}{2}$	$\frac{1}{4}$	$\frac{1}{10}$
Number of containers needed	24						

b. Write an equation that describes the relationship between the volume of the container (v) and the number of containers needed (n) to hold 240 liters of juice.

23. A chemistry student is analyzing the contents of rust, and she finds that it is made of iron and oxygen. She tests several amounts of rust and produces the following data. (Note: g is the abbreviation for grams.)

Amount of rust (g)	Amount of iron (g)	Amount of oxygen (g)
50	35.0	15.0
100	70.0	30.0
135	94.5	40.5
150	105.0	45.0

a. If the student analyzed 400 grams of rust, how much iron and how much oxygen would she find?

b. Is the ratio of the amount of iron to the amount of rust constant? If so, what is the ratio?

Mathematical Reflections

In this investigation, you learned about a special way to compare quantities called a *rate*. You learned to compare rates, to find unit rates, and to use rates to make tables and graphs and to write equations. These questions will help you summarize what you have learned:

1 Give three examples of rates.

2 How can rates or unit rates help you to make comparisons?

3 How do you convert a rate to a unit rate? Illustrate your answer with one of the examples you gave in part 1.

4 How can information about unit rates be used to make tables and graphs showing how two variables are related? Use your example to illustrate your answer.

5 How can a unit rate be used to write an equation relating two variables? Use your example to illustrate your answer.

Think about your answers to these questions, discuss your ideas with other students and your teacher, and then write a summary of your findings in your journal.

Estimating Populations and Population Densities

Since counting is one of the first mathematics skills you learned, you might expect solving a counting problem to be easy. However, sometimes counting things can get complicated.

Think about this!

How would you count the number of people attending a Fourth of July fireworks show or a human-rights rally on the mall of our nation's capital?

How would you count the number of deer in a forest, the number of fish in a stream, or the number of bees in a hive?

Share your ideas about these problems with your class. Be sure to discuss the factors that make the counting in each situation difficult.

5.1 Estimating the Size of a Crowd

News reports often give estimates of the sizes of crowds at political rallies, parades, and festivals. In 1994, television reporters announced that 350,000 people had attended a Fourth of July concert and fireworks display in front of the Capitol in Washington, D.C. How do you think this estimate was made? Do you think someone actually counted each individual in the crowd?

Problem 5.1

Sometimes the size of a crowd is estimated from aerial photographs. Imagine that the illustration below is an aerial photograph of a crowd at a rally. Each dot represents one person.

Estimate how many people attended the rally. Explain the method you used to arrive at your answer.

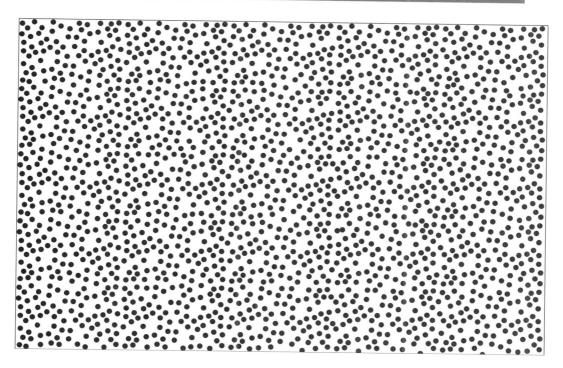

■ Problem 5.1 Follow-Up

In your group, discuss ways your method might lead to a poor estimate of the crowd size.

5.2 Estimating a Deer Population

In states with large populations of white-tailed deer, like Michigan, biologists in the Department of Natural Resources are asked to make estimates of deer populations. The estimates are used to set hunting seasons and regulations. But how is it possible to count all the deer in Michigan—or even in a small part of the state?

One method biologists use to count animal populations is the *capture-tag-recapture* method. You can simulate this method by using a jar or box filled with white beans. Imagine that each bean is a deer in the upper peninsula of Michigan. Your job is to estimate the number of deer without actually counting them all.

Problem 5.2

Your group will need a container with a lid and a large number of white beans. Work with your group to perform this experiment.

- Remove exactly 100 beans from the container, and mark them with a pen or marker.

- Put the marked beans back into the container, and shake or mix them with the unmarked beans.

- Without looking at the beans, scoop out a handful of about 30 beans. Record the numbers of marked and unmarked beans in this sample. Return the sample to the jar, and mix the beans together again.

- Repeat this scoop-and-count procedure four more times. In each case, record the number of marked and unmarked beans.

A. Study the data you collected. Use the data to estimate the number of beans in your container. Explain how you made your estimate.

B. Based on what you have learned from this experiment, how do you think biologists count deer populations?

■ Problem 5.2 Follow-Up

In your group, discuss ways in which this method might give a poor estimate of the actual number of deer in a population. Record your ideas.

5.3 Finding Population Densities

Sometimes a simple count does not tell you the whole story. To understand some situations, you need to count or measure two or more things and determine how the measures or counts are related. For example, suppose you are interested in how crowded a city, state, country, or other geographic region is. It is not enough to consider the number of people in the region. You must also consider the amount of available land.

Think about this!

When we reach the year 2000, there will be over 6 billion people living on our planet. But we are not evenly distributed over the 58 million square miles that make up the seven continents; some cities, states, and countries are much more crowded than others.

What do you think are the most and least crowded places on earth? How could you use land area and population data to test your ideas?

Below is a map of the United States divided into the nine regions used in reporting data from the census.

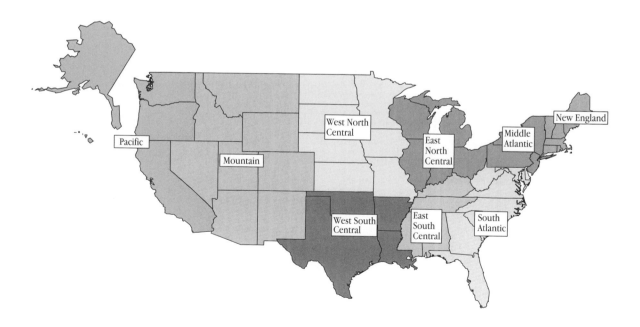

This table shows the 1994 population and land area for the nine census regions.

Region	Population	Area (square miles)
New England	13,270,000	62,811
Middle Atlantic	38,125,000	99,463
South Atlantic	46,398,000	266,221
East North Central	43,184,000	243,539
East South Central	15,890,000	178,615
West North Central	18,210,000	507,981
West South Central	28,404,000	426,234
Mountain	15,214,000	856,121
Pacific	41,645,000	895,353

Source: *Statistical Abstract of the United States 1995.* Published by the Bureau of the Census, Washington, D.C., pp. 28 and 225.

Problem 5.3

The "crowdedness" of a region is commonly reported by giving the number of people (or animals or plants) per unit of area. This rate is called the **population density** of the region.

A. What is the population density of the census region in which your school is located?

B. Divide the remaining eight census regions among the groups in your class. Find the population density of the region you are assigned. Share your group's results with the rest of the class, so that every group has data for all nine regions.

C. Order the regions from least crowded to most crowded.

D. Compare the population density of the region in which you live to the population density of each neighboring region. Write complete sentences explaining which regions you are comparing and describing how their population densities compare.

■ Problem 5.3 Follow-Up

What do you think accounts for the differences in population densities among the regions? In other words, why do you think some areas are densely populated and others are more sparsely populated?

5.4 Comparing the Dakotas

South Dakota and North Dakota rank 45 and 47 in population of all the states in the United States. South Dakota has 721,000 people in 75,896 square miles of land, and North Dakota has 638,000 people in 68,994 square miles of land.

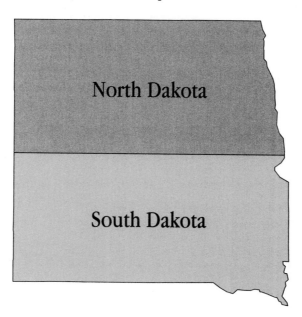

Problem 5.4

A. Which state, North Dakota or South Dakota, has the greater population density?

B. How many citizens of one state would have to move to the other state to make the population densities in the two states equal? Explain how you arrived at your answer.

■ Problem 5.4 Follow-Up

Find the population density of your state. How does it compare to the population densities of North and South Dakota?

5.5 Predicting Traffic Jams

You have probably been in a traffic jam or two. What kinds of things cause traffic jams? How can you predict where traffic jams are likely to occur?

One way to identify places where traffic jams are likely is by calculating traffic densities. Hong Kong is reported to have the highest traffic density in the world. In 1992, there were 418 registered cars and trucks per mile of road, or about 12.63 feet per registered vehicle!
(Source: *Guinness Book of Records 1994.* Ed. Peter Matthews. New York: Bantam Books, 1994, p. 318.)

Problem 5.5

A. The city of Ole has 450,237 registered vehicles for 3000 miles of road. What is the traffic density of Ole? Calculate the number of vehicles per mile of road and the number of feet of road per vehicle.

B. The city of Driftwood Bay has 396 registered vehicles for 10 miles of road. What is the traffic density of Driftwood Bay? Calculate the number of vehicles per mile of road and the number of feet of road per vehicle.

C. Which of the three cities—Hong Kong, Ole, or Driftwood Bay—do you think is most likely to have traffic jams? Explain your answer.

D. Which of the three cities do you think is least likely to have traffic jams? Explain your answer.

■ Problem 5.5 Follow-Up

1. Other than traffic density, what factors might affect the likelihood of traffic jams?

2. A typical four-passenger car is about 13 feet long. Compare this statistic to the amount of road per mile in Hong Kong. What does this say about traffic in Hong Kong? What might Hong Kong do if this situation gets worse?

As you work on these ACE questions, use your calculator whenever you need it.

Applications

1. Yung-nan wants to estimate the number of beans in a jar. She took out a sample of 150 beans, marked them, returned them to the jar, and mixed them with the unmarked beans. She then gathered some data by taking samples. Use her data to predict the number of beans in the jar.

Sample 1
Number of marked beans: 2
Beans in sample: 25

Sample 3
Number of marked beans: 23
Beans in sample: 150

Sample 2
Number of marked beans: 10
Beans in sample: 75

Sample 4
Number of marked beans: 38
Beans in sample: 250

2. Describe a method for estimating (not counting!) the blades of grass on a football field.

3. After testing many samples, an electric company determined that approximately 2 of every 1000 light bulbs on the market are defective. Americans buy over a billion light bulbs every year. Estimate how many of these bulbs are defective.

4. Angela Krebs, a biologist, spends summers on an island off the coast of Alaska. For several summers she studied the puffin, a black-and-white seabird with a flat, brightly colored bill. Two summers ago, Angela trapped 20 puffins, then tagged and released them. This past summer, she trapped 50 puffins and found that 2 of them were tagged. She used this information to estimate the total puffin population on the island.

a. Using Angela's findings, estimate the number of puffins on the island. Explain how you made your estimate.

b. How confident are you that your estimate is accurate? Explain your answer.

In 5–8, use the data in the following table.

Population and Land Area of Selected States

State	Population	Area (square miles)
California	31,431,000	155,973
Connecticut	3,275,000	4845
New Hampshire	1,137,000	8969
North Dakota	638,000	68,994
South Dakota	721,000	75,896
Vermont	580,000	9249
Wyoming	476,000	97,105

Source: *Statistical Abstract of the United States 1995.* Published by the Bureau of the Census, Washington, D.C., pp. 28 and 225.

5. **a.** Find the population density of each state in the table.

    b. Which state has the highest population density?

    c. Which state has the lowest population density?

6. How many people would have to move from Connecticut to Wyoming to make the population densities in the two states the same? Explain.

7. How many times would the land area of Connecticut fit into the land area of Wyoming? Explain.

8. How many times greater is the population of Connecticut than the population of Wyoming? Explain.

9. The city of Canton has three parks: Flyaway Park has an area of 5000 m^2, Golden Park has an area of 7235 m^2, and Pine Park has an area of 3060 m^2.

    a. At 2 P.M. last Saturday, 400 children were playing in Flyaway Park, 630 were in Golden Park, and 255 were in Pine Park. Rank the parks from least crowded to most crowded. Explain how you got your answer.

    b. Oak Park is located in the suburbs of Canton. It has area of 5240 m^2. At 2 P.M. last Saturday, 462 children were playing in Oak Park. How crowded was Oak Park at this time compared to Flyaway, Golden, and Pine?

Connections

10. At Raccoon Middle School, Ms. Picadello's students conducted a class survey about their favorite rock bands. Of the 35 students in the class, 20 picked the Nerds, 8 picked the Promise, and 7 picked Willie and the Wonders.

    a. If you randomly selected 10 students in the halls of Raccoon Middle School and asked what their favorite rock band was, would you expect the same ratio as in Ms. Picadello's class? Why or why not?

    b. Would you expect the same ratio if you asked 10 middle-school students from another state the same question? Why or why not?

11. Shanda and Michi play a lot of basketball, and they keep a record of their free-throw attempts in practices and games. Shanda has made 500 of 1000 free-throw attempts in the last month, and Michi has made 175 of 350.

   a. Compare Shanda's and Michi's free-throw shooting.

   b. How would their success rates change if they each make their next 10 free-throw attempts? Are you surprised at the results? Why or why not?

12. The map on page 55 has a scale of about 1 inch = 600 miles. (Alaska and Hawaii are not drawn to this scale.) Excluding Alaska and Hawaii, the map is about 5 inches wide and 2.5 inches high.

   a. How could you draw a version of the map that is about 10 inches by 5 inches?

   b. What would the scale of your enlarged map be?

13. A jar contains 150 marked beans. Scott took several samples from the jar and got these results:

Beans in sample	25	50	75	100	150	200	250
Marked beans	3	12	13	17	27	38	52
Percent marked beans	12%						

   a. Copy the table, and complete the last row to show the percent of marked beans in each sample.

   b. Graph the (beans in sample, marked beans) data. Describe the pattern of data points in your graph. What does the pattern tell you about the relationship between the number of beans in a sample and the number of marked beans you can expect to find in the sample?

   c. Make a graph of the (beans in sample, percent marked beans) data. Describe the pattern of data points in your graph. What does the pattern tell you about the relationship between the number of beans in a sample and the percent of marked beans you can expect to find in the sample?

Extensions

14. Conduct an experiment in your neighborhood or school to help you predict the number of people in the United States who are left-handed. Make the assumption that your neighborhood or school is representative of the general population in left-handedness. Assume that the population of the United States is about 260 million. Describe your experiment and the results you predict for the population of the United States.

Mathematical Reflections

In this investigation, you used sampling and ratios to estimate the size of a population. You also used the idea of population density to describe and compare the "crowdedness" of geographic regions and roads. These questions will help you summarize what you have learned:

1 For each situation, explain how you could use the given information to estimate the total population of fish in the pond. Be sure to include any assumptions you make.

  a. Biologists caught 25 fish in a net, tagged them, and returned them to the pond. In a later catch of 20 fish, 3 had tags.

  b. Park officials tagged and released 40 fish. They kept records of the fish caught over the next month and found that 30% had tags.

2 In the problems in this investigation, what data did you need to find the densities of populations?

3 **a.** What data would you need to estimate the density of deer in a wildlife area?

  b. What data would you need to estimate the density of trees in a forest?

4 Which of the following comparison statements is most like the population-density comparisons? Explain your reasoning.

  a. People prefer Bolda Cola to Cola Nola by a ratio of 3 to 2.

  b. Mary's car gets 30.5 miles per gallon of gas.

  c. The population of California is 28,156,000 greater than the population of Connecticut.

Think about your answers to these questions, discuss your ideas with other students and your teacher, and then write a summary of your findings in your journal.

Choosing Strategies

So far in this unit, you have used fractions, percents, ratios, rates, and unit rates to make comparisons and to estimate populations and population densities. In this investigation, you will explore several problem situations in which you need to choose a strategy for solving the problem and explain why your strategy makes sense. There will usually be several ways to think about a problem. You will begin to see what kind of reasoning works best for a particular type of problem.

6.1 Scaling Up or Down

Dinosaurs (which means "terrible lizards") roamed the earth for 125 million years. By studying the bones, teeth, and footprints of these ancient reptiles, paleontologists learn more about them. Reconstructing dinosaur skeletons helps these scientists estimate the height, weight, and length of different species of dinosaur.

One of the largest predators of all time was *Tyrannosaurus rex* (which means "king tyrant lizard"). This carnivorous dinosaur lived 70 million years ago in many areas of North America, including the present states of Montana, Wyoming, and Texas. Scientists determined that *T. rex* was a meat eater by studying the shape and size of its head and teeth.

T. rex weighed about 8,100 kilograms and reached heights of up to 6 meters—almost as tall as a two-story house! Archeologists have uncovered *T. rex* skulls 1 meter long and *T. rex* incisors (the longest teeth) 15 centimeters long.

A "larger than average" human being can be about 2 meters tall and weigh 90 kilograms. Human incisors are about 1 centimeter long, and a large human skull can be about 20 centimeters long.

How big was *T. rex* compared to a "larger than average" human being?

Write a paragraph to help someone younger than you understand how the size of *T. rex* compares to the size of a human. Be very specific about the comparisons you are making.

■ **Problem 6.1 Follow-Up**

1. Suppose an infant *T. rex* was the same height as the human described in the problem and was similar to an adult *T. rex*. What would be the scale factor between a grown *T. rex* and the infant *T. rex*?

2. How long were the incisors of this young *T. rex*?

3. How long was the skull of this young *T. rex*?

Using Rules of Thumb

Carpenters, bakers, tailors, designers, and people in many other occupations use rules of thumb to make quick estimates. A *rule of thumb* is a method of estimating, based on experience and common sense, that is practical but not necessarily precise. For example, you may have heard someone say, "A pint is a pound the world around." This rule of thumb tells how to compare liquid measures with weight. Since 1 quart is equal to 2 pints, you can use this rule of thumb to estimate that 1 quart of milk weighs about 2 pounds. In this problem, you will be working with several rules of thumb.

Problem 6.2

In A–D, use the given rule of thumb to solve the problem. Explain how you found each answer.

A. *It takes about 100 maple trees to make 25 gallons of maple syrup.*
Mr. Paulo made maple syrup from all of his sugar maple trees. He ended up with 16 gallons of syrup. About how many sugar maple trees does he have?

B. *A 5-minute shower requires about 18 gallons of water.*
About how much water do you use for an 8-minute shower? How much water will you use if you take an 8-minute shower every day for a year?

C. *A double-spaced page of text contains about 250 words if it is printed in Times with a font size of 12, and about 330 words if it is printed in Times with a font size of 10.*
Jeremy printed his term paper in the computer lab. He used 10-point Times, and the paper came to 15 double-spaced pages. Jeremy's teacher requires term papers be 20 double-spaced pages long. If Jeremy changes the font to 12-point Times, how long will his paper be?

D. *Jogging burns about 100 calories per mile.*
Elizabeth jogs at a rate of 4.5 miles per hour. How long will it take her to burn off the 1200-calorie lunch she ate at Burger Heaven?

Adapted from *Rules of Thumb* by Tom Parker. Boston: Houghton Mifflin, 1993.

■ **Problem 6.2 Follow-Up**

Ask adults you know if they use any rules of thumb in their jobs or at home. Write down one of the rules you learn. Write a problem that can be solved using the rule.

6.3 Selecting Delegates

Young people all over the world are concerned about protecting and improving the environment. American Students for the Environment is hosting a two-week environmental studies conference for 1000 middle-school students from all over the United States. Delegates for the conference will be selected to represent the diversity of the United States population—geographically, ethnically, and economically. Imagine that you are a member of the delegate selection committee.

American Students for the Environment
present

The First Annual

ENVIRONMENTAL STUDIES CONFERENCE

Welcome Delegates!

Think about this!

To make fair decisions about the delegates, you must consider several questions. Tell what information you would need to make each decision below.

- How many of the 1000 delegates should come from each of the nine census regions of the United States?

- What percent of the delegates should represent metropolitan areas, and what percent should represent rural areas?

- What percent of the delegates should represent minority groups?

You and the rest of the delegate selection committee will be using data from the 1990 United States Census to help you make your selections. To choose the number of delegates from each region, you can compare the population of each region to the population of the United States. This ratio can be written as a fraction.

$$\frac{\text{population of the region}}{\text{population of the U.S.}}$$

To give each region a fair number of delegates, it makes sense to make the ratio of delegates equivalent to the ratio of populations. This can be written as an equation:

$$\frac{\text{population of the region}}{\text{population of the U.S.}} = \frac{\text{delegates from the region}}{\text{total number of delegates}}$$

A statement about equivalent ratios or fractions, such as the one above, is called a **proportion.**

To figure out how many delegates should be chosen from a given region, you need to solve the corresponding proportion. For example, the 1990 population of the South Atlantic region of the United States was about 45 million people, and the total population of the United States was about 250 million people. To find the number of conference delegates who should come from the South Atlantic region, you need to solve the proportion

$$\frac{45,000,000}{250,000,000} = \frac{\text{delegates from South Atlantic region}}{1000}$$

Using what you know about equivalent fractions, you could write

$$\frac{45,000,000}{250,000,000} = \frac{45}{250}$$
$$= \frac{180}{1000}$$

and conclude that the South Atlantic region should have 180 delegates.

Problem 6.3

The table on pages 71 and 72 gives data about the United States population. Use the table to help you answer these questions.

A. How many of the 1000 delegates should be chosen from each of the nine geographic regions?

B. How many of the 1000 delegates should be from metropolitan areas, and how many should be from rural areas?

C. How many of the delegates should be of Hispanic origin?

D. Four racial groups are named in the data: white; black; Native American–Eskimo–Aleut; and Asian–Pacific Islander. How many of the total 1000 delegates should represent each of these races? How many should represent the category "all other races" (which is not mentioned in the data)?

E. Use your answers to A–D to help you develop a plan for selecting the delegates. Describe your plan in a report that you could submit to the conference organizers.

■ Problem 6.3 Follow-Up

If you could add another criterion to help choose the delegates so that the representation would be fair, what criterion would you add and why?

U.S. 1990 Population by Region, Race, and Metro/Rural Location
(All Numbers in 1000s)

	Total	Metro areas	Rural areas	White	Black	Hispanic*	Native American, Eskimo, Aleut	Asian, Pacific Islander
United States	**248,710**	**192,726**	**55,984**	**199,686**	**29,986**	**22,354**	**1959**	**7274**
New England	**13,207**	**10,598**	**2609**	**12,033**	**628**	**568**	**33**	**232**
Maine	1228	441	787	1208	5	7	6	7
New Hampshire	1109	622	487	1087	7	11	2	9
Vermont	563	131	431	555	2	4	2	3
Massachusetts	6016	5438	578	5405	300	288	12	143
Rhode Island	1003	928	75	917	39	46	4	18
Connecticut	3287	3038	250	2859	274	213	7	51
Middle Atlantic	**37,602**	**34,193**	**3409**	**30,036**	**4986**	**3186**	**92**	**1104**
New York	17,990	16,386	1605	13,385	2859	2214	63	694
New Jersey	7730	7730	n/a	6130	1037	740	15	273
Pennsylvania	11,882	10,077	1805	10,520	1090	232	15	137
East North Central	**42,009**	**32,557**	**9452**	**35,764**	**4817**	**1438**	**150**	**573**
Ohio	10,847	8567	2280	9522	1155	140	20	91
Indiana	5544	3796	1748	5021	432	99	13	38
Illinois	11,431	9450	1981	8953	1694	904	22	285
Michigan	9295	7446	1850	7756	1292	202	56	105
Wisconsin	4892	3298	1593	4513	245	93	39	54
West North Central	**17,660**	**10,132**	**7528**	**16,254**	**899**	**289**	**188**	**195**
Minnesota	4375	2960	1415	4130	95	54	50	78
Iowa	2777	1223	1554	2683	48	33	7	25
Missouri	5117	3387	1730	4486	548	62	20	41
North Dakota	639	257	381	604	4	5	26	3
South Dakota	696	205	491	638	3	5	51	3
Nebraska	1578	766	812	1481	57	37	12	12
Kansas	2478	1333	1145	2232	143	94	22	32
South Atlantic	**43,567**	**32,461**	**11,106**	**33,391**	**8924**	**2133**	**172**	**631**
Delaware	666	442	224	535	112	16	2	9
Maryland	4781	4439	343	3394	1190	125	13	140
District of Columbia	607	607	n/a	180	400	33	1	11
Virginia	6187	4483	1704	4792	1163	160	15	159
West Virginia	1793	653	1140	1726	56	8	2	7
North Carolina	6629	3758	2871	5008	1456	77	80	52
South Carolina	3487	2113	1374	2407	1040	31	8	22
Georgia	6478	4212	2266	4600	1747	109	13	76
Florida	12,938	11,754	1184	10,749	1760	1574	36	154
East South Central	**15,176**	**8513**	**6663**	**12,049**	**2977**	**95**	**41**	**84**
Kentucky	3685	1714	1971	3392	263	22	6	18
Tennessee	4877	3300	1577	4048	778	33	10	32
Alabama	4041	2723	1317	2976	1021	25	17	22
Mississippi	2576	776	1798	1633	915	16	9	13

	Total	Metro areas	Rural areas	White	Black	Hispanic*	Native American, Eskimo, Aleut	Asian, Pacific Islander
West South Central	**26,703**	**19,614**	**7,089**	**20,142**	**3929**	**4539**	**350**	**407**
Arkansas	2351	943	1408	1945	374	20	13	13
Louisiana	4220	2935	1285	2839	1299	93	19	41
Oklahoma	3146	1870	1276	2584	234	86	252	34
Texas	16,987	13,867	3119	12,775	2022	4340	66	319
Mountain	**13,659**	**9179**	**4480**	**11,762**	**374**	**1992**	**481**	**217**
Montana	799	191	608	741	2	12	48	4
Idaho	1007	206	801	950	3	53	14	9
Wyoming	454	134	319	427	4	26	9	3
Colorado	3294	2686	608	2905	133	424	28	60
New Mexico	1515	733	782	1146	30	579	134	14
Arizona	3665	2896	769	2963	111	688	204	55
Utah	1723	1336	387	1616	12	85	24	33
Nevada	1202	996	206	1013	79	124	20	38
Pacific	**39,127**	**35,479**	**3648**	**28,255**	**2454**	**8114**	**453**	**3831**
Washington	4867	3976	891	4309	150	215	81	211
Oregon	2842	1947	895	2637	46	113	38	69
California	29,760	28,493	1267	20,524	2209	7688	242	2846
Alaska	550	226	324	415	22	18	86	20
Hawaii	1108	836	272	370	27	81	5	685

*Persons of Hispanic origin may be of any race.

Totals include other races, which are not shown separately. N/A means not applicable.

Source: *Statistical Abstract of the United States 1993.* Published by the Bureau of the Census, Washington, D.C., p. 254.

As you work on these ACE questions, use your calculator whenever you need it.

Applications

1. In a free-throw contest at the environmental studies conference, Clifford, a delegate from New England, made 10 out of 15 shots. Suppose Clifford's success rate stays the same for his next 100 shots. Write and solve proportions to answer these questions.

   a. How many shots will Clifford make out of his next 60 shots?

   b. How many shots will Clifford make out of his next 80 shots?

   c. How many shots will it take for Clifford to make 30 more free-throws?

   d. How many shots will it take for him to make 45 more free-throws?

2. The conference organizers ordered environmental buttons for the participants to wear. They paid $18 for 12 dozen buttons. Write and solve proportions to answer these questions.

   a. How much do 4 dozen buttons cost?

   b. How much do 50 dozen buttons cost?

   c. How many dozens of buttons can the organizers buy for $27?

   d. How many dozens of buttons can the organizers buy for $63?

3. Middletown decided to sponsor a two-day meeting for its own middle-school students to study local environmental problems. There are three middle schools in Middletown: Red Middle School with 618 students, White Middle School with 378 students, and Blue Middle School with 204 students. If 20 student delegates in all will attend the conference, how many should be selected from each school?

4. This table gives the total land area of each census region in the United States.

Census region	Area (square miles)
New England	62,811
Middle Atlantic	99,463
East North Central	266,221
West North Central	243,539
South Atlantic	178,615
East South Central	507,981
West South Central	426,234
Mountain	856,121
Pacific	895,353

a. Suppose the delegates for the environmental conference in Problem 6.3 were selected using the ratio of the area of the census region to the area of the United States. Use the data above to figure out how many delegates should attend from each region.

b. In part a, you determined the number of delegates from each region by comparing land areas. In part A of Problem 6.3, you determined the number of delegates from each region by comparing populations. For each region, discuss how these numbers compare.

c. Give one reason why each system of choosing delegates (using land areas or using populations) might be fair.

5. Swimming a quarter of a mile burns about the same number of calories as running a mile.

a. Gilda runs a 26-mile marathon. How far would her sister have to swim to burn the same number of calories Gilda burned during the marathon?

b. Jack swims 5 miles a day. How many miles would he have to run to burn the same number of calories he burns during his daily swim?

Connections

6. Which is the better buy: a 14-ounce box of Cruncho cereal for $1.98, or a 36-ounce box of Cruncho cereal for $2.59?

7. Which is the better average: 10 free-throws out of 15, or 8 free-throws out of 10?

8. Which is the better home-run rate: hitting 2 home runs in 6 times at bat, or hitting 5 home runs in 12 times at bat?

9. The population of the United States in 1994 was about 260,651,000. The land area of the United States is 3,536,338 square miles. If the people in the United States were spread uniformly throughout the states, how many people would there be per square mile? Compare your answer with the population density of your state.

10. The picture below is drawn on a centimeter grid.

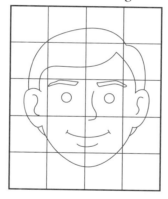

    a. On a grid made of larger squares than those shown here, draw a figure similar to this figure. What is the scale factor between the original figure and your drawing?

    b. Draw another figure similar to this one, but use a grid made of smaller squares than those shown here. What is the scale factor between the original and your drawing?

11. Anna is making a circular spinner to be used at the school carnival. She wants the spinner to be divided so that 30% of the area is blue, 20% is red, 15% is green, and 35% is yellow. Design a spinner that meets her specifications.

Extensions

12. Below is a table of data from a middle school class showing each student's household's water use for one week and the number of people in the household.

Our Water Use

Student (initials)	People in household	Water use (gallons)	Rate of water use (gallons/person)
RE	5	1901	
TW	4	1682	
HW	5	1493	
WE	4	1336	
GK	5	1332	
DJ	6	1309	
MJ	5	1231	
WD	5	1231	
MA	5	1204	
LR	5	1031	
FP	4	986	
HA	5	985	
TB	3	940	
CH	5	938	
ME	4	924	
JW	4	910	
PR	4	843	
NP	3	819	
BH	4	807	
EB	4	755	
PJ	4	726	
HJ	4	641	
HM	3	554	
JZ	2	493	

a. Calculate the rate of water use per person in each household.

b. Combine all the data to find the rate of water use overall.

c. Round your answers in part a to the nearest 10. Make a stem plot showing the rate of water use per person in each household. Start your stem plot like this:

```
4 | 2
3 | 8  0
2 |                    Key
1 |            4 | 2 means 420
```

d. The two *histograms* below and on the next page display the information about gallons of water used per person in each household. Compare the two histograms and explain how they differ.

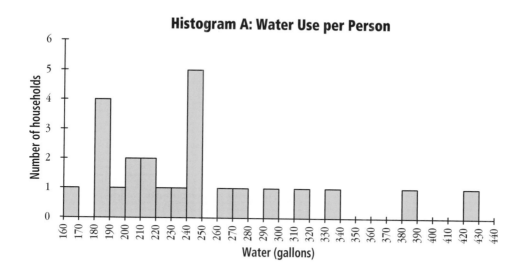

Histogram A: Water Use per Person

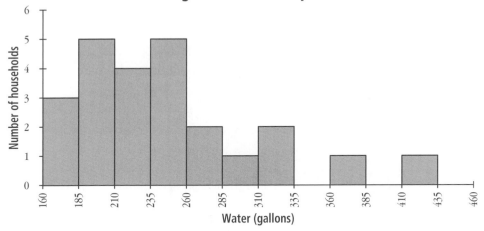

Histogram B: Water Use per Person

e. Does your stem plot from part c look like either histogram?

f. Suppose a new student joined the class and her household used 270 gallons of water per person. How would this student's data be indicated on Histogram A and Histogram B?

g. What is the typical number of gallons of water used per person in one week? Justify your answer, using Histograms A and B and your stem plot to help you explain.

h. Make Histogram C by grouping the data in intervals of 30 gallons. Now which graph—A, B, or C—would be the most useful to help you answer the question in part g? Why?

13. The people of the United States are represented in Congress in two ways: each state has representatives in the House of Representatives, and each state has senators in the Senate.

a. The number of representatives from each state in the House of Representatives varies from state to state. How is the number of representatives from each state determined?

b. How is the number of senators from each state determined?

c. Compare the two methods of determining representation in Congress. What are the advantages and disadvantages of these two forms of representation?

A meeting of the House of Representatives

14. The very small country of Trig has three states: Sine, Cosine, and Tangent, with populations of 59, 76, and 14, respectively. The Trig Congress has 35 members.

a. Using a method that you think is fair to all states, determine the number of representatives from each state. Explain your reasoning.

b. How would the number of representatives from each state change if there were 37 members of Congress?

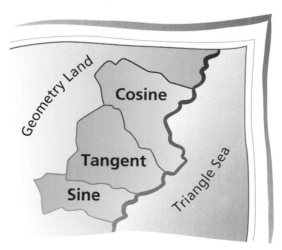

15. Ryan asked his family to mark on a chart whenever they washed a load of laundry. Here is his family's chart for one week:

	Sun.	Mon.	Tues.	Wed.	Thurs.	Fri.	Sat.
Large load					X		
Medium load		X		X	X		
Small load			X		X		

a. Using the following information about rate of water use, estimate the total amount of water Ryan's family used for washing laundry during the week. Explain your answer.

Large-capacity washing machines use approximately
- 9.5 gallons of water for a small load
- 13.4 gallons of water for a medium load
- 17.3 gallons of water for a large load

b. If this is a typical week, how much water does Ryan's family use in one year for washing laundry?

Mathematical Reflections

In this investigation, you used ratios, rates, percents, fractions, and proportions to solve problems. You thought about which methods of making comparisons would be helpful in solving particular types of problems. These questions will help you summarize what you have learned:

1 **a.** Describe a situation in which finding a rate is a good strategy for making comparisons. Tell why you think your situation calls for finding a rate.

b. Describe a situation in which finding a unit rate is a good strategy for making comparisons. Tell why you think your situation calls for finding a unit rate.

2 There are 17 girls and 13 boys in Mr. Baldridge's class. Write every comparison you can think of that can be formed from this information. Describe what each comparison shows.

3 Rodrigo drove his car 400 miles and used 12 gallons of gas. Write two rates that tell about this situation, and explain what each shows.

4 If you know that 4 cans of chili feed 6 people, how many cans of chili will feed 240 people? How many people can you feed with 45 cans of chili? Explain your answers.

5 How do you recognize a situation in which you need to use a ratio comparison rather than simply finding differences?

Think about your answers to these questions, discuss your ideas with other students and your teacher, and then write a summary of your findings in your journal.

Paper Pool

The project is a mathematical investigation of a new game called Paper Pool. For a pool table, use grid paper rectangles like the one shown at right. Each corner is a pocket where a ball could stop.

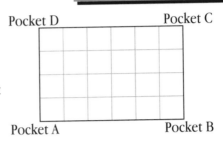

How To Play Paper Pool

- The ball always starts at corner A.
- To start the imaginary ball rolling, hit it with an imaginary cue stick.
- The ball always moves on a 45° diagonal across the grid.
- When the ball hits a side of the table it bounces off at a 45° angle and continues its travel.
- If the ball hits a corner pocket, it falls in and stops.

The dotted lines on the table at the right show the ball's path.

- The ball stopped at corner D.
- It got 5 hits (including the starting hit and the final hit).
- The dimensions of the table are 6 by 4 (always mention the horizontal length first).

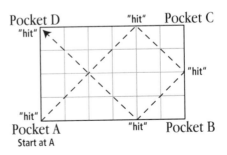

Part 1: Investigate Two Questions

Use Paper Pool Labsheets UP.A, UP.B, and UP.C to play the game. Try to find a rule that tells you (1) the corner where the ball will stop and (2) the number of hits it will make along the way. Keep track of the dimensions because they may give you clues to a pattern.

Part 2: Write a Report

When you find some patterns and reach some conclusions, write a report that includes:

1. A list of the rules you found and why you think they are correct.

2. Drawings of grid paper tables that show your rule.

3. Any tables, charts, or other tools that helped you find patterns.

4. Other patterns or ideas about Paper Pool.

Extension Question

Can you predict the length of the ball's path on any size Paper Pool table? Each time the ball crosses a square, the length is 1 diagonal unit. Find the length of the ball's path in diagonal units for any dimension.

Looking Back and Looking Ahead

Unit Reflections

The problems in this unit all required comparison of measured quantities. In solving those problems you learned when it seems best to use subtraction, division, percents, *rates*, *ratios*, and *proportions* to make those comparisons. You developed a variety of strategies for writing and solving proportions, including writing *equivalent ratios* to scale a pattern up or down.

Using Your Understanding of Proportional Reasoning— To test your understanding and skill with percents, rates, ratios, and proportions, consider the following problem situations.

1 *There are 300 students in East Middle School. To plan transportation services for the new West Middle School, the school system surveyed East students to find out how many ride a bus to school and how many walk.*

- In Mr. Archer's homeroom 20 students ride the bus and 15 students walk.
- In Ms. Baker's homeroom 14 students ride the bus and 9 students walk.
- In Ms. Carnick's homeroom 20 students ride the bus and the ratio of bus riders to walkers is 5 to 3.

a. In what ways could you compare the number of students in Mr. Archer's homeroom who are bus riders with the number who are walkers? Which seems the best comparison statement?

b. In what ways could you compare the numbers of bus riders and walkers in Ms. Baker's homeroom with those in the same categories in Mr. Archer's homeroom? Again, which seems the best way to make the comparison?

c. How many students in Ms. Carnick's homeroom walk to school?

d. Based on the information from these three homerooms, how many East Middle School students would you expect to walk to school? To ride a bus?

e. If the new West Middle School will have 450 students and a ratio of bus riders and walkers that is about the same as that in East Middle School, how many West students can be expected in each category?

2 *The Purr & Woof Kennel buys the food shown for the animals that are boarded. The amounts of food eaten by cats, small dogs, and large dogs are as follows:*

Cats: 1/4 pound per day

Small dogs: 1/3 pound per day

Large dogs: 1/2 pound per day

a. Which is cheaper per pound—cat food or dog food?

b. Which is the cheapest to feed—a cat, a small dog, or a large dog?

c. On an average day, the kennel has 20 cats, 30 small dogs, and 20 large dogs.

    i. Which bag of food will last longer—a bag of cat food or a bag of dog food?

    ii. How many bags of dog food and how many bags of cat food will be used in the month of January?

3 *On their way to school Jeff and Tat-Ming saw several stray cats. They decided to do a social studies project on the number of homeless cats. In their research they found that their own town of Centerville has about 100 stray cats, while the neighboring town of Mason has about 60 stray cats. Centerville covers an area of about 12 square miles, and Mason covers about 8 square miles.*

a. Which town has the greater population density of stray cats?

b. How many stray cats would have to move from one town to the other to make the population densities of stray cats in the two towns equal?

4 *Use proportional reasoning to answer the following questions from other* Connected Mathematics *units.*

a. A spinner used in the "Wheel of Destiny" was spun 250 times. The number of wins was 80, and the number of losses was 170. Based on this experience, how many wins would you expect in the next 10 spins?

b. Arnoldo and Bill rode their bikes to soccer practice. Arnoldo rode 7 miles in 25 minutes, and Bill rode 5 miles in 20 minutes. Who rode faster?

c. Maria reduced a 100 cm by 150 cm poster by 60%.

    i. What are the dimensions of the new poster?

    ii. How do the perimeter and the area of the new poster compare with the perimeter and the area of the original?

Explaining Your Reasoning—Answering comparison questions often requires knowledge of rates, ratios, percents, and proportional reasoning. As you answer the following questions about your reasoning strategies, use preceding problems and other examples from this unit to illustrate your ideas.

1. How do you decide when it makes sense to compare numbers using ratios, rates, or percents rather than by finding the difference of the two numbers?

2. If you are given information that the ratio of two quantities is 3 to 5, how can you express that relationship in other written forms?

3. The ratio of two quantities is 24 to 18.

    a. State five other equivalent ratios in the form "p to q."

    b. What is the equivalent ratio expressed with smallest possible whole numbers?

4. What strategies could you use to solve proportions such as $\frac{5}{8} = \frac{12}{?}$ and $\frac{5}{8} = \frac{?}{24}$?

5. How does proportional reasoning enter into the solution of problems like these?

    a. You want to prepare enough of your favorite recipe to serve a large crowd.

    b. You want to find the actual distance between two points in a large park from their locations on a map and the scale of the map.

    c. You want to find which package of raisins in a store is the most economical.

    d. You want to use a design drawn on a coordinate grid to make several larger and several smaller copies of that design.

Proportional reasoning is one of the most important ways to compare measured quantities. It gives a way of comparing numerical information by rates and percents. It is also used in geometry to enlarge and reduce figures while retaining their shapes. You will apply proportional reasoning in most of the future *Connected Mathematics* units like *Data Around Us*, *Filling and Wrapping*, *Moving Straight Ahead*, and *What Do You Expect?*

population density The population density is the average number of things (people, animals, and so on) per unit of area (or, less commonly, the average amount of space per person or animal). Population density indicates how crowded a region is and can be calculated as the ratio of population to area.

proportion An equation stating that two ratios are equal. For example:

$$\frac{\text{hours spent on homework}}{\text{hours spent in school}} = \frac{2}{7}$$

Note that this does not necessarily imply that "hours spent on homework" = 2 or that "hours spent in school" = 7. During a week, 10 hours may have been spent on homework while 35 hours were spent in school. The proportion is still true because $\frac{10}{35} = \frac{2}{7}$.

rate A comparison of the quantities of two different units or objects is called a rate. A rate can be thought of as a direct comparison of two sets (20 cookies for 5 children) or as an average amount (4 cookies per child). A rate such as 5.5 miles per hour can be written as $\frac{5.5 \text{ miles}}{1 \text{ hour}}$, or 5.5 miles : 1 hour.

ratio A ratio is a comparison of two quantities that tells the scale between them. Ratios may be expressed as quotients, fractions, decimals, percents, or given in the form a:b. Here are some examples of uses of ratios:

- The ratio of females to males on the swim team is 2 to 3, or $\frac{2 \text{ females}}{3 \text{ males}}$.
- The train travels at a speed of 80 miles per hour, or $\frac{80 \text{ miles}}{1 \text{ hour}}$.
- If a small figure is enlarged by a scale factor of 2, the new figure will have an area four times its original size. The ratio of the small figure's area to the large figure's area will be $\frac{1}{4}$. The ratio of the large figure's area to the small figure's area will be $\frac{4}{1}$ or 4.

- In the example above, the ratio of the length of a side of the small figure to the length of the corresponding side of the large figure is $\frac{1}{2}$. The ratio of the length of a side in the large figure to the length of the corresponding side in the small figure is $\frac{2}{1}$, or 2.

scale, scaling The scale is the number a ratio is multiplied by to find an equivalent ratio. Scaling a ratio produces any number of equivalent ratios, which all have the same units. For example, multiplying the rate of 4.5 gallons per hour by a scale of 2 yields the rate of 9 gallons per 2 hours. Scales are also used on maps to give the relationship between a measurement on the map to the actual physical measurement.

unit rate A unit rate compares an amount to a single unit. For example, 1.9 children per family, 32 mpg, and $\frac{3 \text{ flavors of ice cream}}{1 \text{ banana split}}$ are unit rates. Unit rates are often found by scaling other rates.

Index

Density, 55–58

Difference

ACE, 10–14

comparing with, 5–9

Equation, for rate, 43

Equivalent rate, 38

Equivalent ratio, 27

Estimation

using ratio, 4, 55–58

using samples, 52–54

Fraction

ACE, 10–14, 31–35

comparing with, 5–9

proportion and, 69–70

as a ratio, 26–30

Graph

histogram, 77–78

stacked bar, 48–49

Histogram, 77–78

Investigation

Choosing Strategies, 65–81

Comparing by Finding Percents, 16–25

Comparing by Finding Rates, 37–51

Comparing by Using Ratios, 26–36

Estimating Populations and Population Densities, 52–64

Making Comparisons, 5–15

Journal, 15, 25, 36, 51, 64, 81

Looking Back and Looking Ahead: Unit Reflections, 84–86

Mathematical Highlights, 4

Mathematical Reflections, 15, 25, 36, 51, 64, 81

Part-to-part ratio, 27

Part-to-whole ratio, 27

Percent

ACE, 10–14, 20–24, 73–80

comparing with, 4, 5–9, 16–19, 65–72

finding, 16–19

Population density, 55–56

Proportion, 4, 69–70

ACE, 73–80

Rate, 4, 37

ACE, 44–50, 73–80

comparing with, 4, 37–43, 65–72

equation, 43

equivalent, 38

forms, 37

graph of, 42

scaling, 38

unit, 40–43

Rate table, 41

Ratio, 26–27

ACE, 10–14, 31–35, 59–63, 73–80

comparing with, 5–9, 26–30, 65–72
equivalent, 27, 65–70
estimating with, 55–58
forms, 26–27
part-to-part, 27
part-to-whole, 27
proportion and, 69–70
scaling, 4, 38, 27–30
Rule of thumb, 67

Samples, estimating from, 52–54
Scale, 38

Scaling, 38, 148
ACE, 10–14, 31–35, 59–63
estimation and, 52–55
to make a comparison, 5–9, 65–66
rate, 38
using ratios, 27–30
Stacked bar graph, 48–49

Unit rate, 40–43

Connected  Mathematics®

Accentuate the Negative

Integers

Student Edition

Glenda Lappan
James T. Fey
William M. Fitzgerald
Susan N. Friel
Elizabeth Difanis Phillips

Prentice
Hall

Glenview, Illinois
Needham, Massachusetts
Upper Saddle River, New Jersey

Connected Mathematics® was developed at Michigan State University with the support of National Science Foundation Grant No. MDR 9150217.

This project was supported, in part, by the
National Science Foundation
Opinions expressed are those of the authors and not necessarily those of the Foundation

The Michigan State University authors and administration have agreed that all MSU royalties arising from this publication will be devoted to purposes supported by the Department of Mathematics and the MSU Mathematics Education Enrichment Fund.

Contents

Mathematical Highlights   4

Investigation 1: Extending the Number Line   5
     1.1 Playing MathMania   6
     1.2 Winning the Game   8
     1.3 Measuring Temperature   9
     Applications—Connections—Extensions   12
     Mathematical Reflections   17

Investigation 2: Adding Integers   18
     2.1 Adding on a Number Line   19
     2.2 Inventing a New Model   21
     Applications—Connections—Extensions   26
     Mathematical Reflections   33

Investigation 3: Subtracting Integers   34
     3.1 Subtracting on a Chip Board   35
     3.2 Subtracting on a Number Line   40
     3.3 Exploring Patterns   43
     3.4 "Undoing" with Addition and Subtraction   44
     Applications—Connections—Extensions   46
     Mathematical Reflections   52

Investigation 4: Multiplying and Dividing Integers   53
     4.1 Rising and Falling Temperatures   53
     4.2 Studying Multiplication Patterns   56
     4.3 Playing the Integer Product Game   57
     4.4 Dividing Integers   59
     Applications—Connections—Extensions   60
     Mathematical Reflections   66

Investigation 5: Coordinate Grids   67
     5.1 Extending the Coordinate Grid   67
     5.2 Breaking Even   71
     5.3 Using a Calculator to Explore Lines   72
     5.4 Exploring Window Settings   73
     5.5 Revisiting Jean's Problem   75
     Applications—Connections—Extensions   77
     Mathematical Reflections   82

Looking Back and Looking Ahead: Unit Reflections   83

Glossary   86

Index   88

Accentuate the Negative

If a negative number is subtracted from a negative number, then the difference is a negative number. *Decide whether this statement is always true, sometimes true, or always false. Give examples to illustrate your thinking.*

On Tuesday, a cold front passed through, causing the temperature to change ⁻2°F per hour from noon until 10:00 A.M. the next morning. The temperature at noon on Tuesday was 75°F. What was the temperature at 4:00 P.M. Tuesday?

In the first quarter of the big game, the Littleton Lions gain 5 yards on every play. They are now on their own 25-yard line. On what yard line were the Lions three plays ago?

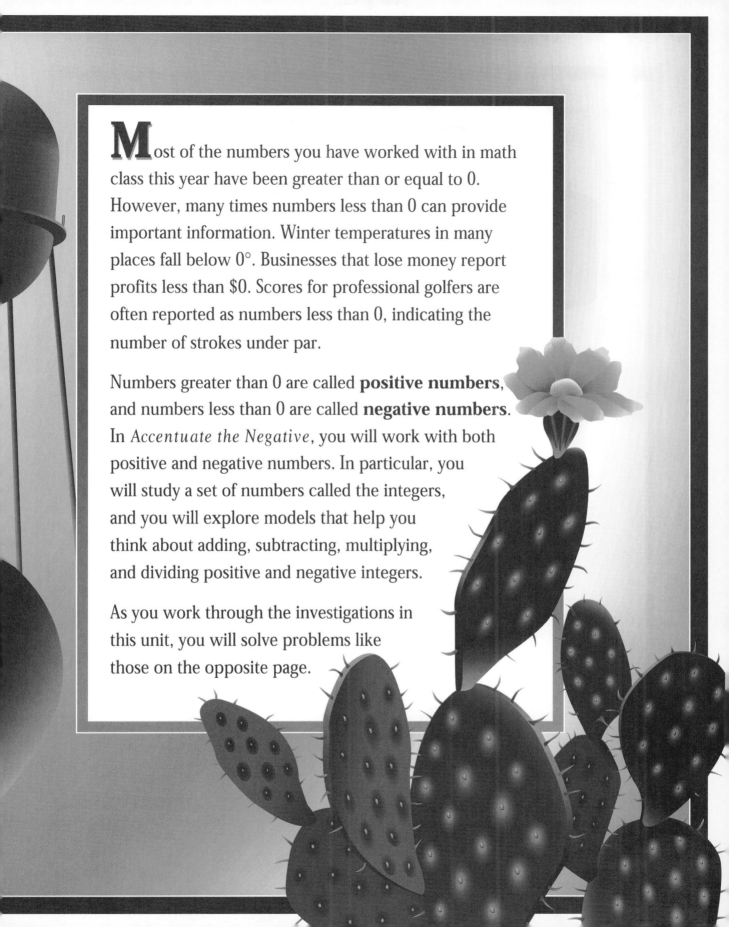

Most of the numbers you have worked with in math class this year have been greater than or equal to 0. However, many times numbers less than 0 can provide important information. Winter temperatures in many places fall below 0°. Businesses that lose money report profits less than $0. Scores for professional golfers are often reported as numbers less than 0, indicating the number of strokes under par.

Numbers greater than 0 are called **positive numbers**, and numbers less than 0 are called **negative numbers**. In *Accentuate the Negative*, you will work with both positive and negative numbers. In particular, you will study a set of numbers called the integers, and you will explore models that help you think about adding, subtracting, multiplying, and dividing positive and negative integers.

As you work through the investigations in this unit, you will solve problems like those on the opposite page.

Mathematical Highlights

In *Accentuate the Negative* you will develop understanding of and algorithms for operations with integers. The unit should help you to:

● Compare and order integers;

● Represent integers on a number line;

● Understand the relationship between an integer and its inverse and the absolute value of numbers;

● Develop ways to model sums, differences, and products of integers, including number line models and chip models;

● Develop strategies and algorithms for adding, subtracting, multiplying, and dividing integers;

● Model situations and solve problems using integers;

● Graph in four quadrants; and

● Graph linear equations using a graphing calculator to observe the effects of changing a coefficient to its inverse or adding a constant to $y = ax$.

As you work the problems in this unit, make it a habit to ask yourself questions about situations that involve integers: *What quantities in the problem can be represented with positive and negative numbers? How can you tell which of two integers is the greater? What models or diagrams might help decide which operation is useful in solving a problem? What is the approximate answer to the computation?*

Extending the Number Line

In math class this year, you have worked with numbers greater than or equal to 0. Numbers greater than 0 are called *positive numbers*. You can write a positive number with a plus sign, as in +150, with a raised plus sign, as in ⁺150, or without a plus sign, as in 150. For example, a temperature of 10 degrees above zero can be written +10°, ⁺10°, or 10°.

Often we need to talk about numbers less than 0. For example, on a very cold day, the temperature might drop below 0°. A company may spend more money than it earns and report a profit less than $0. Numbers less than 0 are called **negative numbers.** You can write a negative number with a minus sign, as in −150, or with a raised minus sign, as in ⁻150. For example, a temperature of 10 degrees below zero can be written −10° or ⁻10°.

Did you know?

You have probably seen golf scores reported with negative numbers. A golf hole is assigned a value called par. *Par* is the number of strokes a skilled golfer might take to reach the hole. For example, a skilled golfer should be able to complete a par-4 hole in four strokes. If a golfer completes a par-4 hole in six strokes, then her score for the hole could be reported as ⁺2, or "two over par." If a golfer completes a par-4 hole in two strokes, her score for the hole could be reported as ⁻2, or "two under par." Some scores for a hole are given special names. A score of ⁺1 is a *bogey,* a score of ⁻1 is a *birdie,* and a score of ⁻2 is an *eagle.* A player's score for a round of golf can be reported as the total number of strokes she is above or below par for the entire course.

1.1 Playing MathMania

Ms. Bernoski's third-period class is playing MathMania, a game similar to the *Jeopardy!*® game show. The game board is shown below. The top row gives six math categories. Below each category name are five cards. The front of each card shows a point value, and the back of each card has a question related to the category. Cards with higher point values have more difficult questions.

Operations with fractions	Similarity	Probability	Area and perimeter	Tiling the plane	Factors and multiples
50	50	50	50	50	50
100	100	100	100	100	100
150	150	150	150	150	150
200	200	200	200	200	200
250	250	250	250	250	250

The game is played by teams. One team starts the game by choosing a category and a point value. The teacher asks the question on the back of the corresponding card. The first team to answer the question correctly gets the point value on the card, and the card is removed from the board. If a team misses the question, the point value is subtracted from their score. The team that answers correctly gets to choose the next category and point value.

At one point in the game, the scores for Ms. Bernoski's class are as follows:

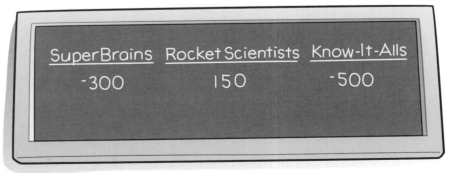

SuperBrains	Rocket Scientists	Know-It-Alls
-300	150	-500

There are several ways each team could have reached their score. For example, to earn their 150 points, the Rocket Scientists may have answered a 100-point question and a 50-point question correctly, or they may have answered a 200-point question correctly and then missed a 50-point question.

Problem 1.1

A. Which team has the highest score? Which team has the lowest score? Explain how you know your answers are correct.

B. How many points separate the highest score and the lowest score?

C. The discussion above describes two possible ways the Rocket Scientists may have reached their score. Describe another possible way. For each of the other two teams, give one possible way the team could have reached their score.

After achieving the scores shown above, the teams continue to play the game. Here is what happens:

- The SuperBrains answer a 200-point question correctly, a 150-point question incorrectly, a 50-point question correctly, and another 50-point question correctly.

- The Rocket Scientists answer a 50-point question incorrectly, a 200-point question incorrectly, a 100-point question correctly, and a 150-point question incorrectly.

- The Know-It-Alls answer a 100-point question incorrectly, a 200-point question correctly, a 150-point question correctly, and a 50-point question incorrectly.

D. What is each team's score now?

E. Which team is in last place? How far behind each of the other two teams is this team?

■ Problem 1.1 Follow-Up

In Ms. Bernoski's fifth-period class, the Smarties have ⁻300 points, and the Brain Surgeons have ⁻150 points. After answering the next four questions, the Smarties are tied with the Brain Surgeons. Give two possible ways the Smarties could have done this.

At the end of the MathMania game, the scoreboard looks like this:

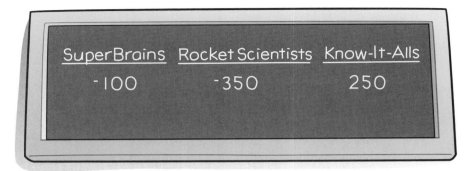

SuperBrains	Rocket Scientists	Know-It-Alls
⁻100	⁻350	250

The Know-It-Alls are the winners because they have the highest score. The Rocket Scientists are in last place because they have the lowest score. The SuperBrains are in second place because they have a lower score than the Know-It-Alls but did not lose as many points as the Rocket Scientists. You can write this as

⁻350 is less than ⁻100, which is less than 250.

Or, you can use symbols to write

$$^{-}350 < {}^{-}100 < 250$$

Problem 1.2

Mr. Hazan plays MathMania with his class. He divides the class into five teams. At the end of the game, the scores are as follows:

Team A: 200   Team B: ⁻250   Team C: ⁻400   Team D: 350   Team E: ⁻100

A. Order the teams by score, from first place through fifth place.

B. By how many points is the first-place team ahead of the second-place team?

C. By how many points is the first-place team ahead of the third-place team?

D. By how many points is the second-place team ahead of the fourth-place team?

E. By how many points is the third-place team ahead of the fifth-place team?

■ Problem 1.2 Follow-Up

1. Copy each pair of numbers below, inserting > or < to make a true statement.

   a. 53   35   **b.** ⁻50   0   **c.** ⁻30   15   **d.** ⁻70   ⁻90

2. Order the numbers below from least to greatest.

    25, 2, 5, ⁻3, 15, ⁻7, ⁻25, 12, 1, ⁻4, 0

1.3 Measuring Temperature

You have used the number line to help you think about whole numbers and fractions and decimals greater than 0. These are all examples of positive numbers. The number line can be extended to the left of 0 to include negative numbers.

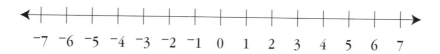

A thermometer can be thought of as a vertical number line with the positive numbers above 0 and the negative numbers below 0. The temperature in many places falls below 0° during the winter months. The thermometer below shows a temperature reading of ⁻4°F:

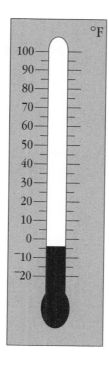

Problem 1.3

A. Arrange the following temperatures in order from lowest to highest:

−8°, 4°, 12°, −2°, 0°, −15°

B. The temperature reading on a thermometer is 5°F. Tell what the new reading will be if the temperature

    1. rises 10°   **2.** falls 2°   **3.** falls 10°   **4.** rises 7°

C. The temperature reading on a thermometer is −5°F. Tell what the new reading will be if the temperature

    1. falls 3°   **2.** rises 3°   **3.** falls 10°   **4.** rises 10°

D. In 1–6, give the temperature halfway between the two given temperatures.

    1. 0° and 10°   **2.** −5° and 15°   **3.** 5° and −15°

    4. 0° and −20°   **5.** −8° and 8°   **6.** −6° and −16°

E. In 1–4, tell which temperature reading is farther from −2°.

    1. −6° or 6°   **2.** −7° or 3°   **3.** 2° or −5°   **4.** −10° or 5°

F. Explain how you determined your answer for part 4 of question E.

■ Problem 1.3 Follow-Up

The numbers −3 and 3 are represented on the number line below.

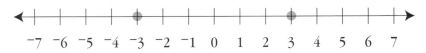

Notice that both numbers are 3 units from 0, but 3 is to the right of 0, and −3 is to the left of 0.

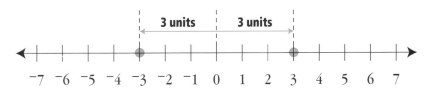

The numbers −3 and 3 are called opposites. **Opposites** are numbers that are the same distance from 0 but on different sides of 0. If you folded the number line at 0, each number would match up with its opposite.

If a team playing the MathMania game starts with 0 points and then answers a 50-point question correctly, they will have $^+50$ points. If they miss the question, they will have $^-50$ points. The numbers $^+50$ and $^-50$ are opposites: they are the same distance from 0 on the number line, but in different directions. The sign of a number tells its direction from 0.

1. Give the opposite of each number.

    a. $^-7$ **b.** 18   **c.** $^-42$ **d.** 0

2. Name two numbers on the number line that are the same distance from $^-2$. Are these numbers opposites?

At the end of Mr. Hazan's MathMania game, the scores of the five teams are as follows:

Team A: $^-50$ Team B: 150   Team C: $^-300$ Team D: 0   Team E: 100

3. Order the teams from first place through fifth place.

4. Draw a number line. Mark and label each team's score. Label the point for each team with both the team letter and the score.

5. On the number line, what is the distance between the scores of Team A and Team B?

6. On the number line, what is the distance between the scores of Team C and Team A?

7. On the number line, what is the distance between the scores of Team D and Team E?

8. Tell how each team, by answering one question, could change their score to 0. Give the point value of the question, and tell whether the team must answer the question correctly or incorrectly. If this is not possible for a particular team, explain why.

As you work on these ACE questions, use your calculator whenever you need it.

Applications

In 1–3, tell what the MathMania team's score would be after the events described. Assume the team starts with 0 points.

1. The Protons answer a 250-point question correctly, a 100-point question correctly, a 200-point question correctly, a 150-point question incorrectly, and a 200-point question incorrectly.

2. The Neutrons answer a 200-point question incorrectly, a 50-point question correctly, a 250-point question correctly, a 150-point question incorrectly, and a 50-point question incorrectly.

3. The Electrons answer a 50-point question incorrectly, a 200-point question incorrectly, a 100-point question correctly, a 200-point question correctly, and a 150-point question incorrectly.

In 4–7, a MathMania score is given. Describe a sequence of five events that would produce the score.

4. 300   5. ⁻200   6. ⁻250   7. 0

8. **a.** Draw a number line, and mark and label points for the following numbers:

   ⁻10, ⁻15, 18, ⁻5, 8, 0, 15, ⁻1

   Use your number line to help you with parts b–f.

   b. What is the opposite of 18?

   c. What is the opposite of ⁻10?

   d. Find a number greater than ⁻5.

   e. Find a number less than ⁻15.

   f. Which numbers are 6 units from ⁻2?

In 9–14, copy the pair of numbers, inserting > or < to make a true statement.

9. 3   0

10. ⁻23   25

11. 46   ⁻79

12. ⁻75   ⁻90

13. ⁻300   100

14. ⁻1000   ⁻999

In 15–17, give the distance between the two numbers on the number line.

15. 53 and 35

16. ⁻50 and ⁻90

17. ⁻30 and 15

In 18–20, use the thermometer shown to help you answer the questions. The thermometer shows temperatures on the Celsius temperature scale. On this scale, 0°C is the freezing point of water.

18. What is the temperature change from ⁻12°C to ⁺13°C?

19. What is the temperature change from ⁺32°C to ⁺12°C?

20. What is the temperature change from ⁺8°C to ⁻7°C?

21. Copy the table below. Study the first two rows, and then complete the table.

Temperature at 9:00 A.M.	Temperature at 9:00 P.M.	Change in temperature from 9:00 A.M. to 9:00 P.M.
−3°	5°	8°
5°	−3°	−8°
−10°	3°	
−2°	−10°	
−13°	−5°	
2°	−12°	
−10°		−7°
	6°	15°
−2°		−10°

22. The highest temperature ever recorded in the United States was 56.7°C (about 134°F) in Death Valley, California, on July 10, 1913. The lowest recorded U.S. temperature was −62.2°C (about −80°F) in Prospect Creek, Alaska, on January 23, 1971.

a. In Celsius degrees, what is the difference between the record high and record low temperatures?

b. In Fahrenheit degrees, what is the difference between the record high and record low temperatures?

Connections

23. In MathMania, winning 100 points and then losing 100 points have the effect of "undoing" each other. In other words, since they are opposites, 100 and −100 combine to give 0. Describe three real-life situations in which two events undo each other.

In 24 and 25, copy the number line below. Mark and label the number line to show the approximate locations of the numbers given.

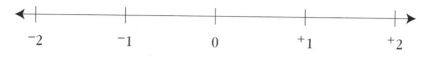

24. $-\frac{2}{3}$, $+\frac{2}{5}$, -1.5, $+1\frac{3}{4}$

25. -1.25, $-\frac{1}{3}$, $+1.5$, $-\frac{1}{6}$

26. The list below gives average temperatures (in °C) for Fairbanks, Alaska, for each month of the year from January through December.

-25, -20, -13, -2, $+9$, $+15$, $+17$, $+14$, $+7$, -4, -16, -23

    a. What is the median of these monthly temperatures?

    b. What is the range of these monthly temperatures (lowest to highest)?

Extensions

27. At the start of December, Shareef has a balance of $595.50 in his checking account. The following is a list of transactions he makes during the month.

Date	Transaction	Balance
December 1		$595.50
December 5	Writes a check for $19.95	
December 12	Writes a check for $280.88	
December 15	Deposits $257.00	
December 17	Writes a check for $58.12	
December 21	Withdraws $50	
December 24	Writes checks for $17.50, $41.37, and $65.15	
December 26	Deposits $100	
December 31	Withdraws $50	

    a. What is Shareef's balance at the end of December?

    b. On what day is his balance greatest? On what day is his balance least?

28. In the first quarter of the big game, the Littleton Lions gain 5 yards on every play. They are now on their own 25-yard line.

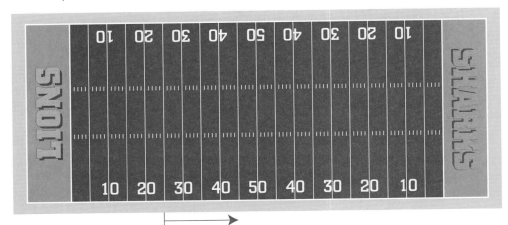

The Lions are here now and are moving from left to right—
that is, they move right when they gain yards.

a. On what yard line were the Lions three plays ago?

b. On what yard line will they be after the next two plays?

29. In the last quarter of the big game, the Littleton Lions (see question 28) lose 5 yards on every play. They are now on their own 25-yard line. They move left when they lose yards.

a. On what yard line were the Lions two plays ago?

b. On what yard line will they be after the next two plays?

Mathematical Reflections

In this investigation, you worked with positive and negative numbers. You analyzed sequences of events in the MathMania game, looked at temperature, and extended the number line to represent numbers less than 0. You also learned how to decide whether one number is less than or greater than another number. These questions will help you summarize what you have learned:

1 Describe what positive numbers, negative numbers, and 0 mean in terms of

   a. keeping score in MathMania.

   b. temperature readings.

2 Describe how you can compare the following types of numbers to decide which is greater. Use examples to illustrate your thinking.

   a. two positive numbers

   b. two negative numbers

   c. a positive number and a negative number

3 Describe how to locate numbers on a number line. Use examples to illustrate your thinking. Be sure to include positive and negative numbers as well as fractions and decimals in your examples.

Think about your answers to these questions, discuss your ideas with other students and your teacher, and then write a summary of your findings in your journal.

Adding Integers

The numbers 0, 1, 2, 3, 4, . . . are *whole numbers.* These numbers are labeled on the number line below.

If we extend this pattern to the left of 0, we get . . . , ⁻4, ⁻3, ⁻2, ⁻1, 0, 1, 2, 3, 4, ...

This larger set of numbers is called the **integers**. The numbers 1, 2, 3, 4, . . . are *positive integers,* and the numbers . . . , ⁻4, ⁻3, ⁻2, ⁻1 are *negative integers.* The number 0 is neither positive nor negative.

In many situations, you need to combine integers to find a sum. In this investigation, you will use two models that will help you think about how to add positive and negative integers.

Did you know?

The Hindus were the first to use negative numbers. The Hindu mathematician Brahmagupta used negative numbers as early as A.D. 628, and even stated the rules for adding, subtracting, multiplying, and dividing with negative numbers. Many European mathematicians of the sixteenth and seventeenth centuries did not accept the idea of negative numbers, referring to them as "absurd" and "fictitious." Mathematicians of that time who did accept negative numbers often had strange beliefs about them. For example, John Wallis believed that negative numbers were greater than infinity!

2.1 Adding on a Number Line

Monique and Ethan were thinking about how to show addition of integers on a number line. They decided to start by working with whole numbers. Monique came up with the following method for representing the **number sentence** 3 + 2 = 5:

> Start at 0, and move 3 units to the right. To show the addition of 2, move 2 more units to the right. You end up at 5, so 3 + 2 = 5.

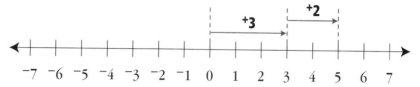

Ethan thought a similar method would work for adding negative integers. He came up with the following plan for finding ⁻3 + ⁻2:

> Start at 0, and move 3 units to the left (the negative direction) to represent the ⁻3. To show the addition of ⁻2, move 2 more units to the left. You end up at ⁻5, so ⁻3 + ⁻2 = ⁻5.

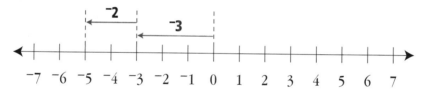

When Ethan wrote ⁻3 + ⁻2 = ⁻5, he used raised negative symbols to help him separate the sign of the integer from the operation sign for addition.

Then, Ethan wanted to try adding a negative integer and a positive integer on a number line. He followed these steps to find ⁻3 + ⁺2:

> Start at 0, and move 3 units to the left (the negative direction) to represent ⁻3. To show the addition of ⁺2, move two units to the right (the positive direction). You end up at ⁻1, so ⁻3 + ⁺2 = ⁻1.

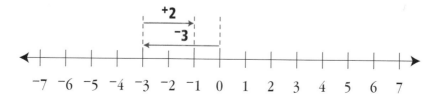

Monique asked Ethan what he thought they would get if they used a number line to find $^+2 + {}^-3$. What do you think?

Problem 2.1

A. Write the addition sentence illustrated by each figure.

1.
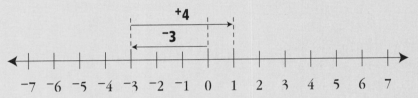

2.
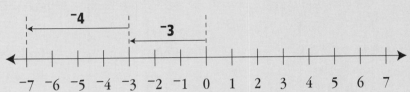

3.
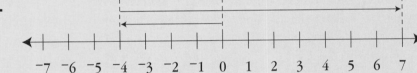

4.
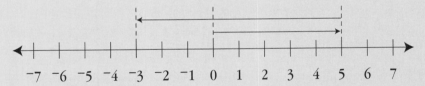

B. Illustrate each addition problem on a number line, and give the answer.

1. $^-5 + {}^+8$ 2. $^-4 + {}^-3$ 3. $^-2 + {}^-3 + {}^+10$

C. When you add two integers, does the order of the numbers make a difference? Illustrate your answer by showing each of these pairs of sums on a number line.

1. $^-5 + {}^+10$ and $^+10 + {}^-5$ 2. $^-4 + {}^-6$ and $^-6 + {}^-4$

3. $^+8 + {}^-8$ and $^-8 + {}^+8$ 4. $^+6 + {}^-7$ and $^-7 + {}^+6$

■ Problem 2.1 Follow-Up

1. You can think of the scoring in MathMania as follows: When a team answers a question correctly, a positive integer is added to their score. When a team answers a question incorrectly, a negative integer is added to their score. For each of the following situations, write an addition sentence that will give the team's score. Assume each team starts with 0 points.

a. The Brainiacs answer a 200-point question correctly and a 150-point question incorrectly.

b. The Aliens answer a 100-point question correctly and a 100-point question incorrectly.

c. The Prodigies answer a 50-point question incorrectly, a 100-point question incorrectly, and a 250-point question correctly.

2. Illustrate each addition problem on a number line and give the answer.

a. $^-2 + {}^+2$ **b.** $^+8 + {}^-8$ **c.** $^-1 + {}^+1$

3. What happens when you add opposites? Explain how you know your answer is correct.

2.2 Inventing a New Model

In the last problem, you used the number line to help you think about adding integers. In this problem, you will explore another way to model the addition of integers.

Amber's mother is an accountant. One day, Amber heard her mother talking to a client on the phone. During the conversation, her mother used the phrases "in the red" and "in the black."

That evening at dinner, Amber asked her mother what these terms meant. Her mother said:

"When people in business talk about income and expenses, they often use colors to describe the numbers they are dealing with. Black refers to profits (or income); red refers to losses (or expenses). A company that is making money, or has money, is 'in the black'; a company that is losing money, or owes money, is 'in the red.'"

Amber was studying integers in her math class and thought she could use these ideas of "in the black" and "in the red" to model the addition of positive and negative integers. Her model uses a chip board and black and red chips. Each black chip represents $^+1$, and each red chip represents $^-1$.

For example, this chip board shows a value of $^+5$:

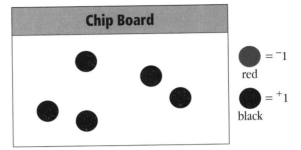

This chip board shows a value of $^-5$:

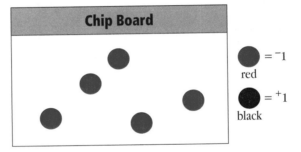

To represent $^-4 + ^-3$, Amber started with an empty chip board. She represented $^-4$ by putting four red chips on the board.

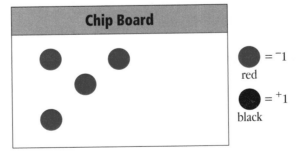

To represent the addition of ⁻3, she put three more red chips on the board.

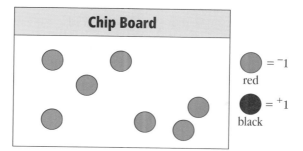

Since there were seven red chips on the board, Amber concluded that the sum of ⁻4 and ⁻3 is ⁻7. She wrote the number sentence ⁻4 + ⁻3 = ⁻7 to represent what she did on the chip board.

Amber showed her idea to her friend Adil. Adil liked Amber's model, but he wasn't sure how to use it to add a negative integer and a positive integer. Amber explained by modeling ⁻4 + ⁺5. She started by clearing the board. She then put four red chips on the board to represent ⁻4.

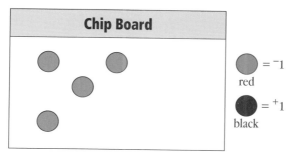

To add ⁺5, Amber added five black chips to the board.

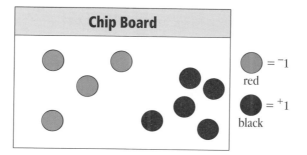

Amber said that next she had to simplify the board so that the answer would be easier to read. She reminded Adil that since $^+1$ and $^-1$ are opposites, they add to 0. So, a pair consisting of one black chip ($^+1$) and one red chip ($^-1$) represents 0. Amber formed as many black-red pairs as she could.

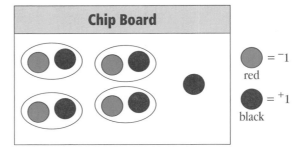

Since each black-red pair represents 0, all the black-red pairs can be removed from the board without changing the total value on the board. After Amber removed these "zeros" from the board, only one black chip remained, representing a sum of $^+1$.

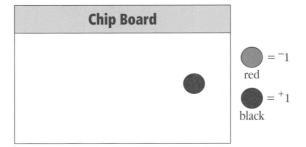

Adil wrote $^-4 + {}^+5 = {}^+1$ to represent the problem Amber had modeled.

Problem 2.2

A. Use a chip board and black and red chips to find each sum. Draw a series of chip boards to illustrate your work.

   1. $^-8 + {}^-7$ **2.** $^-8 + {}^+7$ **3.** $^+8 + {}^-7$ **4.** $^+8 + {}^+7$

B. Find two combinations of black and red chips that will simplify to represent the given integer. Draw a series of chip boards to prove that each combination works.

   1. $^-3$ **2.** $^+5$

C. Write each combination you found in part B as an addition sentence.

Problem 2.2 Follow-Up

1. What integer added to $^-8$ gives a sum of $^-4$?

2. Give two integers with a sum that is less than either of the two integers.

3. Give two integers with a sum that is greater than either of the two integers.

Conrado was adding the integers $^-5$ and $^+8$ on a chip board. First, he represented $^-5$ and $^+8$.

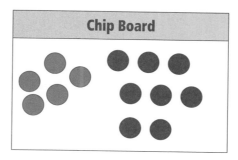

He then rearranged the chips to form a group of five red chips (representing $^-5$) and a group of five black chips (representing $^+5$). Since the two groups add to 0, he removed them from the board.

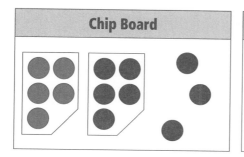 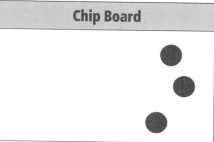

He wrote a series of equations to represent what he had done on the chip board.

$$
\begin{aligned}
^-5 + {}^+8 &= {}^-5 + {}^+5 + {}^+3 \\
&= (^-5 + {}^+5) + {}^+3 \\
&= 0 + {}^+3 \\
&= {}^+3
\end{aligned}
$$

Conrado thought that this method of regrouping to find numbers with a sum of 0 would be a good way to compute sums in his head.

4. Use Conrado's method to compute the following sums in your head.
   a. $^+9 + {}^-7$ **b.** $^-80 + {}^+50$ **c.** $^+35 + {}^-27$ **d.** $^-8 + {}^-5$

As you work on these ACE questions, use your calculator whenever you need it.

Applications

In 1–3, illustrate the addition problem on a number line, and give the answer.

1. $6 + {}^-6$

2. ${}^-4 + {}^-3 + {}^-8$

3. ${}^+8 + {}^-11 + {}^-9$

In 4–7, write the addition sentence illustrated by the figure.

4.

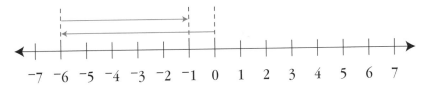

5.

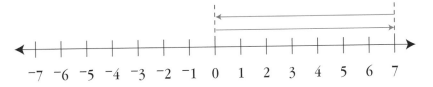

6.

7.

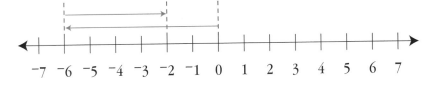

In 8 and 9, use the chip board below.

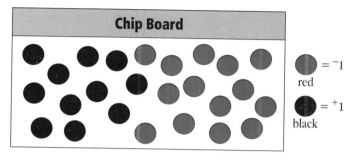

Chip Board

red $= {}^-1$

black $= {}^+1$

8. **a.** After you simplify the board by removing zeros (black-red pairs), what chips would remain? What integer do these chips represent?

b. Give another combination of black and red chips that would simplify to give the same result you got in part a.

9. Starting with the board as shown above, the following series of actions takes place. Write an addition sentence to describe each action. (A correct addition sentence will show the previous value represented by the board, the value of the chips that are added, and the new value represented by the board.)

a. Seven black chips are added.

b. Three more black chips are added.

c. Three red chips are added.

10. **a.** Find two combinations of black and red chips that simplify to represent $^-11$.

b. Draw a chip board to represent each combination from part a.

c. Write an addition sentence to represent each combination from part a.

11. **a.** Find two combinations of black and red chips that simplify to represent $^+7$.

b. Draw a chip board to represent each combination from part a.

c. Write an addition sentence to represent each combination from part a.

In 12 and 13, use the chip board shown below.

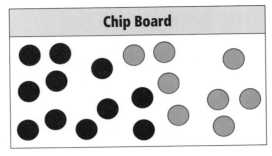

Chip Board

= ⁻1
red

= ⁺1
black

12. After you simplify the board by removing zeros (black-red pairs), what chips would remain? What integer do these chips represent?

13. Starting with the board as shown above, the following series of actions takes place. Write an addition sentence to describe each action. (A correct addition sentence will show the previous value represented by the board, the value of the chips that are added, and the new value represented by the board.)

    a. Four black chips are added.

    b. Ten red chips are added.

    c. Six black chips are added.

    d. Eight more black chips are added.

    e. Eight red chips are added.

In 14–17, illustrate the addition problem on a number line or a series of chip boards, and give the answer.

14. $^+12 + {}^-4$ **15.** $^-5 + {}^+5$

16. $^+5 + {}^-9$ **17.** $^-3 + {}^-6$

In 18–26, find the sum.

18. $^-105 + {}^+65$ **19.** $^+1050 + {}^-150$ **20.** $^-99 + {}^-47$

21. $^+37 + {}^-12 + {}^-15$ **22.** $0 + {}^-400$ **23.** $^-120 + {}^-225$

24. $^-90 + {}^-90$ **25.** $^-90 + 0$ **26.** $^+35 + {}^-35$

In 27 and 28, decide whether the statement is always true, sometimes true, or always false. Give examples to illustrate your answer.

27. The sum of two negative integers is a negative integer.

28. The sum of a negative integer and a positive integer is a positive integer.

Connections

29. In Duluth, Minnesota, the temperature at 6:00 A.M. on January 1 was ⁻30°F. During the next 8 hours, the temperature rose 38°. Then, during the next 12 hours, the temperature dropped 12°. Finally, in the next 4 hours, it rose 15°. What was the temperature at 6:00 A.M. on January 2?

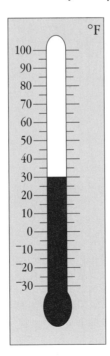

30. Most businesses try hard to make a profit. However, new businesses usually have start-up costs that put them "in the hole" at first. Suppose your family decides to open a bike shop. To get started, you'll have to make a down payment on the rent for your shop, buy bicycles and other supplies to stock the shop, and invest in business equipment and paper to keep track of income and expenses.

Below is a series of business transactions for the bike shop. For each transaction, write an addition sentence that shows how the new balance is calculated from the old balance.

a.   Down payment of two months' shop rent: $1800

b.   Payment for 20 new bicycles: $2150

c.   Down payment of rent on office equipment: $675

d.   Business insurance for 6 months: $2300

e.   Sale of three bicycles: $665

f.   Sale of two helmets and one baby seat: $95

g.   Advertising in the yellow pages: $250

h.   Sale of six bicycles: $1150

i.   Refund for unhappy customer: $225

j.   Sale of two bicycles, two helmets, and two air pumps: $750

k.   Refund from return of five bicycles to manufacturer: $530

Extensions

31. **a.** Which integers, when added to ⁻15, give a sum greater than 0?

  b. Which integers, when added to ⁻15, give a sum less than 0?

  c. Which integers, when added to ⁻15, give a sum of 0?

32. A chip board starts out with five black chips. Chips are added to the board. After the board is simplified by removing zeros (black-red pairs), nine black chips remain.

  a. What chips might have been added? Give two possibilities. (For example, adding five black chips and one red chip results in ten black chips and one red chip. After you remove zeros, nine black chips remain.)

  b. Write an addition sentence for each of the possibilities you gave in part a. (For the example given in part a, the addition sentence would be ⁺5 + ⁺5 + ⁻1 = ⁺9).

33. A chip board starts out empty. Chips are added to the board. After the board is simplified by removing zeros (black-red pairs), one black chip remains.

  a. What chips might have been added? Give two possibilities.

  b. Write an addition sentence for each of the possibilities you gave in part a.

34. A chip board starts out with one black chip. Chips are added to the board. After the board is simplified by removing zeros (black-red pairs), five red chips remain.

  a. What chips might have been added? Give two possibilities.

  b. Write an addition sentence for each of the possibilities you gave in part a.

35. A chip board starts out with five red chips. Chips are added to the board. After the board is simplified by removing zeros (black-red pairs), eight red chips remain.

  a. What chips might have been added? Give two possibilities.

  b. Write an addition sentence for each of the possibilities you gave in part a.

36. A chip board starts out empty. Chips are added to the board. After the board is simplified by removing zeros (black-red pairs), two red chips remain.

    a. What chips might have been added? Give two possibilities.

    b. Write an addition sentence for each of the possibilities you gave in part a.

37. A chip board starts out with two red chips. Chips are added to the board. After the board is simplified by removing zeros (black-red pairs), five black chips remain.

    a. What chips might have been added? Give two possibilities.

    b. Write an addition sentence for each of the possibilities you gave in part a.

Mathematical Reflections

In this investigation, you explored two ways to model the addition of integers—on a number line and with a chip board. These questions will help you summarize what you have learned:

1 When you add two integers, how can you decide whether their sum will be positive, negative, or zero?

2 Describe how to add any two integers.

3 Explain how you can find the opposite of a number. Use the following examples to illustrate your explanations.

a. 7   **b.** 0   **c.** ⁻12

Think about your answers to these questions, discuss your ideas with other students and your teacher, and then write a summary of your findings in your journal.

Subtracting Integers

In the last investigation, you used number lines and chip boards to help you learn about the addition of integers. These tools are also helpful for modeling subtraction of integers. In this investigation, you will start by using a chip board to explore subtraction. Next, you will use the relationship between addition and subtraction to subtract numbers on the number line. Finally, you will study patterns involving subtraction of integers and use these patterns to make predictions.

Think about this!

You can use positive and negative numbers to describe elevations. If you think of sea level as 0 feet, you can express elevations above sea level with positive numbers and elevations below sea level with negative numbers.

The highest point in the United States is Mount McKinley (also known as Denali), Alaska, with an elevation of 20,320 feet above sea level. You can express this elevation as $^{+}$20,320 feet. The lowest point in the United States is Death Valley, California, with an elevation of 282 feet below sea level. You can express this elevation as $^{-}$282 feet.

Death Valley, California

How many feet higher is the highest point in the United States than the lowest point?

Subtracting on a Chip Board

Amber's friends Jing-mei and Drew liked Amber's chip board model for adding integers. They decided to use a chip board to explore subtracting integers.

To model 9 − 5, Jing-mei started with an empty chip board and then put nine black chips on the board to represent ⁺9.

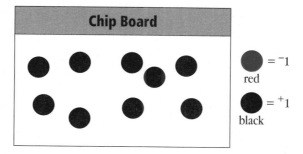

Jing-mei thinks about subtracting as "taking away." Therefore, to represent subtracting 5, she *removed* five black chips from the board.

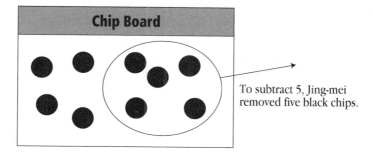

To subtract 5, Jing-mei removed five black chips.

After removing the five black chips, four black chips remained.

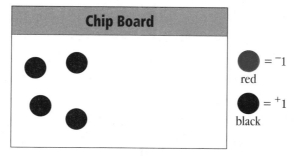

Jing-mei wrote the number sentence 9 − 5 = 4 to represent her work on the chip board.

Drew tried Jing-mei's method to find ⁻11 − ⁻5. He started with an empty board and then put on 11 red chips to represent ⁻11.

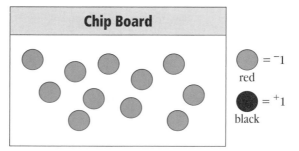

Like Jing-mei, Drew thought of subtracting as "taking away." To represent subtracting ⁻5, he removed five red chips from the board.

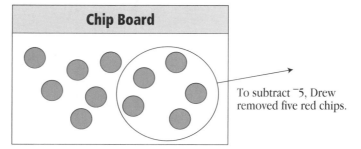

To subtract ⁻5, Drew removed five red chips.

Six red chips remained on the board.

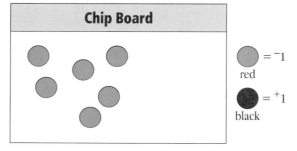

Drew wrote the number sentence ⁻11 − ⁻5 = ⁻6 to represent his work on the chip board.

Think about this!

Why does it makes sense that the difference between 9 and 5 is 4 (that is, 9 − 5 = 4) and the difference between ⁻11 and ⁻5 is ⁻6 (that is, ⁻11 − ⁻5 = ⁻6)?

Problem 3.1

A. Use a chip board and black and red chips to find each sum or difference.

   1. $^-8 - {}^-7$ **2.** $^+8 + {}^-7$

   3. $^-6 - {}^-2$ **4.** $^+6 + {}^-2$

B. In Problem 2.2, you simplified chip boards to find the number represented. For example, each chip board below represents $^+3$.

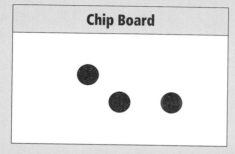
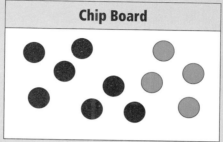

Find three ways to represent $^-8$ on a chip board.

C. Jing-mei wants to find $^-8 - {}^-10$ by using a chip board. She puts eight red chips on the board to represent $^-8$ but then gets stuck because she cannot remove ten red chips to represent subtracting $^-10$.

How can Jing-mei show $^-8$ on a chip board so that she can remove ten red chips? What is $^-8 - {}^-10$? Explain how you determined your answer.

D. Drew wants to find $^+5 - {}^+7$ by using a chip board. How can he show $^+5$ on a chip board so that he can remove seven black chips to represent subtracting $^+7$? What is $^+5 - {}^+7$? Explain how you determined your answer.

E. Use a chip board and black and red chips to find each difference. For each difference, tell how many chips of each color you used to represent the first integer so that you could take away chips to represent subtracting the second integer.

   1. $10 - 12$ **2.** $7 - {}^-2$

   3. $^-5 - 6$ **4.** $^-3 - {}^-7$

■ Problem 3.1 Follow-Up

To find $^+5 - {}^+7$, Drew started by showing $^+5$ as five black chips.

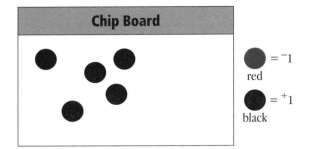

He could not represent subtracting $^+7$ because there were not seven black chips to remove from the board.

He recalled that adding or removing a black-red pair does not change the value of the board because such a pair represents 0 ($^+1$ and $^-1$ are opposites, so they combine to 0). He added a black-red pair to the board.

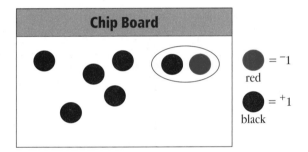

The board now had six black chips and one red chip. To subtract $^+7$, Drew needed to remove seven black chips, so he added one more black-red pair.

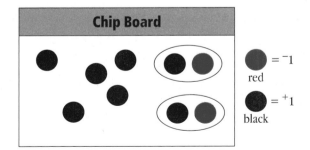

Then Drew was able to represent the subtraction. He removed seven black chips from the board. Two red chips remained.

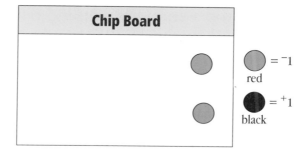

Drew wrote the number sentence $^+5 - {}^+7 = {}^-2$ to represent his work on the chip board.

1. Find three ways to show $^-5$ on the chip board. For each representation, write a subtraction problem that would be easy to solve if you started with that representation.

You have seen that there are lots of ways to represent a given integer on a chip board. For example, you could represent $^+5$ with eight black chips and three red chips or with six black chips and one red chip. However, there is only one way to represent a given integer with only one color. For example, the only way to represent $^+5$ with one color is by using five black chips, and the only way to represent $^-5$ with one color is by using five red chips.

The number of chips needed to represent an integer *with only one color* is the **absolute value** of the integer. Thus, the absolute value of 5 is 5, and the absolute value of $^-5$ is 5. We represent the absolute value of a number by writing a straight, vertical line segment on each side of the number. The equation $|{}^-5| = 5$ is read, "The absolute value of negative five equals five."

2. Find each absolute value.
   a. $|{}^-7|$ **b.** $|18|$ **c.** $|{}^-42|$ **d.** $|0|$

3. Tell which numbers have the given number as their absolute value.
   a. 12   **b.** 3   **c.** 31   **d.** 100

3.2 Subtracting on a Number Line

When you add integers by using a chip board, you add chips to the board. When you subtract integers, you remove chips from the board. Just as you can think of adding and removing chips as opposite "moves," you can think of adding and subtracting integers as opposite, or *inverse*, operations. This idea can help you understand how subtraction is modeled on a number line.

opposites attract

To model the *addition* sentence $^+7 + ^+5 = ^+12$ on a number line, you start at 0 and move 7 units to the right to represent $^+7$.

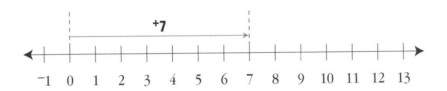

To *add* $^+5$, you move 5 more units to the *right*.

To model the *subtraction* sentence $^+7 - ^+5 = ^+2$, you can use the idea of opposite operations. Start at 0, and then move 7 units to the right to represent $^+7$.

To *subtract* $^+5$, move to the *left*—opposite the direction you moved to add $^+5$.

In other words, since subtraction is the opposite of addition, you subtract a number on the number line by moving in the opposite direction you would to add the number.

Let's use this idea to find $^-11 - {^-5}$. First, start at 0, and move 11 units to the left to represent $^-11$.

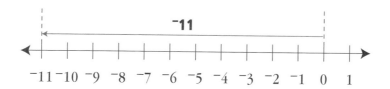

Next, you must subtract $^-5$. To add $^-5$, you would move 5 units to the left, so to subtract $^-5$, you must move 5 units to the right. You end at $^-6$.

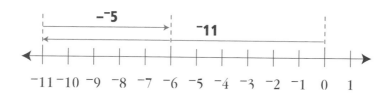

You can write the number sentence $^-11 - {^-5} = {^-6}$ to represent your work on the number line.

Notice in the example above that *subtracting* $^-5$ is the same as *adding* $^+5$.

Problem 3.2

A. Use a number line to find each difference. Use a chip board to check your work.

    1. $^{+}7 - {}^{+}9$ **2.** $^{-}7 - {}^{+}9$ **3.** $^{+}7 - {}^{-}9$ **4.** $^{-}7 - {}^{-}9$

B. Use a number line to find each sum or difference.

    1. $^{+}12 - {}^{+}3$ **2.** $^{+}12 + {}^{-}3$ **3.** $^{-}10 - {}^{-}7$ **4.** $^{-}10 + {}^{+}7$

C. Find the distance between each pair of numbers on a number line. In each case, tell how the distance is related to the difference between the two numbers.

    1. 1 and 5   **2.** $^{-}1$ and 5   **3.** $^{-}5$ and $^{-}9$ **4.** $^{-}3$ and 3

D. Write two number sentences illustrated by this figure.

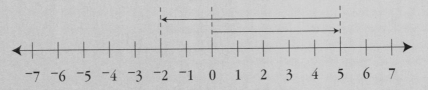

■ Problem 3.2 Follow-Up

1. When you add two positive integers, you get a positive sum. When you subtract two positive integers, do you always get a positive difference? Explain.

2. When you use the number line model, you can think of the *absolute value* of a number as its distance from 0. For example, 3 and $^{-}3$ are each 3 units from 0, so the absolute value of each number is 3.

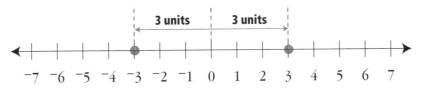

Use a number line to help you find a pair of numbers with the given absolute value.

    a. 10   **b.** 5   **c.** 1   **d.** 7

3.3 Exploring Patterns

Studying and describing patterns are an important part of mathematics. Study the patterns in the equations below, and then work on the problem.

$$15 - 5 = 10$$
$$15 - 4 = 11$$
$$15 - 3 = 12$$
$$15 - 2 = 13$$
$$15 - 1 = 14$$
$$15 - 0 = 15$$

Problem 3.3

A. Describe any patterns you observe in the way the differences change as the integers subtracted from 15 get smaller.

B. Use the patterns you observed to predict the answer to $15 - {}^-1$. Check your prediction by using a chip board or number line.

C. Predict the answer to $15 - {}^-4$. Explain your reasoning.

■ Problem 3.3 Follow-Up

1. Study the equations below.

$$^-10 - 5 = {}^-15$$
$$^-10 - 4 = {}^-14$$
$$^-10 - 3 = {}^-13$$
$$^-10 - 2 = {}^-12$$
$$^-10 - 1 = {}^-11$$
$$^-10 - 0 = {}^-10$$

a. Describe any patterns you observe in the way the differences change as the integers subtracted from $^-10$ get smaller.

b. Use the patterns you observed to predict the answer to $^-10 - {}^-1$. Check your answer by using a chip board or number line.

c. Predict the answer to $^-10 - {}^-6$. Explain your reasoning.

2. When you add two negative integers, you get a negative sum. When you subtract two negative integers, do you always get a negative difference? Explain.

3.4 "Undoing" with Addition and Subtraction

You can use the chip boards below to think about the addition sentence $11 + 3 = 14$. The chip board on the left shows 11 black chips. On the chip board on the right, 3 more black chips have been added for a total of 14 black chips.

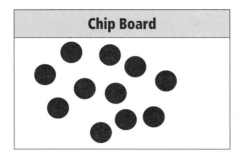

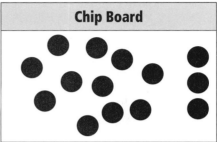

If you removed 3 black chips from the 14 black chips on the second board, you would end up with 11 chips, as you had on the starting board. In other words, removing chips from the board "undoes" placing chips on the board. You can represent this "undoing" with the subtraction sentence $11 = 14 - 3$. So, just as you can think of removing 3 chips from the board as "undoing" placing 3 chips on the board, you can think of the subtraction sentence $11 = 14 - 3$ as "undoing" the addition sentence $11 + 3 = 14$.

You can use this idea of undoing addition to find a subtraction sentence for a given addition sentence.

Problem 3.4

A. 1. Complete the addition sentence $^-17 + 13 = ?$.

   2. Write a subtraction sentence that "undoes" the addition sentence you found in part 1.

B. 1. Complete the addition sentence $^-4 + {}^-18 = ?$.

   2. Write a subtraction sentence that "undoes" the addition sentence you found in part 1.

C. Write a subtraction sentence that solves each problem.

   1. $? + {}^-18 = 6$ **2.** $? + {}^-13 = {}^-41$

   3. $? + 6.1 = {}^-3.2$ **4.** $? + {}^-\frac{1}{3} = \frac{1}{3}$

D. Write an addition sentence that solves each problem.

   1. $? - {}^-6 = {}^-6$ **2.** $? - {}^-2 = 3$

   3. $? - 5.3 = {}^-7.1$ **4.** $? - {}^-\frac{1}{4} = {}^-\frac{3}{4}$

■ Problem 3.4 Follow–Up

1. In the introduction to this problem, we wrote the number sentence $11 = 14 - 3$ from the sentence $11 + 3 = 14$. We could also write $3 + 11 = 14$. Can you write a different subtraction sentence to go with this addition sentence?

2. a. Complete the addition sentence $3.8 + {}^-2.6 = ?$.
   b. Write all the subtraction sentences you can that are related to the addition sentence you found in part a.

3. a. Complete the subtraction sentence $^-11 - 6 = ?$.
   b. Write all the addition sentences you can that are related to the subtraction sentence you found in part a.

4. When you add positive and negative integers, sometimes you get a positive sum and sometimes you get a negative sum. Is the same true when you subtract positive and negative integers? Explain.

As you work on these ACE questions, use your calculator whenever you need it.

Applications

1. When the finance committee for the Westover School Dance met on October 22, they had a balance of $50.25 in their checking account. Since then, the following transactions have taken place. Find the balance in the checking account after each transaction.

a. The committee deposited $44 they received from ticket sales.

b. Two students asked for refunds for their tickets. These tickets were worth a total of $8. The committee treasurer wrote these students checks for their refunds.

c. The finance committee got a $25 refund from the bakery because the refreshments committee decided to bake their own cookies and cakes. They deposited the refund into the checking account.

d. The committee gave the school principal $50 to pay the custodian who would open, clean, and close the school on the night of the party.

e. The DJ called to say she couldn't work at the party because her sound system was broken. She returned the committee's $50 deposit, which they deposited into the checking account.

In 2–10, find the sum or difference. Be prepared to explain how you got your answer.

2. $^+12 + {}^+4$ **3.** $^+5 - {}^+9$ **4.** $^+5 + {}^-9$

5. $^-3 - {}^+6$ **6.** $^-3 + {}^-6$ **7.** $^+7 - {}^-5$

8. $^+7 - {}^+5$ **9.** $^-7 - {}^-5$ **10.** $^+3.8 - {}^-4.2$

11. Write an addition sentence to describe this chip board.

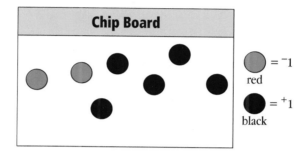

In 12–14, draw chip boards to help you find the difference.

12. $3 - 5$ **13.** $5 - 3$ **14.** $3 - {}^-2$

In 15 and 16, write an addition sentence and a subtraction sentence to represent what is shown on the number line.

15.

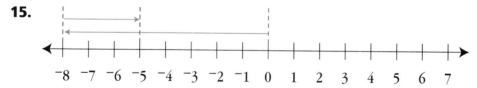

16.

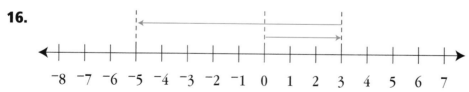

In 17–20, find the distance between the two numbers on the number line.

17. 9 and 4   **18.** $^-9$ and 4   **19.** $^-9$ and $^-4$ **20.** 0 and $^-7$

In 21 and 22, refer to the chip board below.

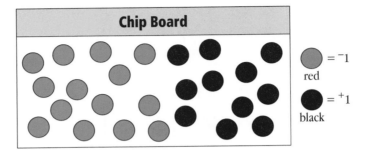

21. After you simplify the board by removing zeros (black-red pairs), what chips would remain? What integer do these chips represent?

22. Starting with the board as shown above, the following series of actions takes place. Write a number sentence to describe each action.

a. Nine black chips are added.

b. Seven black chips are removed.

c. Four red chips are removed.

d. Three black chips are removed.

In 23 and 24, refer to the chip board below. Each black chip represents $1, and each red chip represents ⁻$1.

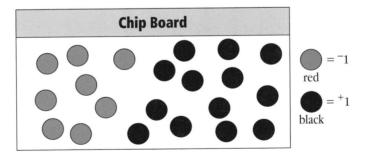

23. What "balance" is shown on this board?

24. Starting with the board as shown on the previous page, the following series of "transactions" takes place. Find the new balance after each transaction.

   a. Four black chips are added.

   b. Ten red chips are added.

   c. Six black chips are added.

   d. Eight black chips are removed.

   e. Five red chips are removed.

In 25 and 26, decide whether the statement is always true, sometimes true, or always false. Give examples to illustrate your thinking.

25. If a negative integer is subtracted from a positive integer, the difference is a negative integer.

26. If a negative integer is subtracted from a negative integer, the difference is a negative integer.

In 27–32, find the sum or difference.

27. $^-756 + 398$

28. $^-756 + ^-398$

29. $3138 + ^-2149$

30. $3138 - ^-2149$

31. $3138 - 5149$

32. $^-3138 - 5149$

33. **a.** Name all integers that have an absolute value of 12.

   b. Name all integers that are 12 units from 0 on the number line.

   c. Name all integers that are 12 units from $^-8$ on the number line.

   d. Write two subtraction problems that relate to your answer in part c.

Connections

34. Records at Jefferson Hospital showed the following information about the number of patients received and discharged:

Day 1: received 12 patients and discharged 9 patients
Day 2: received 14 patients and discharged 21 patients
Day 3: received 5 patients and discharged 14 patients
Day 4: received 11 patients and discharged 10 patients

How did the number of patients in the hospital at the end of the four-day period compare with the number of patients at the start of the four-day period?

35. Write three addition problems that have ⁻7 as a sum.

36. Write three addition problems that have 12 as a sum.

37. Write three subtraction problems that have ⁻7 as a difference.

38. Write three subtraction problems that have 12 as a difference.

Extensions

39. Juan said that he had discovered a new method for subtracting integers. He gave this example to illustrate his method:

$$^+7 - {}^+9 = {}^+7 - ({}^+7 + {}^+2) = ({}^+7 - {}^+7) - {}^+2 = 0 - {}^+2 = {}^-2$$

    a. Is Juan's method correct? Draw chip boards to explain your answer.

    b. Explain Juan's method in words.

40. On many scientific calculators, you use the ⌞+/−⌟ or ⌞(−)⌟ key to enter a negative number. This means that evaluating problems with lots of negative numbers like the ones below requires many keystrokes. For each problem below, find an equivalent problem that you could enter into a calculator to avoid using the ⌞+/−⌟ or ⌞(−)⌟ key as much as possible.

    a. $^-12 - {}^-7 - {}^-9 - {}^-10 - {}^-4$

    b. $^-12 - 7 - {}^-9 + 10 - {}^-4 + 13 + {}^-20$

Mathematical Reflections

In this investigation, you explored situations that involve subtraction of integers. You explored subtraction by using chip boards and number lines and by looking at patterns. These questions will help you summarize what you have learned:

1. Write a strategy for finding the difference of two integers. Be sure to consider all possible combinations of positive integers, negative integers, and 0. Verify your strategy by finding the following differences.

   a. $5 - 9$ **b.** $^-5 - {}^+3$ **c.** $^-5 - {}^-3$ **d.** $5 - {}^-9$

2. Without actually calculating the sum, how can you decide if the sum of two integers is positive? Negative? Zero?

3. Without actually calculating the difference, how can you decide if the difference of two integers is positive? Negative? Zero?

4. Describe how addition and subtraction of integers are related.

5. Describe how to find the absolute value of any number.

   Think about your answers to these questions, discuss your ideas with other students and your teacher, and then write a summary of your findings in your journal.

Multiplying and Dividing Integers

In the previous investigations, you looked at various ways to think about and model addition and subtraction of integers. In this investigation, you will explore ways to think about multiplying and dividing integers.

4.1 Rising and Falling Temperatures

In Investigation 1, you used a thermometer to explore positive and negative numbers. In this problem, you will use a thermometer to help you think about multiplying integers.

In this investigation, we will use a positive symbol to represent a rise in temperature and a negative symbol to represent a drop in temperature. That means, for example, if the temperature rises 3°, we will say that it changes by ⁺3°, and if the temperature drops 3°, we will say that it changes by ⁻3°.

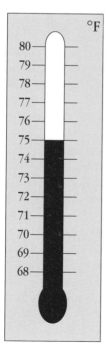
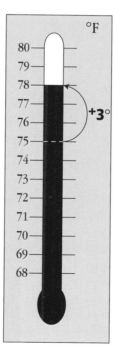
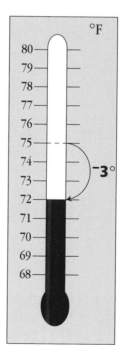

Problem 4.1

A. 1. Suppose the temperature changed by an average of $^+3°$ per hour for a 10-hour period. Copy and complete the table below, and use it to find the total temperature change for the first 5 hours.

Number of hours	1	2	3	4	5
Total temperature change	$^+3°$	$^+6°$			

2. Write a multiplication sentence that represents the total change in temperature for the first 5 hours. Write a multiplication sentence that represents the total change in temperature for the entire 10-hour period.

B. 1. Suppose the temperature changed by an average of $^-3°$ per hour for a 10-hour period. Copy and complete the table below, and use it to find the total temperature change for the first 5 hours.

Number of hours	1	2	3	4	5
Total temperature change	$^-3°$	$^-6°$			

2. Write a multiplication sentence that represents the total change in temperature for the first 5 hours. Write a multiplication sentence that represents the total change in temperature for the entire 10-hour period.

C. 1. Write the addition sentence illustrated by each diagram below.

2. Write the multiplication sentence illustrated by each diagram below.

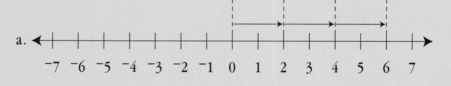

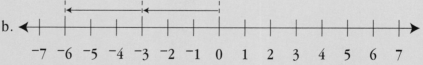

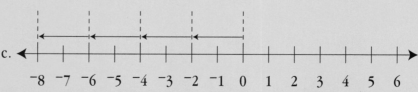

D. Make up a situation about temperatures that can be expressed as $4 \times {}^-10$.

E. Find each product.

1. $5 \times {}^-4$ **2.** $20 \times {}^-4$ **3.** $^-4 \times 20$ **4.** $^-5 \times 4$

1. Suppose the temperature changed by an average of $^+2°$ per hour from its low of $^-4°F$ at 3:00 A.M. What was the temperature at 1:00 P.M.?

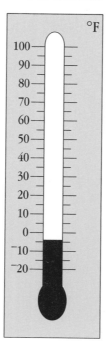

2. Suppose the temperature changed by an average of $^-1.5°$ per hour from its high of $^+25°F$ at noon. What was the temperature at 10:00 P.M.?

3. When you add a positive integer and a negative integer, you sometimes get a positive result and sometimes get a negative result. Is the same true when you multiply a positive integer and a negative integer? Explain.

Did you know?

The temperature at the center of the Sun is estimated to be about 15,000,000°C. The temperature at the center of a thermonuclear fusion bomb is about 400,000,000°C! Temperature does not appear to have an upper limit. However, there does seem to be a lower limit. Scientists believe that $^-273.15°C$, a temperature known as *absolute zero*, is the lowest temperature attainable. At this temperature the molecules and atoms of a substance have the least possible energy.

4.2 Studying Multiplication Patterns

In Investigation 3, you studied patterns to help you understand subtraction of integers. Studying patterns can also help you think about multiplication of integers. Study the equations below, and then work on the problem.

$$5 \times 5 = 25$$
$$5 \times 4 = 20$$
$$5 \times 3 = 15$$
$$5 \times 2 = 10$$
$$5 \times 1 = 5$$
$$5 \times 0 = 0$$

Problem 4.2

A. Describe any patterns you observe in the way the products change as the integers multiplied by 5 get smaller.

B. 1. Use the patterns you observed to predict $5 \times {}^-1$. Explain your reasoning.

   2. Write the next four equations in the pattern.

C. Complete the equations below, and use them to help you answer parts D and E.

$$5 \times {}^-4 = ?$$
$$4 \times {}^-4 = ?$$
$$3 \times {}^-4 = ?$$
$$2 \times {}^-4 = ?$$
$$1 \times {}^-4 = ?$$
$$0 \times {}^-4 = ?$$

D. Describe any patterns you observe in the way the products change as the integers multiplied by $^-4$ get smaller.

E. 1. Use the patterns you observed to predict $^-1 \times {}^-4$. Explain your reasoning.

   2. Write the next four equations in the pattern.

F. Find the following products.

   1. $^-3 \times 7$ **2.** $5 \times {}^-8$ **3.** $^-11 \times {}^-12$ **4.** $^-3.6 \times 2.7$

1. a. Find ⁻6 × 7 and 7 × ⁻6.

   b. When you multiply integers, does the order of the numbers matter?

2. a. Find ⁻6 + 7 and 7 + ⁻6.

   b. When you add integers, does the order of the numbers matter?

3. a. Find ⁻6 – 7 and 7 – ⁻6.

   b. When you subtract integers, does the order of the numbers matter?

4. When you add two negative integers, you get a negative result. Is the same true when you multiply two negative integers? Explain.

4.3 Playing the Integer Product Game

In this problem, you will practice multiplying integers by playing the Integer Product Game. The Integer Product Game board consists of a list of factors and a grid of products. Two players compete to get four squares in a row—up and down, across, or diagonally. To play the game, you will need Labsheet 4.3, two paper clips, and colored markers or game chips. The rules for the game and the game board are given on the next page.

> **Problem 4.3**
>
> Play the game with a partner. Look for interesting patterns and ideas that might help you devise a winning strategy. Make notes of your observations.

■ **Problem 4.3 Follow-Up**

1. Give every combination of two factors from the factor list that will give each of the following products.

   a. 5   **b.** ⁻12   **c.** 12   **d.** ⁻25

2. Your opponent starts the game by putting a paper clip on ⁻4. What products are possible on your turn?

3. At the end of your opponent's turn, the paper clips are on ⁻5 and ⁻2. What move would you make to get a product of ⁻15?

4. At the end of your opponent's turn, the paper clips are on ⁻3 and ⁻2. What move would you make to get a product of ⁻6?

5. Why doesn't ⁻35 appear on the board?

Integer Product Game Rules

1. Player A puts a paper clip on a number in the factor list. Player A does not cover a square on the product grid because only one factor has been marked; it takes two factors to make a product.

2. Player B puts the other paper clip on any number in the factor list (including the same number marked by Player A) and then shades or covers the product of the two factors on the product grid.

3. Player A moves *either one* of the paper clips to another number and then shades or covers the new product using a different color from Player B.

4. Each player, in turn, moves a paper clip and marks a product. If a product is already marked, the player does not get a mark for that turn. The winner is the first player to mark four squares in a row—up and down, across, or diagonally.

The Integer Product Game

1	⁻1	2	⁻2	3	⁻3
4	⁻4	5	⁻5	6	⁻6
8	⁻8	9	⁻9	10	⁻10
12	⁻12	15	⁻15	16	⁻16
18	⁻18	20	⁻20	24	⁻24
25	⁻25	30	⁻30	36	⁻36

Factors:
⁻6 ⁻5 ⁻4 ⁻3 ⁻2 ⁻1 1 2 3 4 5 6

4.4 Dividing Integers

In Investigation 3, you saw that subtraction is the opposite, or inverse, of addition. You observed that for any addition sentence, you can write a subtraction sentence that undoes the addition. Similarly, division is the opposite, or inverse, of multiplication, and for any multiplication sentence, you can write a division sentence that undoes the multiplication.

For example, given the multiplication sentence $5 \times 6 = 30$, you can write two division sentences:

$$5 = 30 \div 6 \text{ and } 6 = 30 \div 5$$

Problem 4.4

A. 1. Complete the multiplication sentence $^-5 \times 6 = ?$.
2. Write two division sentences that are equivalent to the multiplication sentence you found in part 1.

B. 1. Complete the multiplication sentence $^-8 \times {}^-4 = ?$.
2. Write two division sentences that are equivalent to the multiplication sentence you found in part 1.

C. Write a division sentence that solves each problem.

1. $? \times 12 = {}^-132$ **2.** $^-8 \times ? = {}^-56$
3. $? \times {}^-4 = 132$ **4.** $5.2 \times ? = {}^-8.84$

D. Write a division or a multiplication sentence that solves each problem.

1. $? \div {}^-3 = {}^-8$ **2.** $91 \div ? = {}^-7$
3. $? \div 11 = {}^-17$ **4.** $^-19.95 \div ? = 9.5$

■ Problem 4.4 Follow-Up

1. Find each quotient.
a. $^-121 \div 11$ **b.** $121 \div {}^-11$ **c.** $^-96 \div {}^-4$ **d.** $96 \div 4$

2. a. Find $18 \div 3$.
b. How does your answer from part a help you find $^-18 \div 3$, $18 \div {}^-3$, and $^-18 \div {}^-3$?

As you work on these ACE questions, use your calculator whenever you need it.

Applications

1. On Tuesday, a cold front passed through, causing the temperature to change ⁻2°F per hour from noon until 10:00 A.M. the next morning. The temperature at noon on Tuesday was 75°F.

  a. What was the temperature at 4:00 P.M. Tuesday?

  b. What was the temperature at 9:00 A.M. Wednesday?

2. a. Write the addition sentence illustrated by the number line below.

  b. Write the multiplication sentence illustrated by the number line below.

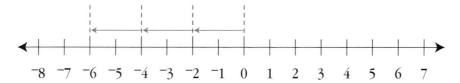

3. a. Write the addition sentence illustrated by the number line below.

  b. Write the multiplication sentence illustrated by the number line below.

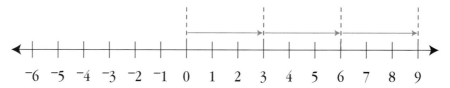

In 4–7, list all the integer factor pairs for the number.

4. 11   **5.** ⁻21   **6.** 12   **7.** ⁻12

8. Iseku and Kylie are making a version of the Integer Product Game in which players need three products in a row to win. What factors do they need for their game?

Iseku and Kylie's Product Game

4	⁻4	6	⁻6
9	⁻9	10	⁻10
15	⁻15	25	⁻25

In 9–16, find the sum, difference, product, or quotient.

9. 52×75 **10.** $52 \times {}^{-}75$ **11.** $2262 \div 58$ **12.** $10{,}680 \div {}^{-}120$

13. $137 + 899$ **14.** $5679 - 7890$ **15.** ${}^{-}4329 - {}^{-}1234$ **16.** ${}^{-}9908 \div {}^{-}89$

Connections

In 17–21, write a number sentence to represent the situation described. Then tell whether more than one number sentence is possible, and explain your reasoning.

17. The temperature at noon was ⁻13°C. For the next 6 hours, the temperature changed by an average of ⁺1.8° per hour. What was the temperature at 6:00 P.M.?

18. The temperature at noon was ⁻13°C. From 6:00 A.M. until noon, the temperature had changed by an average of ⁺5° per hour. What had the temperature been at 6:00 A.M.?

19. In a game of MathMania, the Extraterrestrials had a score of ⁻300, and then they answered four 50-point questions incorrectly. What was their score after missing the four questions?

20. After answering three 100-point questions correctly, the Supermutants had 200 points. What was their score before answering the three questions?

21. The Bigtown Bears were on their own 25-yard line. For the next three plays, they lost an average of 4 yards per play. Where did the Bears end up after the three plays?

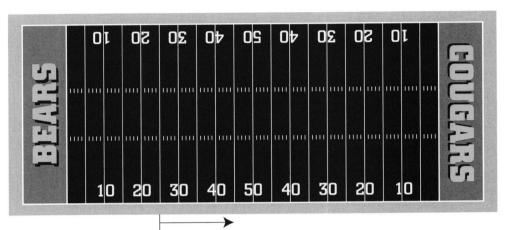

The Bears are here now and are moving from left to right—
that is, they move right when they gain yards.

In 22–25, complete the number sentence, and then write an equivalent sentence using the inverse operation.

22. $^-34 \times ^+15 = ?$

23. $^-12 \times ^-23 = ?$

24. $^+532 \div ^-7 = ?$

25. $^-777 \div ^-37 = ?$

26. **a.** Suppose the temperature changes by an average of $^-7°$ per hour. Write an equation you can use to determine the temperature change, *C*, after *H* hours.

b. Use your equation to find the temperature change after 3 hours.

c. How many hours will it take for the temperature to change by $^-42°$?

27. The list below gives average temperatures (in °C) for Fairbanks, Alaska, for each month of the year from January through December. What is the mean of these monthly temperatures?

$^-25, ^-20, ^-13, ^-2, ^+9, ^+15, ^+17, ^+14, ^+7, ^-4, ^-16, ^-23$

28. The R-80 Trucking Company carried freight along interstate 80 from New York City to San Francisco. The home base of R-80 Trucking was in Omaha, Nebraska, which is roughly midway between the ends of its line. R-80 truckers averaged about 50 miles per hour on this route, allowing time for rest stops.

R-80 Trucking Company Route Map

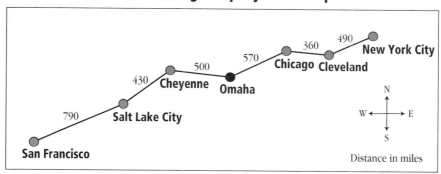

a. Make a number line to represent this truck route. Put Omaha at 0, and use positive numbers for cities east of Omaha and negative numbers for cities west of Omaha.

b. A truck left Omaha, heading east, and traveled for 7 hours. About how far did the truck go? Where on the number line did it stop? Show all your calculations.

c. A truck left Omaha, heading west, and traveled for 4.5 hours. About how far did the truck go? Where on the number line did it stop? Show all your calculations.

d. A truck heading east arrived in Omaha. About where on the number line was the truck 12 hours before it reached Omaha? Show all your calculations.

e. A truck heading west arrived in Omaha. About where on the number line was the truck 11 hours before it reached Omaha? Show all your calculations.

29. The list below shows the yards gained and lost on each play by the Mathville Mudhens in the fourth quarter of their last football game. What was their average gain or loss per play?

-8, 20, 3, 7, -15, 4, -12, 32, 5, 1

In 30 and 31, write a set of number sentences that shows the related multiplication and division facts for the set of integers. For example, for the integers 27, 9, and 3, the sentences would be

$$9 \times 3 = 27 \qquad 3 = 27 \div 9 \qquad 9 = 27 \div 3$$

30. 7, -3, and -21

31. -4, -5, and 20

32. Without actually multiplying, how can you decide whether the product of two integers is

   a. positive

   b. negative

   c. 0

33. Without actually dividing, how can you decide whether the quotient of two integers is

   a. positive

   b. negative

   c. 0

Extensions

34. Make a Sum Game with a 6-by-6 grid of sums. Each sum in the grid must be the sum of two integers (addends) listed below the grid.

In 35–38, use the following information: Many towns and small cities have water towers to store water and help maintain water pressure. Water flows into and out of the towers all day long. Generally, flow out of the tower is greatest during the hours when most people are awake and active. The flow into the towers is greatest at night when most people are asleep.

35. If water flows into a tower at the rate of 5000 gallons per hour, how will the supply in the tower change over a 4-hour period? Assume no water flows out of the tower during this time. Show your calculations.

36. If water flows into a tower at the rate of 4000 gallons per hour for a 7-hour period, by how much will the supply at the end of the 7 hours differ from the supply at the beginning of the 7 hours? Assume no water flows out of the tower during this time. Show your calculations.

37. If water flows out of a tower at the rate of 7500 gallons per hour, how will the supply in the tower change over a 3-hour period? Assume no water flows into the tower during this time. Show your calculations.

38. If water flows out of a tower at the rate of 5000 gallons per hour for a 6.5-hour period, by how much will the supply at the end of the 6.5 hours differ from the supply at the beginning of the 6.5-hour period? Assume no water flows into the tower during this time. Show your calculations.

Mathematical Reflections

In this investigation, you explored the multiplication and division of integers. These questions will help you summarize what you have learned:

1. Write a strategy for multiplying two integers. Be sure to consider all possible combinations of positive integers, negative integers, and 0. Verify your strategy by finding the following products.

   a. $^-13 \times 7$ **b.** $11 \times ^-20$

   c. $^-12 \times 0$ **d.** $^-18 \times ^-22$

2. Write a strategy for dividing two integers. Be sure to consider all possible combinations of positive integers, negative integers, and 0. Verify your strategy by finding the following quotients.

   a. $126 \div ^-9$ **b.** $^-36 \div ^-12$

   c. $^-2592 \div 32$ **d.** $0 \div 18$

Think about your answers to these questions, discuss your ideas with other students and your teacher, and then write a summary of your findings in your journal.

Coordinate Grids

In previous units, you created and studied coordinate graphs. Coordinate graphs let you look at the relationship between two variables and observe how a change in one variable affects the other variable. All the points on the graphs you have worked with so far have had coordinates greater than or equal to 0. In this investigation, you will see how the coordinate grid can be extended in order to plot points with negative coordinates.

5.1 Extending the Coordinate Grid

The *x*-axis on a coordinate grid is a horizontal number line, and the *y*-axis is a vertical number line. On the coordinate grids you have worked with so far, all the values on the *x*- and *y*-axes have been greater than or equal to 0.

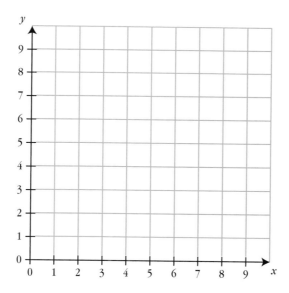

Just as we extended the number line in Investigation 1 to include negative numbers, we can extend the *x*- and *y*-axes of the coordinate grid to include negative numbers.

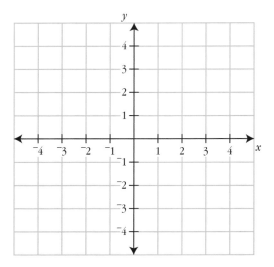

When the axes are extended, they divide the grid into four regions called *quadrants*. We can number these quadrants, starting with the region at the upper right and continuing counterclockwise. The quadrants are usually numbered by using roman numerals as shown below.

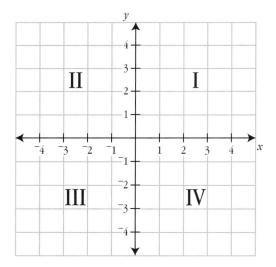

Melina made a coordinate grid and plotted the points (4, 3), (⁻3, 1), (⁻4, ⁻5), and (3, ⁻3). Study her work, and see if you can figure out what she did.

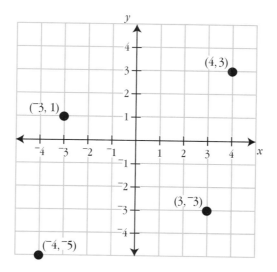

Recall that the two numbers that describe a point are called the *coordinates* of the point. The first number is the *x-coordinate,* and the second number is the *y-coordinate.* For example, the first point Melina plotted has coordinates (4, 3); the *x*-coordinate is 4, and the *y*-coordinate is 3.

Problem 5.1

A. Describe how Melina located each of the four points on the coordinate grid.

B. What polygon could you make by connecting the four points? Justify your answer.

C. On a coordinate grid, plot four points that are the vertices of a square, such that both coordinates of each point are positive integers.

D. On a coordinate grid, plot four points that are the vertices of a square, such that both coordinates of each point are negative integers.

E. On a coordinate grid, plot four points that are the vertices of a square, such that one point has two negative-integer coordinates, one point has two positive-integer coordinates, and each of the other points has one positive-integer coordinate and one negative-integer coordinate.

F. Two vertices of a square are (3, 1) and (⁻1, 1). Find the coordinates for every pair of points that could be the other two vertices.

■ Problem 5.1 Follow-Up

Imagine that you can walk on a coordinate grid. Each integer unit is one step, and you must stay on the grid lines. Suppose you want to walk from point (4, 2) to point (2, 1), taking the least number of steps possible.

You could go 2 steps to the left and then 1 step down.

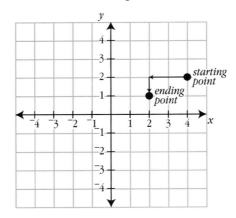

Or you could go 1 step down and then 2 steps to the left.

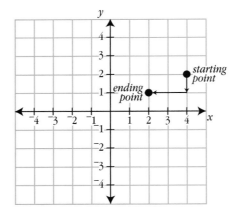

Paths between two points that require the least possible number of steps are called *minimal paths.*

1. For each pairs of points, describe two minimal paths from the first point to the second point.
   - **a.** (⁻4, ⁻2) to (5, 3)
   - **b.** (⁻4, 3) to (5, 2)
   - **c.** (2, ⁻4) to (⁻1, ⁻2)

2. **a.** Locate two points on the coordinate grid such that it will take 12 steps to travel from one of the points to the other on a minimal path.
   b. Will everyone name the same two points for part a? Why do you think this is so?

5.2 Breaking Even

Jean is planning to start a bicycle tune-up business. She figures out that her start-up costs will be $800 to buy the tools and parts she needs. She decides to charge $60 for each tune-up. She comes up with the following equation to determine her profit:

$$P = 60t - 800$$

where P is her profit in dollars, and t is the number of tune-ups.

If she does 30 tune-ups ($t = 30$), her profit will be

$$P = (60 \times 30) - 800 = \$1000$$

Jean wants to use her equation to calculate her *break-even point*. That is, she wants to find out the number of tune-ups she will have to do before she begins to make a profit. Then, she wants to figure out how her profit will change with each tune-up after this break-even point.

Problem 5.2

A. Make a table that shows the profit Jean will earn for 0 through 20 tune-ups.

B. Plot the (tune-ups, profit) data from your table on a coordinate grid. Be sure to label the axes. Explain how you chose the scale for each axis.

C. What will Jean's profit be if she does only four tune-ups? How is this shown on the graph?

D. How many tune-ups will Jean have to do before she breaks even? How is this shown on the graph?

E. How does Jean's profit change with each tune-up she does? How is this shown on the graph?

■ **Problem 5.2 Follow-Up**

1. Jean figures out that she could decrease her start-up cost to $600 by buying used tools. She writes a new equation, $P = 60t - 600$, to determine her profit. What is the break-even point for this profit equation?

2. Jean's friend Chuck thinks Jean should advertise her business in the local paper. This would increase her costs, giving her the profit equation $P = 60t - 1200$. What is the break-even point for this profit equation?

5.3 Using a Calculator to Explore Lines

Jean has several profit equations, each based on a different start-up cost. She borrows her brother's graphing calculator so she can explore the graphs of the equations. Since she has never used the calculator before, she decides to start by experimenting with some simple equations.

Problem 5.3

A. 1. Enter the equation $y = 4x$ into your graphing calculator as Y_1, and then press GRAPH to see a graph of the equation. Make a sketch of the graph you see.

2. Predict how the graph of $y = {}^-4x$ will differ from the graph of $y = 4x$. Then, enter the equation $y = {}^-4x$ as Y_2, and press GRAPH to see the graphs of both equations in the same window. Add a sketch of $y = {}^-4x$ to your sketch from part 1.

3. How are the graphs alike? How are they different?

B. 1. Press TABLE to look at the table showing data for both equations ($y = 4x$ and $y = -4x$). You may need to use the ▶ key to see the Y_2 column. Copy part of the table onto your paper.

2. For each value of x in the table, look at the two corresponding values of y (Y_1 and Y_2). How are the two y values for a given x value related? How does this relationship show up in the graph?

C. With your graphing calculator, experiment with each set of equations. Look at the graphs and the tables. Record your observations.

1. $y = 4x + 5$ and $y = {}^-4x + 5$

2. $y = 4x - 5$ and $y = {}^-4x - 5$

■ **Problem 5.3 Follow-Up**

In 1–3, predict what the graphs of the equations will look like. Then test your predictions by using a graphing calculator.

1. $y = 3x$ and $y = {}^-3x$

2. $y = 3x + 3$ and $y = {}^-3x + 3$

3. $y = 3x - 3$ and $y = {}^-3x - 3$

4. Give three other pairs of equations that will have a relationship similar to the pairs above.

5.4 Exploring Window Settings

Jean's brother tells her that she can change the section of the graph displayed on the calculator by using the $\boxed{\text{WINDOW}}$ key. Jean decides to experiment with this key, using the equation $y = 3x + 2$.

Below are the window settings Jean used. You will need to refer to these settings as you work on Problem 5.4.

Window settings 1

```
WINDOW
 XMIN=0
 XMAX=10
 XSCL=1
 YMIN=0
 YMAX=10
 YSCL=1
```

Window settings 2

```
WINDOW
 XMIN=⁻10
 XMAX=10
 XSCL=1
 YMIN=⁻10
 YMAX=10
 YSCL=1
```

A. On paper, make a table of x and y values for the equation $y = 3x + 2$.

B. On grid paper, sketch a graph of $y = 3x + 2$.

C. Enter the equation $y = 3x + 2$ into your graphing calculator, and press GRAPH . Make a sketch of the graph you see. How does this graph compare with the graph you drew by hand?

D. If you press WINDOW , you will see a screen that allows you to change the section of the graph displayed in the window. Change the settings to those shown in "Window settings 1" on the previous page, and then press GRAPH to see the graph of $y = 3x + 2$ in the new window.

   1. Make a sketch of the graph you see.

   2. How does this graph compare with the graph you drew by hand in part B?

   3. How does this graph compare with the graph you made with your calculator in part C?

   4. Explain what you think each entry on the "Window settings 1" screen means.

E. On paper, make a table of x and y values for the equation $y = 2x$.

F. On grid paper, sketch a graph of $y = 2x$.

G. Enter the equation $y = 2x$ into your graphing calculator, and press GRAPH . Make a sketch of the graph you see.

H. Change the window settings to those shown in "Window settings 2" on the previous page, and then press GRAPH to see the graph of $y = 2x$ in the new window.

   1. Make a sketch of the graph you see.

   2. How does this graph compare with the graph you drew by hand in part F?

   3. How does this graph compare with the graph you made with your calculator in part G?

   4. Explain what you think each entry on the "Window settings 2" screen means.

1. In part D of Problem 5.4, what happened to the coordinate grid on your calculator when you changed the window settings? Why?

2. Change the window settings so that only quadrant III of the coordinate grid is displayed. Record the window settings you used.

3. Graph $y = 2x$ in this new window. Make a sketch of the graph you see.

4. Except for the point (0,0), which quadrants contain none of the points on the graph of $y = 2x$?

5. Which window settings would you use to display only quadrant II? Quadrant IV?

5.5 Revisiting Jean's Problem

Jean uses her brother's graphing calculator to display the graph of her original profit equation, $P = 60t - 800$. She lets the number of tune-ups, t, be the x variable and the profit, P, be the y variable. She uses the window settings shown below at the left and gets the display shown below at the right.

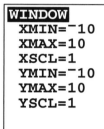

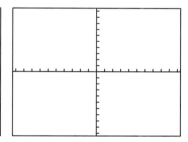

Only the axes appear in the display. There is no sign of the graph anywhere! Jean reasons that the window shown on the screen does not include any of the points on her graph. She needs to change her window settings so that the graph of her equation will show.

Think about this!

What information could Jean use to help her choose an appropriate window setting?

Problem 5.5

In the following questions, use Jean's profit equation $P = 60t - 800$ and your work from Problem 5.2.

A. 1. In the table of data you made in Problem 5.2, what range of values did you use for the number of tune-ups?

  2. What range of values did you use for the profit?

B. Enter Jean's profit equation into your calculator. Use the number of tune-ups as the x variable and the profit as the y variable. Use your answers to part A to help you decide how to adjust the window settings so that you will be able to see the graph of the profit equation. Press $\boxed{\text{GRAPH}}$ to display the graph. Make a sketch of the graph you see on the screen.

C. How is the break-even point shown on the graph?

D. Look at the table of data on your calculator. How is the break-even point shown in the table?

■ Problem 5.5 Follow-Up

1. Recall that Jean wrote the equation $P = 60t - 600$ to represent the profit she would make if she bought used tools instead of new tools. Find an appropriate window for viewing the graph of this profit equation. Graph the equation on a calculator. Make a sketch of what you see.

2. Jean wrote the equation $P = 60t - 1200$ to represent the profit she would make if she advertised in the local paper. Find an appropriate window for viewing the graph of this profit equation. Graph the equation on a calculator. Make a sketch of what you see.

3. Find the break-even points for the equations in 1 and 2.

As you work on these ACE questions, use your calculator whenever you need it.

Applications

1. **a.** When the window settings on the left are used, the coordinate axes look like those shown on the right. Copy the axes, and label the tick marks with the appropriate scale values.

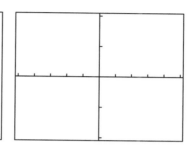

```
WINDOW
 XMIN=⁻10
 XMAX=10
 XSCL=2
 YMIN=⁻10
 YMAX=10
 YSCL=5
```

b. Sketch a graph of the equation $y = {}^-2x$ on the axes.

In 2–5, use the coordinates of the points to figure out what scale interval was used on each axis.

2.

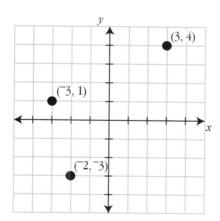

3.

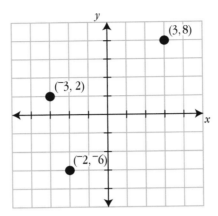

4.

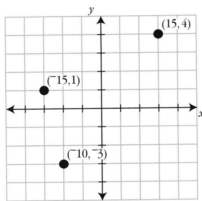

5.

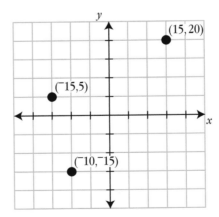

6. The graph at the right shows the relationship between the number of riders on a bike tour and the cost of providing snacks for the riders.

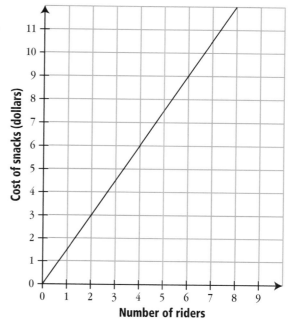

Number of riders

a. What is the cost of a snack for one rider?

b. What is the total cost of snacks for eight riders?

c. If snacks for all the riders cost $18, how many riders are there?

d. If there were 100 riders, what would be the total cost for the snacks? Explain how you got your answer.

In 7–10, tell which graph on the screen on the left below matches the equation, and explain how you know you are right. The screen on the right shows the settings that were used for the display window.

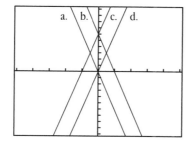

```
WINDOW
  XMIN=⁻5
  XMAX=5
  XSCL=1
  YMIN=⁻10
  YMAX=10
  YSCL=1
```

7. $y = 5x$

8. $y = {}^-5x$

9. $y = 5x + 6$

10. $y = {}^-5x + 6$

Connections

11. Explain why $85 - 73$ is equivalent to $85 + {}^{-}73$.

12. Three students—Sami, Manoj, and Aimee—started a lawn-mowing business. They made this table and graph to relate their income in dollars (the y values) to the number of weeks worked (the x values). The third screen shows the window settings they used for the graph.

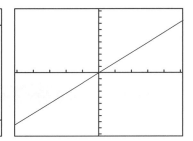

X	Y1
1	80
2	160
3	240
4	320
5	400
6	480

X=1

```
WINDOW
 XMIN=⁻10
 XMAX=10
 XSCL=2
 YMIN=⁻1000
 YMAX=1000
 YSCL=100
```

a. How much income would the students make if they worked 0 weeks? How is this shown on the graph?

b. Locate the point $({}^{-}2, {}^{-}160)$ on the graph. What does this point represent in the context of the situation presented? Is this situation possible? Explain your thinking.

13. The following table gives the temperature (in °C) in Fairbanks, Alaska, for each month over two consecutive years.

Month	Temperature in year 1 (°C)	Temperature in year 2 (°C)
January	−25	−27
February	−20	−23
March	−13	−12
April	−2	−4
May	+9	+10
June	+15	+12
July	+17	+15
August	+14	+16
September	+7	+9
October	−4	0
November	−16	−16
December	−23	−23

a. Find the median and mean temperatures for these two years.

b. Make a coordinate graph that shows how the temperature changed over these two years.

Extensions

14. a. Name five pairs of numbers with a sum of −3.

b. Plot the pairs of numbers from part a, and connect the points.

c. Find the coordinates of a point on the connecting line. (Choose a point that is different from the points you plotted in part b.) What is the sum of these coordinates? Pick another point on the line and find the sum of its coordinates. If you picked a third point on this line, what do you think the sum of its coordinates would be?

d. What would a graph of pairs of numbers whose sum is +8 look like? Justify your answer.

Mathematical Reflections

In this investigation, you extended the coordinate grid to include points with negative coordinates, and you used your graphing calculator to explore graphs of equations. These questions will help you summarize what you have learned:

1 How can you tell which quadrant a point will fall in by looking at its coordinates?

2 You have looked at several problem situations in which you figured out how to make a table of data. You also learned that if you can write an equation to describe how the variables are related, you can use a graphing calculator to graph the equation. How do you figure out what part of the entire graph actually makes sense in the real problem situation? Use an example to help explain.

Think about your answers to these questions, discuss your ideas with other students and your teacher, and then write a summary of your findings in your journal.

Looking Back and Looking Ahead

Unit Reflections

While working on problems in this unit, you investigated properties, operations, and applications of *positive* and *negative* numbers and zero. The numbers {... , −3, −2, −1, 0, 1, 2, 3, ... } are called the *integers*. You learned how to represent integers on a number line and how to add, subtract, multiply, and divide integers. Answering questions about thermometers, distance on a number line, elevations, and scoring games focused your attention on important uses of integers.

Using Your Understanding of Integers — To test your understanding and skill in use of integers, consider the questions that arise in the following games and problem situations.

1 *Kaylee and Cassie designed a board game that involves a number line. In their game, players take turns flipping a penny and moving a marker to the left or the right on a number line like this one.*

These are the rules of the game.

- *At the start of the game each player puts a marker on the point labeled 0.*
- *In round one each player flips a coin and moves 2 spaces to the left if the penny shows a tail (T) or two spaces to the right if the penny shows a head (H).*
- *In round two, each player flips the coin but moves 5 spaces left (T) or right (H).*
- *In round three, each player flips the coin but moves 10 spaces left (T) or right (H).*
- *At the end of three rounds, the player whose marker is on the greater number wins.*

a. Where will Jose's marker end up if he flips HHT on his three turns?

b. Where will Maria's marker end up if she flips THT on her three turns?

c. Consider the possible outcomes of this game and their probabilities.

i. Make a list showing all possible final numbers in the game.

ii. Write number sentences using integer addition to confirm your answers.

iii. Find the probability of ending on each possible final number.

d. Repeat the directions of part c. to show what will happen if the moves in each round are 2, 4, and 6 spaces to the left or right.

2 *Write number sentences involving integer operations that answer the following questions.*

a. In four plays of a football game, one team gained 12 yards, lost 8 yards, lost 3 yards, and gained 7 yards. What was the team's net gain or loss for those four plays?

b. Bill and Susan were comparing the depths of two submarines. One was 890 feet below sea level, and the other was 1425 feet below sea level.

i. Which submarine was at the greater depth?

ii. What change in the first submarine's depth would put it at the same depth as the other submarine?

c. The Blue Devil Booster Club sells snacks at Duke Middle School activities. To get a good price on supplies, the club ordered food worth $125 for each of eight major events and paid in full at the start of the year. After the first four events, the club's total income was $745. How much profit or loss did they have at that time?

d. In Mooseville, the high temperature on one Monday in January was 40°F. It rose 12°F on Tuesday, dropped 10°F on Wednesday, dropped another 6°F on Thursday, and rose 12°F on Friday. What was the high temperature on Friday?

e. Sunday was a cold day in Wolfville. Then the low temperature dropped an average of 8°F per day for the next five days. On Friday, the low temperature was −30°F. What had the low temperature been on Sunday?

3 **a.** Copy and complete the pyramid below so that each number represents the sum of the two numbers directly beneath it.

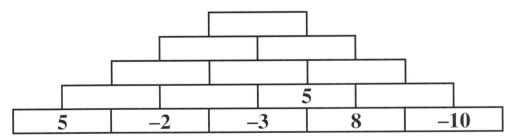

b. Copy and complete the pyramid below so that each number represents the product of the two numbers directly beneath it.

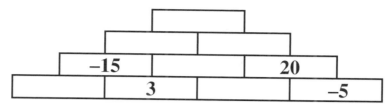

Explaining Your Reasoning—Prior to this unit, you worked only with whole numbers and positive fractions and decimals. Answering the questions in Problems 1–3 required knowledge of integers and operations with integers. You should be able to justify the ways that you used that knowledge in each problem.

1. What operation(s) can you do with the set of integers that you could not do with just the set of whole numbers?

2. Arrange the following numbers from least to greatest and be prepared to justify your answer.

-20, 15, -55, 30, 0

3. Use sketches of number line or chip models to demonstrate each of these calculations:
   a. $5 + (-7) = -2$ **b.** $(-2) + (-9) = -11$ **c.** $3 \times (-2) = -6$
   d. $(-3) \times (-2) = 6$

4. If you are given two integers, how do you find the sign of their
   a. sum?
   b. difference?
   c. product?
   d. quotient?

Positive and negative numbers are useful in solving a variety of problems that involve losses and gains. They also provide coordinates for points on an extended number line and coordinate plane. These ideas will be useful when you study graphs of functions in future *Connected Mathematics* units like *Moving Straight Ahead*, *Thinking with Mathematical Models*, and *Growing, Growing, Growing*. You will also use negative and positive numbers when you solve equations in these units and in the algebraic reasoning of *Say It with Symbols*.

absolute value The absolute value of a number is its distance from 0 on a number line. It can be thought of as the value of a number when its sign is ignored. For example, ⁻3 and 3 both have an absolute value of 3.

integers The whole numbers and their opposites. 0 is an integer, but it is neither positive nor negative. The integers from ⁻4 to 4 are shown on the number line below.

inverse operations Operations that "undo" each other. Addition and subtraction are inverse operations. For example, the subtraction equation $7 - 4 = 3$ is undone by the addition equation $3 + 4 = 7$. Multiplication and division are inverse operations. For example, for multiplication equation $2 \times 6 = 12$ is undone by the division equations $12 \div 2 = 6$ and $12 \div 6 = 2$.

negative number A number less than 0. On a number line, negative numbers are located to the left of 0 (on a vertical number line, negative numbers are located below 0).

number sentence A mathematical statement that gives the relationship between two expressions, which are composed of numbers and operation signs. For example, $3 + 2 = 5$ and $6 \times 2 > 10$ are number sentences; $3 + 2$, 5, 6×2, and 10 are expressions.

opposites Two numbers whose sum is 0. For example, ⁻3 and 3 are opposites. On a number line, opposites are the same distance from 0 but in different directions from 0. The number 0 is its own opposite.

positive number A number greater than 0. (The number 0 is neither positive nor negative.) On a number line, positive numbers are located to the right of 0 (on a vertical number line, positive numbers are located above 0).

quadrants The four sections into which the coordinate plane is divided by the x- and y-axes. The quadrants are labeled as follows:

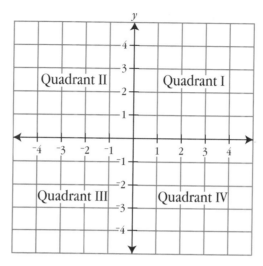

Index

Absolute value, 39

Absolute zero, 55

Addition
 ACE, 26–32
 integer, 4, 18–25
 inverse of subtraction, 40–42, 44–45

Break-even point, 71–72, 75–76

Calculator, graphing linear equations,
 72–76

Chip board
 integer addition on, 22–25
 integer subtraction on, 35–39, 44

Comparison
 ACE, 12–16
 integer, 7–11

Coordinate grid, 4, 67–70
 ACE, 77–81
 graphing linear equations on, 72–76
 paths on, 70
 points on, 69

Coordinates, integer, 4, 67–70

Division
 ACE, 61–65
 integer, 59
 inverse of multiplication, 59

Equation
 addition, 19–25

division, 59
 graphing linear, 72–76
 linear, 71–76
 multiplication, 54–56
 subtraction, 34–45

Game
 Integer Product Game, 4, 57–58
 MathMania, 6–9

Golf, positive and negative scores in, 5

Graph
 ACE, 77–81
 coordinate, 67–76
 linear, 72–76

Graphing calculator, linear equations
 on, 72–76

Integer, 3, 4
 ACE, 12–16, 26–32, 46–51, 60–65,
  77–81
 addition, 4, 18–25
 comparison, 7–11
 coordinates, 4
 definition, 18
 division, 59
 multiplication, 4, 53–58
 order, 7–11
 patterns, 43, 56–57
 subtraction, 4, 34–45

Integer Product Game, 4, 57–58

Inverse operations
  addition and subtraction, 40–42,
    44–45
  multiplication and division, 59
Investigation
  Adding Integers, 18–33
  Coordinate Grids, 67–82
  Extending the Number Line, 5–17
  Multiplying and Dividing Integers,
    53–66
  Subtracting Integers, 34–52

Journal, 17, 33, 52, 62, 66

Linear equation, 71–76
  graphing pairs of, 72–76
Looking Back and Looking Ahead:
  Unit Reflections, 83–85

Mathematical Highlights, 4
Mathematical Reflections, 17, 33, 52,
  62, 66
MathMania, 6–9
Minimal path, 70
Model
  chip board, 22–25, 27–28, 34–39, 44
  integer addition, 4, 18–25
  integer division, 4
  integer multiplication, 4, 53–58
  integer subtraction, 4, 34–45
  number line, 5–11, 19–21, 40–42,
    53–55

Multiplication
  ACE, 60–65
  integer, 4, 53–58
  Integer Product Game, 4, 57–58
  inverse of division, 59

Negative number, 3, 5, 18
  sign for, 5
Number
  integer, 18
  negative, 3, 5, 18
  opposites, 10–11
  positive, 3, 5, 18
  whole, 18
Number line
  absolute value on, 42
  ACE, 12–16, 26, 29, 47
  adding integers on, 19–21
  locating integers on, 5–11
  multiplying integers on, 53–55
  subtracting integers on, 40–42
  thermometer as, 9–10
Number sentence, 19
  addition, 19–25
  division, 59
  multiplication, 54–56
  subtraction, 34–45

Opposites, integer, 10–11
Order
  ACE, 12–16
  integer, 7–11

Path, minimal, 70
Pattern
  integer multiplication, 56–57
  integer subtraction, 43
Point, integer coordinates of, 69–70
Positive number, 3, 5, 18
  sign for, 5

Quadrant, 68–70

Scale
  ACE, 77–81
  on an integer grid, 71–76
Subtraction
  ACE, 46–51

integer, 34–45
inverse of addition, 40–42, 44–45
Symbol
  integer, 19
  minus, 5
  operation, 19
  plus, 5

Temperature
  integers and, 9–10, 53–55
  limits, 55
Thermometer, as a vertical number
  line, 9–10, 53, 55

Whole number, 18

Connected  Mathematics®

Linear Relationships

Student Edition

Glenda Lappan
James T. Fey
William M. Fitzgerald
Susan N. Friel
Elizabeth Difanis Phillips

Prentice
Hall

Glenview, Illinois
Needham, Massachusetts
Upper Saddle River, New Jersey

Connected Mathematics® was developed at Michigan State University with the support of National Science Foundation Grant No. MDR 9150217.

This project was supported, in part,
by the
National Science Foundation
Opinions expressed are those of the authors
and not necessarily those of the Foundation

The Michigan State University authors and administration have agreed that all MSU royalties arising from this publication will be devoted to purposes supported by the Department of Mathematics and the MSU Mathematics Education Enrichment Fund.

Photo Acknowledgements: 8 © Gary S. Settles/Photo Researchers, Inc.; 15 © Alan Carey/The Image Works; 18 © Thelma Shumsky/The Image Works; 19 © Bob Daemmrich/The Image Works; 29 © Bob Martin/Allsport; 51 © Peter Southwick/Stock, Boston; 60 © Jack Dermid/Photo Researchers, Inc.; 65 © Daniel Wray/The Image Works; 75 © Zigy Kaluzny/Tony Stone Images; 88 Special Collections, California Academy of Science; © G. Goodwin/Superstock, Inc.

Contents

Mathematical Highlights   4

Investigation 1: Predicting from Patterns   5
    1.1 Conducting an Experiment   5
    Applications—Connections—Extensions   9
    Mathematical Reflections   14

Investigation 2: Walking Rates   15
    2.1 Walking to the Yogurt Shop   17
    2.2 Changing the Walking Rate   18
    2.3 Walking for Charity   19
    2.4 Walking to Win   21
    2.5 Crossing the Line   22
    Applications--Connections—Extensions   24
    Mathematical Reflections   34

Investigation 3: Exploring Lines with a Graphing Calculator   35
    3.1 Getting to the Point   36
    3.2 Graphing Lines   37
    3.3 Finding Solutions   39
    3.4 Planning a Skating Party   41
    Applications—Connections—Extensions   44
    Mathematical Reflections   52

Investigation 4: Solving Equations   53
    4.1 Paying in Installments   53
    4.2 Using the Symbolic Method   54
    4.3 Analyzing Bones   57
    Applications—Connections—Extensions   59
    Mathematical Reflections   63

Investigation 5: Exploring Slope   64
    5.1 Climbing Stairs   64
    5.2 Finding the Slope of a Line   66
    5.3 Connecting Points   68
    Applications—Connections—Extensions   70
    Mathematical Reflections   79

Investigation 6: Writing an Equation for a Line   80
    6.1 Solving Alphonso's Puzzle   80
    6.2 Converting Temperatures   81
    6.3 Solving the Mystery of the Irish Elk   82
    Applications—Connections—Extensions   84
    Mathematical Reflections   91

Looking Back and Looking Ahead: Unit Reflections   92

Glossary   95

Index   100

Moving Straight Ahead

Henri challenges his older brother Emile to a walking race. Emile figures out that his walking rate is 2.5 meters per second, and Henri's walking rate is 1 meter per second. Emile agrees to give Henri a 45-meter head start. Emile knows Henri would enjoy winning the race, but he does not want to make the race so short that it is obvious his brother will win. What distance would allow Henri to win in a close race?

Rosa's grandfather gives her some money as a birthday gift. She plans to put her birthday money in a safe place and add the same amount from her allowance to it each week. After five weeks, she will have a total of $175, and after eight weeks, she will have $190. How much money is Rosa planning to save each week? How much money did her grandfather give her for her birthday?

To estimate the outside temperature, count cricket chirps. If a cricket chirps n times in one minute, then the temperature, t, in degrees Fahrenheit can be computed with the formula $t = \frac{1}{4}n + 40$. What is the temperature if a cricket chirps 150 times in a minute?

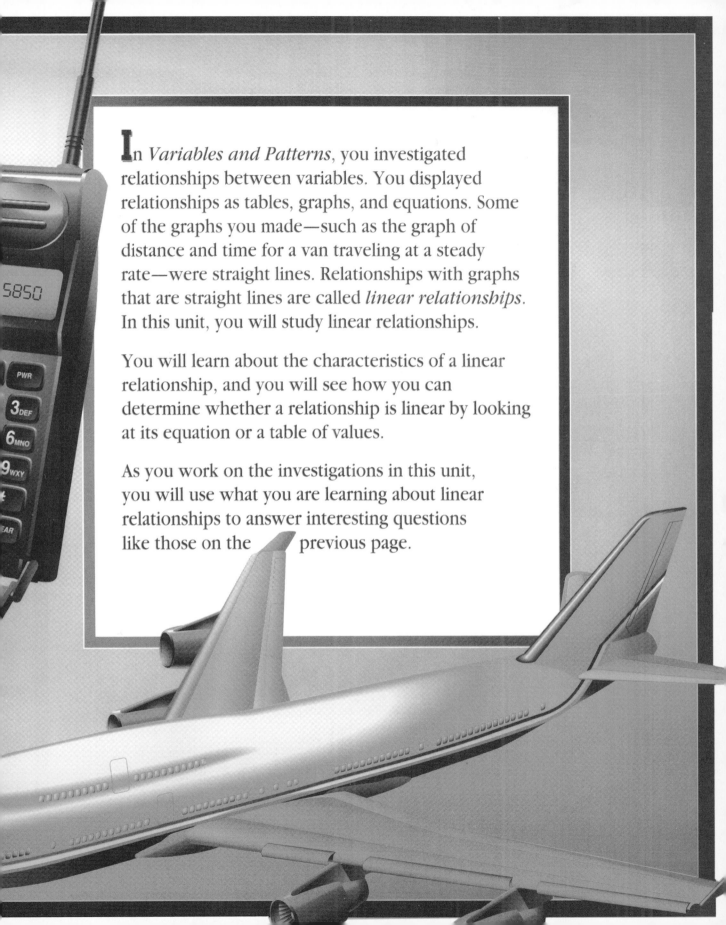

In *Variables and Patterns*, you investigated
relationships between variables. You displayed
relationships as tables, graphs, and equations. Some
of the graphs you made—such as the graph of
distance and time for a van traveling at a steady
rate—were straight lines. Relationships with graphs
that are straight lines are called *linear relationships*.
In this unit, you will study linear relationships.

You will learn about the characteristics of a linear
relationship, and you will see how you can
determine whether a relationship is linear by looking
at its equation or a table of values.

As you work on the investigations in this unit,
you will use what you are learning about linear
relationships to answer interesting questions
like those on the   previous page.

Mathematical Highlights

In *Moving Straight Ahead* you will explore properties of the most important type of relationship among variables, linearity. The unit should help you to

● Recognize problem situations in which two or more variables have a linear relationship to each other;

● Construct tables, graphs, and symbolic equations that express linear relationships;

● Translate information about linear relations given in a table, a graph, or an equation to one of the other forms;

● Understand the connections between linear equations and patterns in the tables and graphs of those relations—rate of change, slope, and *y*-intercept;

● Solve linear equations;

● Solve problems and make decisions about linear relationships using information given in tables, graphs, and symbolic expressions; and

● Use a graphing calculator to make tables and graphs of linear relations between variables and to answer questions about those relations.

As you work on the problems of this unit, ask questions about problem situations that involve related quantities: *What are the variables in the problem? Do the variables in this problem have a linear relationship to each other? What patterns in the problem suggest that it is linear? How can the linear pattern in a table, graph, or problem statement be expressed with an equation? How can tables, graphs, and equations of linear relationships be used to express and answer given questions?*

Predicting from Patterns

All around you, things occur in patterns. Once you observe a pattern, you can predict information beyond and between the data observed. The ability to use patterns to make predictions makes it possible for you to run to the right position to catch a fly ball or to guess how a story will end. Often, you are not even aware that you are thinking about patterns until something surprises you because it does not fit a familiar pattern. For example, the first time you bounced a superball, you may have had trouble catching it because you weren't expecting it to bounce so high. You were basing your expectations on patterns you had observed for other types of balls.

In many situations, patterns become apparent only after sufficient data are collected, organized, and displayed. In this investigation, you will conduct an experiment and use patterns in the data to make predictions.

1.1 Conducting an Experiment

Problems 1.1A and 1.1B are experiments. Your group should carry out *only one* of these experiments. Read the directions carefully *before you start.* Be prepared to explain your findings to the rest of the class.

- In Problem 1.1A, you investigate the rate at which a leaking faucet loses water.
- In Problem 1.1B, you investigate how the drop height of a ball is related to its bounce height.

1.1A: Wasting Water

In this experiment, you will simulate a leaking faucet and collect data about the volume of water lost at 5-second intervals. You will then use the patterns in your results to predict how much water is wasted when a faucet leaks for one month.

Equipment: a paper cup, water, a sharp object (such as a paper clip or a small nail), a clear measuring container, and a watch or clock with a second hand

Directions: You will need to figure out how to divide the work among the members of your group.

1. Make a table with columns for recording time and amount of water lost. Fill in the time column with values from 0 seconds to 60 seconds in 5-second intervals (that is, 5, 10, 15, and so on).
2. Use the sharp object to punch a small hole in the bottom of the cup. Cover the hole with your finger.
3. Fill the paper cup with water.
4. Hold the paper cup over the measuring container.
5. When you are ready to begin timing, uncover the hole so that the water drips into the measuring container.
6. In a table, record the amount of water in the measuring container at 5-second intervals, up to a total time of 60 seconds.

Problem 1.1A

A. Make a coordinate graph of the data you collected.

B. What variables did you investigate in this experiment? Describe the relationship between the variables.

C. If a faucet dripped at the same rate as your cup does, how much water would be wasted in 2 minutes? In 2.5 minutes? In 3 minutes and 15 seconds? Explain how you made your predictions. Did you use the table, the graph, or some other method? What clues in the data helped you?

■ Problem 1.1A Follow-Up

1. If a faucet dripped into the measuring container at the same rate as your paper cup does, how long would it take for the container to overflow?
2. Besides time, what other variables affect the amount of water in the measuring container?
3. If a faucet leaked at the same rate as your paper cup, how much water would be wasted in one month? Explain how you arrived at your answer.
4. Find out how much water costs in your area. Use this information and your answer from question 3 to figure out the cost of the water wasted by a leaking faucet in one month.

1.1B: Bouncing Balls

You have probably bounced lots of kinds of balls. After bouncing a ball many times, you are better able to predict its behavior. For example, practicing bouncing a basketball can help you make a more accurate bounce pass in a game. In this experiment, you will investigate how the height from which a ball is dropped is related to the height it bounces.

Equipment: a meterstick and a ball that bounces

Directions: You will need to figure out how to divide up the work among the members of your group.

1. Make a table with columns for recording drop height and bounce height.
2. Hold the meterstick perpendicular to a flat surface, such as an uncarpeted floor, a table, or a desk.
3. Choose and record a height on the meterstick as the height from which you will drop the ball. Hold the ball at this height.
4. *Drop* the ball, and record the height of the first bounce. (You may have to do this several times before you feel confident you can make a good estimate of the bounce height.)
5. Repeat this for several different drop heights.

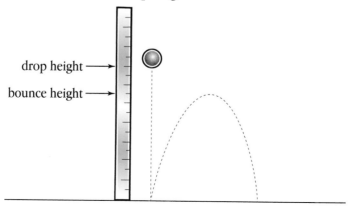

■ Problem 1.1B Follow-Up

Besides the drop height, what other variables affect the bounce height of the ball?

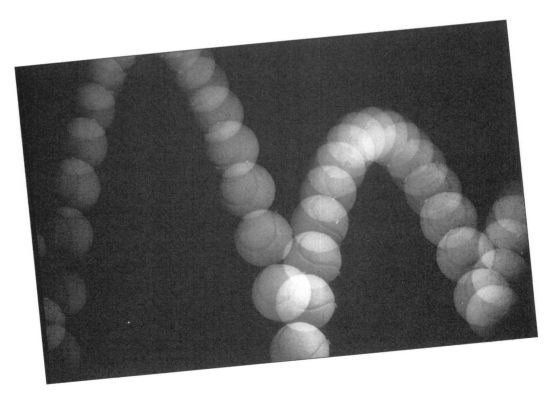

As you work on these ACE questions, use your calculator whenever you need it.

Applications

1. The table of data below was produced by students who did the bouncing-ball experiment.

Drop height (centimeters)	20	30	40	50	60	70	80
Bounce height (centimeters)	10	18	25	32	38	45	50

   a. Make a coordinate graph of these data.

   b. Predict the bounce height for a drop height of 45 centimeters. What method did you use to make your prediction?

   c. Predict the bounce height for a drop height of 140 centimeters.

   d. Predict the drop height needed for a bounce height of 60 centimeters.

   e. Are you equally confident about each prediction you made in parts b–d? Explain.

2. The table of data below was produced by students who did the leaking-faucet experiment. The measuring container they used held only 100 milliliters. If the students had continued their experiment, after how many seconds would the measuring container have overflowed?

Time (seconds)	10	20	30	40	50	60	70
Water loss (milliliters)	2	5	8.5	11.5	14	16.5	19.5

3. a. Think of two variables whose relationship can be represented by a straight-line graph like the one at the right. Copy the graph, and add labels for the variables you chose.

   b. Make up a question about your variables that could be answered by using the graph.

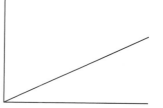

Connections

4. In *Variables and Patterns,* you saw that the distance traveled by the tour van depended on time. Suppose the van averaged a steady 60 miles per hour on the interstate highway. The table below shows the relationship between the time traveled and the distance.

Time (hours)	0.5	1.0	1.5	2.0	2.5	3.0	3.5
Distance (miles)	30	60					

   a. Copy and complete the table.

   b. Make a coordinate graph of the data in the table.

   c. Write a rule that describes the relationship between distance and time.

   d. Predict the distance traveled in 8 hours.

   e. Predict the time needed to travel 300 miles.

   f. Pick a pair of (time, distance) values from the table. How is the pair related to the graph and the rule?

5. The soccer boosters make $5 on each T-shirt they sell. This can be described by the equation $A = 5n$, where A is the amount of money made and n is the number of T-shirts sold.

   a. Make a table and a graph showing the amount of money made by selling up to ten T-shirts.

   b. Compare the table and the graph from part a with the table and the graph you made for your experiment in Problem 1.1A or 1.1B. How are the tables similar? How are they different? How are the graphs similar? How are they different? What do you think causes the similarities and differences?

   c. Compare the table, graph, and rule for the T-shirt sale with the table, graph, and rule in question 4. Describe the similarities and differences.

6. Denise and Takashi worked together on the leaking-faucet experiment. Each of them made a graph of the data they collected. What might have caused their graphs to look so different?

Denise's Graph   **Takashi's Graph**

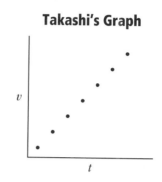

7. What might the following graph mean with regard to the leaking-faucet experiment?

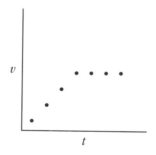

8. Jack does the bouncing-ball experiment and collects the following data.

Drop height (centimeters)	30	40	50	60	70	80	90
Bounce height (centimeters)	20	24	31	37	43	51	60

Jack says he does not need to make a graph to predict the bounce height for a drop height of 130 centimeters. He says the rule is that the bounce height is always two thirds of the drop height. Is his rule reasonable? Explain.

Extensions

9. Mr. Delgrosso's class conducted an experiment using a spring and some weights. They placed each weight on the end of the spring and measured the length of the stretched spring.

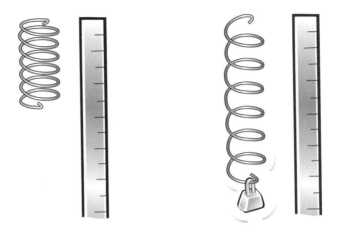

a. One student made the graph below to display the class's data from the experiment. What are the variables? Describe the general relationship between the variables.

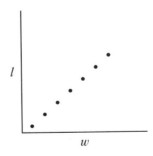

b. Another student used the same data to make the graph below. How is this graph different from the graph in part a? Is it possible that both graphs are correct? Explain.

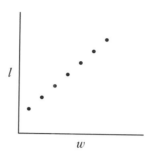

Mathematical Reflections

In this investigation, you conducted an experiment. By organizing your data into a table and a graph, you observed patterns and used the patterns to make predictions. These questions will help you summarize what you have learned:

1 One of the goals of this unit is to discover ways to identify a linear relationship from its table. Look at the table you made for your experiment and the tables you have made for other straight-line relationships. What do you think characterizes the table of a linear relationship?

2 What other relationships that you have investigated, in this class or somewhere else, do you now suspect to be linear?

Think about your answers to these questions, discuss your ideas with other students and your teacher, and then write a summary of your findings in your journal.

INVESTIGATION

Walking Rates

In *Variables and Patterns,* you read about five college students who set up a bicycle-touring business. The students used tables, graphs, and equations to look for patterns relating variables such as cost, income, and profit.

For example, the total cost to rent bikes depends on the number of people on the tour. We say that the rental cost is a *function of* the number of people on the tour. The variables in this situation are the number of people and the cost. If you were interested in how these variables are related, you might ask questions like these:

As the number of people on the tour increases, what happens to the cost to rent the bikes?

If the tour partners want to decrease the cost of renting bikes, how will this affect the number of people who can go on the tour?

For example, one bike shop charges $300 plus $20 per bike to rent bikes for one week. If we let C be the total cost to rent the bikes and n the number of people who go on the tour, we can write this equation to show the relationship between the number of people on the tour and the total rental cost:

$$C = 300 + 20n$$

Remember that $20n$ means 20 *times n.* If a variable is multiplied by a number, we can omit the times sign.

In *Variables and Patterns,* you also looked at the number of miles a van covers in a specified period of time. For example, if a van averages 60 miles per hour, then the distance covered depends on the number of hours the van travels. In other words, the distance is a *function of* the number of hours of travel. The variables are distance traveled and time. The relationship between these variables can be expressed as

$$d = 60t$$

where d represents the distance traveled in miles and t represents the time in hours.

The graphs of $C = 300 + 20n$ and $d = 60t$ are straight lines.

Rental Costs

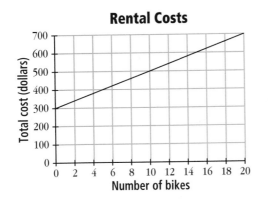

Van Distances

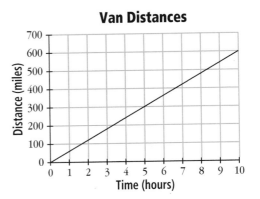

From the graphs, it is easy to see that the relationships between the number of bikes and the rental cost, and between the miles traveled and the time are **linear relationships**. In this investigation, you will consider this question:

> *How can you determine whether a situation is linear by examining a table of data or an equation?*

Once you have determined—from the table, the graph, or the equation—that a relationship is linear, you can explore this question:

> *How does changing one of the quantities in a situation affect the table, the graph, or the equation?*

For example, how does changing the cost per bike affect the table, the graph, and the equation of the relationship between the number of customers and the total rental cost? How does increasing the average speed at which the van travels affect the table, the graph, and the equation of the relationship between distance and time?

2.1 ## Walking to the Yogurt Shop

Mr. Goldberg's gym class does an experiment to determine their walking rates. Here are the results for three students.

Name	Walking rate
Terry	1 meter per second
Jade	2 meters per second
Jerome	2.5 meters per second

Jerome wonders how a person's walking rate would affect the amount of time it takes him or her to walk from school to the frozen yogurt shop.

Problem 2.1

A. If Terry, Jade, and Jerome leave school together and walk toward the frozen yogurt shop at the rates given in the table, how far apart will they be after 1 minute?

B. If the yogurt shop is 750 meters from school, how long will it take each student to walk there?

C. When Jerome arrives at the yogurt shop, how far away will Terry be?

■ Problem 2.1 Follow-Up

1. In Problem 2.1, what strategies did you use to get your answers?

2. Does Problem 2.1 involve linear relationships? Explain why or why not.

2.2 Changing the Walking Rate

In Problem 2.1, you saw that a person's walking rate determines the time it takes him or her to walk a given distance. In this problem, you will more closely examine the effect that walking rate has on the relationship between time and distance walked. Your findings will give you some important clues about how to identify linear relationships from tables, graphs, and equations.

Problem 2.2

A. In Problem 2.1, each student walked at a different rate. Use the walking rates given in that problem to make a table showing the distance walked by each student after different numbers of seconds. How does the walking rate affect the data in the table?

Time (seconds)	Distance (meters)		
	Terry	Jade	Jerome
0	0	0	0
1	1	2	2.5
2			
3			
.			
.			
.			

B. Graph the time and distance data for the three students on the same coordinate axes. Use a different color for each student's data. How does the walking rate affect the graphs?

C. For each student, write an equation that gives the relationship between the time and the distance walked. Let d represent the distance in meters and t represent the time in seconds. How does the walking rate affect the equations?

■ Problem 2.2 Follow-Up

While reading a sports magazine, Abby finds the following time and distance data for an athlete in an Olympic race. She wonders whether the data represent a linear relationship. Abby knows that if the relationship is linear, the data will lie on a straight line when graphed.

Time (seconds)	Distance (meters)
0	0
1	2
2	4
3	8
4	13
5	17

1. Use the table to determine how the distance changes as the time increases. How can you use this information to predict whether or not the data will lie on a straight line when graphed?

2. Describe the race that might have produced these data.

2.3 Walking for Charity

Ms. Chang's class decides to participate in a walkathon to raise money for a local hospital. Each participant in the walkathon must find sponsors to pledge a certain amount of money for each mile the participant walks.

Ms. Chang says that some sponsors might ask the students to suggest a pledge amount. The class wants to agree on how much they will ask for. Leanne says that $1 per mile would be appropriate. Gilberto says that $2 per mile would be better because it would bring in more money. Alana points out that if they ask for too much money, not as many people will want to be sponsors. She suggests that they ask each sponsor for a $5 donation plus 50¢ per mile.

In this problem, we will refer to Leanne, Gilberto, and Alana's suggestions as pledge plans.

A. 1. Make a table showing the amount of money a sponsor would owe under each pledge plan if a student walked distances between 0 and 10 miles.

2. Graph the three pledge plans on the same coordinate axes. Use a different color for each plan.

3. For each pledge plan, write an equation that can be used to calculate the amount of money a sponsor owes, given the total distance the student walks.

B. What effect does increasing the amount pledged per mile have on the table? On the graph? On the equation?

C. If a student walks 8 miles in the walkathon, how much would a sponsor owe under each pledge plan? Explain how you got your answer.

D. For a sponsor to owe a student $10, how many miles would the student have to walk under each pledge plan? Explain how you got your answer.

E. Alana suggested that each sponsor make a $5 donation and then pledge 50¢ per mile. How is this fixed $5 donation represented in the table? In the graph? In the equation?

■ **Problem 2.3 Follow-Up**

1. a. On the graph of a pledge plan, the point (2, 6) means that a student who walks 2 miles earns $6 from each sponsor. On which of the graphs is the point (2, 6)?

b. Find a point on each graph, and describe what the coordinates of the point mean in the context of the walkathon.

2. a. Write an equation for a pledge plan whose graph is a steeper line than any of the lines you graphed in the problem. Check your equation by graphing it on the coordinate axes with the other three lines.

b. Write an equation for a pledge plan whose graph is less steep than any of the lines you graphed in the problem. Check your equation by graphing it on the coordinate axes with the other lines.

Walking to Win

In Mr. Goldberg's gym class, Emile finds out that his walking rate is 2.5 meters per second. When he gets home from school, he times his little brother Henri, as Henri walks 100 meters. He figures out that Henri's walking rate is 1 meter per second.

Henri challenges Emile to a walking race. Because Emile's walking rate is faster, Emile gives Henri a 45-meter head start.

Problem 2.4

Emile knows his brother would enjoy winning the race, but he does not want to make the race so short that it is obvious his brother will win.

What would be a good distance to make the race so that Henri will win in a close race? Describe your strategy, and give evidence to support your answer.

■ **Problem 2.4 Follow-Up**

What would be a good distance to choose if Emile wants to beat his brother but wants the race to be close? Explain.

In Problem 2.4, there are many strategies you can use to determine a good distance for the race. Some strategies are more efficient or useful than others. Here are three powerful ways to tackle the problem:

1. Make a table showing time and distance data for both brothers.

2. On the same set of axes, graph time and distance data for both brothers.

3. Write an equation for each brother showing the relationship between the time and the distance from the starting line.

Problem 2.5

Use the information from Problem 2.4.

A. 1. Make a table showing the distance each brother is from the starting line at several different times during the first 40 seconds.

2. On the same set of axes, graph the time and the distance from the starting line for both brothers.

3. Write an equation for each brother showing the relationship between the time and the distance from the starting line.

B. How far from the starting line will Emile overtake Henri? Explain how you can use the table and the graph to answer this question.

C. After how many seconds will Emile overtake Henri? Explain how you can use the table and the graph to answer this question.

■ Problem 2.5 Follow-Up

1. After 3 seconds, who will be ahead? By how much?

2. How far will Henri be from the starting line when Emile has walked 10 meters?

3. a. Which graph is steeper?

b. How can you determine which of two lines will be steeper from their tables? From their equations?

4. Explain how you can use the table, the graph, and the equations to determine how far from the starting line each brother will be after 5 minutes.

5. a. At what points do Emile's and Henri's graphs cross the y-axis? What do these points mean in terms of the race?

b. How can you predict where a graph will cross the y-axis from a table? From an equation?

6. Emile's friend Yvette joins the race. Yvette has a head start of 20 meters and walks at 2 meters per second.

a. Copy and complete the table below to show Yvette's distance from the starting line for 0 to 7 seconds.

Time (seconds)	Distance (meters)
0	20
1	
2	
3	
4	
5	
6	
7	

b. Which of the following equations gives the relationship between Yvette's distance from the starting line, d, and the time, t?

i. $d = 20 + 2t$

ii. $d = 2 + 20$

iii. $d = 20t + 2$

iv. $d = 20 + t$

v. none of the above

As you work on these ACE questions, use your calculator whenever you need it.

Applications

In 1–3, use the following information: José, Mario, and Melanie went on a weeklong cycling trip. The table below gives the distance each person traveled for the first 3 hours of the trip. The table shows only the time when the riders were actually biking, not when they stopped to rest, eat, and so on.

Cycling time (hours)	Distance (miles)		
	José	Mario	Melanie
0	0	0	0
1	5	7	9
2	10	14	18
3	15	21	27

1. a. How fast did each person travel for the first 3 hours? Explain how you got your answer.

   b. Assume that each person continued at this rate. Find the distance each person traveled in 7 hours.

2. a. Graph the time and distance data for all three riders on the same coordinate axes.

   b. Use the graphs to find the distance each person traveled in $6\frac{1}{2}$ hours.

   c. Use the graphs to find the time it took each person to travel 70 miles.

   d. How does the rate at which each person rides affect the graphs?

3. a. For each rider, write an equation that can be used to calculate the distance traveled after a given number of hours.

   b. Use your equations from part a to calculate the distance each person traveled in $6\frac{1}{2}$ hours.

   c. How does a person's biking rate show up in his or her equation?

4. Mike was on the bike trip with José, Mario, and Melanie (from questions 1–3). He made the following table of the distances he traveled during day 1 of the trip.

Time (hours)	Distance (miles)
0	0
1	6.5
2	13
3	19.5
4	26
5	32.5
6	39

a. Assume Mike continued riding at this rate for the entire bike trip. Write an equation for the distance Mike traveled after t hours.

b. Sketch a graph of the equation.

c. When you made your graph, how did you choose the range of values for the time axis? For the distance axis?

d. How can you find the distance Mike traveled in 7 hours and in $9\frac{1}{2}$ hours, using the table? The graph? The equation?

e. How can you find the number of hours it took Mike to travel 100 miles and 237 miles, using the table? The graph? The equation?

f. For parts d and e, give the advantages and disadvantages of using each form of representation—a table, a graph, and an equation—to find the answers.

g. Compare the rate at which Mike rides with the rates at which José, Mario, and Melanie ride. Who rides the fastest? How can you determine this from the tables? From the graphs? From the equations?

5. Alicia was also on the bike trip. The distance she traveled in t hours is represented by this equation:

$$d = 7.5t$$

a. At what rate did Alicia travel?

b. If the graph of Alicia's distance and time were put on the same set of axes as Mike's graph, where would it be located in relationship to Mike's graph? Describe the location without actually making the graph.

c. If the graph of Alicia's distance and time were put on the same set of axes as José's, Mario's, and Melanie's graphs, where would it be located in relationship to the other graphs? Describe the location without actually making the graph.

6. The students in Ms. Chang's class decide to order T-shirts that advertise the walkathon. Miguel obtains two different quotes for the costs for the shirts.

> One Size Fits All charges $4 per shirt.
> You Draw It/We Print It charges $75 plus $3 per shirt.

a. For each company, write an equation Miguel could use to calculate the cost for any number of shirts.

b. On the same set of axes, graph both equations from part a.

c. Which company do you think the class should buy shirts from? What factors influenced your decision?

d. For what number of T-shirts is the cost the same for both companies? Explain how you got your answer.

In 7–9, refer to tables a–c.

a.

x	y
−2	3
−1	3
0	3
1	3
2	3
3	3

b.

x	y
−3	9
−2	4
−1	1
0	0
1	1
2	4

c.

x	y
0	0
2	−4
3	−8
4	−12
8	−16

7. How are the patterns in tables a–c similar? How are they different?

8. Make a graph of the data in each table.

9. Which tables represent a linear relationship? Explain how you decided.

10. The equation $C = 10 + 2n$ represents the cost in dollars, C, for n painter's caps advertising the walkathon. Which pair of values could represent a number of caps and the cost for that number of caps, (n, C)? Explain your answer.

(0, 10) (7, 24) (15, 30)

11. The equation $d = 3.5t + 50$ represents the distance in meters, d, that a cyclist is from his home after t seconds. Which pair of values represents a point on the graph of this equation? Explain your answer.

(10, 85) (0, 0) (3, 60.5)

12. Ingrid stops at Tara's house on her way to school. Tara's mother says that Tara left 4 minutes ago. Ingrid leaves Tara's house, running to catch up with Tara. The graph below shows the distance each girl is from Tara's house, starting from the time Ingrid leaves Tara's house.

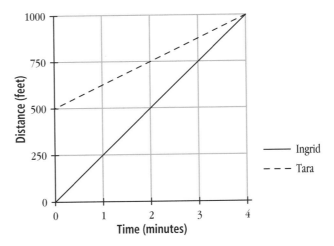

a. In what way is this situation like the race between Henri and Emile? In what way is it different?

b. After how many minutes does Ingrid catch up with Tara?

c. How far from Tara's house does Ingrid catch up with Tara?

d. Each graph intersects the distance axis (the *y*-axis). What information do the points of intersection give about the problem?

e. Which line is steeper? How can you tell from the graph? How is the steepness of each line related to the rate at which the person travels?

f. What do you think the graphs would look like if we extended them to show distance and time after the girls meet?

13. The organizers of the walkathon want to have brochures printed to advertise the event. They get cost estimates from two printing companies. The costs are given by the equations

Company A: $C = 15 + 0.10n$
Company B: $C = 0.25n$

where C is the cost in dollars and n is the number of brochures.

a. Graph both equations on the same set of axes.

b. For what number of brochures is the cost the same for both companies?

c. The organizers have $65 to spend on brochures. How many brochures can they have printed if they use company A? If they use company B? Describe the method you used to get your answers.

d. At what point does each graph intersect the vertical axis? What information does each of these points give?

e. Explain what the numbers 15 and 0.10 represent in the equation for company A.

f. Explain what the number 0.25 represents in the equation for company B.

Connections

14. The 1996 Olympic gold medal winner for the 20-kilometer walk was Jefferson Perez from Ecuador. His time was 1 hour, 20 minutes, 7 seconds. Perez's time was not good enough to beat the Olympic record set in 1988 by Josef Pribilinec from Czechoslovakia. Pribilinec's record for the 20-kilometer walk was 1 hour, 19 minutes, 57 seconds. What was the walking rate of each person?

Josef Pribilinec

15. The longest one-day bike race goes from Bordeaux, France, to Paris, France. The record for this race was set in 1981 by Herman van Springel of Belgium. He finished the 363.1-mile race in 13 hours, 35 minutes, 18 seconds. What was Springel's average speed for the race?

16. The longest human-powered sporting event is the Tour de France cycling race. The record average speed for this race is 24.547 miles per hour, which was obtained by Miguel Indurain of Spain in 1992. If the race is 3569 miles long, how long did it take Indurain to complete the race?

17. In 1990, Beate Anders of East Germany set the women's world record for the 3000-meter walk. She completed the race in 11 minutes, 59.36 seconds.

    a. What was Anders' average walking speed?

    b. In 1991, Kerry Ann Saxby of Australia beat Anders' record. She completed the 3000-meter walk in 11 minutes, 51.26 seconds. How much faster did Saxby walk than Anders?

18. **a.** Generate a table and a graph for $y = 5x - 2$. Look back at the graphs you made in this investigation. How is the graph of this equation different from the other graphs you made?

    b. Generate a table and a graph for $y = {}^-2x + 3$. How is the graph different from the other graphs you made in this investigation?

    c. Generate a table and write an equation for the graph below. How is this graph different from the other graphs you made in this investigation?

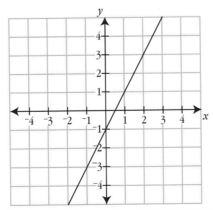

19. The table below shows the amount of orange juice concentrate and water needed to make a given number of batches of juice.

Batches of juice *(b)*	Concentrate *(c)*	Water *(w)*	Juice *(j)*
1	2 cups	3 cups	5 cups
2	4 cups	6 cups	10 cups
3	6 cups	9 cups	15 cups

a. The relationship between the number of batches of juice and the number of cups of concentrate is linear. The equation for this relationship is $c = 2b$. Are there other linear relationships in this table? Make graphs or write equations for the linear relationships you find.

b. A different recipe calls for 3 cups of concentrate and 5 cups of water. Which recipe gives the more "orangey" drink? Explain how you found your answer.

20. The tables below give information about two fruit punch recipes. Each table shows the number of cups of orange juice, pineapple juice, and soda water needed for different quantities of punch. The relationship between cups of orange juice and cups of pineapple juice is linear, and the relationship between cups of orange juice and cups of soda water is linear.

Recipe 1

j	*p*	*s*
1		
2	6	3
3		
4	12	6
5		
6		

Recipe 2

j	*p*	*s*
1		
2		
3	8	6
4		
5		
6	16	12

a. Shannon made recipe 1, using 6 cups of orange juice. How many cups of pineapple juice and how many cups of soda water did she use?

b. Patrick made recipe 2, using 4 cups of orange juice. How many cups of pineapple juice and how many cups of soda water did he use?

Extensions

21. Wind can affect the speed of an airplane. Suppose a plane is making a round-trip from New York City to San Francisco. The plane has a cruising speed of 300 miles per hour. The wind is blowing from west to east at 30 miles per hour. When the plane flies into (in the opposite direction of) the wind, its speed decreases by 30 miles per hour. When the plane flies with (in the same direction as) the wind, its speed increases by 30 miles per hour. The distance between New York City and San Francisco is 3000 miles.

a. Make a table that shows the total time the plane has traveled after each 200-mile interval on its trip from New York City to San Francisco and back.

Distance (miles)	NYC to SF time (hours)	SF to NYC time (hours)
0		
200		
400		
600		
.		
.		
.		

b. On the same set of axes, make graphs of time and distance data for travel in both directions.

c. For each direction, write an equation for the distance, *d*, traveled in *t* hours.

d. How long would it take this plane to fly 5000 miles against a 30-mile-per-hour wind? With a 30-mile-per-hour wind? Explain how you found your answers.

22. The table below shows the population of four cities for the past eight years.

Year	Population Deep Valley	Nowhere	Swampville	Mount Silicon
0 (Start)	1000	1000	1000	1000
1	1500	900	1500	2000
2	2000	800	2500	4000
3	2500	750	3000	8000
4	3000	700	5000	16,000
5	3500	725	3000	32,000
6	4000	900	2500	64,000
7	4500	1500	1500	128,000
8	5000	1700	1000	256,000

a. Describe how the population of each city changed over the eight years.

b. Graph the data for each city. Describe how you selected ranges of values for the horizontal and vertical axes.

c. What are the advantages of each representation?

Mathematical Reflections

In this investigation, you learned how to recognize a linear relationship from a table, and you explored the effect that changing the rate has on the table, graph, and equation of a linear relationship. These questions will help you summarize what you have learned:

1 How can you decide whether a relationship is linear by looking at its table or its equation?

2 In the situations you explored, how did the rate—such as the meters per second a student walks or the dollars per mile a sponsor pledges—show up in the table, the graph, and the equation of a linear relationship?

3 How can you compare the rates for two linear relationships by looking at their graphs? Their tables? Their equations?

4 When might you use a graph to answer a question about a linear relationship? When might you use a table? When might you use an equation?

Think about your answers to these questions, discuss your ideas with other students and your teacher, and then write a summary of your findings in your journal.

INVESTIGATION 3

Exploring Lines with a Graphing Calculator

In the last investigation, you read about the walkathon that Ms. Chang's class is participating in. You considered three possible pledge plans. If *A* represents the dollars owed and *d* represents the number of miles walked, we can express these plans with the equations below.

- Leanne's plan: $A = d$
- Gilberto's plan: $A = 2d$
- Alana's plan: $A = 5 + 0.5d$

In this investigation, you will learn how to use a graphing calculator to help you answer questions like these:

What does Leanne's equation mean?

Using Gilberto's plan, how much will a sponsor owe a student who walks 5 miles?

Using Alana's plan, how far will a student have to walk to earn $17 from each sponsor?

Did you know?

Have you ever seen a walking race? You may have thought the walking style of the racers seemed rather strange. Race walkers must follow two rules:

1. The walker must always have one foot in contact with the ground.

2. The walker's leg must be straight from the time it strikes the ground until it passes under the body.

A champion race walker can cover a mile in about 6.5 minutes. It takes most people 15 to 20 minutes to walk a mile.

3.1 Getting to the Point

To work on this problem, you will need the tables and graphs you made in Problem 2.3.

Problem 3.1

Look at the table and the graph you made for Alana's pledge plan.

A. The point (14, 12) is on the graph of Alana's plan. Write a question you could answer by locating this point.

B. How can you use the equation for Alana's plan to check the answer to the question you wrote in part A?

C. 1. For a sponsor to owe a student $17 under Alana's pledge plan, how many miles would the student have to walk?

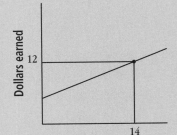

2. Was the graph or the equation more helpful in answering part 1?

■ Problem 3.1 Follow-Up

1. Aretha is trying to answer a question about Alana's pledge plan. She writes $A = 5 + 0.5(28)$. What question is she trying to answer?

2. a. Daniel is trying to answer a question about Alana's pledge plan. He writes $46 = 5 + 0.5d$. What question is he trying to answer?

b. Daniel decides to use a calculator to help him answer the question from part a. He enters Alana's equation as $Y_1 = 5 + 0.5X$ and presses GRAPH. He uses the TRACE key to search for an answer. Help Daniel interpret the information in the window below to determine an answer to his question.

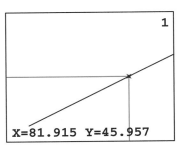

c. Daniel could have answered the question by making a table. Use your calculator to make a table for $Y_1 = 5 + 0.5X$. Copy a section of the table you could use to answer Daniel's question.

3.2 Graphing Lines

A graphing calculator can be helpful for answering questions like those in Problem 3.1 and Problem 3.1 Follow-Up. When you use a graphing calculator, you need to make decisions about the range of values and the scale interval for each axis. These values are called *window settings* because they determine what part of the graph will be displayed in the calculator's window.

Below are two examples of window settings and the corresponding graph windows. For each example, try to make sense of what the ranges and the scale intervals are for the *x*- and *y*-axes.

Window 1

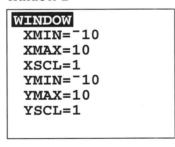
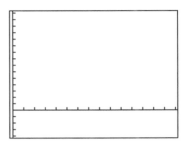

Window 2

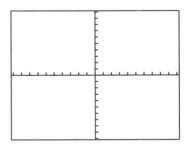

The settings for window 1 use a different range for each axis. The range of *x* values is from 0 to 15, which is a spread of 15 units. The range of *y* values is from ⁻4 to 15, which is a spread of 19 units. The scale interval for both axes is 1, which means that each tick mark represents 1 unit.

Window 2 is the *standard window* on many graphing calculators. These are the settings the calculator uses unless you change them. In this window, both axes have a range from ⁻10 to 10 and a scale interval of 1.

Notice that, in each window, the length of 1 unit (the distance between tick marks) is different on the *x*-axis than it is on the *y*-axis. Can you explain why?

Think about this!

How far would a student have to walk to raise $8.50 from each sponsor under Alana's plan?

Ali and Tamara are using graphing calculators to answer this question. They both enter the equation $Y_1 = 5 + 0.5X$. Ali uses window 1 for his graph, and Tamara uses window 2. Both students use TRACE to find the solution.

Window 1 (Ali's Graph)

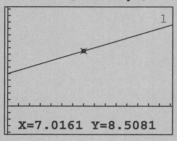

X=7.0161 Y=8.5081

Window 2 (Tamara's Graph)

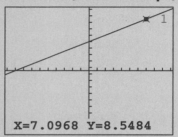

X=7.0968 Y=8.5484

- What does the X value displayed at the bottom of each window mean? What does the Y value mean?

- How could you interpret the information displayed in the windows to answer the question above? How could you check your answer?

You have explored pledge plans suggested by Leanne, Gilberto, and Alana. In this problem, you will explore some plans suggested by other students.

Problem 3.2

In A–D, consider the following suggested pledge plans. In each equation, y is the amount owed in dollars, and x is the number of miles walked.

i. $y = 3x$ **ii.** $y = {}^-2x$ **iii.** $y = 5x - 3$
iv. $y = {}^-x + 6$ **v.** $y = 2$

A. What does each pledge plan mean?

B. Without using your graphing calculator, make a table of x and y values for each pledge plan. Use the x values 1, 2, 3, 4, and 5. Use your tables to help you decide which plans are reasonable. Explain how you made your decisions.

C. Graph each pledge plan with a graphing calculator. Use a window that shows the graph clearly. Make a sketch of the graph you see.

D. For each pledge plan, tell whether the y values increase, decrease, or stay the same as the x values increase. How can you tell from the graph? From the table? From the equation?

■ Problem 3.2 Follow-Up

1. For each of the five pledge plans, give the coordinates of the points where the line crosses the x- and y-axes. (Check that the coordinates you give fit the equation. Sometimes the decimal values your calculator gives are only approximations.)

2. Ali says that $x = {}^-1$ makes the equation ${}^-8 = {}^-3 + 5x$ true. Tamara tries this value in the equation. She says Ali is wrong because ${}^-3 + 5({}^-1)$ is ${}^-2$, not ${}^-8$. Why do you think these students found different answers?

3.3 Finding Solutions

In this problem, you will explore the relationship between a general equation, such as $y = 5 + 0.5x$, and the equation you get by substituting a value for either x or y, such as $8 = 5 + 0.5x$ or $y = 5 + 0.5(3)$. You will continue to work with the pledge plan equations from Problem 3.2.

By now you've probably noticed that values for x and y come in pairs. In the pledge equations, if you know the distance walked, x, you can find the amount a sponsor owes, y. If you know the amount a sponsor owes, y, you can find the distance walked, x. You can express related x and y values as **coordinate pairs** in the form (x, y). For example, the pairs (6, 8) and (3, 6.5) fit Alana's equation. Can you explain what each pair means?

Problem 3.3

In A–D, consider the following equations.

i. $y = 3x$ **ii.** $y = {}^-2x$ **iii.** $y = 5x - 3$
iv. $y = {}^-x + 6$ **v.** $y = 2$

A. 1. Which equation has a graph you can trace to find the value of x that makes $^-8 = 5x - 3$ a true statement?

2. Use your graphing calculator to find the value of x. We call this value the *solution* to the equation $^-8 = 5x - 3$.

B. 1. Which equation has a table you can use to find the value of x that makes $6.8 = {}^-2x$ a true statement?

2. Make a table with your graphing calculator, and find the value of x. Copy the part of the table you used to find the solution.

C. Find solutions for the equations $^-8 = 5x - 3$ and $6.8 = {}^-2x$ by reasoning about what the equations mean rather than by using graphs or tables. Explain how you found the solutions.

D. 1. How does finding the solution to $^-8 = 5x - 3$ help you find a coordinate pair that fits the equation $y = 5x - 3$?

2. Find three other coordinate pairs that fit the equation $y = 5x - 3$. How can you prove your coordinate pairs fit the equation?

■ **Problem 3.3 Follow-Up**

1. Are the points for the coordinate pairs you found for $y = 5x - 3$ on the graph of $y = 5x - 3$? Explain your answer.

2. In part B of Problem 3.3, you found the solution to the equation $6.8 = {}^-2x$. Based on the solution, what coordinate pair do you know must fit the equation $y = {}^-2x$? How is this coordinate pair related to the graph of $y = {}^-2x$?

3. a. By substituting values for y, write three equations that are related to the equation $y = {}^-3x + 6$.

b. Solve each of your equations from part a. Explain how you found each solution.

c. Use the solutions from part b to find the coordinates of three points on the graph of $y = {}^-3x + 6$.

d. Use your graphing calculator to check your answers to part c. Explain how you know your answers are correct.

3.4 Planning a Skating Party

You have studied lots of linear equations. Here are some examples:

$$y = x \qquad y = 2x \qquad y = 5 + 0.5x \qquad y = 45 + x \qquad y = {}^-3x + 6$$

All the linear equations you have studied can be written in the form $y = mx + b$. For the equation $y = x$, m is 1 and b is 0. For $y = 2x$, m is 2 and b is 0. For $y = 5 + 0.5x$, m is 0.5 and b is 5. What are the values of m and b for $y = 45 + x$ and $y = {}^-3x + 6$?

When we substitute 0 for x in $y = mx + b$, we get $y = b$. This means that the point $(0, b)$ lies on the line. The point $(0, b)$ is called the **y-intercept.** It is the point where the line crosses the y-axis. To save time, we sometimes refer to the number b, rather than the point $(0, b)$, as the y-intercept. You found y-intercepts for some equations in Problem 3.2 Follow-Up.

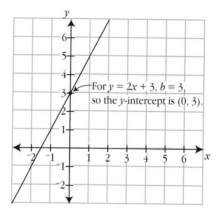

For $y = 2x + 3$, $b = 3$, so the y-intercept is $(0, 3)$.

If the b in $y = mx + b$ is 0 (in other words, if the equation is of the form $y = mx$) then the y-intercept is $(0, 0)$, or the **origin**. For example, the graphs of Leanne's pledge plan $y = x$ and Gilberto's pledge plan $y = 2x$ both pass through the origin.

The m in $y = mx + b$ is called the **coefficient** of x. In Investigation 2, you found that the value of m indicates the steepness of the line. For example, when you graphed equations for students' walking rates, you found that the graph of $y = 2x$ was steeper than the graph of $y = x$ but less steep than the graph of $y = 2.5x$. You also discovered that the sign of m—that is, whether m is positive or negative—determines whether a line slants upward or downward.

In the last problem, you used a graphing calculator to find specific points on the graphs of linear equations. In this problem, you will use a graphing calculator to find the point where two graphs cross. This point is called the **point of intersection** of the graphs.

Problem 3.4

Suppose your class is planning a skating party to celebrate the end of the school year. Your committee is in charge of finding a place to rent in-line skates for a reasonable price. You get quotes from two companies:

Roll-Away Skates charges $5 per person.
Wheelie's Skates and Stuff charges $100 plus $3 per person.

Which company should you choose if you want to keep the cost to a minimum? Explain how you made your choice.

■ Problem 3.4 Follow-Up

In these problems, let y be the total cost to rent the skates and x be the number of people attending the party.

1. a. For each company, write an equation for the relationship between the number of people and the cost.
   b. In the same window, graph the equations for both companies.
   c. What range of values did you use for the number of people? For the rental cost? How did you select these ranges?
2. a. On which graph is the point (8, 40)? What does this point mean in terms of the cost to rent skates?
   b. On which graph is the point (8, 124)? What does this point mean in terms of the cost to rent skates?
   c. Find the point of intersection of the two graphs. What does this point mean in terms of the cost to rent skates?

3. If you write a linear equation in the form $y = mx + b$, the y-intercept is $(0, b)$.
   a. Find the y-intercepts for the equations you graphed in question 1.
   b. What do the y-intercepts mean in terms of the cost to rent skates?
   c. How do the y-intercepts appear on the graphs?
   d. Display the table for the equations. How do the y-intercepts appear in the table?
4. What are the coefficients of x in the equations you graphed in question 1? What do these coefficients mean in terms of the cost to rent skates? What effect do the coefficients have on the graphs?
5. Which company would you choose if 100 students are planning to attend the party? Why?
6. If your budget for skate rental is $250, how many pairs of skates can you rent from each company?

As you work on these ACE questions, use your calculator whenever you need it.

Applications

In 1–4, do parts a–e.

1. $y = 1.5x$ **2.** $y = {}^-3x + 10$ **3.** $y = {}^-2x + 6$ **4.** $y = 2x + 5$

  a.   Graph the equation on your calculator, and make a sketch of the line you see.

  b.   Give the ranges of values you used for the x- and y-axes.

  c.   Do the y values increase, decrease, or stay the same as the x values increase?

  d.   Give the y-intercept.

  e.   List the coordinates of three points on the line.

5.   The school band decides to sell chocolate bars to raise money for an upcoming trip. The cost and the revenue (total sales, or income) of selling the candy bars are represented on the graph below.

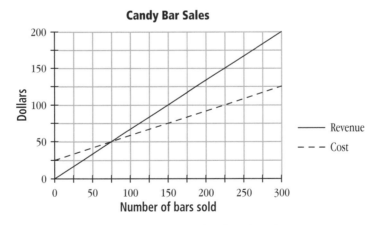

Candy Bar Sales

  a.   How many candy bars must the band sell to break even?

  b.   What would be the revenue from selling 50 candy bars? 125 candy bars?

  c.   How many candy bars must the band sell for the revenue to be $200? How much of this revenue would be profit?

6. a. At the left below, the graphs from question 5 are shown in a calculator's graph window. The window settings are shown at the right. Copy the graph window, and use the window settings to label the axes to show where the scale values 50, 100, 150, and so on are located.

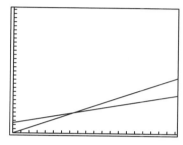

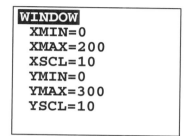

```
WINDOW
 XMIN=0
 XMAX=200
 XSCL=10
 YMIN=0
 YMAX=300
 YSCL=10
```

b. Below are the same two graphs shown in a different graph window. Copy the graph window, and use the window settings to label the tick marks.

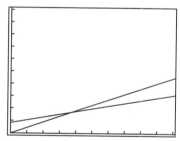

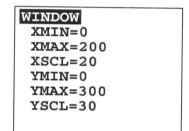

```
WINDOW
 XMIN=0
 XMAX=200
 XSCL=20
 YMIN=0
 YMAX=300
 YSCL=30
```

7. In a–c, use the equation $y = 2x + 10$.

a. By making a graph on your calculator, find the value of y when $x = 15$.

b. By making a graph on your calculator, find the value of x when $y = 35$.

c. Make a sketch of the graph of $y = 2x + 10$, and label the points that represent the pairs of values you found in parts a and b.

8. In a–c, use the equation $y = {}^-3.5x - 9$.

a. By making a graph on your calculator, find the value of y when $x = 5$.

b. By making a graph on your calculator, find the value of x when $y = {}^-40$.

c. Make a sketch of the graph of $y = {}^-3.5x - 9$, and label the points that represent the pairs of values you found in parts a and b.

In 9–12, do parts a–c.

9. $y = 5x + 24$ and $y = {}^-3x - 8$

10. $y = {}^-2.5x + 15$ and $y = x - 10$

11. $y = x + 10$ and $y = 8 - 2x$

12. $y = 6$ and $y = 4 + 2x$

a. With your graphing calculator, graph both equations in the same window. Use window settings that allow you to see the point where the two graphs intersect. What ranges of x and y values did you use for your window?

b. Find the point of intersection for the graphs.

c. Test the point of intersection you found by substituting its coordinates into the equations. Do the coordinates fit the equations exactly? Explain why or why not.

13. In Problem 2.4, Emile gave Henri a head start of 45 meters. Now suppose Emile does not give his brother a head start.

a. Write a new equation for the distance Henri is from the starting line after a given number of seconds. Describe the graph of this new equation.

b. How do this new graph and equation compare with the original graph and equation?

c. What effect did Henri's head start have on the original graph? On the original equation?

14. For Valentine's Day, students at Holmes Middle School will sell roses to raise money for a school party. The students can buy the roses from a wholesaler for 50¢ each. In addition to buying the roses, they need to spend $60 for ribbon and paper to wrap the flowers and for materials to advertise the sale. They will sell each flower for $1.30. They will take orders in advance so that they know how many roses they will need.

a. How many roses must the students sell to break even?

b. How much profit will the students earn if they sell 50 roses? 100 roses? 200 roses?

15. A new movie theater opened in Lani's neighborhood. The theater offers a yearly membership for which customers pay a fee of $50, after which they pay only $1 per movie. Nonmembers pay $4.50 per movie. Lani is trying to figure out whether to buy a membership. She writes these cost equations.

$$C_M = 50 + n \qquad \text{and} \qquad C_N = 4.5n$$

where n is the number of movies seen in one year, C_M is the yearly cost in dollars for a member, and C_N is the yearly cost in dollars for a nonmember.

a. If Lani sees ten movies this year, what would be her cost under each plan?

b. How many movies must Lani see this year to make the yearly membership a better deal?

c. What does the y-intercept in each equation tell you about this situation?

d. What does the coefficient of n in each equation tell you about this situation?

In 16 and 17, use the following information: You are on the committee to select a DJ for a school party. The committee has obtained price quotes from three DJs:

Tom's Tunes charges $60 an hour.
Solidus' Sounds charges $100 plus $40 an hour.
Light Plastic charges $175 plus $30 an hour.

16. a. Which DJ would you choose? What variables might affect your decision?

b. For each DJ, write an equation you could use to calculate the total cost from the number of hours worked. Let y be the total cost and x be the number of hours worked.

c. Graph all three equations in the same window of your calculator. Make a sketch of the graphs you see.

d. What information does the coefficient of x represent in each equation?

e. What information does the y-intercept represent in each equation?

17. Use your calculator to answer a–c.

    a. For what number of hours are the costs for Tom's Tunes and Solidus' Sounds equal? What is the cost for that time?

    b. What would be the cost for each DJ if he or she worked $8\frac{1}{2}$ hours?

    c. You have $450 to spend on a DJ. How many hours could each DJ work for this price?

Connections

In 18–21, tell what values of x make y negative.

18. $y = {}^{-}2x - 5$ **19.** $y = {}^{-}5$ **20.** $y = 2x - 5$ **21.** $y = \frac{3}{2}x - \frac{1}{4}$

22. In a–c, explain how you could use the display shown to find the solution to $22 = 100 - 3x$.

    a.

X	Y₁
21	37
22	34
23	31
24	28
25	25
26	22

$Y_1 = 100 - 3X$

    b.

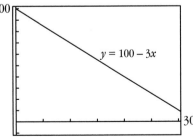

$y = 100 - 3x$

c.

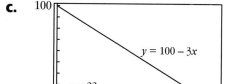

23. In a and b, explain how you could use the display shown to find the solution to $100 - 3x = 2x - 50$.

a.

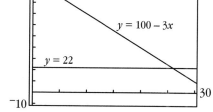

X	Y₁	Y₂
25	25	0
26	22	2
27	19	4
28	16	6
29	13	8
30	10	10

$Y_2 \equiv 2X-50$

b.

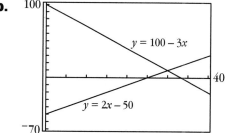

In 24–26, tell whether or not the equation represents a linear relationship, and explain your answer.

24. $y = 2x$　　　　**25.** $y = \dfrac{2}{x}$　　　　**26.** $y = x^2$

Extensions

27. a. On grid paper, graph each pair of lines below on the same set of axes. Use the same scale for the *x*- and *y*-axes for each pair. When you are finished, look at the graphs for all four pairs of equations. What patterns do you observe? Use what you know about the influence of *m* and *b* on the graph of $y = mx + b$ to explain why these patterns might occur.

i. $y = 1.2x + 3$ and $y = 1.2x$ **ii.** $y = 4$ and $y = {}^-2$

iii. $y = x - 19$ and $y = 4 + x$ **iv.** $y = {}^-3.6x$ and $y = 5 - 3.6x$

b. On grid paper, graph each pair of lines below on the same set of axes. Use the same scale for the *x*- and *y*-axes. When you are finished, look at the graphs for all four pairs of equations. What patterns do you observe? Compare the coefficients of *x* in each pair, and describe any relationships you see.

i. $y = 2x + 1$ and $y = -\frac{1}{2}x - 2$ **ii.** $y = x - 3$ and $y = {}^-x$

iii. $y = x$ and $y = {}^-x$ **iv.** $y = \frac{5}{4}x$ and $y = -\frac{4}{5}x + 4$

c. Graph the equations from part b on your graphing calculator, using the same scales you used in your hand-drawn graphs. Explain any differences you see between the hand-drawn graphs and the calculator graphs.

d. Use your observations from parts a and b to predict the relationship between the graphs of the pairs of equations below. Check your predictions by graphing the equations.

i. $y = 4x$ and $y = -\frac{1}{4}x$ **ii.** $y = x + 2$ and $y = {}^-x + 5$

iii. $y = 0.5x + 2$ and $y = 0.5x - 2$ **iv.** $y = 2x + 1$ and $y = 2x$

28. For a given latitude and longitude, the temperature decreases as the altitude increases. The formula for calculating the temperature, T, at a given altitude is

$$T = t - \frac{d}{150}$$

where t is the ground temperature in degrees Celsius and d is the altitude in meters.

   a. If the ground temperature is 0°C, what is the temperature at an altitude of 1500 meters?

   b. If the temperature at an altitude of 300 meters is 26°C, what is the ground temperature?

29. **a.** Which one of the following points is on the line $y = 3x - 7$?

      (3, 3)   (3, 2)   (3, 1)   (3, 0)

      Describe where each of the other three points is in relationship to the line.

   b. Find another point on the line $y = 3x - 7$ and three more points above the line.

   c. The equation $y = 3x - 7$ is true for (4, 5) and (7, 14). Find two points for which the inequality $y < 3x - 7$ is true and two points for which the inequality $y > 3x - 7$ is true.

Mathematical Reflections

In this investigation, you learned how to use tables and graphs to solve problems about linear relationships, and you discovered how a point in a table or on a graph relates to the corresponding equation. You also learned how to find the *y*-intercept of a relationship from a table, graph, or equation. These questions will help you summarize what you have learned:

1. What are some of the advantages and disadvantages of using a graphing calculator to answer questions about linear situations?

2. Explain how to find the *y*-intercept of a linear relationship from a table, from a graph, and from an equation.

3. In Investigation 2, you explored the effect that the rate has on the graph of a linear relationship. In this investigation, you looked at the meaning of particular points on the graph, including the *y*-intercept. Summarize what you know about the graph of a linear equation of the form $y = mx + b$.

4. To check whether a given point fits a linear relationship, you can make a table, trace a graph, or substitute the coordinates into an equation. When you substitute values into an equation, you need to be careful about the order in which you do the calculations. Check whether the point (−2, 13) is on the line $y = 5 - 4x$ by substituting the coordinates into the equation. Show and explain each step you take so that it is easy to see the order in which you did your calculations.

Think about your answers to these questions, discuss your ideas with other students and your teacher, and then write a summary of your findings in your journal.

Solving Equations

In previous investigations, you answered questions about linear relationships by using graphs and tables and by reasoning about the numbers involved. In this investigation, you will learn how to answer such questions by writing and solving linear equations.

4.1 Paying in Installments

The Unlimited Store allows any customer who buys merchandise costing over $30 to pay on an installment plan. The customer pays $30 down and then pays $15 a month until the item is paid for.

Problem 4.1

Suppose you buy a $195 CD-ROM drive from the Unlimited Store on an installment plan. How many months will it take you to pay for the drive? Describe how you found your answer.

■ Problem 4.1 Follow-Up

1. Write down the sequence of steps you used to find the solution to Problem 4.1. Try to use mathematical symbols and not just words to describe your steps.

2. Make up a problem similar to Problem 4.1, and solve it using your method from question 1.

4.2 Using the Symbolic Method

The students in your class may have found several ways to solve Problem 4.1. Some may have used a table or a graph. Others may have found a way to reason about the quantities in the problem. For example, in Ms. Winslow's class, one student reasoned as follows:

"If I pay $30 down, I will have $195 – $30, or $165, left to pay. If I pay $15 a month, then it will take me $165 ÷ 15 = 11, months to pay for the drive."

You can also solve Problem 4.1 by writing and solving an equation. To write an equation, you could reason as follows:

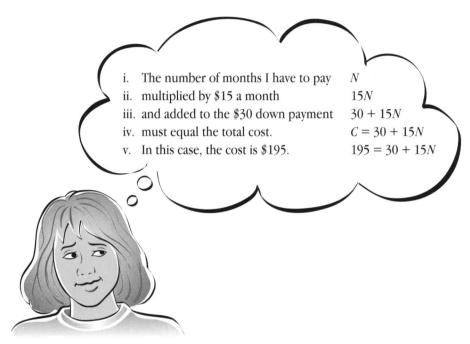

i. The number of months I have to pay	N
ii. multiplied by $15 a month	$15N$
iii. and added to the $30 down payment	$30 + 15N$
iv. must equal the total cost.	$C = 30 + 15N$
v. In this case, the cost is $195.	$195 = 30 + 15N$

To find the number of months you must pay, you need to find the value of N that makes the equation $195 = 30 + 15N$ a true statement. This is called *solving the equation* for the variable N.

From your work in the last investigation, you know you can solve $195 = 30 + 15N$ by making a table or a graph of the general equation $C = 30 + 15N$. Now you will learn to solve $195 = 30 + 15N$ by *operating on the symbols* in the equation.

Thinking	Manipulating the Symbols
	$195 = 30 + 15N$
"I want to buy a CD-ROM drive that costs $195. To pay for the drive on the installment plan, I must pay $30 down and $15 a month."	$195 = 30 + 15N$
"After I pay the $30 down payment, I can subtract this from the cost. To keep the sides of the equation equal, I must subtract 30 from both sides."	$195 - 30 = 30 - 30 + 15N$
"I now owe $165, which I will pay in monthly installments of $15."	$165 = 15N$
"I need to separate $165 into payments of $15. This means I need to divide it by 15. To keep the sides of the equation equal, I must divide both sides by 15."	$\frac{165}{15} = \frac{15N}{15}$
"There are 11 groups of $15 in $165, so it will take 11 months."	$11 = N$

After you solve an equation, you should always check your solution by substituting it back into the original equation. Here are the steps you would follow to check the solution to the equation above.

$$195 = 30 + 15N$$
$$195 = 30 + 15(11)$$
$$195 = 30 + 165$$
$$195 = 195$$

Review the table above. The strategy we used to solve the equation was to *undo*, or *reverse*, the operations until the variable was alone on one side of the equation. Notice that we applied each reverse operation to *both* sides of the equation. We will refer to this strategy for solving an equation as the *symbolic method*.

Problem 4.2

Karen wants to buy a stove from the Unlimited Store on an installment plan. The stove costs $305.

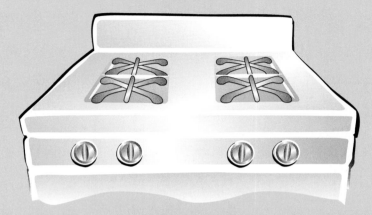

A. Write an equation you could solve to find the number of months it will take Karen to pay for the stove.

B. Solve your equation by using the symbolic method. How many months will it take Karen to pay for the stove?

■ Problem 4.2 Follow-Up

1. In a–d, use the symbolic method to solve the equation for x. Check your answers.
   a. $y = 2.5x$ when $y = 175$
   b. $y = 19 + 3x$ when $y = 64$
   c. $y = 2x - 50$ when $y = 15$
   d. $y = {}^-2x + 14$ when $y = 60$

2. What other methods could you use to solve for x in the equations in question 1?

4.3 Analyzing Bones

Forensic scientists can estimate a person's height by measuring the length of certain bones, including the femur, the tibia, the humerus, and the radius.

The table below gives equations for the relationships between the length of each bone and the height for males and females. These relationships were found by scientists after much study and data collection. In the table, F represents the length of the femur, T the length of the tibia, H the length of the humerus, R the length of the radius, and h the person's height. All measurements are in centimeters.

Bone	Male	Female
Femur	$h = 69.089 + 2.238F$	$h = 61.412 + 2.317F$
Tibia	$h = 81.688 + 2.392T$	$h = 72.572 + 2.533T$
Humerus	$h = 73.570 + 2.970H$	$h = 64.977 + 3.144H$
Radius	$h = 80.405 + 3.650R$	$h = 73.502 + 3.876R$

Source: George Knill. "Mathematics in Forensic Science." *Mathematics Teacher* (February 1981): 31–32.

Problem 4.3

Use the equations on page 57 to answer parts A–D.

A. How tall is a female if her femur is 46.2 centimeters long?

B. How tall is a male if his tibia is 50.1 centimeters long?

C. If a woman is 152 centimeters (about 5 feet) tall, how long is her femur? Her tibia? Her humerus? Her radius?

D. If a man is 183 centimeters (about 6 feet) tall, how long is his femur? His tibia? His humerus? His radius?

■ Problem 4.3 Follow-Up

For one of the bones discussed above, graph the equations for males and females on the same set of axes. What do the x- and y-intercepts represent in terms of this problem? Does this make sense? Why?

Did you know?

Forensic scientists use scientific methods to solve crimes. Today, fingerprints and DNA evidence are used to identify criminals, but early forensic scientists used methods based on body measurements. Beginning in 1879, the Bertillon system—developed by the French criminologist Dr. Alphonse Bertillon—was used to identify criminals and suspects. The Bertillon system involves measuring characteristics that do not change as a person ages. The system first classifies a person as having a short, medium, or long head. Similar divisions are then made based on the length of the middle finger, the length of the forearm, the length of the little finger, and height. Final subdivisions are made according to eye color and ear length. Many criminals underwent surgical procedures to escape their Bertillon classifications.

As you work on these ACE questions, use your calculator whenever you need it.

Applications

1. Find x if $326 = 4x$.

2. Find p if $93 = 16 - 5p$.

3. Find n if $321.5 = 16n - 25.5$.

In 4–6, do parts a and b by using the symbolic method and by using a graphing calculator.

4. $y = x - 15$
   a. Find y if $x = 9.4$.   **b.** Find x if $y = 29$.

5. $y = 10 - 2.5x$
   a. Find y if $x = 3.2$.   **b.** Find x if $y = 85$.

6. $y = 5x - 15$
   a. Find y if $x = 1$.   **b.** Find x if $y = 50$.

7. In questions 4–6, you solved linear equations by using the symbolic method and by using a graphing calculator. Compare these two methods. Which do you prefer? Why?

8. Below is a student's solution to the equation $58.5 = 3.5x - 6$. The student made an error. Find the error, and give the correct solution.

$$58.5 = 3.5x - 6$$
$$58.5 - 6 = 3.5x$$
$$52.5 = 3.5x$$
$$\frac{52.5}{3.5} = x$$
$$\text{so } 15 = x$$

9. The number of times a cricket chirps in a minute is a function of the temperature. You can use the formula

$$n = 4t - 160$$

to determine the number of chirps, n, a cricket makes in a minute when the temperature is t degrees Fahrenheit. If you want to estimate the temperature by counting cricket chirps, it is easier to use the following form of the equation:

$$t = \tfrac{1}{4}n + 40$$

a. At 60°F, how many times does a cricket chirp in a minute?

b. What is the temperature if a cricket chirps 150 times in a minute?

c. At what temperature does a cricket stop chirping?

d. Sketch a graph of the equation with number of chirps on the x-axis and temperature on the y-axis. What information does the y-intercept give you?

10. At Fabulous Fabian's Bakery, the cost, C, and revenue, R, to make and sell N cakes per month are given by the equations below.

$$C = 800 + 3.20N \qquad \text{and} \qquad R = 8.50N$$

a. Fabian sold 100 cakes in January. What were his cost and his revenue? Did he make a profit?

b. In April, Fabian's revenue was $1105. How many cakes did he sell?

c. What was the cost of producing the number of cakes from part b?

d. What is the break-even point between cost and revenue?

e. In each equation, what information do the y-intercept and the coefficient of N give you?

11. In a and b, find the mystery number, and explain your reasoning.

    a. If you add 15 to 3 times this mystery number, you get 78. What is the mystery number?

    b. If you subtract 27 from 5 times this mystery number, you get 83. What is the mystery number?

    c. Make up clues for a riddle whose answer is 9.

Connections

12. When a person reaches the age of 30, his or her height starts decreasing by approximately 0.06 centimeter per year.

    a. If a basketball player is 6 feet, 6 inches tall on his thirtieth birthday, about how tall will he be at age 80? (Remember, 1 inch ≈ 2.5 centimeters.)

    b. Myron's 80-year-old grandmother is 160 centimeters tall. About how tall was she at age 30?

13. World Connections long-distance phone company charges $50 a month plus 10¢ a minute for each call.

    a. Write an equation for the total monthly cost, C, for m minutes of long-distance calls.

    b. A customer made $10\frac{1}{2}$ hours of long-distance calls in a month. How much was his bill for that month?

    c. A customer received a $75 long-distance bill for last month's calls. How many minutes of long-distance calls did she make?

    d. The International Links long-distance phone company has no monthly fee and charges 18¢ a minute for long-distance calls. Compare the World Connections long-distance plan to the International Links plan. Under what circumstances is it cheaper to use International Links?

14. Give the formulas for finding the circumference and the area of a circle if you know its radius. Tell whether each equation represents a linear relationship.

15. **a.** Write an equation for the distance covered by a car traveling 50 miles per hour for a given number of hours.

b. Write an equation for the time it takes to go 20 miles at a given rate of speed.

c. Is either of the equations in parts a and b linear?

Extensions

16. The Small World long-distance phone company charges 55¢ for the first minute of a long-distance call and 23¢ for each additional minute.

a. How much would a 10-minute long-distance call cost?

b. If a call costs $4.55, how long did the call last?

c. Write an equation for the total cost, C, of an m-minute long-distance call.

17. The maximum weight allowed in an elevator is 1500 pounds.

a. If ten children are in the elevator, how many adults can get in? Assume the average weight per adult is 150 pounds and the average weight per child is 40 pounds.

b. If six adults are in the elevator, how many children can get in?

c. Write an equation for the number of adults, A, and the number of children, C, the elevator can hold.

Mathematical Reflections

In this investigation, you learned how to solve equations by operating on the symbols. These questions will help you summarize what you have learned:

1 Describe the symbolic method for solving an equation of the form $y = mx + b$ for the variable x when you know the value of y. Use an example to illustrate the method.

2 Describe how you would use a graphing calculator to solve a linear equation of the form $y = mx + b$ for the variable x when you know the value of y. Use an example to illustrate the process.

Think about your answers to these questions, discuss your ideas with other students and your teacher, and then write a summary of your findings in your journal.

Exploring Slope

All the linear situations you have explored in this unit involve rates. For example, you worked with walking rates expressed as meters per second and pledge rates expressed as dollars per mile. In these situations, you found that the rate affects the following things:

- the steepness of the graph
- the coefficient, *m*, of *x* in the equation $y = mx + b$
- the amount the *y* values in the table change for each unit change in the *x* values

All of these things are related to the *slope* of the line. In this investigation, you will learn what the slope of a line is, and you will discover how you can determine the slope from the graph, equation, or table of values for a linear relationship.

5.1 Climbing Stairs

Climbing stairs is good exercise. Some athletes run up and down stairs as part of their training. The steepness of stairs determines how difficult they are to climb. Stairs that are very steep are more difficult to climb than stairs that rise gradually. Examining the steepness of stairs can help you understand the idea of steepness, or slope, of a line.

Think about this!

Consider the following questions about the stairs you encounter at home, in your school, and in other buildings:

- How can you describe the steepness of the stairs?

- Is the steepness the same between any two consecutive steps for a particular set of stairs?

The steepness of stairs is determined by the ratio of the **rise** to the **run** for each step. The rise and run are labeled in the diagram below.

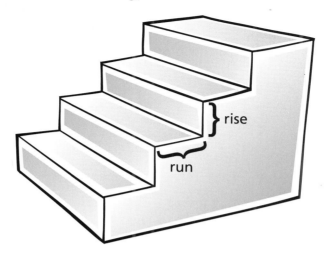

Carpenters have developed guidelines to ensure the stairs they build are relatively easy for a person to climb. In some states, carpenters work with these guidelines:

- The ratio of rise to run for each step should be between 0.45 and 0.60.
- The rise plus the run for each step should be between 17 and 17.5 inches.

Problem 5.1

Determine the steepness of a set of stairs.

To calculate the steepness you will need to measure the rise and the run of a step. Measure at least two steps in the set of stairs you choose. Make a sketch of the stairs, and label it with the measurements you found.

How do the stairs you measured compare with the guidelines above?

1. Make and label a scale drawing of stairs that don't meet the carpenters' guidelines. Explain why the stairs you drew are steeper (or less steep) than the stairs described in the guidelines.

2. You can use the ideas about the steepness of stairs to find the steepness of a ramp.

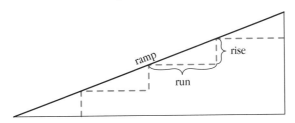

In one state, the construction code for an access ramp is a rise of 1 foot for a run of 12 feet. The access ramp at a football stadium in this state has a rise of 1 foot for a run of 8 feet. Many people in wheelchairs cannot get their chairs up the ramp without help. Make scale drawings of the stadium ramp and a ramp meeting the state code.

5.2 Finding the Slope of a Line

The method for finding the steepness of stairs suggests a way to find the steepness of a line. A line drawn from the bottom step to the top step of a set of stairs will touch each step in one point. The rise and the run of a step are the vertical and the horizontal changes, respectively, between two points on the line.

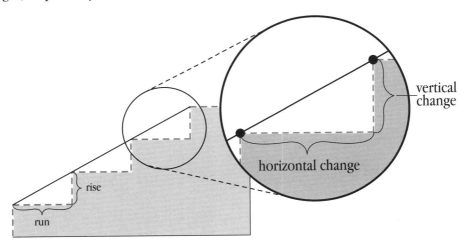

If you choose two points on a line, you can draw a "step" from one point to the other.

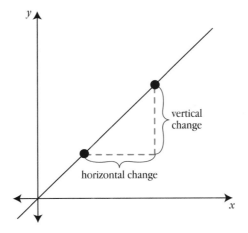

The steepness of the line is the ratio of rise to run, or vertical change to horizontal change, for this step. We call the steepness of a line its **slope.**

$$\text{slope} = \frac{\text{vertical change}}{\text{horizontal change}}$$

Unlike the steepness of stairs, the slope of a line can be negative. To determine the slope of a line, you need to consider the direction, or sign, of the vertical and horizontal change from one point to another. If one of these changes is negative, the slope will be negative. Lines that slant *upward* from left to right have *positive slope;* lines that slant *downward* from left to right have *negative slope.*

Line with Positive Slope

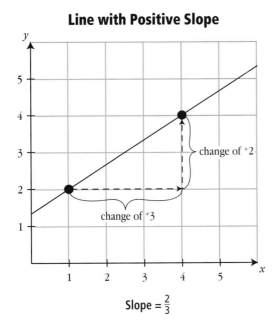

Slope $= \frac{2}{3}$

Line with Negative Slope

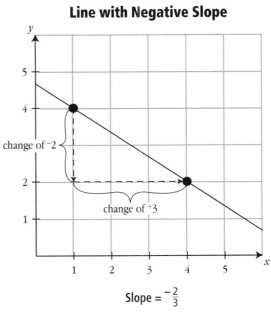

Slope $= \frac{-2}{3}$

Problem 5.2

Do parts A–D for each equation below.

i. $y = 2x$ **ii.** $y = {}^-3x$ **iii.** $y = 5 + 2x$
iv. $y = \frac{1}{2}x + 2$ **v.** $y = 2 - 3x$

A. Make a table of x and y values for the equation. Use the x values $^-3$, $^-2$, $^-1$, 0, 1, 2, 3, and 4.

B. On grid paper, make a graph of the equation.

C. Choose two points on the line, and compute the ratio of the vertical change to the horizontal change from one point to the other. Would you get the same ratio if you had chosen two different points? Choose two different points, and check your answer.

D. The ratio you computed in part C is the slope of the line. How is the slope of the line related to the table of values for the line? How is it related to the equation for the line?

■ **Problem 5.2 Follow-Up**

Use the ideas you have learned about slope and about vertical and horizontal change to explain why the line for $y = 3x$ is steeper than the line for $y = x$.

5.3 Connecting Points

For any two points, there is exactly one straight line that can be drawn through both points. In this problem, you will be given the coordinates of two points. Your task will be to find information about the line through these points—including its slope, its y-intercept, and the coordinates of other points that lie on the line.

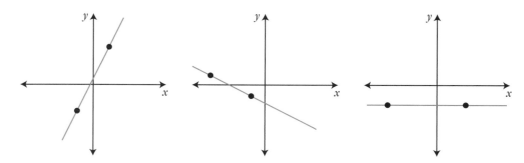

Problem 5.3

Do parts A–E for each pair of points below.

i. (2, 6) and (0, 4)   **ii.** (2, 3) and (4, 6)   **iii.** (0, 3) and (1, 4)
iv. (⁻1, 3) and (1, 0)   **v.** (1, 4) and (3, 4)   **vi.** (4, 1) and (⁻4, 2)

A. Plot the points on a coordinate grid, and draw the line that passes through them.

B. Do the y values for points on the line increase, decrease, or stay the same as the x values increase?

C. Find the slope of the line.

D. Mark and label at least three other points on the line, and record the x and y values for the points in an organized table. Does the pattern in your table confirm the slope you found in part B?

E. Use the graph or the table to find the y-intercept of the line.

Problem 5.3 Follow-Up

1. How can you use the slope of a line to determine whether the line slants upward from left to right, slants downward from left to right, or is horizontal?

2. The table below represents a linear relationship. Copy the table, and use the pattern to fill in the missing entries. Find the slope and the y-intercept of the graph of this relationship. Explain how you found your answers.

x	?	⁻6	⁻5	⁻4	⁻3	⁻2	⁻1	?	?
y	?	⁻10	⁻7	⁻4	⁻1	2	5	?	?

3. Confirm that the table below represents a linear relationship. What is the slope of the graph of this relationship?

x	46	47.1	48.1	49	50.1
y	31.5	34.14	36.54	38.7	41.34

As you work on these ACE questions, use your calculator whenever you need it.

Applications

In 1–4, find the slope and the y-intercept of the line represented by the equation.

1. $y = 10 + 3x$

2. $y = 0.5x$

3. $y = {}^-3x$

4. $y = {}^-5x + 2$

In 5–9, the table represents a linear relationship.

- Give the slope and the y-intercept of the graph of the relationship.
- Determine which of the following equations fits the relationship:

$y = 5 - 2x \quad y = 2x \quad y = {}^-3x - 2 \quad y = 2x - 1 \quad y = x + 3.5$

5.

x	0	1	2	3	4
y	0	2	4	6	8

6.

x	0	1	2	3	4
y	3.5	4.5	5.5	6.5	7.5

7.

x	0	1	2	3	4
y	$^-1$	1	3	5	7

8.

x	0	1	2	3	4
y	5	3	1	$^-1$	$^-3$

9.

x	1	2	3	4	5
y	$^-5$	$^-8$	$^-11$	$^-14$	$^-17$

In 10–13, find the slope of the line, and write an equation for the line.

10.

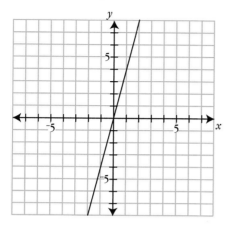

11.

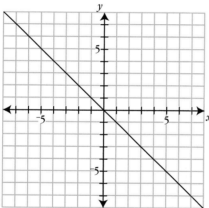

12.

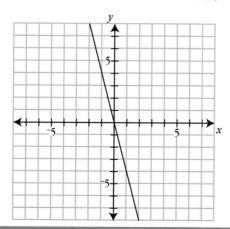

13.

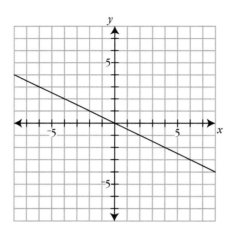

In 14–17, do parts a–d.

14. (0, 0) and (3, 3)   **15.** (⁻1, 1) and (3, ⁻3)

16. (0, ⁻5) and (⁻2, ⁻3)   **17.** (3, 6) and (5, 6)

    a. Plot the points on a coordinate grid, and draw a line through them.

    b. Find the slope of the line.

    c. Estimate the y-intercept from the graph.

    d. Use your answers from parts b and c to write an equation for the line.

In 18–20, do parts a–c.

18. $y = x$ **19.** $y = 2x + {}^-2$ **20.** $y = {}^-0.5x + 2$

    a. Make a table of x and y values for the equation.

    b. Make a graph of the equation.

    c. Find the slope of the graph.

In 21–23, determine which linear relationships in a–j fit the description.

21. The line for this relationship has positive slope.

22. The line for this relationship has a slope of ⁻2.

23. The line for this relationship has a slope of 0.

a.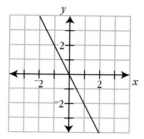

b.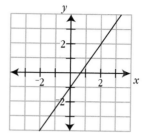

c.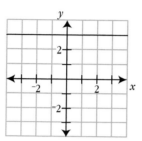

d.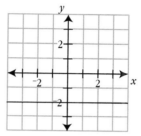

e.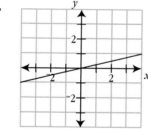

f.

x	$^-3$	$^-2$	$^-1$	0
y	7	5	3	1

g.

x	$^-4$	$^-2$	$^-1$	0
y	2	2	2	2

h. $y = 1.5$ **i.** $y = {}^-5 + 3x$ **j.** $y = 4 + {}^-2x$

24. a. Find the slope of the line represented by the equation $y = x - 1$.

    b. Make a table of x and y values for the equation $y = x - 1$. How is the slope related to the table entries?

25. **a.** Find the slope of the line represented by the equation $y = {}^-2x + 3$.

b. Make a table of x and y values for the equation $y = {}^-2x + 3$. How is the slope related to the table entries?

26. At noon, the temperature was 12°F. For the next 24 hours, the temperature fell by an average of 3°F an hour.

a. Write an equation for the temperature, T, n hours after noon.

b. What is the y-intercept of the line the equation represents? What does the y-intercept tell you about this situation?

c. What is the slope of the line the equation represents? What does the slope tell you about this situation?

27. Natasha never manages to make her allowance last for a whole week, so she borrows money from her sister. Suppose Natasha borrows 50 cents every week.

a. Write an equation for the amount of money, m, Natasha owes her sister after n weeks.

b. What is the slope of the graph of the equation from part a?

Connections

28. In Europe, many hills have signs indicating their steepness, or slope. Here are some examples:

 This means for each 4 meters in run the hill rises by 1 meter.

 This means for each 15 meters in run the hill falls by 1 meter.

On a coordinate grid, sketch hills with the above slopes.

29. In 1980, the town of Rio Rancho, located on a mesa outside Santa Fe, New Mexico, was destined for obscurity. But as a result of hard work by its city officials, it began adding manufacturing jobs at a fast rate. As a result, the city's population grew 239% from 1980 to 1990, making Rio Rancho the fastest-growing "small city" in the United States. The population of Rio Rancho in 1990 was 37,000.

    a. What was the population of Rio Rancho in 1980?

    b. If the same rate of population increase continues, what will the population be in the year 2000?

30. James and Janna share a veterinary practice. They each make farm visits two days a week. They take cellular phones on these trips to keep in touch with the office. James makes his farm visits on weekdays. His cellular phone rate is $14.95 a month plus $0.50 a minute. Janna makes her visits on Saturday and Sunday and is charged a weekend rate of $29.95 a month plus $0.25 a minute.

    a. Write an equation for each billing plan.

    b. Is it possible for James' cellular phone bill to be more than Janna's? Explain how you know this.

    c. Is it possible for James' and Janna's phone bills to be for the same amount? How many minutes of phone calls would each person have to make for their bills to be equal?

    d. Janna finds another phone company that offers one rate for both weekday and weekend calls. The billing plan for this company can be expressed by the equation $A = 25 + 0.25m$, where A is the total monthly bill and m is the number of minutes of calls. Compare this billing plan with the other two plans.

Extensions

31. **a.** Find the slope of each line below, and write an equation for the line.

i.

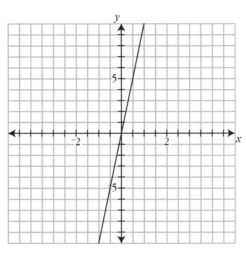

ii.

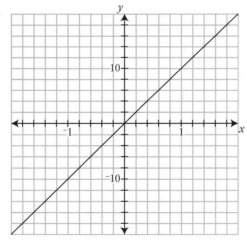

iii.

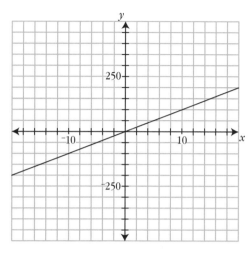

b. Compare the slopes of the three lines.

c. How are the three graphs similar? How are they different?

32. On a flight from Boston to Detroit last March, passengers were able to watch a monitor that gave the altitude and the outside temperature. Two middle school teachers on the flight decided to try to figure out a formula for the temperature, *t,* in degrees Fahrenheit at an altitude of *a* feet above sea level. One teacher said the formula is $t = 46 - 0.003a$, and the other said it is $t = 46 + 0.003a$.

a. Which formula makes more sense to you? Why?

b. The Detroit Metropolitan Airport is 620 feet above sea level. Use the formula you chose in part a to find the temperature at the airport.

c. Does the temperature you found in part b seem reasonable? Why or why not?

33. The graph below shows the altitude of a spaceship from 10 seconds before liftoff through 7 seconds after liftoff.

a. Describe the relationship between the altitude of the spaceship and time.

b. What is the slope for the part of the graph that is a straight line? What does this slope represent in this situation?

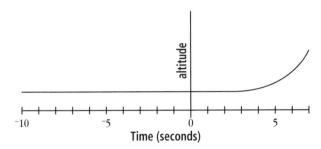

Time (seconds)

Mathematical Reflections

In this investigation, you learned about the slope, or steepness, of a line, and you discovered how to determine the slope from a table, a graph, or an equation. These questions will help you summarize what you have learned:

1 Explain what the slope of a line is.

2 How can you find the slope of a line from its equation? From its graph? From a table of values for the line? From the coordinates of two points on the line?

3 Describe how information about *y*-intercept and slope allows you to compare two equations. For example, how can you decide which equation has a steeper graph? How can you can you determine where the graphs of the equations cross the *y*-axis?

4 In *Comparing and Scaling,* you used ratios to make comparisons. What similarities are there between the way you used ratios in *Comparing and Scaling* and the way you have used slope in this unit?

Think about your answers to these questions, discuss your ideas with other students and your teacher, and then write a summary of your findings in your journal.

Writing an Equation for a Line

If you know the slope and the *y*-intercept of a line, it is easy to write an equation of the form $y = mx + b$ for the line. Unfortunately, you are not always given this information. How would you write an equation for a line if you knew only the coordinates of two points on the line? How would you write an equation for a line if you knew only the slope and the coordinates of a point that is not the *y*-intercept? In this investigation, you will work on some interesting problems in which you will consider questions like these.

6.1 Solving Alphonso's Puzzle

Today is Alphonso's birthday. Alphonso's grandfather gave Alphonso some money as a birthday gift. Alphonso says he will put his birthday money in a safe place and add part of his allowance to it each week. His sister Maria asks him how much his grandfather gave him and how much of his allowance he is planning to save each week. As usual, Alphonso does not answer his sister directly. Instead, he gives her some information and lets her puzzle out the answer for herself.

> **Problem 6.1**
>
> **A.** Alphonso tells Maria he will save the same amount from his allowance each week. He says that after five weeks he will have a total of $175 and after eight weeks he will have $190. How much money is Alphonso planning to save each week?
>
> **B.** How much money did Alphonso's grandfather give him for his birthday?

■ Problem 6.1 Follow-Up
Write an equation for the total amount of money Alphonso will have saved after a given number of weeks. Describe the reasoning you used to write your equation.

6.2 Converting Temperatures

Detroit, Michigan, is just across the Detroit River from the Canadian city of Windsor, Ontario. Since Canada uses the Celsius temperature scale, weather reports in Detroit often give temperatures in both Fahrenheit and Celsius degrees. The relationship between Fahrenheit degrees and Celsius degrees is linear. In this problem, you will write an equation you can use to convert temperatures from one scale to the other.

Problem 6.2

Two important reference points for temperature are the boiling point and the freezing point of water. Water freezes at 0°C, or 32°F. Water boils at 100°C, or 212°F.

0°C, or 32°F   100°C, or 212°F

Use this information to write an equation for the relationship between Fahrenheit degrees and Celsius degrees.

■ Problem 6.2 Follow-Up

1. Find the y-intercept for the equation you wrote in Problem 6.2. What does the y-intercept tell you about this situation?

2. Find the slope for the equation you wrote in Problem 6.2. What does the slope tell you about this situation?

3. If it is 85°F outside, what is the Celsius temperature?

4. If it is 30°C outside, what is the Fahrenheit temperature?

6.3 Solving the Mystery of the Irish Elk

The data below were gathered by evolutionary biologists studying an extinct animal called the Irish elk. The Irish elk grew to sizes much larger than any modern elk. The biologists were studying fossils to try to find patterns that might help them explain why this animal became extinct.

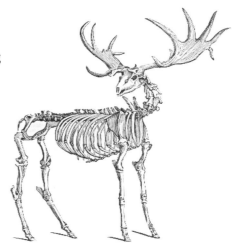

x	46	47.1	48.1	49	50.1
y	31.5	34.14	36.54	38.7	41.34

Source: *Ever Since Darwin.* Stephen Jay Gould. New York: Norton, 1977. Data have been modified slightly.

The data are skull and antler measurements for five different Irish elk fossils: x is the length of the skull in centimeters, and y is the length of one antler in centimeters.

In Problem 5.3 Follow-Up, you looked at the data in the above table. You showed that the data are linear and found that the slope of the line that fits the data is 2.4. This means that, for every 1-centimeter increase in the skull length, the antler length increases by 2.4 centimeters. You can use this information to write an equation that describes the relationship between skull length and antler length. Your equation might give you clues about why the Irish elk became extinct.

Problem 6.3

A. Since the relationship represented in the table is linear, its equation can be written in the form $y = mx + b$. You know the slope is 2.4, so the equation becomes $y = 2.4x + b$. Now you need to find the value of b, the y-intercept.

To find b, pick a pair of x and y values from the table, and substitute them into the equation

$$\square = 2.4\,\square + b$$

What value must b have? Substitute this value into $y = 2.4x + b$ to complete the equation.

B. Use your equation from part A to predict the antler length for a skull length of 55 centimeters.

C. For each Irish elk represented in the table, the antler length is shorter than the skull length. However, the Irish elk skeleton shown on page 82 has antlers much longer than its skull. Can you explain how the skull and antler data for this elk could fit the equation you wrote?

■ Problem 6.3 Follow-Up

1. Graph the data from the table on a coordinate grid. Use the graph to estimate the y-intercept. Do you get the same y-intercept you found in part A of Problem 6.3?

2. a. Use your graph to predict the antler length for a skull length of 55 centimeters. Do you get the same answer you got by using the equation? Explain.

b. Use the table to predict the antler length for a skull length of 55 centimeters. How does the result compare with the results you got by using the equation and the graph?

Did you know?

The Irish elk was not really an elk, and it wasn't exclusively Irish. It was actually a giant deer that inhabited parts of Europe, Asia, and northern Africa. The Irish elk evolved during the last million years and became extinct about 11,000 years ago. Fossils have been found showing that Irish elk had antlers with spreads of up to 12 feet! These antlers could not have been carried by any modern deer. Indeed, the antlers of the largest Irish elk are so out of proportion with the rest of the skeleton that biologists believe they were an encumbrance rather than an asset.

As you work on these ACE questions, use your calculator whenever you need it.

Applications

1. Write an equation for the line with slope $^-3$ and y-intercept 5.

2. Write an equation for the line with slope $\frac{3}{2}$ that passes through $(0, 2)$.

3. Write an equation for the line that passes through $(0, 1.5)$ and $(1, 2.5)$.

4. Write an equation for the line that passes through $(1, 5)$ and $(4, 6)$.

5. Write an equation for the line that passes through $(2, 6)$ and $(3, 6)$.

In 6–9, write an equation for the line.

6.
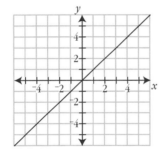

7.
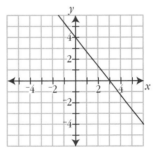

8.
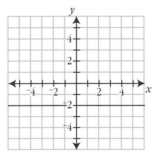

9.
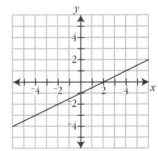

In 10 and 11, write a linear equation that represents the data in the table.

10.

x	$^-1$	0	1	2	3
y	1	3	5	7	9

11.

x	1	2	3	4	5
y	3	2	1	0	$^-1$

12. On the Talk for Less long-distance phone plan, the relationship between the number of minutes a call lasts and the cost of the call is linear. A 5-minute call costs $1.25, and a 15-minute call costs $2.25.

   a. Write an equation for the relationship between the cost and the length of a call.

   b. Find the slope and the y-intercept for the equation, and explain what this information means in the context of this problem.

   c. How much will a 25-minute call cost?

   d. How long can a customer talk for $5.00?

13. The hardware store sells batteries individually. Five batteries cost $4.50, and seven batteries cost $6.30.

   a. Write an equation for the relationship between the cost and the number of batteries.

   b. Find the slope and the y-intercept for the equation, and explain what this information means in the context of this problem.

   c. How much do eight batteries cost?

   d. Dominique spent $10.80 on batteries. How many batteries did she buy?

14. Mr. Brock's class is planning a cookie sale to raise money for the local food bank. They took a survey to help them figure out how much to charge for each cookie. They found that the relationship between the price and the number of cookies they would sell is linear. According to the survey, they will sell about 200 cookies if they charge 50¢, and they will sell about 50 cookies if they charge $1.

    a. Write an equation for the relationship between the cost and the number of cookies.

    b. Find the slope and the y-intercept for the equation, and explain what this information means in the context of this problem.

    c. If they charge 70¢ for each cookie, about how many cookies will they sell?

    d. If they want to sell 300 cookies, how much should they charge?

15. You can figure out how far away lightning is by counting the number of seconds between a flash of lightning and the following clap of thunder. The speed of sound is about 1100 feet per second. Thus, if you hear thunder 3 seconds after you see lightning, the lightning hit about $3 \times 1100 = 3300$ feet away.

    a. Write an equation you can use to predict the distance lightning is from you from the number of seconds between the lightning and the thunder.

    b. Find the slope and the y-intercept for the equation, and explain what this information means in the context of this problem.

    c. If lightning hits 1 mile away, how many seconds will elapse before you hear the thunder?

    d. If you hear thunder $6\frac{1}{2}$ seconds after you see lightning, how far away did the lightning hit?

16. **a.** Describe a situation involving a linear relationship whose graph has the given slope.

        i. positive slope   **ii.** negative slope   **iii.** a slope of 0

      b. For each situation you described in part a, tell what information the slope and the *y*-intercept give about the situation.

Connections

17. The drawing below shows "trains" of triangles made from toothpicks.

Number of toothpicks	3	5	7
Number of triangles	1	2	3
Perimeter of train	3	4	5

      a. Write an equation for the relationship between the number of triangles in a train and the perimeter of the train. Check your equation by testing it on the next few trains in the pattern.

      b. Write an equation for the relationship between the number of triangles in a train and the number of toothpicks.

18. Repeat question 17 for trains of squares.

19. Repeat question 17 for trains of hexagons.

20. a. There is 0.62 mile in 1 kilometer. Write an equation for the relationship between miles and kilometers.

b. How many miles are in 15 kilometers?

c. How many kilometers are in 10 miles?

21. In January 1991, a huge oil slick appeared in the Persian Gulf. A couple of days after it was reported, it covered a rectangular area 50 kilometers long and 13 kilometers wide. One day later, it covered a rectangular area 57 kilometers long and 16 kilometers wide.

a. Assume that the area of the oil slick continued to change at the rate described above. What was the average rate of change of the area of the slick with respect to the number of days? Explain.

b. Assume the relationship between the area of the slick and time is linear. Write an equation that describes the area of the slick as a function of time.

c. Draw a graph showing the relationship between area and time.

d. Estimate how long the oil had been spreading at the time of the first report of its area.

e. Do you think the oil really spread at a constant rate? Why or why not?

22. The radius of a circular oil spill from a certain underwater drilling site grows at a rate of 10 feet per minute.

a. Use a table, a graph, and an equation to describe the growth of the radius of the spill over time.

b. Use a table, a graph, and an equation to describe the growth of the circumference of the spill over time.

c. Use a table, a graph, and an equation to describe the growth of the area of the spill over time.

d. Which of the relationships in parts a–c are linear? How did you decide?

23. The distance required to stop a car depends on the speed at which the car is traveling. This stopping distance can be divided into two parts. The *reaction distance* is the distance the car travels from the time the driver realizes there is a need to stop until she applies the brakes. The *braking distance* is the distance the car travels from the moment the brakes are applied until the car stops. The table below shows the reaction distance and the braking distance for travel at different speeds. The *total distance* is the sum of the reaction distance and the braking distance. Below the table, the graphs of reaction distance, braking distance, and total distance are shown on the same set of axes.

Speed (kilometers per hour)	0	20	40	60	80	100	120
Reaction distance (meters)	0	5	10	15	20	25	30
Braking distance (meters)	0	2.5	10	22	40	63	90
Total distance (meters)	0	7.5	20	37	60	88	120

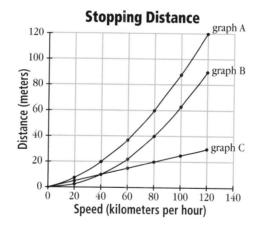

Stopping Distance

a. Which graph shows the relationship between reaction distance and speed?

b. Which graph shows the relationship between braking distance and speed?

c. Is either relationship linear? Explain your reasoning.

d. Match each equation with its graph.

   i. $d = 0.006s^2$ **ii.** $d = 0.25s$ **iii.** $d = 0.25s + 0.006s^2$

Extensions

24. Write an equation of the line that is parallel to the line $y = \frac{3}{2}x + 1$ and has a y-intercept of $(0, 3)$.

25. Write an equation of a line that is parallel to the line $y = 6$.

26. When Glenda travels in Europe, she uses a rule of thumb to convert Celsius temperatures to Fahrenheit temperatures: she doubles the Celsius temperature and adds $30°$.

   a. Write an equation for Glenda's rule of thumb.

   b. Convert a few Celsius temperatures to Fahrenheit temperatures, using both Glenda's rule of thumb and the equation you found in Problem 6.2. How do the results of the two conversion methods compare?

   c. Graph the equation for Glenda's rule and the equation from Problem 6.2 on the same set of axes.

   d. For what range of Celsius temperatures does Glenda's rule give Fahrenheit temperatures fairly close to those obtained by applying the equation from Problem 6.2?

27. Write an equation for a line that passes through the point $(3, {}^-3)$.

28. Write an equation for a line that passes through the point $(\frac{2}{3}, 4)$.

29. **a.** On a coordinate grid, draw a nonrectangular parallelogram, and write equations for the four lines that contain the sides of the parallelogram.

   b. On a coordinate grid, draw a rectangle, and write equations for the four lines that contain the sides of the parallelogram.

30. **a.** Repeat question 17 for trains of regular, eight-sided polygons.

   b. Repeat question 17 for trains of regular, ten-sided polygons.

   c. Can you make any generalizations about these equations for a figure with any number of sides?

Mathematical Reflections

In this investigation, you learned methods for finding an equation that fits given information. These questions will help you summarize what you have learned:

1 Explain how you can write an equation of a line from the given information. Use examples to illustrate your thinking.

    a. the slope and the y-intercept of the line

    b. two points on the line

    c. the slope of the line and a point on the line that is not the y-intercept

2 Why would you want to write an equation of a line? Use examples to illustrate your answer.

3 In this unit, you did a lot of work with equations. You wrote equations for linear relationships and then used the equations to find solutions and make predictions. Through your work, you probably developed ways to work efficiently with symbols. Apply what you learned to answer these questions.

    a. A student claims that $y = 3x + 10$ and $y = 10 + 3x$ are two ways to represent the same relationship. Do you agree? Why or why not? Can you think of some other ways to represent the relationship $y = 3x + 10$?

    b. What steps would you follow to find the value of y in $y = 10 + 3(^-4)$?

Think about your answers to these questions, discuss your ideas with other students and your teacher, and then write a summary of your findings in your journal.

Looking Back and Looking Ahead

Unit Reflections

Working on the problems of this unit you explored many examples of *linear relationships* between variables. You learned how to recognize linear patterns in *graphs* and in *tables* of numerical data and how to express those patterns in words and in symbolic *equations* or *formulas*. Most important of all, you learned how to study tables, graphs, and equations to answer questions about linear relationships. Examples of linear relationships and equations arise in many situations, but there are also important *nonlinear relationships*.

Using Your Algebraic Reasoning—To test your understanding and skill in work with linear relationships, consider some questions that arise in the operation of a movie theater. During daytime hours, the admission prices and operating costs of many theaters are somewhat different from those for ordinary evening hours.

1. *Suppose that a theater charges a school group $4.50 per student to show a special film. Suppose that the theater's operating expenses include $130 for the staff and film rental fee of $1.25 per student.*

   a. What equation relates the number of students, x, to the theater's income, I?

   b. What equation relates the theater's operating expenses, E, to x?

   c. Copy and complete the following table of sample income and expenses for the theater.

Number of Students, x	0	10	20	30	40	50	60	70
Income, I, in dollars								
Expenses, E, in dollars								

   d. On the same set of axes, graph both income and operating expenses of the theater for any number of students from 0 to 100.

e. Describe the patterns by which income and operating expenses increase as the number of students increases.

f. Write and solve an equation whose solution will answer the question "How many students need to attend the movie so that the theater's income will equal its operating expenses?"

2 *At another theater, the income and expenses combine to give the equation* $y = 3x - 115$ *relating operating profit,* y, *to the number of students in a group.*

a. What do the numbers 3 and -115 tell about

   i. the relation between number of students in a group and the theater's profit?

   ii. the pattern of entries that would appear in a table of sample (students, profit) pairs?

   iii. a graph of the relation between number of students and profit?

b. Write and solve equations to find the number of students necessary for the theater to

   i. break even (make $0 profit).

   ii. make a profit of $100.

c. Write and solve an equation that will find the number of students for which the two theaters will make the same profit. Then find the amount of that profit.

Explaining Your Reasoning—When you use mathematical calculations to solve a problem or make a decision, it is important to be able to justify each step in your reasoning.

1. Consider the variables and relationships studied in the two problems.

   a. What are the variables?

   b. Which pairs of variables are related to each other?

   c. In each pair of related variables, how does change in the value of one variable cause change in the value of the other?

2. Which relationships are linear and which are not? What patterns in the tables, graphs, and symbolic rules support your conclusions?

3. For those relationships that are linear, what do the slopes and intercepts of the graphs indicate about the relationships involved?

4. How do the slopes and intercepts relate to data patterns in the various tables of values?

5. Consider the strategies for solving linear equations such as those in Problem 1, part f. and Problem 2, part c.

   a. How can the equations be solved using tables of values?

   b. How can you solve those equations by using the graphs?

   c. How can you solve the equations by reasoning about the equations alone?

6. If you were asked to write a report describing the relationships among number of students, theater income, and operating costs, what value might be gained by including the table? The graph? The equation? What are the limitations of each type of display?

The algebra ideas and techniques you've used in this unit will be applied and extended in many future units of *Connected Mathematics* such as *Thinking with Mathematical Models* and *Say It with Symbols* as well as in work on problems of science and business.

coefficient A number that is multiplied by a variable in an equation or expression. In a linear equation of the form $y = mx + b$, the number m is the coefficient of x *and* the slope of the line. For example, in the equation $y = 3x + 5$, the coefficient of x is 3. This is also the slope of the line.

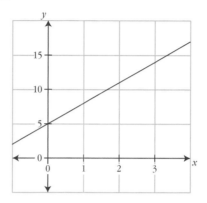

constant term A number in an equation that is not multiplied by a variable, or an amount added to or subtracted from the terms involving variables. In an equation of the form $y = mx + b$, the y-intercept, b, is a constant term. The effect of the constant term on a graph is to raise or lower the graph. The constant term in the equation $y = 3x + 5$ is 5. The graph of $y = 3x$ is raised vertically 5 units to give the graph of $y = 3x + 5$.

coordinate pair A pair of numbers of the form (x, y) that gives the location of a point in the coordinate plane. The x term gives the distance left or right from the origin $(0, 0)$, and the y term gives the distance up or down from the origin.

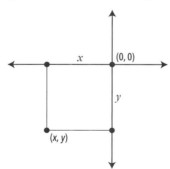

function A relationship between two variables in which the value of one variable depends on the value of the other variable. For example, the distance, *d*, in miles covered in *t* hours by a car traveling at 55 mph is given by the equation $d = 55t$. The relationship between distance and the time is a function, and we say that the distance is a *function of* the time. This function is a *linear function*, and its graph is a straight line whose slope is 5. In future units, you will learn about functions that are not linear.

intersecting lines Lines that cross or *intersect*. The coordinates of the point where the lines intersect are solutions to the equations for both lines. The graphs of the equations $y = x$ and $y = 2x - 3$ intersect at the point (3, 3). This number pair is a solution to each equation.

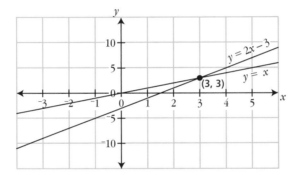

linear relationship A relationship in which there is a constant rate of change between two variables; for each unit increase in one variable, there is a constant change in the other variable. A linear relationship between two variables can be represented by a straight-line graph and by an equation of the form $y = mx + b$. The rate of change is m, the coefficient of x. For example, if you save \$2 each month, the relationship between the amount you save and the number of months is a linear relationship which can be represented by the equation $y = 2x$. The constant rate of change is 2.

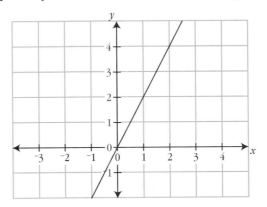

origin The point where the x- and y-axes intersect on a coordinate graph. With coordinates (0, 0), the origin is the center of the coordinate plane.

rise The vertical change between two points. The slope of a line is the rise divided by the run.

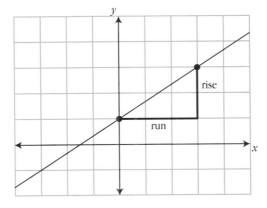

run The horizontal change between two points. The slope of a line is the rise divided by the run.

scale The distance between tick marks on the *x*- and *y*-axes of a coordinate grid. When graphing, an appropriate scale must be selected so that the resulting graph will be clearly shown. For example, when graphing the equation $y = 60x$, a scale of 1 for the *x*-axis and a scale of 15 or 30 for the *y*-axis would be reasonable.

slope The number that expresses the steepness of a line. The slope is the ratio of the vertical change to the horizontal change between any two points on the line. Sometimes this ratio is referred to as *the rise over the run*. The slope of a horizontal line is 0. Slopes are positive if the *y* values increase from left to right on a coordinate grid and negative if the *y* values decrease from left to right. The slope of a vertical line is undefined.

The slope of a line is the same as the constant rate of change between the two variables. For example, the points (0, 0) and (3, 6) lie on the graph of $y = 2x$. Between these points, the vertical change is 6 and the horizontal change is 3, so the slope is $\frac{6}{3} = 2$, which is the coefficient of *x* in the equation.

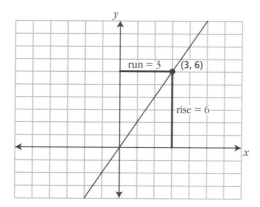

x-intercept The point where a graph crosses the *x*-axis. The *x*-intercept of the equation $y = 3x + 5$ is $(-\frac{5}{3}, 0)$ or $-\frac{5}{3}$.

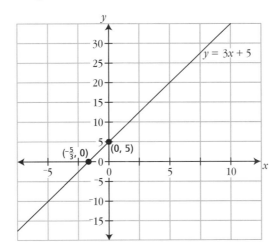

y-intercept The point where the graph crosses the *y*-axis. In a linear equation of the form $y = mx + b$, the *y*-intercept is the constant, *b*. In the graph above, the *y*-intercept is (0, 5) or 5.

Index

Bertillon, Alphonse, 58

Coefficient, 41
Constant term, 41
Coordinate pair, 39

Experiment
  bouncing balls, 7–8
  leak rate, 6–7

Function, 15–16

Graphing calculator
  graphing lines with, 4, 35–43
  locating points with, 36
  solving linear equations with, 39–40
  tables on, 4, 40
  window settings for, 37–38

Investigation
  Exploring Lines with a Graphing
    Calculator, 35–52
  Exploring Slope, 64–79
  Predicting from Patterns, 5–14
  Solving Equations, 53–63
  Walking Rates, 15–34
  Writing an Equation for a Line, 80–91

Journal, 14, 34, 52, 63, 79, 91

Linear equation
  ACE, 24–33, 44–51, 60–62, 70–78,
    84–90
  checking solutions, 55
  fitting an equation to data, 80–83
  general form of, 41
  graphing on a graphing calculator,
    35–43
  rate of change and, 15–23
  writing an equation for a line, 80–83
  writing and solving, 53–58
Linear graph
  ACE, 9–13, 24–33, 44–51, 84–90
  on a graphing calculator, 35–43
  predicting from, 5–8
  rate and, 15–23
  writing an equation for, 80–83
Linear relationship, 3, 16
  ACE, 9–13, 24–33, 44–51, 60–62,
    70–78, 84–90
  on a graphing calculator, 35–43
  predicting from, 5–8
  rate of change and, 4, 15–23
  slope and, 64–69
  writing and solving equations for,
    53–58, 80–83
Looking Back and Looking Ahead:
  Unit Reflections, 92–94

Mathematical Highlights, 4
Mathematical Reflections, 14, 34, 52, 63, 79, 91

Origin, 41

Pattern
  ACE, 9–13
  predicting from, 4, 5–8
Point of intersection, for linear graphs, 41
Prediction
  ACE, 9–13, 24–33
  using patterns, 4, 5–8
  using rate, 15–23

Range, values on a graphing calculator, 37–38
Rate of change, 15–23
  ACE, 24–33
  comparing, 17–23
  linear relationship and, 4, 15–23
  predicting from, 5–8
  slope and, 64–69

Rise, steepness and, 64–66
Run, steepness and, 64–66
Scale, 37
Slope, 4, 64–66
  ACE, 70–78
  of a line, 66–68
  of a line between two points, 68–69
  negative, 67
  positive, 67
Steepness, 41, 64–66

Table
  graphing calculator function, 40
  predicting from, 5–8
  rate of change and, 16–23
  slope and, 69
  for solving a linear equation, 39, 40

Variables, relationships between, 15–16

x-intercept, 41

y-intercept, 4, 41

Connected  Mathematics®

Three-Dimensional Measurement

Student Edition

Glenda Lappan
James T. Fey
William M. Fitzgerald
Susan N. Friel
Elizabeth Difanis Phillips

Prentice
Hall

Glenview, Illinois
Needham, Massachusetts
Upper Saddle River, New Jersey

Connected Mathematics® was developed at Michigan State University with the support of National Science Foundation Grant No. MDR 9150217.

This project was supported, in part,
by the
National Science Foundation
Opinions expressed are those of the authors
and not necessarily those of the Foundation

The Michigan State University authors and administration have agreed that all MSU royalties arising from this publication will be devoted to purposes supported by the Department of Mathematics and the MSU Mathematics Education Enrichment Fund.

Contents

Mathematical Highlights   4

Investigation 1: Building Boxes   5
    1.1 Making Cubic Boxes   5
    1.2 Making Rectangular Boxes   7
    1.3 Flattening a Box   8
    1.4 Testing Flat Patterns   9
    Applications—Connections—Extensions   10
    Mathematical Reflections   14

Investigation 2: Designing Packages   15
    2.1 Packaging Blocks   16
    2.2 Saving Trees   17
    Applications—Connections—Extensions   19
    Mathematical Reflections   23

Investigation 3: Finding Volumes of Boxes   24
    3.1 Filling Rectangular Boxes   24
    3.2 Burying Garbage   26
    3.3 Filling Fancy Boxes   26
    Applications—Connections—Extensions   29
    Mathematical Reflections   36

Investigation 4: Cylinders   37
    4.1 Filling a Cylinder   38
    4.2 Making a Cylinder from a Flat Pattern   39
    4.3 Designing a New Juice Container   40
    Applications—Connections—Extensions   41
    Mathematical Reflections   45

Investigation 5: Cones and Spheres   46
    5.1 Comparing Spheres and Cylinders   47
    5.2 Comparing Cones and Cylinders   49
    5.3 Melting Ice Cream   50
    Applications—Connections—Extensions   51
    Mathematical Reflections   56

Investigation 6: Scaling Boxes   57
    6.1 Building a Bigger Box   58
    6.2 Scaling Up the Compost Box   59
    6.3 Looking at Similar Prisms   60
    Applications—Connections—Extensions   61
    Mathematical Reflections   67

Investigation 7: Finding Volumes of Irregular Objects   68
    7.1 Displacing Water   68
    Applications—Connections—Extensions   70
    Mathematical Reflections   72

The Unit Project   73
Looking Back and Looking Ahead: Unit Reflections   74
Glossary   77
Index   81

Filling and Wrapping

Baseballs, basketballs, and soccer balls are spheres, but they often come in boxes shaped like cubes. Why do you think these balls are packaged in this way?

Salt, juice concentrate, oatmeal, and tuna are often sold in packages shaped like cylinders. Why do you think these items are packaged in cylindrical containers instead of rectangular boxes?

At the Bijou theater, popcorn is sold in rectangular boxes with a height of 20 centimeters and a square base with 12-centimeter sides. At the Roxy theater, popcorn is sold in cylindrical boxes with a height of 20 centimeters and a diameter of 12 centimeters. Both theaters charge $2.50 for a box of popcorn. At which theater will you get the most popcorn for your money?

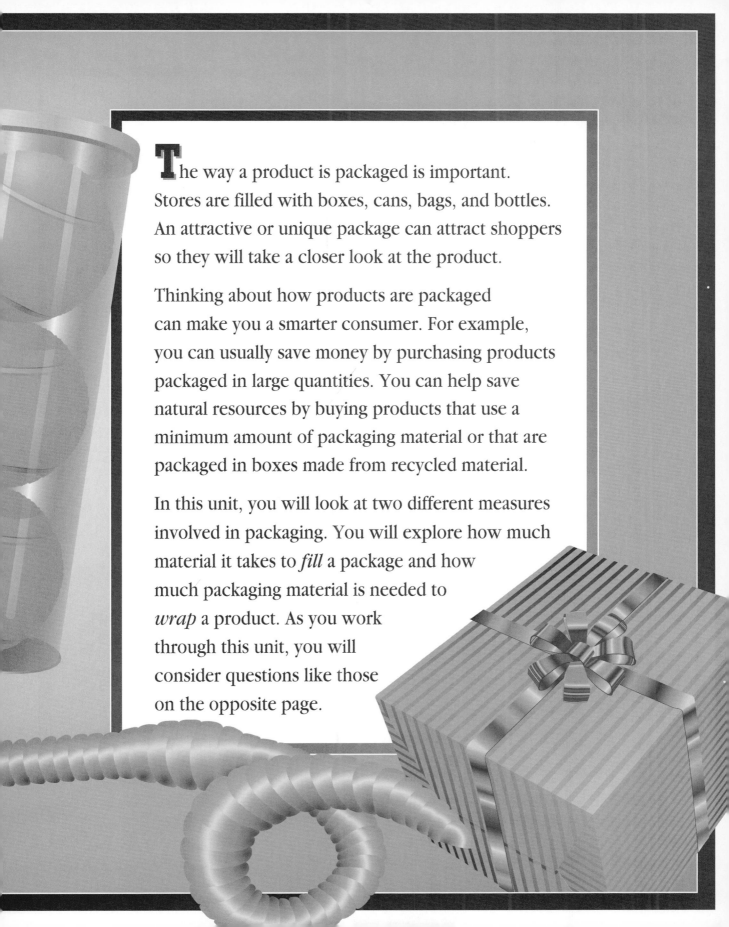

The way a product is packaged is important. Stores are filled with boxes, cans, bags, and bottles. An attractive or unique package can attract shoppers so they will take a closer look at the product.

Thinking about how products are packaged can make you a smarter consumer. For example, you can usually save money by purchasing products packaged in large quantities. You can help save natural resources by buying products that use a minimum amount of packaging material or that are packaged in boxes made from recycled material.

In this unit, you will look at two different measures involved in packaging. You will explore how much material it takes to *fill* a package and how much packaging material is needed to *wrap* a product. As you work through this unit, you will consider questions like those on the opposite page.

Mathematical Highlights

In *Filling and Wrapping* you will explore surface area and volume of objects, in particular, rectangular prisms, cylinders, cones, and spheres. The unit should help you to

● Understand volume as a measure of *filling* an object and surface area as a measure of *wrapping* an object;

● Develop strategies and formulas for finding the volume and surface area of objects including rectangular prisms and cylinders;

● Find patterns among the volumes of cylinders, cones, and spheres;

● Design flat patterns for rectangular prisms given certain specifications;

● Investigate the effects of varying the dimensions of rectangular prisms and cylinders on volume and surface area;

● Estimate the volume of irregular shapes by measuring the amount of water displaced by the solid; and

● Recognize and solve problems involving volume and surface area.

As you work on the problems of this unit, ask yourself questions about problem situations that involve volume and surface area: *What quantities are involved in the problem? Which measures of an object are involved—volume or surface area? Is an exact answer required? What method should I use to determine these measures? What strategies or formulas might help?*

Building Boxes

The most common type of package is the rectangular box. Rectangular boxes come filled with everything from cereal to shoes and from pizza to paper clips. Most rectangular boxes begin as flat sheets of cardboard. The sheets are cut and then folded into a box shape and glued or taped together.

1.1 Making Cubic Boxes

Some boxes are shaped like cubes. A **cube** is a three-dimensional shape with six identical square **faces**. What kinds of things might be packaged in cubic boxes?

In this problem, you will make **flat patterns** that can be folded to form boxes. The diagram on the left below shows one possible flat pattern for a cubic box.

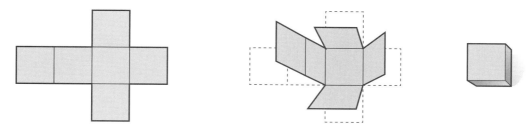

The boxes you will work with in this problem are shaped like unit cubes. A **unit cube** is a cube with **edges** that are 1 unit long. Cubes that are 1 inch on each edge are called inch cubes, and cubes that are 1 centimeter on each edge are called centimeter cubes.

A. How many different flat patterns can you make that will fold into a box shaped like a unit cube? Make a sketch of each pattern you find on inch grid paper. Test each pattern by cutting it out and folding it into a box.

B. Find the total area of each pattern.

■ **Problem 1.1 Follow-Up**

1. Choose one of your flat patterns from Problem 1.1, and make a copy of it on grid paper. Add the least possible number of flaps you need to be able to fold the pattern and glue it together to make a box with a lid that opens. The lid should have a flap that you tuck in to close the box. On your drawing indicate which flap will be part of the lid and which flaps will be glued. Cut your pattern out and fold it to make sure that it works.

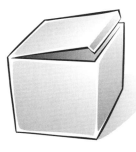

2. Below is Benjamin's work for question 1. Does his pattern meet the requirements given in that question?

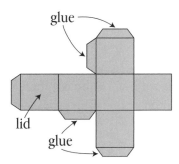

3. Copy Benjamin's flat pattern and add a different set of flaps so that his pattern meets the requirements in question 1.

Many boxes are not shaped like cubes. The box below has square ends, but the remaining faces are nonsquare rectangles. Next to the box is a flat pattern that could be folded to make the box.

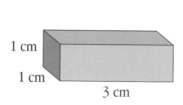

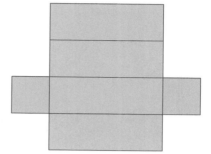

Problem 1.2

A. On grid paper, draw a flat pattern for a rectangular box that is *not* a cube. Each side length of your pattern should be a whole number of units. Then, make a different flat pattern for the same box. Test each pattern by cutting it out and folding it into a box.

B. Find the total area of each flat pattern you made in part A.

C. Describe the faces of the box formed from each flat pattern you made. What are the dimensions of each face?

D. How many unit cubes will fit into the box formed from each flat pattern you made? Explain how you got your answer.

■ **Problem 1.2 Follow-Up**

Choose one of your flat patterns from Problem 1.2, and make a copy of it on grid paper. Add the least possible number of flaps you need to be able to fold the pattern and glue it together to make a box with a lid that opens. The lid should have a flap that you tuck in to close the box. On your drawing indicate which flap will be part of the lid and which flaps will be glued.

1.3 Flattening a Box

A **rectangular prism** is a three-dimensional shape with six rectangular faces. A cube is a special type of rectangular prism. All the boxes you have made so far have been shaped like rectangular prisms. The size of a rectangular prism can be described by giving its dimensions—the length, the width, and the height.

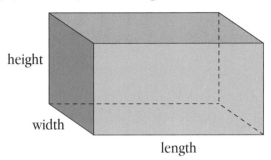

The **base** of a rectangular prism is the face on the bottom, or the face that rests on the table or floor. The length and width of a prism are the length and width of its rectangular base, and the height is the distance from the base of the prism to its top.

Amy is a packaging engineer at the Save-a-Tree packaging company. Mr. Shu asked Amy to come to his class and explain her job to his students. To help the class understand her work, she gave the students boxes and scissors and asked them to do some exploring.

Problem 1.3

Your teacher will give you a box.

A. Find the dimensions of your box in centimeters.

B. Use the dimensions you found in part A to make a flat pattern for your box on grid paper.

C. Cut your box along the edges so that, when you lay it out flat, it will match your flat pattern from part B.

■ Problem 1.3 Follow-Up

1. Amy explained that one thing she considers when designing a box is the cost of the material. If the material for your box costs $\frac{1}{10}$ of a cent per square centimeter, what is the total cost of the material for your box? Why might this information be useful?

2. What other information or constraints do you think would be important to consider when designing a box?

1.4 Testing Flat Patterns

The flat patterns below were drawn by one of the engineers at the Save-a-Tree packaging company. The engineer lost his notes that indicated the dimensions of the boxes. Can you help him determine the dimensions?

Box P

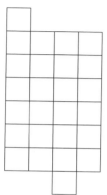

Box Q

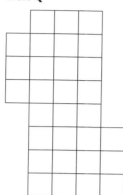

Box R

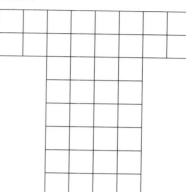

Problem 1.4

A. Cut out each pattern on Labsheet 1.4, and fold it to form a box.

B. Find the dimensions of each box.

C. How are the dimensions of each box related to the dimensions of its faces?

D. Find the total area of all the faces of each box.

E. Fill each box with unit cubes. How many cubes does it take to fill each box?

■ Problem 1.4 Follow-Up

Design a flat pattern for a box that has a different shape from box P (from Labsheet 1.4) but that holds the same number of cubes as box P.

As you work on these ACE questions, use your calculator whenever you need it.

Applications

1. An *open box* is a box without a top.

    a. On grid paper, sketch three different flat patterns for an open cubic box. Find the area of each flat pattern you found.

    b. On grid paper, sketch three different flat patterns for an open rectangular box (not a cubic box) with square ends. Find the area of each flat pattern you found.

In 2–5, tell whether the flat pattern could be folded along the lines to form a closed cubic box. If you are unsure, cut the pattern out of grid paper and experiment.

2.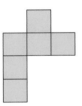

3.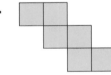

4.

5.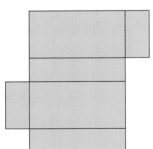

6. Which of these patterns could be folded along the lines to form a closed rectangular box?

    i.   ii.   iii.

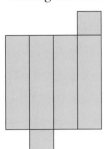
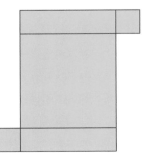

7. Do parts a–c for each pattern from question 6 that forms a box.

unit square

    a. Use the unit square shown to help you find the dimensions of the box.

    b. Find the total area of all the faces of the box.

    c. Find the number of unit cubes it would take to fill the box.

8. This closed rectangular box does not have square ends.

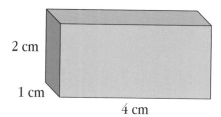

2 cm

1 cm

4 cm

    a. What are the dimensions of the box?

    b. On grid paper, sketch two flat patterns for the box.

    c. Find the area of each flat pattern.

    d. Find the total area of all the faces of the box. How does your answer compare to the areas you found in part c?

Connections

9. **a.** What measurements do you need to find the area and perimeter of a rectangle? Explain how you would use these measurements to find the area and perimeter of a rectangle.

    b. What measurements do you need to find the area and perimeter of a square? Explain how you would use these measurements to find the area and perimeter of a square.

10. a. Draw a flat pattern for a rectangular box with dimensions 2 cm by 3 cm by 5 cm. Find the dimensions and area of each face.

b. What is the total area of all the faces of the box?

In 11–15, use the following information: A *hexomino* is a shape made of six identical squares connected along their sides. The flat patterns for a closed cubic box are examples of hexominos. Below are five different hexominos.

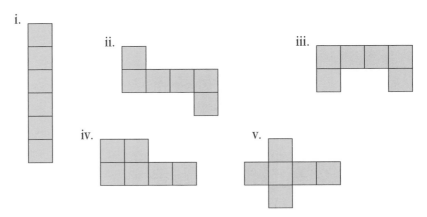

11. Find the perimeter of each hexomino shown above.

12. Which hexominos above could be folded to form a closed cubic box?

13. To which hexominos above can you add one square without changing the perimeter? For each hexomino that works, draw a diagram showing where the square could be added, and explain why the perimeter does not change.

14. To which hexominos above can you add two squares without changing the perimeter? For each hexomino that works, draw a diagram showing where the squares could be added, and explain why the perimeter does not change.

15. To which hexominos above can you add a square that changes the perimeter? For each hexomino that works, draw a diagram showing where the square could be added.

Extensions

16. A number cube is designed so that numbers on opposite sides add to 7. Write the integers from 1 to 6 on one of the flat patterns you found in Problem 1.1 so that it can be folded to form a number cube. You may want to test your pattern by cutting it out and folding it.

17. Could the flat pattern below be folded along the lines to form a rectangular box? If so, explain how.

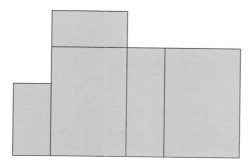

18. Could the flat pattern below be folded along the lines to form an open cubic box? If so, explain how.

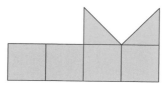

19. Examine the flat patterns you made for cubic boxes in Problem 1.1. Suppose you wanted to make boxes by tracing several copies of the same pattern onto a large sheet of cardboard and cutting them out. Which pattern would allow you to make the greatest number of boxes from a sheet of cardboard? Test your ideas by tiling a piece of grid paper with your box pattern. (*Tiling* is covering a flat surface with copies of a figure with no overlaps or gaps.)

Mathematical Reflections

In this investigation, you explored rectangular boxes, and you made flat patterns for boxes. You found the dimensions of a box, the total area of all its faces, and the number of unit cubes required to fill it. These questions will help you summarize what you have learned:

1. Suppose you were a packaging engineer. Explain why you might want to know the total area of all the faces of a rectangular box.

2. Explain how you would find the total area of all the faces of a rectangular box.

3. Explain how you would find the number of cubes it would take to fill a rectangular box.

4. What features must be the same for any flat pattern for a given box? What features might be different?

Think about your answers to these questions, discuss your ideas with other students and your teacher, and then write a summary of your findings in your journal.

Designing Packages

Finding the right box for a particular product requires a lot of thought and planning. A company must consider how much a box can hold and the amount and cost of the material needed to make the box.

The amount that a box can hold depends on its volume. The **volume** of a box is the number of unit cubes that would fill the box. The amount of material needed to make or cover a box depends on the box's surface area. The **surface area** of a box is the total area of all of its faces.

The box shown below has dimensions 1 centimeter by 3 centimeters by 1 centimeter. It would take three 1-centimeter cubes to fill this box, so the box has a volume of 3 cubic centimeters. Since it takes fourteen 1-centimeter grid squares to make the box, the box has a surface area of 14 square centimeters.

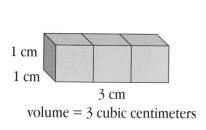

1 cm
1 cm
3 cm
volume = 3 cubic centimeters

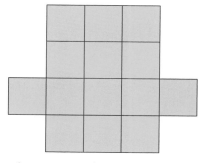

surface area = 14 square centimeters

In this investigation, you will explore the possible surface areas for a rectangular box that holds a given amount. In other words, you will investigate the range of possible surface areas for boxes with a fixed volume.

2.1 Packaging Blocks

ABC Toy Company is planning to market a set of children's alphabet blocks. Each block is a cube with 1-inch edges, so each block has a volume of 1 cubic inch.

Problem 2.1

The company wants to arrange 24 blocks in the shape of a rectangular prism and then package them in a box that exactly fits the prism.

A. Find all the ways 24 cubes can be arranged into a rectangular prism. Make a sketch of each arrangement you find, and give its dimensions and surface area. It may help to organize your findings into a table like the one below.

Possible Arrangements of 24 Cubes

Length	Width	Height	Volume	Surface area	Sketch
			24 cubic inches		
			24 cubic inches		
			24 cubic inches		

B. Which of your arrangements requires the least material to make the box? Which requires the most material?

■ Problem 2.1 Follow-Up

Which arrangement would you recommend to ABC Toy Company? Write a short report giving your recommendation and explaining the reasons for your choice.

2.2 Saving Trees

Were you surprised to discover that 24 blocks can be packaged in ways that use quite different amounts of packaging material? By reducing the amount of material it uses, a company can save money, reduce waste, and conserve natural resources.

Both boxes have the same volume.

Problem 2.2

When packaging a given number of cubes, which rectangular arrangement uses the least amount of packaging material?

To help you answer this question, you can investigate some special cases and look for a pattern in the results. Explore the possible arrangements of the following numbers of cubes. For each number of cubes, try to find the arrangement that would require the least amount of packaging material.

8 cubes   27 cubes   12 cubes

Use your findings to make a conjecture about the rectangular arrangement of cubes that requires the least packaging material.

■ **Problem 2.2 Follow–Up**

1. Test your conjecture from Problem 2.2 on some other examples, such as 30 cubes or 64 cubes. Does your conjecture work for the examples you tried? If not, change your conjecture so it works for any number of cubes. When you have a conjecture that you think is correct, give reasons why you think your conjecture is valid.

2. What rectangular arrangement of cubes uses the most packaging material? Why do you think this is so?

3. What is the surface area of the box below? Explain how you found your answer.

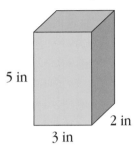

5 in

2 in

3 in

4. Suppose the box in question 3 were resting on a different face. How would this affect its surface area?

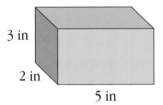

3 in

2 in

5 in

As you work on these ACE questions, use your calculator whenever you need it.

Applications

In 1–3, a rectangular prism made from inch cubes is pictured. Answer parts a–c.

1.

2.

3.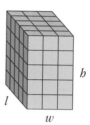

   a. What are the length, width, and height of the prism?

   b. How much material would be needed to make a box for the prism?

   c. How many blocks are in the prism?

4. Suppose you want to make a box to hold exactly thirty 1-inch cubes.

   a. Describe all the possible boxes you could make.

   b. Which box has the least surface area? Which has the greatest surface area?

   c. Why might you want to know the dimensions of the box with the least surface area?

5. **a.** Sketch a rectangular box with dimensions 2 cm by 3 cm by 6 cm.

   b. What is the surface area of your box?

   c. Sketch a flat pattern for your box. What is the relationship between the area of the flat pattern and the surface area of the box?

Connections

6. There is only one way to arrange five identical cubes into the shape of a rectangular prism.

    a. Sketch the rectangular prism made from five identical cubes.

    b. Give some other numbers of cubes that can be arranged into a rectangular prism in only one way. What kind of numbers are these?

7. **a.** Sketch every rectangular prism that can be made from ten identical cubes.

    b. Find the surface area of each prism you sketched in part a.

    c. Give the dimensions of the prism from part a that has the least surface area.

    d. Find one other number of blocks that has this same number of rectangular arrangements.

8. The dimensions of the recreation center floor are 150 ft by 45 ft, and the walls are 10 ft high. A gallon of paint will cover 400 ft^2. About how much paint is needed to paint the walls of the recreation center?

9. **a.** If a small can of paint will cover 1400 in^2, about how many cans are needed to paint the walls of the recreation center described in question 8?

    b. What factors might affect how much paint is actually used?

10. **a.** Graph the relationship between the area of the base and the height for your rectangular arrangements in Problem 2.1.

    b. Describe the relationship between the height and the area of the base.

    c. How might your graph be useful to the packaging engineer at ABC Toys?

11. The 1994 World Cup soccer championships were held in the United States. Some of the games were played in the Silverdome in Pontiac, Michigan. The dimensions of the soccer field in the Silverdome were 71 m by 115 m.

    a. How many square meters of turf were needed to cover the field?

    b. What were the dimensions of the field in feet? (1 in = 2.54 cm and 1 m = 100 cm)

Did you know?

The Pontiac Silverdome, like most domed stadiums, normally has a field made from artificial turf. However, the World Cup Soccer Host Committee required that the Silverdome be fitted with a natural grass field that could survive three weeks of soccer matches. The Detroit World Cup Bid Committee asked scientists at Michigan State University to help.

Because of the lack of natural light in the Silverdome, scientists had to design a turf system that could be grown outside the Silverdome and then brought inside and prepared for play. They grew the turf in about 2000 hexagonal pieces, each 7.5 feet wide. About two weeks before the first soccer game was to be played on the turf, the hexagonal pieces were brought inside and pieced together. Why do you think researchers chose hexagons rather than squares, rectangles, or some other shape?

Extensions

12. Many brands of soft drink are packaged in rectangular boxes of 24 cans.

    a. During the spring of 1993, a major cola company announced that they were going to package 24 cans into a more cube-like shape. Why might the company have done this?

    b. List all the ways 24 cans of soda could be arranged and packaged in a rectangular box. Which arrangement would you recommend that a soft drink company use? Why?

13. Slam Dunk Sporting Goods packages its basketballs in cubic boxes with 1-ft edges.

    a. Slam Dunk ships basketballs from its factory to stores all over the country. To ship the balls, the company packs 12 basketballs (in their boxes) into a large rectangular shipping box. Find the dimensions of every possible shipping box into which the boxes of balls would exactly fit.

    b. Find the surface area of each shipping box you found in part a.

    c. Slam Dunk uses the shipping box that requires the least material. Which shipping box do they use?

    d. Slam Dunk decides to ship basketballs in boxes of 24. They want to use the shipping box that requires the least material. Find the dimensions of the box they should use. How much more packaging material is needed to ship 24 balls than to ship 12 balls?

Mathematical Reflections

In this investigation, you arranged cubes in the shape of rectangular prisms, and you found the arrangements with the least and greatest surface area. These questions will help you summarize what you have learned:

1 For a given number of cubes, what arrangement will give a rectangular prism with the least surface area? What arrangement will give a rectangular prism with the greatest surface area? Use specific examples to illustrate your ideas.

2 Describe how you can find the surface area of a rectangular prism.

Think about your answers to these questions, discuss your ideas with other students and your teacher, and then write a summary of your findings in your journal.

Finding Volumes of Boxes

In the last investigation, you started with a fixed number of cubes and explored the various ways you could arrange them to form a rectangular prism. In this investigation, you will start with boxes shaped like rectangular prisms and determine how many unit cubes they will hold.

3.1 Filling Rectangular Boxes

To package its products, a company may have boxes custom-made. However, a company can save money if it buys ready-made boxes. The Save-a-Tree packaging company sells ready-made boxes in several sizes.

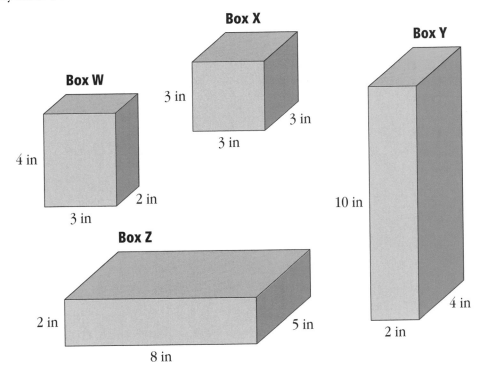

Problem 3.1

ABC Toy Company is considering using one of Save-a-Tree's ready-made boxes to ship their blocks. Each block is a 1-inch cube. ABC needs to know how many blocks will fit into each box and the surface area of each box.

A. How many blocks will fit in each of Save-a-Tree's ready-made boxes? Explain how you got your answer.

B. What is the surface area of each box? Explain how you got your answer.

■ Problem 3.1 Follow-Up

1. How many cubes would fit in a single layer at the bottom of each box in Problem 3.1?

2. How many *identical layers* of cubes could be stacked in each box?

3. The number of unit cubes that fit in a box is the volume of the box. For each box in Problem 3.1, consider the box's dimensions, the number of cubes in a layer, the number of layers, and the volume. What connections do you see among these measurements?

4. Suppose box Y were laid on its side so its base was 4 inches by 10 inches and its height was 2 inches. Would this affect the volume of the box? Explain your reasoning.

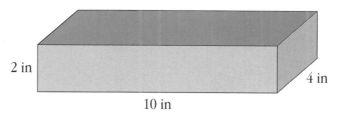

2 in

10 in

4 in

3.2 Burying Garbage

The city of Greendale has set aside a piece of land on which to bury its garbage. The city plans to dig a rectangular hole with a base measuring 500 feet by 200 feet and a depth of 75 feet.

The population of Greendale is 100,000. It has been estimated that, on average, a family of four throws away 0.4 cubic foot of compacted garbage a day. How could this information help Greendale evaluate the plan for a waste site?

Problem 3.2

A. How much garbage will this site hold?

B. How long will it take before the hole is filled?

■ Problem 3.2 Follow-Up

What suggestions would you make to the Greendale city council about their plan?

3.3 Filling Fancy Boxes

Prisms come in many different shapes. A **prism** is a three-dimensional shape with a top and bottom that are congruent polygons, and faces that are parallelograms. The boxes you have investigated so far in this unit have been shaped like rectangular prisms. A prism is named for the shape of its base. For example, the base of a rectangular prism is a rectangle, and the base of a triangular prism is a triangle. Some prisms are shown below.

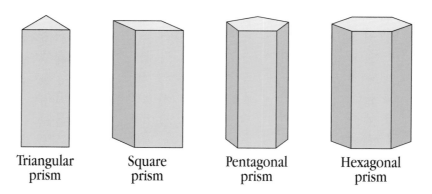

Triangular prism   Square prism   Pentagonal prism   Hexagonal prism

You have seen that you can find the volume of a rectangular prism by thinking about the number of unit cubes that would fit inside the prism. In this problem, you will see if a similar method will work for finding the volume of a nonrectangular prism. First, you need to make some paper prisms. (These paper prisms are actually prism-shaped boxes that are open at the top and bottom.)

Making paper prisms

- Start with four identical sheets of paper.
- Fold one of the sheets of paper into three congruent rectangles. Tape the paper into the shape of a triangular prism.

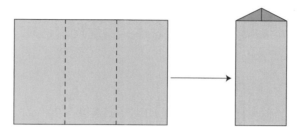

- Fold a second sheet of paper into four congruent rectangles, and tape it into the shape of a square prism.
- Fold and tape the remaining two sheets of paper as shown below to form pentagonal and hexagonal prisms.

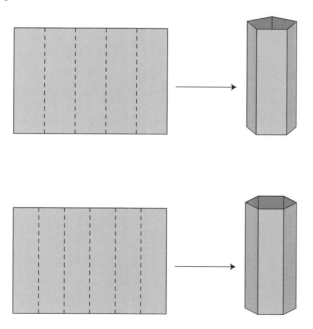

In Problems 3.1 and 3.2, you saw that you could find the volume of a rectangular prism by figuring out how many cubes would fit in a single layer at the bottom of the prism and then figuring out how many layers it would take to fill the prism. Do you think this layering method would work for finding volumes of different types of prisms?

A. Find the volumes of the triangular, square, pentagonal, and hexagonal prisms you made in cubic centimeters. Describe the method you use.

B. Imagine that each of your paper prisms had a top and a bottom. How would you find the surface area of each prism? Which of the four prisms would have the greatest surface area?

■ **Problem 3.3 Follow-Up**

1. Do parts a and b for each paper prism you made.

    a. Set the paper prism on its base on a sheet of centimeter grid paper. Trace the prism's base. Look at the centimeter squares inside your tracing. How many cubes would fit in one layer at the bottom of the prism? Consider whole cubes and parts of cubes.

    b. How many layers of centimeter cubes would it take to completely fill the prism?

2. What connections can you make between the area of a prism's base, the height of the prism, and the volume of the prism?

3. Suppose you used the same size sheets of paper to make prisms with 7 sides, 8 sides, 9 sides, and so on. What would happen to the shape of the prism as the number of sides increased? What would happen to the volume of the prism as the number of sides increased?

Save your paper prisms for the next investigation.

As you work on these ACE questions, use your calculator whenever you need it.

Applications

In 1–3, a rectangular prism made from inch cubes is pictured. Answer parts a–c.

1.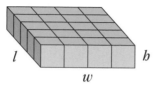

2.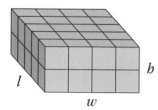

3.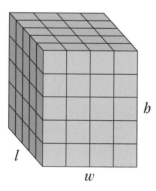

a. What are the length, width, and height of the prism?

b. What is the volume of the prism? Describe how you found the volume.

c. What is the surface area of the prism? Describe how you found the surface area.

4. **a.** How many cubes are needed to fill the closed box below?

    b. What is the surface area of the box?

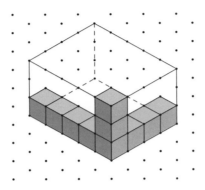

In 5–7, find the volume and surface area of the closed box.

5.

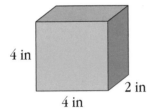

4 in

2 in

4 in

6.

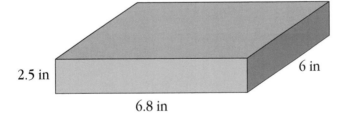

2.5 in

6 in

6.8 in

7.

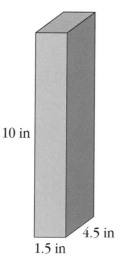

10 in

4.5 in

1.5 in

8. a. Make a sketch of a closed box with dimensions 2 cm by 3 cm by 5 cm.

  b. How many centimeter cubes would fit in one layer at the bottom of the box?

  c. How many layers would be needed to fill the box?

  d. Find the volume of the box.

  e. Find the surface area of the box.

9. Mr. Singh's classroom is 20 ft wide, 30 ft long, and 10 ft high.

  a. Sketch a scale model of Mr. Singh's classroom. Label the dimensions of the classroom on your sketch.

  b. Find the volume of Mr. Singh's classroom. Why might this information be useful to know?

  c. Find the total area of the walls, the floor, and the ceiling. Why might this information be useful to know?

10. a. Sketch a prism with a base of area 40 cm² and a height of 5 cm.

b. What is the volume of the prism you drew?

c. Do you think everyone in your class drew the same prism? Explain.

d. Do you think the prisms your classmates drew have the same volume as your prism? Explain.

11. Below are side and top views of a triangular prism with ends that are equilateral triangles.

a. Describe two ways you could find the volume of the prism. What is the volume?

b. Describe two ways you could find the surface area of the prism. What is the surface area?

Side view

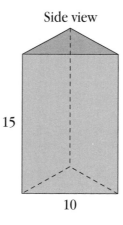

15

10

Top view

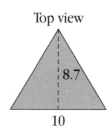

8.7

10

Connections

12. In Problem 3.1, boxes Y and Z have the same volume. Describe the dimensions of another rectangular prism with this same volume but a smaller surface area.

13. a. On isometric dot paper, sketch a closed box with dimensions 4 by 1 by 3.

b. How many unit cubes would fit in a single layer at the bottom of the box you drew?

c. How many layers of unit cubes would be needed to fill the box?

d. Find the volume of the box.

e. Find the surface area of the box.

f. Is there a box with the same volume but less surface area? Explain your answer.

g. Is there a box with the same volume but greater surface area? Explain your answer.

14. The city of Rubberville plans to dig a rectangular landfill. The landfill will have a base with dimensions 700 ft by 200 ft and a depth of 85 ft.

a. How many cubic feet of garbage will the landfill hold?

b. What information would you need to determine how long the landfill can be used until it is full?

c. An excavator was hired to dig the hole for the landfill. How many cubic yards of dirt will he have to haul away?

15. a. Look for an object in your classroom or neighborhood with a volume of about 60 ft^3. Explain how you estimated the volume of the object.

b. Look for an object in your classroom or neighborhood with a volume of about 60 cm^3. Explain how you estimated the volume of the object.

16. Find four rectangular boxes in your home.

   a. Find the dimensions of each box.

   b. Find the volume and surface area of each box.

   c. Is it possible for two boxes to have the same volume but different surface areas? Explain why or why not.

   d. Why do you think most products are not packaged in the shape that uses the least packaging material?

   e. Choose one of the four boxes. See if you can design a box with the same volume as the box you chose but with a smaller surface area. That is, see if you can design a more efficient package.

17. a. Look for objects outside of your classroom that are shaped like prisms. Find three objects that are rectangular prisms and three objects that are nonrectangular prisms.

   b. Without measuring, estimate the volume of each object.

   c. How could you check the volumes you found in part b?

Extensions

18. The drawing below shows a prism with an odd-shaped top and bottom and rectangular sides. The top and bottom each have an area of 10 cm², and the height is 4 cm. What is the volume of the prism? Explain how you found the volume and why you think your method works.

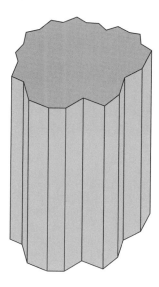

Mathematical Reflections

In this investigation, you developed methods for finding volumes of rectangular and nonrectangular prisms. These questions will help you summarize what you have learned:

1 What is the relationship between the number of unit cubes needed to fill a prism-shaped box and the volume of the box?

2 Describe how you can find the volume of any prism.

Think about your answers to these questions, discuss your ideas with other students and your teacher, and then write a summary of your findings in your journal.

Cylinders

So far in this unit, you have studied boxes shaped like prisms. There are many packages and containers that are not shaped like prisms. For example, salt, juice concentrate, oatmeal, and tuna are often sold in packages shaped like cylinders. A cylinder is a three-dimensional shape with a top and bottom that are congruent circles.

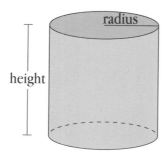

As with a prism, the bottom of a cylinder is called the *base,* and the distance from the base to the top is called the *height.* You can describe a cylinder by giving its dimensions. The *dimensions* of a cylinder are the radius of its base (or top) and its height.

Did you know?

Cylindrical cans often contain liquids. The volume, or *capacity,* of containers that hold liquids are often given in units like quarts, gallons, liters, and milliliters. Although volumes given in these units do not tell you how many unit cubes a container will hold, these units are based on cubic measures. For example, a gallon equals 231 cubic inches. In Investigation 7, you will figure out the cubic equivalent of 1 milliliter.

4.1 Filling a Cylinder

The *volume* of a container is the number of unit cubes it will hold. In the last investigation, you saw that you could find the volume of a prism-shaped box by figuring out how many unit cubes will fit in a single layer at the bottom of the box and then multiplying by the total number of layers needed to fill the box. In this problem, you will develop a method for determining how many cubes will fit inside a cylinder.

Problem 4.1

Make a cylinder by taping together the ends of a sheet of paper. Use the same size paper you used to make the prism shapes in Problem 3.3.

A. Set the cylinder on its base on a sheet of centimeter grid paper. Trace the cylinder's base. Look at the centimeter squares inside your tracing. How many cubes would fit in one layer at the bottom of the cylinder? Consider whole cubes and parts of cubes.

B. How many layers of cubes would it take to fill the cylinder?

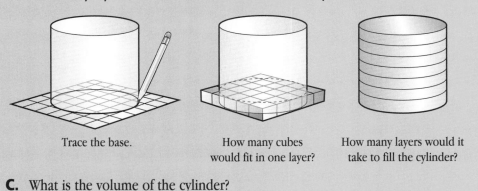

Trace the base.   How many cubes would fit in one layer?   How many layers would it take to fill the cylinder?

C. What is the volume of the cylinder?

■ Problem 4.1 Follow-Up

1. How can you use the dimensions of the cylinder to help you estimate its volume more accurately? Explain.

2. How does the volume of the cylinder compare to the volumes of the prisms you made in Problem 3.3?

Making a Cylinder from a Flat Pattern

In the last problem, you developed a strategy for finding the volume of a cylinder. In this problem, you will develop a strategy for finding the surface area of a cylinder. To do this problem, you will need Labsheet 4.2, which shows a flat pattern for a cylinder.

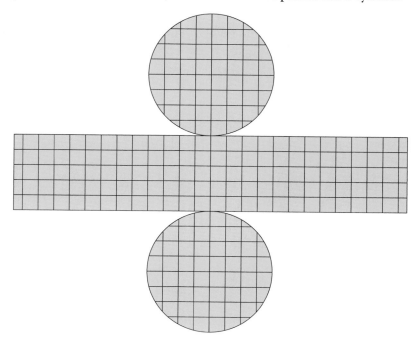

Problem 4.2

Cut out the flat pattern from Labsheet 4.2. Try to cut the pattern so there is a small connector between each circle and the rectangle.

A. What will the dimensions of the cylinder be?

B. What will the surface area of the cylinder be? Explain how you got your answer.

C. Tape the flat pattern together to form a cylinder. How many centimeter cubes will exactly fit in one layer at the bottom of the cylinder? How many cubes will exactly fill the cylinder?

■ **Problem 4.2 Follow-Up**

1. How are the dimensions of the circles and the rectangle in the flat pattern related to the dimensions of the cylinder?

2. How can you use the dimensions of a cylinder to calculate its volume?

3. How can you use the dimensions of a cylinder to calculate its surface area?

4.3 Designing a New Juice Container

Fruit Tree juice company packages its most popular drink, apple-prune juice, in small cylindrical cans. Each can is 8 centimeters high and has a radius of 2 centimeters.

Recent sales reports indicate that sales of Fruit Tree juice are falling, while sales of juice sold by a competitor, the Wrinkled Prune company, are on the rise. Market researchers at Fruit Tree determine that Wrinkled Prune's success is due to its new rectangular juice boxes. Fruit Tree decides to try packaging their juice in rectangular boxes.

Problem 4.3

Fruit Tree wants the new rectangular box to have the same volume as the current cylindrical can.

A. On centimeter grid paper, make a flat pattern for a box that would hold the same amount of juice as the cylindrical can.

B. Cut out your flat pattern. Use colored pencils or markers to design the outside of the box so it will appeal to potential customers. When you are finished, fold and tape your pattern to form a box.

C. Give the dimensions of your box. Are there other possibilities for the dimensions? Explain.

■ Problem 4.3 Follow-Up

1. Compare your juice box with the boxes made by your classmates. Which rectangular box shape do you think would make the best juice container? Why?

2. Make a flat pattern for the current cylindrical can.

3. Compare the surface area of the cylindrical can to the surface area of your juice box. Which container has greater surface area?

As you work on these ACE questions, use your calculator whenever you need it.

Applications

1. A cylindrical storage tank has a radius of 15 ft and a height of 30 ft.

    a. Make a sketch of the tank and label its dimensions.

    b. What is the volume of the tank?

    c. What is the surface area of the tank?

2. A cylinder has a radius of 3 cm. Sand is poured into the cylinder to form a layer 1 cm deep.

    a. What is the volume of sand in the cylinder?

    b. If the height of the cylinder is 20 cm, how many layers of sand—each 1 cm deep—are needed to fill the cylinder?

    c. What is the volume of the cylinder?

3. A soft drink can is a cylinder with a radius of 3 cm and a height of 12 cm. Ms. Doyle's classroom is 6 m wide, 8 m long, and 3 m high. Estimate the number of soft drink cans that would fit inside Ms. Doyle's classroom. Explain how you found your estimate.

4. Below is a scale model of a flat pattern for a cylinder.

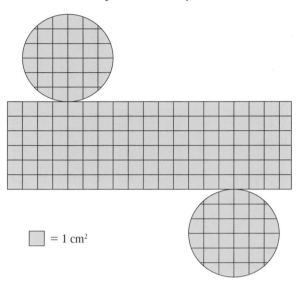

$\square$ = 1 cm²

    a. When the pattern is assembled, what will the volume of the cylinder be?

    b. What will the surface area of the cylinder be?

5. You are the manager of a new movie theater. You need to order popcorn boxes, and you must decide between a cylindrical box and a rectangular box. The cylindrical box has a height of 20 cm and a radius of 7 cm, and the rectangular box has a height of 20 cm and a square base with 12-cm sides. The price of each box is based on the amount of material needed to make the box. The theater plans to charge $2.75 for popcorn, regardless of the shape of the box.

    a. Find the volume and surface area of each container.

    b. Which box would you choose? Give the reasons for your choice. What additional information might help you make a better decision?

Connections

6. How is finding the area of a circle related to finding the volume of a cylinder?

7. Find three different cylindrical objects in your home. For each cylinder, record the dimensions and calculate the volume.

8. A pipeline for carrying oil is 5000 km long and has an inside diameter of 20 cm.

   a. How many cubic centimeters of oil would it take to fill 1 km of the pipeline? (1 km = 100,000 cm)

   b. How many cubic centimeters of oil would it take to fill the entire pipeline?

9. Carlos wants to build a rectangular hot tub that is 4 ft high and holds 1000 ft³ of water. What could the dimensions of the base of Carlos's hot tub be?

10. The Buy-and-Go Mart sells soft drinks in three sizes. Which size is the best buy? Explain your answer.

| 12 oz | 18 oz | 32 oz |
| $1.25 | $1.75 | $3.00 |

11. Tell what features of a cylinder could be measured in the given units.

   a. cm   b. cm²   c. cm³

Extensions

12. A cylindrical can is packed securely in a box as shown at right. The height of the box is 10 cm, and the sides of its square base measure 2 cm.

    a. Find the radius and height of the can.

    b. What is the volume of the empty space between the can and the box?

    c. Find the ratio of the volume of the can to the volume of the box.

    d. Make up a similar example with a different size can and box. What is the ratio of the volume of the can to the volume of the box for your example? How does the ratio compare to the ratio you got in part c?

13. Start with two identical sheets of paper. Tape the long sides of one sheet together to form a cylinder. Form a cylinder from the second sheet by taping the short sides together. Imagine that each cylinder has a top and a bottom.

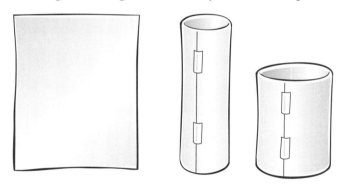

    a. Which cylinder has greater volume? Explain your reasoning.

    b. Which cylinder has greater surface area? Explain your reasoning.

Mathematical Reflections

In this investigation, you developed methods for finding the volume and surface area of a cylinder. These questions will help you summarize what you have learned:

1 Describe how you can find the volume of a cylinder.

2 Describe how you can find the surface area of a cylinder.

3 Discuss the similarities and differences in the methods for finding the volume of a cylinder, a rectangular prism, and a nonrectangular prism.

4 Discuss the similarities and differences in the methods for finding the surface area of a cylinder, a rectangular prism, and a nonrectangular prism.

Think about your answers to these questions, discuss your ideas with other students and your teacher, and then write a summary of your findings in your journal.

Cones and Spheres

Many common and important three-dimensional objects are not shaped like prisms or cylinders. For example, ice cream is often served in *cones.* The planet we live on is very nearly a *sphere.*

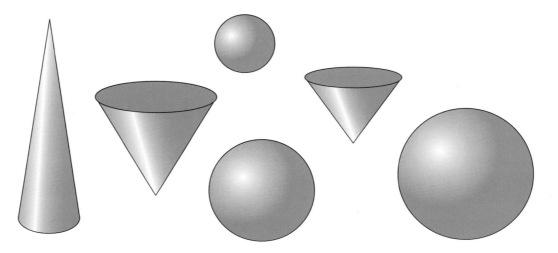

Cones come in many shapes and sizes—from tall and thin to short and wide. As with a cylinder and a prism, we can describe a cone by giving its dimensions. The *dimensions* of a cone are the radius of its circular end and its height.

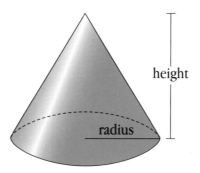

Although spheres may differ in size, they are all the same shape. We can describe a sphere by giving its radius.

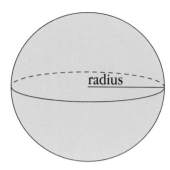

In this investigation, you will explore ways to determine the volume of cones and spheres.

5.1 **Comparing Spheres and Cylinders**

In this problem, you will make a sphere and a cylinder with the same radius and height and then compare their volumes. (The "height" of a sphere is just its diameter.) You can use the relationship you observe to help you develop a method for finding the volume of a sphere.

Did you know?

The Earth is nearly a sphere. You may have heard that, until Christopher Columbus's voyage in 1492, most people believed the Earth was flat. Actually, as early as the fourth century B.C., scientists in Greece and Egypt had figured out that the Earth was round. They observed the shadow of the Earth as it passed across the Moon during a lunar eclipse. It was clear that the shadow was round. Combining this observation with evidence gathered from observing constellations, these scientists concluded that the Earth was indeed spherical. In fact, in the third century B.C., Eratosthenes, a scientist from Alexandria, Egypt, was actually able to estimate the circumference of the Earth.

Problem 5.1

- Using modeling dough, make a sphere with a diameter between 2 inches and 3.5 inches.

- Using a strip of transparent plastic, make a cylinder with an open top and bottom that fits snugly around your sphere. Trim the height of the cylinder to match the height of the sphere. Tape the cylinder together so that it remains rigid.

- Now, flatten the sphere so that it fits snugly in the bottom of the cylinder. Mark the height of the flattened sphere on the cylinder.

height of cylinder

height of empty space

height of flattened sphere

A. Measure and record the height of the cylinder, the height of the empty space, and the height of the flattened sphere.

B. What is the relationship between the volume of the sphere and the volume of the cylinder?

Remove the modeling dough from the cylinder, and save the cylinder for the next problem.

Problem 5.1 Follow-Up

Compare your results with the results of a group that made a larger or smaller sphere. Did the other group find the same relationship between the volume of the sphere and the volume of the cylinder?

5.2 Comparing Cones and Cylinders

In the last problem, you discovered the relationship between the volume of a sphere and the volume of a cylinder. In this problem, you will look for a relationship between the volume of a cone and the volume of a cylinder.

Problem 5.2

- Roll a piece of stiff paper into a cone shape so that the tip touches the bottom of your cylinder.

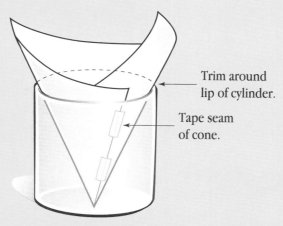

Trim around lip of cylinder.

Tape seam of cone.

- Tape the cone shape along the seam and trim it to form a cone with the same height as the cylinder.

- Fill the cone to the top with sand or rice, and empty the contents into the cylinder. Repeat this as many times as needed to completely fill the cylinder.

What is the relationship between the volume of the cone and the volume of the cylinder?

If a cone, a cylinder, and a sphere have the same radius and the same height, what is the relationship between the volumes of the three shapes?

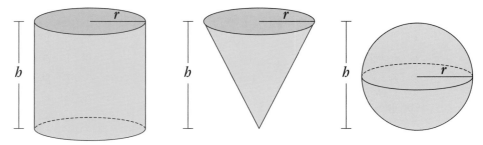

5.3 Melting Ice Cream

Olga and Serge buy ice cream from Chilly's Ice Cream Parlor. They think about buying an ice cream cone to bring back to Olga's little sister but decide the ice cream would melt before they got back home. Serge wonders, "If the ice cream all melts into the cone, will it fill the cone?"

Problem 5.3

Olga gets a scoop of ice cream in a cone, and Serge gets a scoop in a cylindrical cup. Each container has a height of 8 centimeters and a radius of 4 centimeters, and each scoop of ice cream is a sphere with a radius of 4 centimeters.

A. If Serge allows his ice cream to melt, will it fill his cup exactly? Explain.

B. If Olga allows her ice cream to melt, will it fill her cone exactly? Explain.

■ **Problem 5.3 Follow-Up**

How many scoops of ice cream of the size above can be packed into each container?

As you work on these ACE questions, use your calculator whenever you need it.

Applications

1. The city of La Agua has water storage tanks in three different shapes: a cylinder, a cone, and a sphere. Each tank has a radius of 20 ft and a height of 40 ft.

   a. Sketch each tank, and label its dimensions.

   b. What is the volume of the cylindrical tank?

   c. What is the volume of the conical tank?

   d. What is the volume of the spherical tank?

2. a. Find the volume of the cylinder, cone, and sphere shown below.

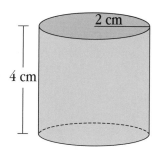
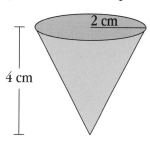
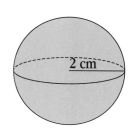

   b. How do the volumes of the three shapes compare?

3. An ice cream cone has a radius of 1 in and a height of 5 in. If a scoop of ice cream is a sphere with a radius of 1 in, how many scoops can be packed into the cone?

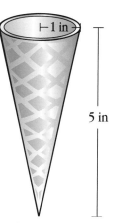

4. The track-and-field club is planning a frozen yogurt sale to raise money for new equipment. The club needs to buy containers to hold the yogurt. They must choose between the cup and cone shown below. The containers cost the same amount of money. The club plans to charge customers $1.25 for a serving of yogurt. Which container should the club buy? Why?

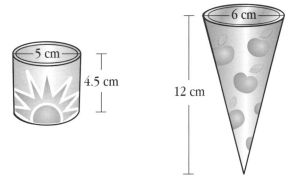

5. Fernando collected popcorn containers from several local movie theaters and recorded the prices and dimensions of the containers. Which is the best buy? Explain your answer.

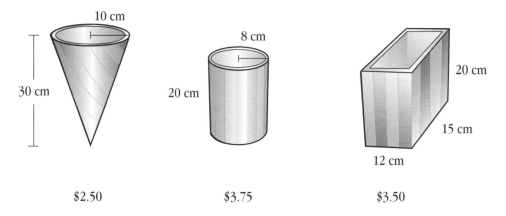

$2.50 $3.75 $3.50

Connections

6. A soft drink can is a cylinder with a radius of 3 cm and a height of 12 cm.

    a. Sketch a soft drink can, and label its dimensions.

    b. What is the circumference of the can?

    c. What is the volume of the can?

    d. What is the surface area of the can?

    e. How many cans of soda would it take to fill a liter bottle? (A liter bottle contains 1000 cm³.)

Extensions

7. Some Inuit Indians build igloos shaped like hemispheres (halves of a sphere). Some Hopi Indians in Arizona build adobes shaped like rectangular boxes. Suppose an igloo has an inner diameter of 40 ft.

    a. Describe the shape of a Hopi dwelling that would provide the same amount of living space as the igloo described above.

    b. For a Hopi dwelling to have the same amount of floor space as the igloo described above, what should the dimensions of the floor be?

8. Laurie made a scale model of a submarine for her science class.

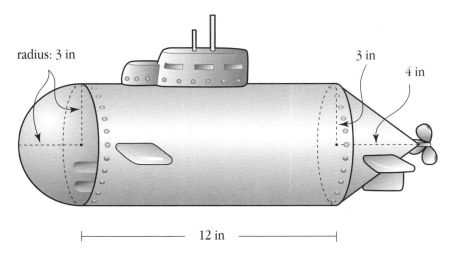

radius: 3 in

3 in

4 in

12 in

a. What is the volume of Laurie's model?

b. If 1 in on the model represents 100 ft on the actual submarine, what is the volume of the actual submarine?

9. a. Give the dimensions of the largest sphere that will fit inside a cubic box with 5-cm edges.

b. Give the dimensions of the largest cylinder that will fit inside a cubic box with 5-cm edges.

c. Give the dimensions of the largest cone that will fit inside a cubic box with 5-cm edges.

d. Which shape—sphere, cylinder, or cone—fits best inside the cubic box? That is, for which shape is there the least space between the shape and the box?

10. The edges of a cube measure 10 cm. Describe the dimensions of a cylinder and a cone with the same volume as the cube. (Hint: Starting with the cylinder is easier.) Explain your reasoning.

11. Pearl measures the circumference of a sphere and finds that it is 54 cm. What is the volume of the sphere? Explain.

12. The shapes below are pyramids. A pyramid is named for the shape of its base. The left shape is a triangular pyramid, the center shape is a square pyramid, and the right shape is a pentagonal pyramid. The sides of all pyramids are triangles.

   a. As the number of sides in the base of a pyramid increases, what happens to the shape of the pyramid?

   b. Describe a method for finding the surface area of a pyramid.

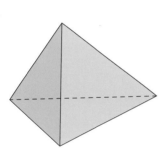 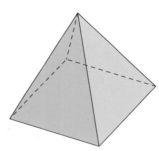 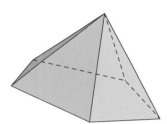

Mathematical Reflections

In this investigation, you studied the relationships between the volumes of a cone, a sphere, and a cylinder with the same radius and height. These questions will help you summarize what you have learned:

1 If a cone, a cylinder, and a sphere have the same radius and height, describe the relationships among the volume of the cone, the volume of the sphere, and the volume of the cylinder. Use examples and sketches to illustrate your answer.

2 If you know the radius of a sphere, how can you find the sphere's volume?

3 If you know the radius and height of a cone, how can you find the cone's volume?

Think about your answers to these questions, discuss your ideas with other students and your teacher, and then write a summary of your findings in your journal.

Scaling Boxes

Discarded paper, plastic, and glass is not the only urban-waste disposal problem. Decaying organic waste from food, grass, and leaves gives off unpleasant odors and explosive methane gas.

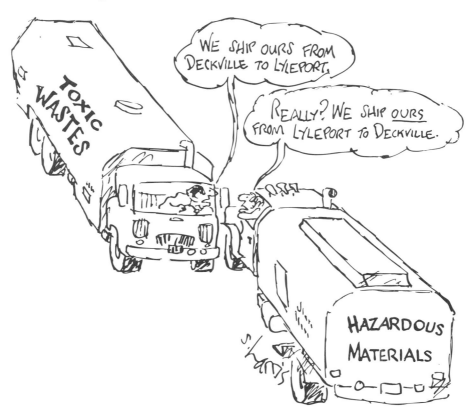

© 1991 by Sidney Harris. From *You Want Proof? I'll Give You Proof!* W. H. Freeman, New York.

Composting is a method for turning organic waste into rich soil. Composting has been used for thousands of years on farms and in gardens. Today, many people have indoor compost boxes that break down kitchen waste quickly and with little odor. The secret is in the worms!

Recipe for a 1-2-3 Compost Box

- Start with an open rectangular wood box that is 1 foot high, 2 feet wide, and 3 feet long. We call this a *1-2-3 box*.
- Mix 10 pounds of shredded newspaper with 15 quarts of water, and put the mixture in the 1-2-3 box.
- Add a few handfuls of soil.
- Add about 1000 redworms (about 1 pound).

Every day, mix collected kitchen waste with the soil in the box. The worms will do the rest of the work, turning the waste into new soil. A 1-2-3 box will decompose about 0.5 pound of garbage each day.

Source: Woldumar Nature Center, Lansing, Michigan.

6.1 Building a Bigger Box

Deshondra chose composting as the topic of her science project. She plans to build a compost box at home and to keep records of the amount of soil produced over several weeks.

Problem 6.1

Deshondra wants her compost box to be larger than the 1-2-3 box. She decides to double each edge of the 1-2-3 box.

A. Use grid paper to make scale models of a 1-2-3 box and Deshondra's 2-4-6 box. The boxes should have open tops.

B. Deshondra wants to increase the composting capacity of her box by the same factor as the volume. How much shredded paper and water will she need for her 2-4-6 compost box?

C. How many worms will she need?

D. How much plywood will she need to build the box?

E. How many pounds of garbage will the box be able to decompose in one day?

Save your model of the 1-2-3 box for the next problem.

■ Problem 6.1 Follow-Up

1. Find the ratio of the length of each side of the 1-2-3 box to the length of the corresponding side of the 2-4-6 box.

2. Find the ratio of the surface area of the 1-2-3 box to the surface area of the 2-4-6 box.

3. Find the ratio of the volume of the 1-2-3 box to the volume of the 2-4-6 box.

6.2 Scaling Up the Compost Box

Ms. Fernandez's class decides that building and maintaining a compost box would be a fascinating project. One student suggests that they could earn money for a class trip by selling the worms and soil they produce to a local nursery.

The class estimates that they throw away about 1 pound of organic waste each day, rather than the 0.5 pound specified in the 1-2-3 box recipe. They need to adjust the recipe to build a box large enough to decompose all the garbage they will produce.

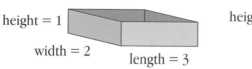
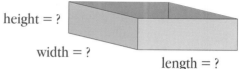

height = 1
width = 2
length = 3

height = ?
width = ?
length = ?

Problem 6.2

How could Ms. Fernandez's class scale up the recipe for the 1-2-3 box to make a box that will decompose 1 pound of organic waste each day?

A. What box dimensions would give the required space for the new quantity of organic waste?

B. Use grid paper to make a scale model of a box that would decompose 1 pound of garbage per day. The box should have an open top.

■ Problem 6.2 Follow-Up

1. How much plywood will the class need to construct their box?

2. How much shredded paper and water will they need?

3. How many worms will they need?

6.3 Looking at Similar Prisms

In *Stretching and Shrinking*, you studied similar two-dimensional figures. The ideas you learned in that unit also apply to three-dimensional figures. For example, two rectangular prisms are similar if the ratios of the lengths of corresponding edges are equal.

The *scale factor* is the number that each dimension of one rectangular prism must be multiplied by to get the dimensions of a similar prism. For example, a 1-2-3 box is similar to a 2-4-6 box. The scale factor from the small box to the large box is 2, because the edge lengths of the small box must be multiplied by 2 to get the corresponding edge lengths of the large box.

Problem 6.3

A. Find three other rectangular boxes that are similar to a 1-2-3 box, and give their dimensions. Give the scale factor from a 1-2-3 box to each box you find.

B. 1. Calculate the surface area of each box you found in part A, and tell how the result compares to the surface area of a 1-2-3 box.

   2. How is the change in surface area from a 1-2-3 box to a similar box related to the scale factor from the 1-2-3 box to the similar box?

C. 1. Calculate the volume of each box you found in part A, and tell how the result compares to the volume of a 1-2-3 box.

   2. How is the change in volume from a 1-2-3 box to a similar box related to the scale factor from the 1-2-3 box to the similar box?

■ Problem 6.3 Follow-Up

Are all rectangular prisms similar? Explain your answer.

As you work on these ACE questions, use your calculator whenever you need it. Remember that height is the first number when dimensions of a box are given.

Applications

1. a.   What is the volume of a 1-2-2 box?

b.   What is the surface area of a closed 1-2-2 box?

2. a.   What is the volume of a 1.5-1.5-3 box?

b.   What is the surface area of a closed 1.5-1.5-3 box?

3. a.   What is the volume of a 2-4-1 box?

b.   What is the surface area of a closed 2-4-1 box?

4. a.   Make a sketch of an open 2-2-3 box and an open 2-2-6 box. Label the edges of the boxes.

b.   Find the volume of each box in part a.

c.   Find the surface area of each box in part a.

d.   If you wanted to adapt the 1-2-3 compost box recipe for the boxes in part a, how many worms and how much paper and water would you need for each box?

5. a.   Make a sketch of a 1-3-5 box. Label the edges of the box.

b.   Sketch three boxes that have twice the volume of a 1-3-5 box. Label each box with its dimensions.

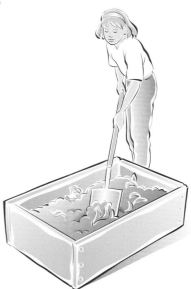

6. **a.** Make scale drawings of three cubes: one with edges measuring 1 ft, one with edges measuring 2 ft, and one with edges measuring 3 ft. For each cube, tell what length in the drawing represents 1 ft. In other words, give the scale for each drawing.

   b. Find the volume of each cube in part a.

   c. Find the surface area of each cube in part a.

   d. Describe what happens to the volume of a cube when the edge lengths are doubled, tripled, quadrupled, and so on.

   e. Describe what happens to the surface area of a cube when the edge lengths are doubled, tripled, quadrupled, and so on.

7. For every ton of paper that is recycled, about 17 trees and 3.3 yd^3 of landfill space are saved. In the United States, 500,000 trees are used each week to produce the Sunday papers. If one Sunday, all the newspapers were made from 100% recycled paper, how much landfill would be saved?

8. In the United States, an average of 2.7 pounds of garbage per person is delivered to available landfills each day. A cubic foot of compressed garbage weighs about 50 pounds.

   a. Estimate the amount of landfill used by a family of four in one year.

   b. Estimate the amount of landfill used by the families of all your classmates in one year. Assume each family has four people.

9. Each year the United States generates about 450 million cubic yards of solid waste. Mr. Costello's classroom is 42 ft long, 30 ft wide, and 12 ft high. How many rooms of this size would be needed to hold all this garbage?

Connections

10. Mary's class decides to build a cylindrical compost box. Mary calculates that a cylindrical container with a height of 2 ft and a radius of 1 ft would decompose 0.5 pound of garbage each day. She calls this container a *1-2 cylinder*.

1 ft

2 ft

    a. How does the volume of the 1-2 cylinder compare to the volume of the 1-2-3 box?

    b. How does the surface area of the 1-2 cylinder compare to the surface area of the 1-2-3 box?

    c. Mary's class estimates that they throw away about 1 pound of organic waste at school each day. What size cylinder should they build to handle this much waste?

11. At the movie theater, Ted is trying to decide whether to buy a large popcorn or two small popcorns. Both sizes come in cylindrical containers. Ted thinks that the heights of the containers are about the same and that the radius of the large container is about twice the radius of the small container. A large popcorn costs $3.00, and a small popcorn costs $1.50. To get the most popcorn for his $3.00, should Ted buy one large popcorn or two small popcorns? Explain your answer.

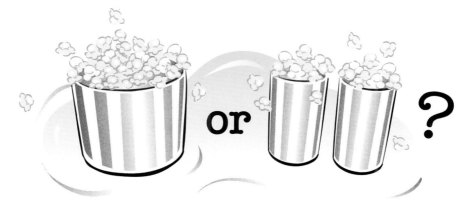

or   ?

12. The Whole Earth Compost Company builds and sells 1-2-3 compost boxes. They need to store a supply of the boxes in their warehouse to fill customers' orders. The sketch below shows a 1-2-3 box and the space in the warehouse allotted for the boxes.

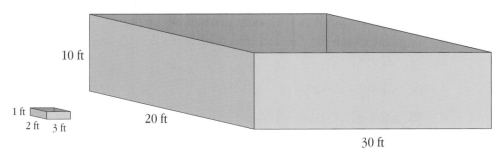

a. How many 1-2-3 boxes could be stored in one layer on the floor of the storage space?

b. How many layers of boxes could be stacked in the storage space?

c. How many boxes could be stored in the storage space?

In 13–15, find the volume and surface area of the box.

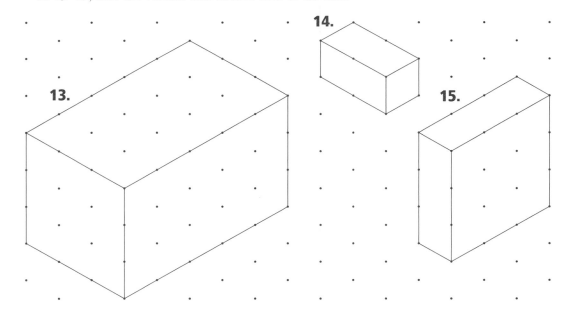

Extensions

16. Is the price of cereal directly related to the volume of the box? Collect some data to help you answer this question.

    a. Record the dimensions and prices of two or three different size boxes of the same cereal brand.

    b. Calculate the volume of each box.

    c. Calculate the cost per unit of volume for each box. Compare the results for the different boxes.

    d. Write a short report summarizing what you learned about the relationship between box size and cereal price.

17. The following sketch shows a "tilted box" in which the base, top, and smaller sides are rectangles, and the other two faces are non-rectangular parallelograms.

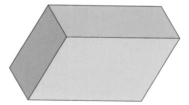

    a. What measurements would you need to find the volume of this box? How would you use these measurements to calculate the volume?

    b. What measurements would you need to find the surface area of this box? How would you use these measurements to calculate the surface area?

18. Think about a "sliceable" rectangular prism, such as a cake, a loaf of bread, or a brick of cheese.

    a. How many different ways can you slice such a prism into two pieces of equal volume?

    b. If the prism were a cube, how many ways could you slice it into two pieces of equal volume?

19. The dimensions of cylinder A are twice the dimensions of cylinder B.

    a. What is the ratio of the radius of cylinder A to the radius of cylinder B?

    b. What is the ratio of the height of cylinder A to the height of cylinder B?

    c. What is the ratio of the surface area of cylinder A to the surface area of cylinder B?

    d. What is the ratio of the volume of cylinder A to the volume of cylinder B?

20. The dimensions of cylinder A are three times the dimensions of cylinder B. Repeat parts a–d of question 19 for these cylinders.

21. The dimensions of cylinder A are four times the dimensions of cylinder B. Repeat parts a–d of question 19 for these cylinders.

22. Natasha built a model cruise ship from a kit. She was trying to imagine what the actual cruise ship would look like. The scale factor from the model ship to the actual ship is 200.

    a. If the length of the model ship is 25 cm, what is the length of the actual ship?

    b. If the cold-storage space of the model has a capacity of 600 cm³, what is the capacity of the cold-storage space of the actual ship?

    c. The area of the dance floor on the actual cruise ship is 250 m². What is the area of the dance floor on the model?

    d. The cylindrical smokestack on the model has a height of 4 cm and a radius of 1.5 cm.

        i. What are the dimensions of the smokestack on the actual ship?

        ii. What is the volume of the smokestack on the actual ship?

        iii. What is the surface area of the smokestack on the actual ship?

Mathematical Reflections

In this investigation, you learned how changing the dimensions of a rectangular box affects its volume and how changing the volume of a rectangular box affects its dimensions. These questions will help you summarize what you have learned:

1. Suppose you wanted to build a rectangular box with twice the volume of a given rectangular box. How could you determine the possible dimensions for the new box?

2. Describe how the volume and surface area of a rectangular prism change as each of its dimensions is doubled, tripled, quadrupled, and so on.

Think about your answers to these questions, discuss your ideas with other students and your teacher, and then write a summary of your findings in your journal.

Finding Volumes of Irregular Objects

You have solved many problems in which you had to calculate the volume or surface area of a prism, a cylinder, a cone, or a sphere. However, many three-dimensional objects do not have such regular shapes. In this investigation, you will explore finding volumes of odd-shaped, or irregular, objects.

7.1 Displacing Water

According to legend, Archimedes, a Greek scientist in the third century B.C., made an important discovery while taking a bath. He noticed that the water level rose when he sat down in the tub. He figured out that he could calculate the volume of his body—or any other object—by submerging it in water and finding the difference between the combined volume of the water and the object, and the volume of the water alone. This difference in volumes is called *water displacement.* It is said that Archimedes was so excited about his discovery that he jumped from his bath and, without dressing, ran into the streets shouting "Eureka!"

Think about this!

Does Archimedes' discovery suggest a way to measure the volume of an irregular shape?

In this problem, you measure the volume of water in *milliliters,* a unit commonly used to express the volume of liquids. As part of the problem, you will figure out how to convert milliliters to cubic centimeters.

Problem 7.1

You will need a measuring box or cylinder with milliliter markings, water, a few centimeter cubes, and some odd-shaped objects like stones.

Fill the measuring container about halfway with water. Record the volume of the water in milliliters.

To find the volume of an object, drop it into the container and find the volume of water that is displaced. That is, find the difference between the combined volume of the water and the object, and the volume of the water alone.

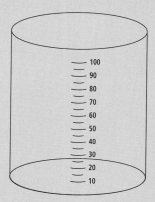

A. How much water is displaced when you drop a centimeter cube into the container? What does this tell you about the relationship between one milliliter and one cubic centimeter?

B. Use this method to find the volume in cubic centimeters of some odd-shaped objects.

■ Problem 7.1 Follow-Up

Give examples of objects whose volume cannot be measured by this method. Explain why this method would not work.

As you work on these ACE questions, use your calculator whenever you need it.

Applications

1. A cylinder with a diameter of 5 cm contains some water. Five identical marbles are dropped into the cylinder, and the water level rises by 1 cm. What is the volume of one marble?

2. A rectangular 1-2-3 box is half full of water.

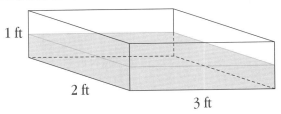

1 ft

2 ft

3 ft

    a. What is the total volume of the box?

    b. What is the water level in the box?

    c. Several large stones are dropped into the box, and the water level rises to $\frac{3}{4}$ full. What is the total volume of the stones?

3. A gallon of paint covers about 400 ft^2 of surface area. When an artist painted a statue he had carved, he used about 0.25 gallon of paint. What is the approximate surface area of the statue?

4. A rectangular juice box contains 250 milliliters of juice. Give the dimensions of a box that will hold this amount of juice.

5. An average adult has a mass of about 78 kilograms and a surface area of about 9675 cm^2. A film of water about 0.05 cm thick clings to our skin when we step out of the bath.

    a. What volume of water clings to an average adult when he steps out of the bath?

    b. If 1 cm^3 of water has a mass of 1 gram, what percent of an average adult's body mass is the mass of the water that clings to him after a shower?

Extensions

6. Paper often comes in packages of 500 sheets, called reams. A particular ream of paper has a length of 28 cm, a width of 21.5 cm, and a height of 5.5 cm.

    a. What is the volume of a sheet of paper?

    b. What is the thickness of a sheet of paper?

7. A particular iceberg is shaped like a mountain with a height of 1250 m above the water level and a distance of 132 km around the base (1 km = 1000 m) at water level.

    a. What shape most closely resembles the top of a mountain?

    b. Estimate the volume of the part of the iceberg that is above water level.

Mathematical Reflections

In this investigation, you found volumes of odd-shaped objects by measuring water displacement. These questions will help you summarize what you have learned:

1. Describe how you can find the volume of an odd-shaped object by measuring water displacement, and give an example of a situation in which this method would be useful.

2. What is the relationship between cubic centimeters and milliliters? How can you prove this relationship?

Think about your answers to these questions, discuss your ideas with other students and your teacher, and then write a summary of your findings in your journal.

Package Design Contest

The Worldwide Sporting Company wants new package designs for its table-tennis balls (Ping-Pong balls). The company's table-tennis balls are about 3.8 cm in diameter. There are three main requirements for the packages:

- The board of directors wants to have three different size packages: small, medium, and large.
- The president of the company wants the cost of the packages to be a primary consideration.
- The sales manager wants the packages to be appealing to customers, to stack easily, and to look good on store shelves.

The company holds a package design contest, and you decide to enter.

- You must design three different packages for the table-tennis balls.
- You must submit your designs and a written proposal to WSC.
- You must try, in your written proposal, to convince WSC to use your designs.

Include the following things in your proposal:

1. A description of the shape or shapes of the packages and an explanation for why you selected these shapes.

2. Patterns for each package that, when they are cut out, folded, and taped together, will make models of your packages. Use centimeter grid paper to make your patterns.

3. Cost estimates to construct your designs. The packaging material costs $0.005 per square centimeter.

4. An explanation of how you have addressed WSC's requirements.

Remember, you are trying to convince WSC that your designs are the best and that they meet the requirements. Your written proposal should be neat, well organized, and easy to read so that the company officials can follow your work and ideas easily.

Unit Reflections

While working on the problems in this unit you developed strategies for finding *surface area*, *volume*, and *flat patterns* for rectangular prisms and cylinders. You used the relationships of other figures to cylinders to find the volume of shapes such as *cones* and *spheres,* and irregular solids. Finally, you discovered the effects of enlargement and reduction on dimensions, surface area, and volume of prisms.

Using Your Understanding of Volume and Surface Area—To test your understanding of volume and surface area, consider the following problems that require knowledge and skills you developed during the investigations of this unit.

1 *The drawing on the right is a flat pattern for a rectangular prism.*

a. What are the dimensions of the box that can be made from the flat pattern?

b. What is the surface area of the box?

c. What is the volume of the box?

d. Draw two other flat patterns that will produce boxes of the same size and shape.

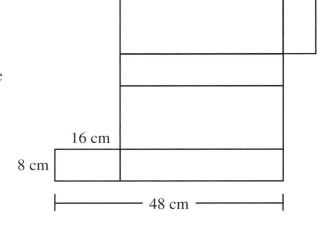

16 cm

16 cm

8 cm

48 cm

2 *Sweet-Tooth Chocolates is marketing a special assortment of caramels. They want to put the 40 individual caramels into a rectangular box. Each caramel is a 1-inch cube. The caramels should completely fill the box.*

    a. Which arrangement of caramels would require the most cardboard for a box?

    b. Which arrangement of caramels would require the least cardboard?

    c. Make sketches of the boxes you described in part a and part b and label the dimensions.

    d. Draw flat plans for each box and add the minimum number of flaps needed to fold and then glue the pattern together so that the top opens.

    e. If each dimension of the box in part b is doubled, how many more caramels could be packaged in the new box?

3 *The Just-Add-Water Company has decided to change the packaging for a breakfast drink, Twang. Twang used to come in cylindrical containers with a base diameter of 6 inches and a height of 10 inches. The new container will be a square prism as shown in this sketch.*

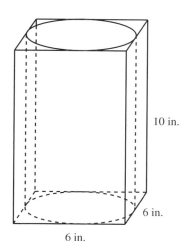

10 in.

6 in.

6 in.

    a. What is the volume of the original cylindrical container?

    b. How much more juice can the rectangular prism hold than the cylindrical container?

    c. Suppose that the cost per cubic inch of Twang is to be the same for both containers. How much should a new box of Twang cost if the original container cost $2.19?

    d. The company is also considering selling the drink in a cone with the same volume as the cylinder. Describe possible dimensions for such a cone.

Explaining Your Reasoning—To answer problems about surface area and volume of solid figures you have to know the meaning of those terms and some strategies for calculating the measurements from given dimensions of various figures.

1. What do *volume* and *surface area* measurements tell about a solid figure?

2. What algebraic formulas will show how to calculate surface area, *A*, and volume, *V*, of the figures drawn here?

a. a rectangular prism

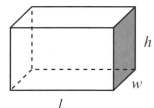

b. a cylinder

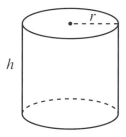

3. How would you convince someone that the formulas given in Question 2 are correct?

4. How are the volumes of cylinders, cones, and spheres related?

5. If you know the volume of an object such as a box, a cylinder, or a cone, can you determine its surface area? If you know the surface area, can you find the volume?

6. How are the surface areas and volumes of similar solid figures related?

Measurement of surface area and volume for solid figures is used in many practical, scientific, and engineering problems. You will encounter the key ideas about area and volume in many future *Connected Mathematics* units, in other mathematics subjects such as geometry and calculus, and in many situations of daily life such as packing, storing and building tasks.

base The bottom face of a three-dimensional shape.

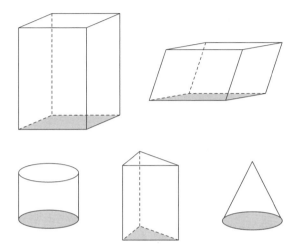

cone A three-dimensional shape with a circular end and a pointed end.

cube A three-dimensional shape with six identical square faces.

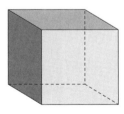

cylinder A three-dimensional shape with two opposite faces that are congruent circles. A rectangle (the lateral surface) is "wrapped around" the circular ends.

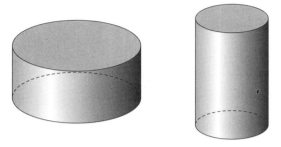

edge The line segment formed where two faces of a three-dimensional shape meet.

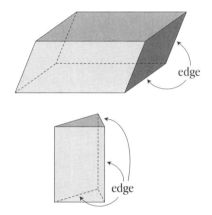

face A polygon that forms one of the flat surfaces of a three-dimensional shape.

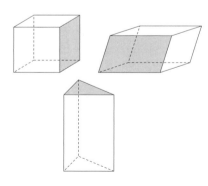

flat pattern An arrangement of attached polygons that can be folded into a three-dimensional shape.

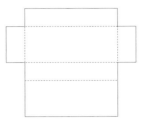

oblique prism A prism whose vertical faces are not all rectangles.

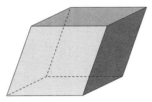

prism A three-dimensional shape with a top and bottom that are congruent polygons and faces that are parallelograms.

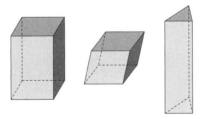

rectangular prism A prism with a top and bottom that are congruent rectangles.

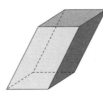

Right rectangular prism

Oblique rectangular prism

right prism A prism whose vertical faces are rectangles.

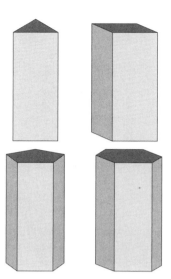

sphere A three-dimensional shape whose surface consists of all the points that are a given distance from the center of the shape.

surface area The area required to cover a three-dimensional shape. In a prism, it is the sum of the areas of all the faces.

unit cube A cube whose edges are 1 unit long. It is the basic unit of measurement for volume.

volume The amount of space occupied by, or the capacity of, a three-dimensional shape. It is the number of unit cubes that will fit into a three-dimensional shape.

Index

Archimedes, 68
Area. *See also* **Surface area**
    ACE, 19–22
    units of, 18

Base
    of a cylinder, 37
    of a nonrectangular prism, 26
    of a pyramid, 55
    of a rectangular prism, 8
Box
    ACE, 10–13, 19–22, 29–35, 61–66
    cubic, 5–6
    rectangular, 7–9
    scaling, 57–60
    surface area of, 15–18
    volume of, 15–18, 24–28

Capacity, units of, 37
Columbus, Christopher, 47
Cone, 46–50
    ACE, 51–55
    dimensions of, 46
    volume of, 49–50
Cube, 4, 5–6
    ACE, 10
    flat pattern for, 5–6
Cubic unit, for volume, 18
Cylinder, 37–40
    ACE, 41–44, 51–54
    capacity of, 37
    dimensions of, 37

    flat pattern for, 39–40
    surface area of, 39–40
    volume of, 38, 47–50

Displacing water, 68–69

Eratosthenes, 47

Flat pattern
    ACE, 10–13, 41–44
    for a cube, 5–6
    for a cylinder, 39–40
    for a hexagonal prism, 27–28
    for a pentagonal prism, 27–28
    for a rectangular prism, 7–9
    surface area and, 4
    for a triangular prism, 27–28

Hexagonal prism, 26–28
Hexomino, 12

Investigation
    Building Boxes, 5–14
    Cones and Spheres, 46–56
    Cylinders, 37–45
    Designing Packages, 15–23
    Finding Volumes of Boxes, 24–36
    Finding Volumes of Irregular Objects,
      68–72
    Scaling Boxes, 57–67
Irregular objects
    ACE, 70–71
    volume of, 4, 68–69

Journal, 14, 23, 36, 45, 56, 67, 72

Looking Back and Looking Ahead:
  Unit Reflections, 74–76

Mathematical Highlights, 4
Mathematical Reflections, 14, 23, 36,
  45, 56, 67, 72

Nonrectangular prism, 26–28

Pattern. *See* **Flat pattern**
Pentagonal prism, 26–28
Pontiac Silverdome, 21
Prism. *See also* **Rectangular prism**,
  Nonrectangular prism, 26
    ACE, 10–13, 19–22, 29–35
    nonrectangular, 26–28
    rectangular, 7–9, 15–18, 24–26
Pyramid, 55

Rectangular prism, 26
  ACE, 10–13, 19–22, 29–35, 61–66
  flat pattern for, 7–9
  scaling, 57–60
  surface area of, 4, 15–18
  volume of, 4, 15–18, 24–28

Scale factor, 60
Scaling, 57–60
  ACE, 61–66
Sphere, 46–50
  ACE, 51–55
  dimensions of, 47

volume of, 47–50
Square prism, 27–28
Surface area, 4, 15
  ACE, 19–22, 29–35, 41–44, 61–66
  of a box, 15–18
  of a cylinder, 39–40
  of a pyramid, 55
  of a rectangular prism, 15–18
  scaling and, 58–60
  units for, 18

Tiling, 13
Triangular prism, 26–28

Unit cube, 5

Volume, 4
  ACE, 19–22, 29–35, 41–44, 51–55,
    61–66, 70–71
  of a box, 15–18, 24–28
  of a cone, 49–50
  of a cylinder, 38, 47–50
  of a hexagonal prism, 27–28
  of irregular objects, 68–69
  of a pentagonal prism, 27–28
  of a rectangular prism, 15–18, 24–28
  scaling and, 58–60
  of a sphere, 47–50
  of a square prism, 27–28
  of a triangular prism, 27–28
  units of, 18, 37, 68
  water displacement and, 68–69

Water displacement, 68–69

Connected Mathematics®

What Do You Expect?

Probability and Expected Value

Student Edition

Glenda Lappan
James T. Fey
William M. Fitzgerald
Susan N. Friel
Elizabeth Difanis Phillips

Prentice
Hall

Glenview, Illinois
Needham, Massachusetts
Upper Saddle River, New Jersey

Connected Mathematics® was developed at Michigan State University with the support of National Science Foundation Grant No. MDR 9150217.

This project was supported, in part,
by the
National Science Foundation
Opinions expressed are those of the authors
and not necessarily those of the Foundation

The Michigan State University authors and administration have agreed that all MSU royalties arising from this publication will be devoted to purposes supported by the Department of Mathematics and the MSU Mathematics Education Enrichment Fund.

Contents

Mathematical Highlights   4

Investigation 1: Evaluating Games of Chance   5
  1.1 What's in the Bucket?   5
  1.2 Matching Colors   6
  1.3 Making Purple   8
  1.4 Making Counting Trees   10
  Applications—Connections—Extensions   13
  Mathematical Reflections   21

Investigation 2: Analyzing Number-Cube Games   22
  2.1 Playing the Addition Game   22
  2.2 Playing the Multiplication Game   23
  Applications—Connections—Extensions   24
  Mathematical Reflections   31

Investigation 3: Probability and Area   32
  3.1 Cracking Level 1   32
  3.2 Cracking Level 2   34
  Applications—Connections—Extensions   36
  Mathematical Reflections   40

Investigation 4: Analyzing Two-Stage Games   41
  4.1 Choosing Paths   41
  4.2 Finding the Best Arrangement   43
  Applications—Connections—Extensions   45
  Mathematical Reflections   49

Investigation 5: Expected Value   50
  5.1 Shooting the One-and-One   50
  5.2 Finding Expected Value   51
  Applications—Connections—Extensions   53
  Mathematical Reflections   58

Investigation 6: Carnival Games   59
  6.1 Drawing Marbles   59
  6.2 Choosing the Best Game   60
  6.3 Taking a Computer Safari   61
  Applications—Connections—Extensions   64
  Mathematical Reflections   68

Investigation 7: Analyzing Sequences of Outcomes   69
  7.1 Counting Puppies   69
  7.2 Guessing Answers   70
  Applications—Connections—Extensions   74
  Mathematical Reflections   78

The Unit Project   79

Looking Back and Looking Ahead: Unit Reflections   81

Glossary   84

Index   86

What Do You Expect?

What Do You Expect?

In the district finals, Nicky has just been fouled and is in a one-and-one free-throw situation. This means that she must make her first shot to try a second shot. Nicky's free-throw average is 60%. Is Nicky most likely to miss the first shot, to make the first shot and miss the second shot, or to make both shots?

Raymundo invented the Prime Number Multiplication game. Two 1-6 number cubes are rolled to get a product. Player A scores 10 points if the product is prime, and Player B scores 1 point if it is not prime. Raymundo thinks his game is fair because there are many more ways to roll a nonprime product than a prime product. Is his game a fair game?

Have you ever had to guess because you forgot to study for a quiz? If you take a five-question true-false quiz and guess on every question, what are your chances of getting every question right?

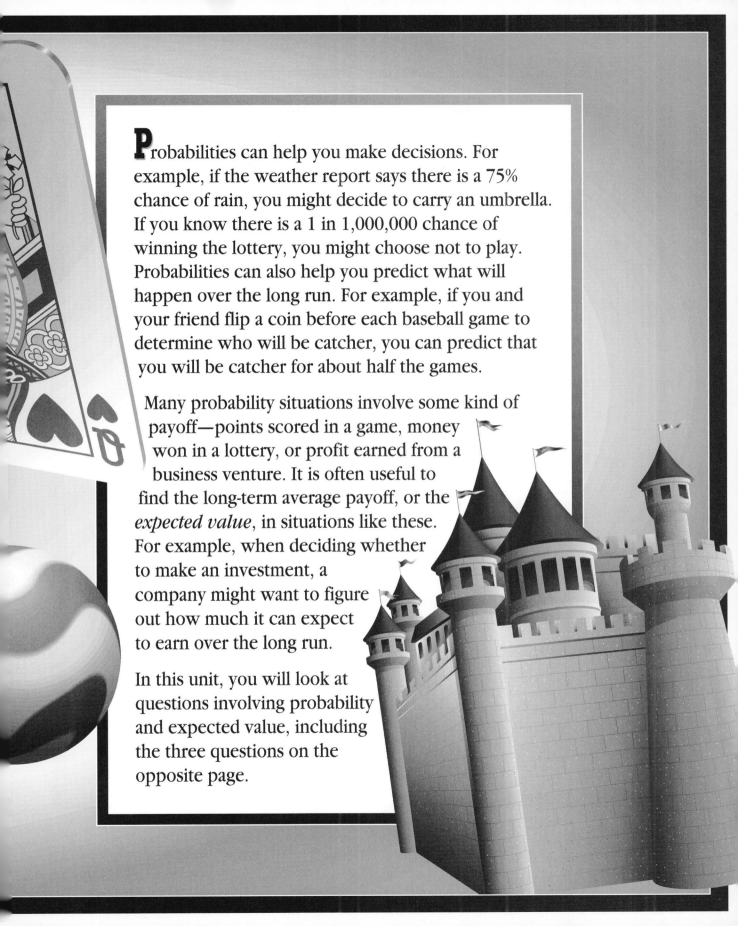

Probabilities can help you make decisions. For example, if the weather report says there is a 75% chance of rain, you might decide to carry an umbrella. If you know there is a 1 in 1,000,000 chance of winning the lottery, you might choose not to play. Probabilities can also help you predict what will happen over the long run. For example, if you and your friend flip a coin before each baseball game to determine who will be catcher, you can predict that you will be catcher for about half the games.

Many probability situations involve some kind of payoff—points scored in a game, money won in a lottery, or profit earned from a business venture. It is often useful to find the long-term average payoff, or the *expected value*, in situations like these. For example, when deciding whether to make an investment, a company might want to figure out how much it can expect to earn over the long run.

In this unit, you will look at questions involving probability and expected value, including the three questions on the opposite page.

Mathematical Highlights

In *What Do You Expect?* you will explore ways to deepen your understanding of basic probability concepts and learn about the expected value of chance situations. This unit will help you to

● Understand experimental and theoretical probabilities and the relationship between them;

● Further develop ways to identify the possible outcomes of an event;

● Understand the distinction between equally likely and non–equally likely events;

● Analyze situations that involve independent events and situations that involve dependent events;

● Develop a variety of strategies for analyzing probabilities, such as using lists, counting trees and area models;

● Determine the expected value of a chance situation; and

● Use probability and expected value to make decisions.

As you work on the problems in this unit, ask yourself questions about situations that involve analyzing probabilities: *What are the possible outcomes for the event(s) in this situation? Are they equally likely? Can I compute the theoretical probabilities or do I need to find experimental probabilities associated with the outcomes of the event(s)? If I'm exploring two or more events, are they independent or dependent events? In the context of games, how can I use expected value to help me determine whether a game is fair or unfair?*

Evaluating Games of Chance

In this investigation, you will explore several games involving chance. In each situation, you are asked to determine the chance, or *probability*, that certain outcomes will occur. In some situations, you will also be asked to determine whether a particular game is fair. What do you think it means for a game to be fair?

1.1 What's in the Bucket?

One day, Ms. MacAfee brought a mysterious bucket to class. She did not show her students what was in the bucket, but she told them that it contained blue, yellow, and red blocks. She asked if they could predict, without emptying the bucket, the fraction of the blocks that were blue, the fraction that were yellow, and the fraction that were red.

The class conducted an experiment to help them make their predictions. Each student randomly selected a block from the bucket, and the result was recorded on the board. After each draw, the block was returned to the bucket before the next student selected a block. In this problem, your class will conduct a similar experiment.

Problem 1.1

Your teacher has prepared a bucket identical to Ms. MacAfee's. One at a time, you and each of your classmates will select a block from the bucket, record the result, and return the block to the bucket.

A. How many blocks drawn by your class were blue? How many were yellow? How many were red?

B. Which color block—blue, yellow, or red—do you think there are the greatest number of in the bucket? Which color block do you think there are the least number of?

C. Based on your experimental data, predict the fraction of blocks in the bucket that are blue, that are yellow, and that are red.

D. After your teacher shows you the blocks in the bucket, find the fraction of blue blocks, the fraction of yellow blocks, and the fraction of red blocks.

E. How do the fractions of blocks that are blue, yellow, and red compare to the fractions of blue, yellow, and red blocks drawn during the experiment?

■ **Problem 1.1 Follow-Up**

1. a. Is each block *equally likely* to be selected from the bucket? That is, does each block have the same chance of being selected? Explain your reasoning.

  b. Is each color equally likely to be selected? Explain your reasoning.

2. What is the probability of drawing a white block from the bucket?

3. How many blue blocks need to be added to the bucket for the probability of drawing a blue block to be $\frac{1}{2}$?

1.2 Matching Colors

April and Tioko invented a two-player spinner game called Match/No-Match. A player spins this spinner twice on his or her turn. If both spins land on the same color (a match), Player A scores. If the two spins land on different colors (a no-match), Player B scores. Since there are two matching combinations—blue/blue and yellow/yellow—they decided that Player A should score only 1 point for a match and Player B should score 2 points for a no-match.

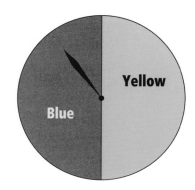

Problem 1.2

Play the Match/No-Match game with a partner. Take a total of 24 turns (12 turns for each player). For each turn, record the color pair on Labsheet 1.2, and award points to the appropriate player.

A. Use the results you collected to find the *experimental probabilities* of a match and a no-match. The experimental probability of a match is

$$P(\text{match}) = \frac{\text{number of turns that are matches}}{\text{total number of turns}}$$

The experimental probability of a no-match is

$$P(\text{no-match}) = \frac{\text{number of turns that are no-matches}}{\text{total number of turns}}$$

B. List all the possible **outcomes** of a turn (two spins). Write the outcomes as pairs of the form *color on first spin / color on second spin,* such as blue/blue. Use your list to determine the *theoretical probabilities* of a match and a no-match. Since all the outcomes are equally likely, the theoretical probability of a match is

$$P(\text{match}) = \frac{\text{number of outcomes that are matches}}{\text{number of possible outcomes}}$$

The theoretical probability of a no-match is

$$P(\text{no-match}) = \frac{\text{number of outcomes that are no-matches}}{\text{number of possible outcomes}}$$

C. How do your results for parts A and B compare?

D. Is Match/No-Match a **fair game**? If you think the game is fair, explain why. If you think it is not fair, explain how the rules could be changed to make it fair.

Problem 1.2 Follow-Up

1. Are a match and a no-match equally likely? Explain your reasoning.
2. In 100 turns of the Match/No-Match game, how many times would you expect each of the following to occur?
  a. two yellows
  b. two blues
  c. one yellow and one blue
  d. at least one yellow

3. a. Look at your results on Labsheet 1.2. If you had stopped after one turn, what would have been the experimental probability of a match? If you had stopped after two turns, what would have been the experimental probability of a match? If you had stopped after three turns, what would have been the experimental probability of a match? Continue to find the experimental probabilities through 24 turns. Record your results in a table.

b. Plot your data from part a on a coordinate grid similar to the one below.

c. What do you think your graph would look like if you had taken 30 turns? 50 turns? 100 turns? 1000 turns?

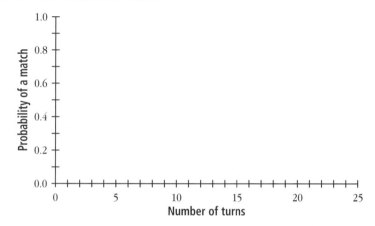

1.3 Making Purple

The most popular game at the school carnival is a spinner game called Making Purple. To play the game, a player spins each of the spinners below once. If the player gets red on spinner A and blue on spinner B, the player wins, because red and blue together make purple.

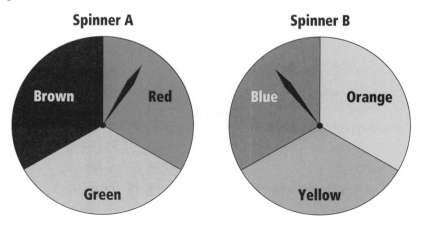

Problem 1.3

A. Play Making Purple 50 times, and record the results on Labsheet 1.3. Based on your results, what is the experimental probability that a player will "make purple" on any single turn?

B. Plot the experimental probability of making purple you would have found if you had stopped after 5 turns, 10 turns, 15 turns, and so on, up to 50 turns.

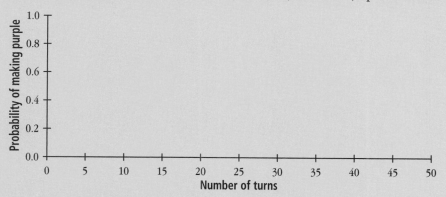

C. What do you think your graph would look like if you had taken 100 turns? 200 turns? 1000 turns?

D. List the possible outcomes for a turn. Write the outcomes as pairs of the form *color on spinner A/color on spinner B*. Are the outcomes equally likely? Explain why or why not.

E. What is the theoretical probability that a player will make purple on a turn?

F. How does the experimental probability of making purple compare with the theoretical probability of making purple? Explain.

■ Problem 1.3 Follow-Up

1. If 36 people play this game, how many would you expect to win? Explain how you got your answer.

2. Tickets at the school carnival cost 50¢ each. It takes four tickets to play the Making Purple game. The prizes awarded to the winners cost the school $5 each. Suppose 36 people play the game.
   a. How much money will the school take in from this game?
   b. How much money would you expect the school to pay out in prizes?
   c. How much profit would you expect the school to make from this game?

Making Counting Trees

You can find all the possible outcomes of a situation by making an organized list. Creating a **counting tree** can help you make sure you find all the possibilities. April used a counting tree to show all the possible outcomes for the Match/No-Match game (from Problem 1.2). First, she listed the equally likely outcomes of the first spin as shown in the tree at right below.

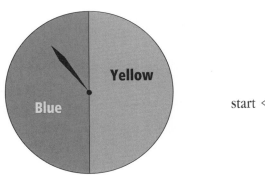

A turn consists of two spins, so from each of the possible results of the first spin, April drew two branches and labeled them to show the possible results of the second spin.

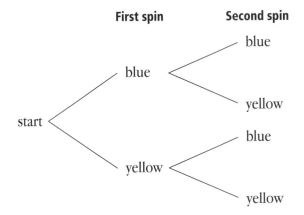

By following the paths from left to right, April can read all the possible outcomes of a turn. For example, she can follow the upper branch from start to blue, and then from there follow the upper branch to blue. This path represents the outcome blue/blue.

The column to the right of the tree below lists the possible outcomes.

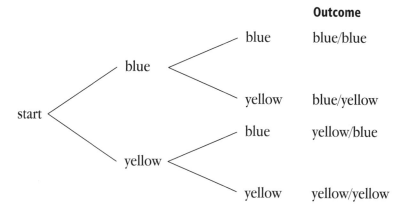

Outcome

blue/blue

blue/yellow

yellow/blue

yellow/yellow

Problem 1.4

April and Tioko decide to play the Match/No-Match game on the spinner below. As in the original game, a turn consists of two spins. Player A scores 1 point if the spins match, and Player B scores 1 point if they do not match.

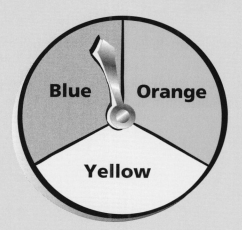

A. Use a counting tree to find all the possible outcomes for this game.

B. What is the theoretical probability of getting a match on a turn?

C. What is the theoretical probability of getting a no-match on a turn?

D. Do you think this is a fair game? If you think the game is fair, explain why. If you think it is not fair, explain how the rules could be changed to make it fair.

■ Problem 1.4 Follow-Up

1. a. Find all the possible outcomes for the Making Purple game in Problem 1.3 by creating a counting tree.

   b. Use your counting tree to find the theoretical probability of making purple on a turn.

   c. How does the theoretical probability you found by using a counting tree compare with the theoretical probability you found in Problem 1.3?

2. Shondra played a game with a spinner and a coin. For each turn, she spun the spinner once and tossed the coin once. For example, one possible outcome would be blue/head.

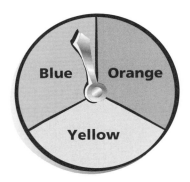 

   a. Create a counting tree to find all the possible outcomes of a turn in Shondra's game.

   b. Are all the outcomes equally likely? Explain why or why not.

   c. What is the probability that Shondra will spin blue and toss a head on a turn?

As you work on these ACE questions, use your calculator whenever you need it.

Applications

In 1–5, decide whether the possible resulting events are equally likely, and briefly explain your answer.

Action	Possible resulting events
1. You roll a number cube.	You roll an even number, or you roll an odd number.
2. A baby is born.	The baby is left-handed, or the baby is right-handed.
3. You toss a marshmallow.	The marshmallow lands on its end, or the marshmallow lands on its side.
4. You draw a card from a standard deck of 52 playing cards with no jokers.	The card is a heart, the card is a club, the card is a diamond, or the card is a spade.
5. You toss a coin three times.	You get three heads, you get two heads and a tail, you get a head and two tails, or you get three tails.

6. The probability of an event is a number between 0 and 1. The greater the probability, the greater the chances the event will happen. If an event is impossible, the probability that it will occur is 0, or 0%. If an event is certain to happen, the probability that it will occur is 1, or 100%.

Copy the number line below. Place the letter of each event below on the number line at the spot that best describes its probability.

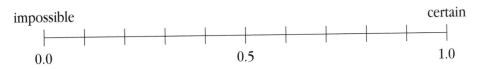

a. You will get a head when you toss a coin.

b. You can run 20 miles in one hour.

c. You will roll a 6 on a number cube.

d. It will snow in Minnesota this winter.

e. The sun will rise tomorrow.

f. You will toss a coin twice and get two heads.

g. You will toss a coin twice and get at least one head.

h. You will listen to a CD today.

i. You will spin the spinner shown below once, and it will land on red.

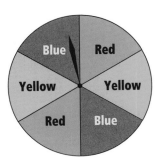

7. Lori's little sister Lulu tore the labels from ten cans of vegetables. Now all of the cans look exactly the same. Lori knows that three of the cans contain corn, two contain spinach, four contain beans, and one contains tomatoes. Lori picks a can at random and opens it.

   a. What is the probability that the can contains corn?

   b. What is the probability that the can contains beans?

   c. What is the probability that the can does *not* contain spinach?

   d. What is the probability that the can contains beans or tomatoes?

   e. Is it equally likely that any one of the vegetables is in the can? Explain.

8. If a tack is dropped on the floor, there are two possible outcomes: the tack lands on its side (point down), or the tack lands on its head (point up). The probability that a tack will land point up or point down can be determined by experimenting. Kalifa tossed a tack 100 times and recorded the results in the table below.

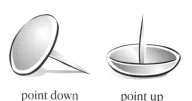

point down   point up

Outcome	Number of times it occurs
Tack lands point up	58
Tack lands point down	42

   a. If you dropped Kalifa's tack once, what is the probability that it would land point up? What is the probability that it would land point down?

   b. If you dropped Kalifa's tack 500 times, how many times would you expect it to land point up?

   c. Is it equally likely that the tack will land point up or point down? Explain.

   d. Is it possible to determine theoretical probabilities for this situation? Why or why not?

9. José is going to a party. He has decided to wear his jeans and a sweater, but he can't decide what else to wear. The counting tree below shows the possible outfits he can make if he randomly selects sneakers or loafers; blue, red, or brown socks; and a black, red, or plaid cap.

a. What are the chances that José will wear loafers, blue socks, and a plaid cap?

b. What are the chances that José will wear sneakers, either red or blue socks, and a black cap?

c. What are the chances that José will wear neither red socks nor a red cap?

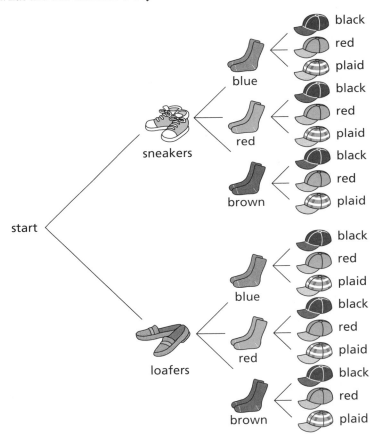

10. Tino and Kim are playing a game with two pennies. The players take turns tossing both pennies. If the pennies match, Tino scores 1 point. If they don't match, Kim scores 1 point.

a. Is this a fair game? Explain.

b. How does this game compare to the Match/No-Match game in Problem 1.2?

c. Kim suggests playing the game with three pennies instead of two. The rules would be the same—Tino would get a point if the three pennies matched, and Kim would get a point if they didn't all match. Is this a fair game? Why or why not?

11. In the Gee Whiz Everyone Wins! television game show, members of the studio audience draw a block randomly from the bucket shown at right. If a blue block is drawn, the contestant wins $5. If a red block is drawn, the contestant wins $10. If the yellow block is drawn, the contestant wins $50. The block is replaced after each draw.

a. What is the probability of drawing each color?

b. If 24 contestants draw a block from the bucket, how much money can the game show expect to pay out?

12. At the school carnival, the Math Club is running a coin-toss game. It costs four 50¢ tickets to play the game. A player tosses two coins. If the coins match, the player wins a prize. Each prize costs the club $5. Can the club expect to make a profit on this game? If so, how much? If not, explain why.

13. Tioko and Dione are using the spinners from the Making Purple game to play a two-person game. They take turns spinning the two spinners. If the colors on the two spinners make purple, Dione scores. If they do not make purple, Tioko scores. For this to be a fair game, how many points should Dione score when the spinners make purple, and how many points should Tioko score when they do not make purple?

14. Suppose the spinners for the Making Purple game were changed to the following.

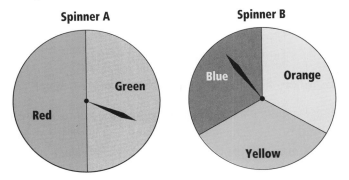

Spinner A

Spinner B

a. Make a counting tree, and list all the possible outcomes for this game.

b. Find the theoretical probability of making purple on a turn.

Connections

15. A dart is thrown at random at each of the dartboards below.

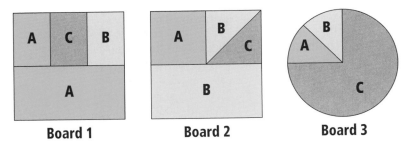

Board 1   Board 2   Board 3

a. For each dartboard, what is the probability that a dart will land in a region marked A? A region marked B? A region marked C?

b. For board 1, what is the probability that a dart will land in a region marked A or B?

c. For board 2, what is the probability that a dart will *not* land in region C?

16. A dartboard is divided into four regions, A, B, C, and D. The probability that a randomly thrown dart will land in region A is 40%. The probabilities that the dart will land in region B, region C, or region D are all equal.

    a. What is the probability that a dart will land in a region other than A?

    b. Make a square dartboard that meets the given conditions.

    c. Make a circular dartboard that meets the given conditions.

17. Jason spins the spinner below several times and tallies the results in a table.

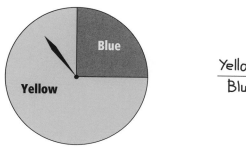

    a. How many times did Jason spin the spinner?

    b. What percent of the spins landed in the blue region? In the yellow region?

    c. According to the theoretical probabilities, what percent of the spins should land in the blue region? In the yellow region?

    d. Compare the experimental probability of the spinner landing in each region with the theoretical probability. If the probabilities are different, explain why.

Extensions

18. A bucket contains 60 marbles—some red, some blue, and some white. The probability of drawing a red marble is 35%, and the probability of drawing a blue marble is 25%. How many marbles of each color are in the bucket?

19. Hannah's teacher brought in a bucket containing 72 blocks—some red, some yellow, and some blue. Hannah wanted to try to figure out how many of the blocks were blue without emptying the bucket. She drew a block from the bucket, recorded its color, and then replaced it. She did this 14 times. Of her 14 draws, 5 were blue. Based on Hannah's experiment, how many of the blocks are blue? Explain your answer.

20. All the winners from the Gee Whiz Everyone Wins! game show get an opportunity to compete for a bonus prize. Each contestant draws one block at random from each of the buckets shown below. If the blocks are the same color, the contestant wins a prize.

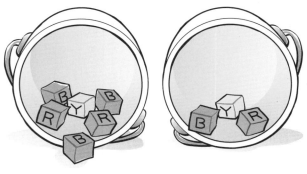

Bucket 1   Bucket 2

a. List all the possible outcomes when a player randomly draws one block from each bucket.

b. What is the probability that a contestant will draw two blocks of the same color?

c. Natasha wants to use a similar game at the school carnival. Contestants would pay two 50¢ tickets to play and would win a prize worth $3 for a match. Could the school expect to make money from this game? Explain.

Mathematical Reflections

In this investigation, you explored games of chance. Working on the problems gave you an opportunity to review ideas about experimental probability and theoretical probability. These questions will help you summarize what you have learned:

1 **a.** Write a brief description of experimental probability.

   b. Describe a strategy you have used to find experimental probabilities.

2 **a.** Write a brief description of theoretical probability.

   b. Describe strategies you have used to find theoretical probabilities.

3 What does it mean for two or more events to be equally likely? Give examples of events that are equally likely.

Think about your answers to these questions, discuss your ideas with other students and your teacher, and then write a summary of your findings in your journal.

Analyzing Number-Cube Games

In Investigation 1, you used various strategies to find probabilities associated with games of chance. You found *experimental probabilities* by playing a game several times and evaluating the results, and you found *theoretical probabilities* by analyzing the possible outcomes of a game. In this investigation, you will explore experimental and theoretical probabilities involved in some number-cube games.

2.1 Playing the Addition Game

In this problem, you will play the Addition Game with a partner and try to determine whether it is fair.

Addition Game Rules

- Player A and Player B take turns rolling two number cubes.
- If the sum of the numbers rolled is odd, Player A scores 1 point.
- If the sum of the numbers rolled is even, Player B scores 1 point.
- The player with the most points after 36 rolls wins.

Problem 2.1

Play the Addition Game with a partner. Keep track of your results.

A. Based on your data, what is the experimental probability of rolling an odd sum? An even sum?

B. List all the possible pairs of numbers you can roll with two number cubes.

C. What is the theoretical probability of rolling an odd sum? An even sum?

D. Do you think the Addition Game is a fair game? Explain why or why not.

---

1. Min-wei invented a game based on the sum of two number cubes. In her game, Player A scores 1 point for sums of 6 or 7, and Player B scores 1 point for any other sum. Min-wei thought this would be a fair game because sums of 6 and 7 occur so often. Is this a fair game? Explain why or why not.

2. Royce invented a game based on the sum of two number cubes. In his game, Player A scores 3 points if the sum is a multiple of 3, and Player B scores 1 point if the sum is *not* a multiple of 3. Is Royce's game a fair game? Explain why or why not.

2.2 Playing the Multiplication Game

In the Addition Game, players score points based on the sum of the numbers rolled on two number cubes. In the Multiplication Game, scoring depends on the *product* of the numbers rolled.

Multiplication Game Rules

- Player A and Player B take turns rolling two number cubes.
- If the product of the numbers rolled is odd, Player A scores 1 point.
- If the product of the numbers rolled is even, Player B scores 1 point.
- The player with the most points after 36 rolls wins.

Problem 2.2

Play the Multiplication Game with a partner. Keep track of your results.

A. Based on your data, what is the experimental probability of rolling an odd product? An even product?

B. What is the theoretical probability of rolling an odd product? An even product?

C. Do you think the Multiplication Game is fair? Explain why or why not.

D. If the game consisted of 100 rolls instead of 36, how many points would you expect each player to have at the end of the game?

■ **Problem 2.2 Follow-Up**

1. How could you make the Multiplication Game a fair game?

2. Invent a fair two-person game based on the product of two number cubes. A player should score 1 point each time he or she scores. You will need to decide which player scores on which kinds of products. Explain why your game is fair.

As you work on these ACE questions, use your calculator whenever you need it.

Applications

In 1–4, find the probability of getting the given result when two number cubes are rolled.

1. a sum of 4

2. a sum less than 6

3. a sum of 7 or 11

4. a pair of 5s

5. Suppose you were to spin the spinner below and then roll a number cube.

a. Make an organized list of the possible outcomes.

b. What is the probability that you will get a 1 on both the number cube and the spinner?

c. What is the probability that you will *not* get a 1 on both the number cube and the spinner?

d. What is the probability that you will get a 1 on the number cube or the spinner?

e. What is the probability that you will get the same number on the number cube and the spinner?

f. What is the probability that the sum of the number on the spinner and the number on the number cube will be greater than 8?

g. What is the probability that the product of the number on the spinner and the number on the number cube will be 0?

6. Chris did an experiment using the spinner and number cube from question 5. For each trial, he spun the spinner and then rolled the number cube. He was surprised to find that he got a 1 on both the spinner and the number cube in 4 out of 36 trials.

a. Based on his results, what is the experimental probability of getting a 1 on both the number cube and the spinner?

b. Chris compared the experimental probability of getting a 1 on both the number cube and the spinner to the theoretical probability. He decided that something must be wrong with the spinner or the number cube, since these probabilities are not the same. Do you agree? Why or why not?

7. Raymundo invented the Prime Number Multiplication game. In this game, two number cubes are rolled. Player A scores 10 points if the product is prime, and Player B scores 1 point if the product is not prime. Raymundo thinks this scoring system is reasonable because there are many more ways to roll a nonprime product than a prime product.

a. If the cubes are rolled 100 times, how many points would you expect Player A to score? How many points would you expect Player B to score?

b. Is Raymundo's game a fair game? Explain why or why not.

8. Rachel says that if she rolls two number cubes 36 times, she will get a product of 1 exactly once. Luis said that she cannot be sure this will happen exactly once, but it will probably happen very few times. Who is right? Explain your reasoning.

9. Rachel told Luis that if she rolls two number cubes 100 times, she will *never* get a product of 23. Luis told her that she can't be sure. Who is right? Explain your reasoning.

10. Juanita is trying to decide whether to play a certain game at an amusement park. It takes one ticket to play the game. A player flips two plastic bottles. If both bottles land standing up, the player wins ten tickets to use for rides and games. Juanita has been watching people play the game for a while and has recorded the results in a table:

Both land on side	One lands on side and one lands standing up	Both land standing up
卌 卌 卌 卌 ‖‖‖	卌 卌 ‖‖‖‖	‖

a. Based on Juanita's results, what is the experimental probability of winning the game?

b. If Juanita played this game 20 times, how many times could she expect to win?

c. How many tickets could Juanita expect to be ahead or behind after playing the game 20 times? Explain your reasoning.

d. Is it possible to find the theoretical probability of winning this game? Why or why not?

In 11–15, tell whether theoretical or experimental probability is being used.

11. Kelly played darts on a board made of concentric blue, red, and yellow regions. The dart landed in the red region 7 times and in the other regions a total of 13 times. Kelly stated that on her next throw, the dart has a 35% chance of landing in the red region.

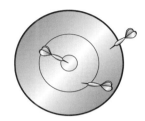

12. For 10 minutes before school each day, some students from Ms. MacAfee's class recorded the types of vehicles that passed by the school. They wanted to figure out whether it was more likely for a car or a truck to pass by. After a week of observing, the students used their data to predict that a car is more likely to pass by than a truck.

13. Emma is in the fun house at the amusement park. She must choose from among three exits. At one exit, visitors get squirted with water. At another exit, visitors get sprayed with whipped cream. At a third exit, visitors must walk through mud. Emma does not know which exit is which. She decides that if she selects an exit at random, she has a $\frac{1}{3}$ chance of getting sprayed with whipped cream.

14. Waldo buys a pair of weighted number cubes at a novelty store. In 30 rolls, he gets a sum of 2 eleven times. Waldo figures that if he rolls the number cubes 100 times, he will get a sum of 2 about 37 times.

15. Tina keeps a pack of 20 colored pencils in her backpack. When her science teacher asks the students to design a cover for their science projects, Tina pulls out a colored pencil without looking. She figures she has about a 5% chance of picking her favorite color, orange.

Connections

16. Marinda and Isaiah are analyzing a game involving two different spinners. For each turn, a player spins each spinner once. To help them find theoretical probabilities, Marinda and Isaiah made the counting tree at right.

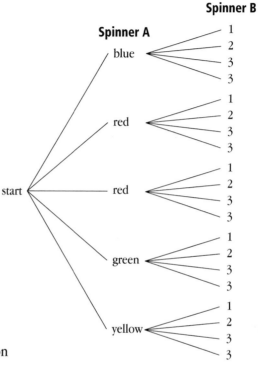

a. Design two spinners that could be the spinners used by Marinda and Isaiah.

b. List all the possible outcomes of spinning each spinner once.

c. Which color/number combination has the greatest probability of occurring?

d. Based on your spinners, what is the probability of getting red on spinner A and 3 on spinner B?

e. Based on your spinners, what is the probability of *not* getting 3 on spinner B?

17. a. When you roll two number cubes, what is the probability that the product of the numbers will be a multiple of 5?

b. If you roll two number cubes 100 times, about how many times can you expect the product to be a multiple of 5?

c. What is the probability of rolling a product that is a multiple of 7?

d. If you roll two number cubes a million times, how many times can you expect to get a product that is a multiple of 7?

18. David went to Miceli's Deli for lunch. He saw the sign below:

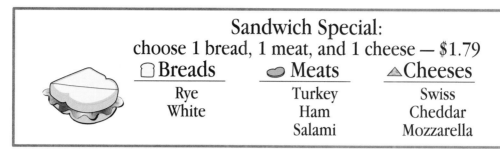

Sandwich Special:
choose 1 bread, 1 meat, and 1 cheese — $1.79

⬭ Breads	⬬ Meats	△ Cheeses
Rye	Turkey	Swiss
White	Ham	Cheddar
	Salami	Mozzarella

David couldn't decide which kind of sandwich he wanted, so he told the sandwich maker to surprise him. If the sandwich maker chooses the bread, meat, and cheese at random, what is the probability that David will get a turkey sandwich on wheat bread with cheddar cheese? Explain your reasoning.

19. Tricia wants to determine the probability of getting two 1s when two number cubes are rolled. She made a counting tree and used it to list the possible outcomes.

Cube 1	Cube 2	Outcome
	1	1/1
1	not 1	1/not 1
	1	not 1/1
not 1	not 1	not 1/not 1

start

She says that, since there are four possible outcomes, the probability of getting 1 on both number cubes is $\frac{1}{4}$. Is Tricia right? Why or why not?

20. The authors of this book surveyed middle school students from several schools across the country to try to determine what interests middle school students. One question they asked was: "How interested are you in bicycling?" The bar graphs below show the results for 44 girls and 42 boys.

Interest in Bicycling

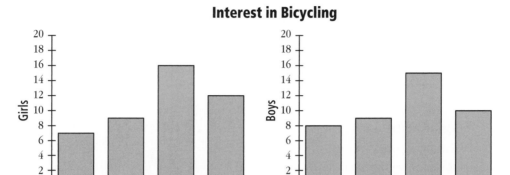

a. Based on the results of the survey, what is the probability that a middle school girl will say she is very interested in bicycling?

b. Based on the results of the survey, what is the probability that a middle school boy will say he is very interested in bicycling?

Extensions

21. Make up a fair game that involves tossing three coins. Describe the rules of your game, and explain why your game is fair.

22. When you roll three number cubes, what is the probability that all three numbers will match?

23. When you roll three number cubes, what is the probability that the product of the numbers will be greater than 200?

24. Matthew invented a two-person game in which players take turns rolling three number cubes. If the sum is even, Player A scores 1 point. If the sum is odd, Player B scores 1 point. Is Matthew's game a fair game? Explain why or why not.

Mathematical Reflections

In this investigation, you looked at games involving number cubes. You determined whether games were fair and figured out how you could change the rules of an unfair game to make it a fair game. These questions will help you summarize what you have learned:

1. What does it mean for a game of chance to be fair?

2. Create a game that is not fair. How can you adjust the system of scoring to make the game fair?

3. In a game of chance, how can you predict the number of times out of 100 a certain outcome will occur? Give an example if it helps you to explain your thinking.

Think about your answers to these questions, discuss your ideas with other students and your teacher, and then write a summary of your findings in your journal.

Probability and Area

In this investigation, you will explore a computer game called Treasure Hunt, which involves searching for treasure in a royal palace. You will see how you can use theoretical probability to improve your chances of winning the game.

3.1 Cracking Level 1

When you play the first level of the Treasure Hunt game, the computer hides a treasure on the first floor of the palace. The floor plan is pictured here.

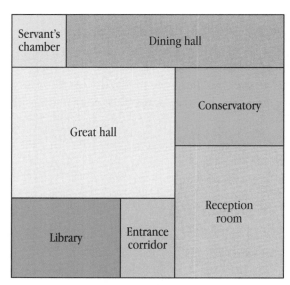

Level 1

The computer gives the player clues about where the treasure is located. After each clue, the player must guess which room the treasure is in. The computer continues to give clues until the player finds the treasure. The fewer clues the player needs to find the treasure, the more points the player gets.

To make good guesses when playing Treasure Hunt, it helps to understand how the computer hides the treasure. The computer "thinks" of the first floor of the palace as a 10 by 10 grid. At the start of a game, the computer **randomly** selects one of the 100 squares as the location for the treasure. For example, if the computer selects the square indicated on the left grid below, the treasure is hidden in the conservatory.

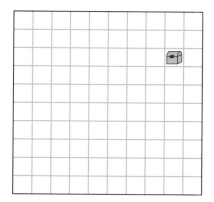

Think about this!

Suppose the computer gives you this first clue:

The treasure is hidden in a room with "hall" in its name.

Which room should you guess first? Explain your answer.

Problem 3.1

A. How can this information about how the computer hides the treasure help you find the treasure?

B. You have just entered level 1 of Treasure Hunt. What is the probability that the treasure is hidden in the great hall? In the servant's chamber?

C. If you play level 1 ten times, how many times can you expect the treasure to be hidden in the great hall? In the servant's chamber?

■ Problem 3.1 Follow-Up

1. The first time you play level 1, the treasure is hidden in the library. What is the probability that the treasure will be hidden in the library the second time you play level 1?

2. Monty says that since the computer randomly picks the location of the treasure, the treasure is just as likely to be hidden in the entrance corridor as in the great hall. Is Monty correct? Explain your answer.

3.2 Cracking Level 2

For the second level of the Treasure Hunt game, a player must find a hidden treasure on the second floor of the palace. The second floor has rooms for the king's and queen's servants. As in level 1, the computer "thinks" of the floor as a grid and hides the treasure by randomly selecting a grid square. However, notice that the floor of level 2 is *not* a square.

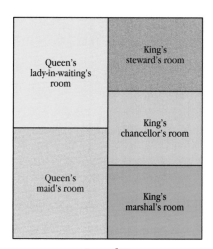

Level 2

Problem 3.2

Answer each question, and explain your reasoning.

A. You have just advanced to level 2 of Treasure Hunt. What is the probability that the treasure is hidden in one of the queen's servants' rooms? In one of the king's servants' rooms?

B. What is the probability that the treasure is hidden in the maid's room? In the steward's room?

C. If you play the second level 100 times, how many times can you expect the treasure to be hidden in one of the queen's servants' rooms? In one of the king's servants' rooms?

D. If you play the second level 100 times, how many times can you expect the treasure to be hidden in the maid's room? In the steward's room?

■ Problem 3.2 Follow-Up

1. You have just advanced to level 2. What is the probability that the treasure is hidden in one of the rooms on the second floor? Explain how you determined your answer.

2. You have just advanced to level 2. What is the probability that the treasure is hidden in the cook's room? Explain how you determined your answer.

As you work on these ACE questions, use your calculator whenever you need it.

Applications

1. The diagram below shows level 3 of the Treasure Hunt game. Before receiving the first clue, a player must guess whether the treasure is in a room used by the king, a room used by the queen, or a room used by the princess. When the treasure is actually located, a player receives bonus points if his or her initial guess was correct.

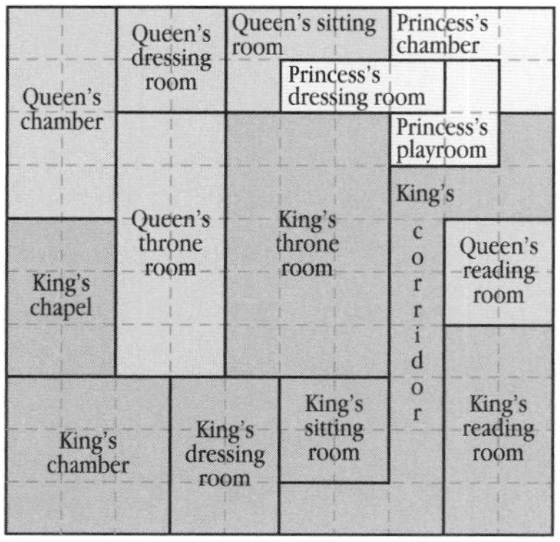

Level 3

a. Suppose you have just entered level 3. To have the best chance of getting the bonus points, should you guess that the treasure is in one of the king's rooms, one of the queen's rooms, or one of the princess's rooms? Give the reasons for your choice.

b. If you played this level 100 times, how many times would you expect the treasure to be in one of the king's rooms? In one of the queen's rooms? In one of the princess's rooms?

c. If you played this level 100 times, how many times would you expect the treasure to be in the princess's playroom?

In 2–4, use the dartboard shown to answer parts a–c.

2. 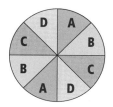   **3.** 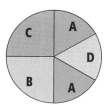   **4.**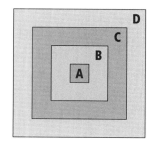

a. If a dart is thrown randomly at the board, what is the probability that it will land in a region marked A? In a region marked B? In a region marked C? In a region marked D?

b. The board is used to play a four-person game. Darts are thrown randomly at the board. Player A receives points when a dart lands in a region marked A, Player B receives points when a dart lands in a region marked B, and so on. Make up a scoring system that would make the game fair.

c. Using your point scheme from part b, what would you expect the score to be after 100 darts have been thrown?

5. Sarah, the designer of the Treasure Hunt game, considered several different floor plans for level 1. Here are two floor plans she rejected. Use these floor plans to answer parts a–d on the next page.

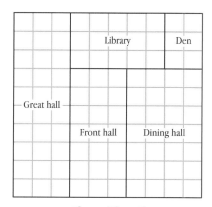

Floor Plan F

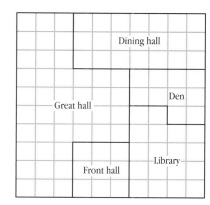

Floor Plan G

a. If level 1 had floor plan F, what would be the probability that the computer would hide the treasure in the library?

b. If level 1 had floor plan G, what would be the probability that the computer would hide the treasure in the library?

c. If level 1 had floor plan F, how many times out of 100 would you expect the computer to hide the treasure in the library?

d. If level 1 had floor plan G, how many times out of 100 would you expect the computer to hide the treasure in the library?

Connections

6. Sarah tested one of the floor plans from question 5. She kept track of the number of times the treasure was hidden in each room and made a bar graph of the results. Which floor plan do you think she was testing? Explain your reasoning.

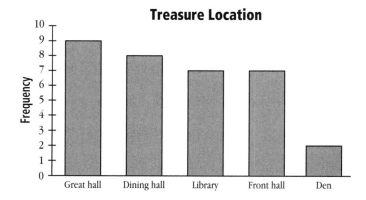

Treasure Location

7. If Sarah had enlarged floor plan F in question 5 by a scale factor of 2 to make a similar floor plan, how would this affect the probabilities?

8. Rich, the programmer of the Treasure Hunt game, tested an early version of the level 1 floor plan. He kept track of the number of times the computer hid the treasure in each room, and he made a line plot of his results:

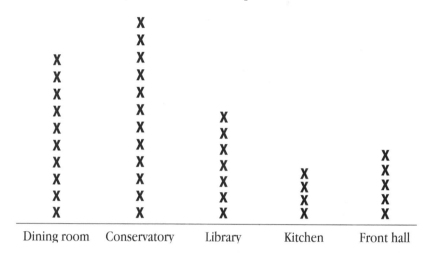

Because of a computer disk error, Rich has no record of the floor plan he was using. Design a floor plan that you would expect to give these data. State the area of each room on your floor plan.

Extensions

9. Create a floor plan for level 4 of the Treasure Hunt game. The floor should have five rooms, and the largest room should have the same area as the other four rooms combined. Label each room, and give its area.

Mathematical Reflections

In this investigation, you solved problems about games of chance in which probabilities were related to area. These questions will help you summarize what you have learned:

1. In games like Treasure Hunt in which probabilities are related to area, how can you tell if two events are equally likely?

2. In the Treasure Hunt game, how can you use the diagram of a level to find the probability that the treasure will be hidden in a particular room?

Think about your answers to these questions, discuss your ideas with other students and your teacher, and then write a summary of your findings in your journal.

Analyzing Two-Stage Games

In the Treasure Hunt game and in games involving spinners and dartboards, you used area to find probabilities. In this investigation, you will learn how to use area in a slightly different way to analyze more situations involving probability.

4.1 Choosing Paths

Kenisha designed a computer game called Deep in the Dungeon. The game pits a player against a computer character named Zark. The game screen is shown below.

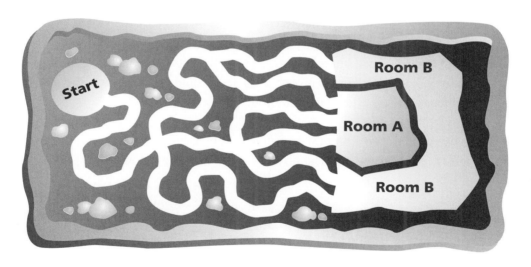

The player puts the treasure in one of the two rooms in the dungeon. Zark begins at "start" and makes his way toward the dungeon, *randomly* selecting a path at each fork. If Zark ends in the room with the treasure, he wins. If he ends in the room without the treasure, the player wins.

Problem 4.1

A. If you were playing Deep in the Dungeon, in which room would you put the treasure in order to have the best chance of beating Zark? Explain your choice.

B. Work with a partner to find a way to simulate Deep in the Dungeon so it can be played without a computer. Your simulation should be a two-person game. One person should hide the treasure, and the other should play the role of Zark. You will need to figure out a way for Zark to make a random selection at each fork.

C. Play your simulation of Deep in the Dungeon 20 times with your partner. Take turns hiding the treasure and playing Zark. For each game, record the room that Zark ends in.

D. Based on your results from part C, what is the experimental probability that Zark will end in room A? What is the experimental probability that Zark will end in room B?

■ **Problem 4.1 Follow-Up**

You and your classmates may have found several ways to simulate Deep in the Dungeon in order to find experimental probabilities. How could you determine the theoretical probabilities of Zark ending in each room?

One way to find the theoretical probabilities is by using an *area model.* To make it easier to talk about the game, we'll number the paths as shown below.

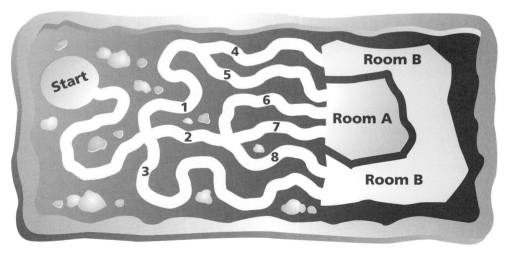

1. Draw a square on your paper. Suppose that the square has an area of 1 square unit, representing a probability of 1. At the first fork, there are three equally likely choices: path 1, path 2, and path 3. Divide and label the square so the areas of the sections represent the probabilities of these three choices.

2. If Zark selects path 1 at the first stage of his journey, he will reach a fork where he must randomly select path 4 or path 5. Subdivide your diagram to represent the probabilities that Zark will choose path 1 and then choose path 4 or path 5.

3. If Zark selects path 2 at the first stage of his journey, he will reach a fork where he must randomly select path 6, path 7, or path 8. Subdivide your diagram to represent the probabilities that Zark will choose path 2 and then choose path 6, path 7, or path 8.

4. On your diagram, color the sections that represent paths leading to room A with one color and the sections that represent paths leading to room B with a second color.

5. What is the theoretical probability that Zark will end in room A? What is the theoretical probability that he will end in room B?

4.2 Finding the Best Arrangement

Brianna and Emmanuel are selected from the studio audience of the Gee Whiz Everyone Wins! game show to play a game. While Emmanuel waits backstage, Brianna is to place two orange marbles and two blue marbles in two identical containers in any way she chooses. After she places the marbles in the containers, Emmanuel will return and select one of the containers at random. Then, without looking, he will reach into the container and pull out a marble. If he draws an orange marble, the friends each win a prize. If he draws a blue marble, or if the container he chooses is empty, the friends do not win anything.

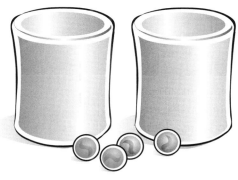

Problem 4.2

A. List all the different ways Brianna can place the four marbles in the two containers.

B. Which arrangement will give Brianna and Emmanuel the best chance of winning? Explain why the arrangement you chose is the best.

C. For the arrangement you chose, what is the probability of drawing an orange marble?

■ Problem 4.2 Follow-Up

1. Which arrangement gives Brianna and Emmanuel the worst chance of winning?

2. Brianna and Emmanuel lost the first game but were given a chance to play a second game. This time Brianna had to place three orange marbles and three blue marbles in three containers. Find the arrangement that gives Emmanuel the best chance of drawing an orange marble.

As you work on these ACE questions, use your calculator whenever you need it.

Applications

1. Kenisha created a new screen for Deep in the Dungeon.

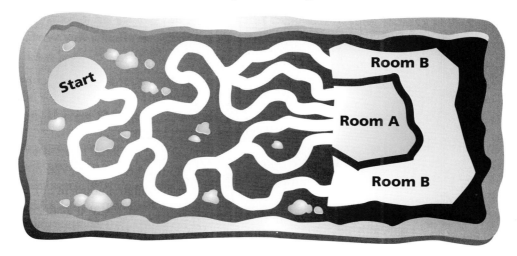

  a. If Zark randomly selects a path at each fork, what is the theoretical probability that he will end in room A? In room B?

  b. If you played this game 100 times, how many times would you expect Zark to end in room A? In room B?

2. Suppose Brianna (from Problem 4.2) was given three blue marbles and two orange marbles to distribute between the two containers. What arrangement would give Emmanuel the best chance of drawing an orange marble?

3. Suppose Brianna (from Problem 4.2) was given two blue marbles and three orange marbles to distribute between the two containers. What arrangement would give Emmanuel the best chance of drawing an orange marble?

4. Kenisha designed a new version of Deep in the Dungeon with a different arrangement of paths and doors leading into rooms A and B. She made the area model below to analyze the probabilities of landing in each room.

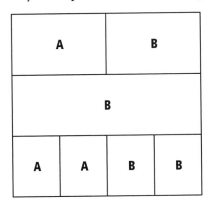

a. For Kenisha's new version, what is the probability that Zark will end up in room A? In room B?

b. Draw a game screen showing the paths, forks, and rooms that represents Kenisha's area model.

Connections

5. The table below shows the results of a survey that asked 100 seniors at Spartan High School the following questions:

- Do you favor a rule that would allow only seniors to drive to school?

- Do you drive to school?

Driving Survey

	Drives to school	Does not drive to school	Row totals
Favors rule	40	30	70
Opposes rule	20	10	30
Column total	**60**	**40**	**100**

a. Based on this survey, what is the probability that a Spartan senior, selected at random, favors the rule?

b. What is the probability that a Spartan senior, selected at random, drives to school *and* favors the rule?

c. What is the probability that a Spartan senior, selected at random, drives to school *or* opposes the rule?

d. Do you think the results of this survey are a good indicator of how all the students at Spartan High School feel about the driving rule? Explain.

6. A bag contains three orange marbles and two blue marbles. You are to choose a marble, return it to the bag, and then choose again.

a. Tell whether each method below is appropriate for finding the possible outcomes of this experiment. If the method is appropriate, explain how you would use it to find the possible outcomes. If the method is not appropriate, explain why.

    i. making a counting tree
    ii. making a list
    iii. using an area model
    iv. making a table or chart

b. If you did this experiment 100 times, how many times would you expect to draw two marbles of the same color?

c. Suppose this experiment were a two-person game in which one player scores if the marbles match, and one player scores if they do not match. Describe a scoring system that would make this a fair game.

Extensions

7. At the school carnival, you are about to play a game using the two spinners below. You get two spins. You may spin each spinner once, or you may spin one of the spinners twice. If you get a red on one spin and a blue on the other spin (the order makes no difference), you win. To have the greatest chance of winning, should you spin spinner A twice, spin spinner B twice, or spin each spinner once? Explain how you got your answer.

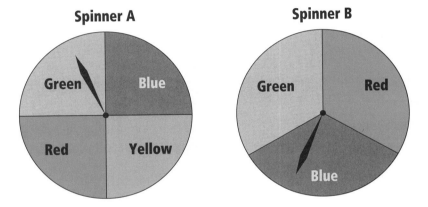

Spinner A

Green Blue

Red Yellow

Spinner B

Green Red

Blue

Mathematical Reflections

In this investigation, you analyzed probabilities by dividing the area of a square. These questions will help you summarize what you have learned:

1 In what kinds of situations is it appropriate to find probabilities by dividing the area of a square? Give an example to illustrate your answer.

2 How can you use the area of a square to analyze a probability situation? Use an example to help explain your answer. At each stage, explain how you decide how to divide the square.

Think about your answers to these questions, discuss your ideas with other students and your teacher, and then write a summary of your findings in your journal.

Expected Value

On April 14, 1993, during half-time of a basketball game between the Chicago Bulls and the Miami Heat, Don Calhoun won 1 million dollars by making a basket from the free-throw line at the opposite end of the court. Don was chosen at random from the audience to attempt the shot as part of a promotional contest. A *Sports Illustrated* article explains:

> The odds against one randomly chosen person given one shot from the opposite foul line and making it are considered astronomical. Scottie Pippen admitted that after practice one day he and Michael Jordan tried to hit the shot but couldn't.*

Not every shot is this difficult to make! In this investigation, you will use a player's free-throw percentage to figure out what is likely to happen in a given free-throw situation.

5.1 Shooting the One-and-One

Nicky is playing basketball on her school team this year. In the district finals, the team is 1 point behind with 2 seconds left in the game. Nicky has just been fouled, and she is in a one-and-one free-throw situation. This means that Nicky will try one shot. If she makes the first shot, she gets to try a second shot. If she misses the first shot, she is done and does not get to try a second shot. Nicky's free-throw average is 60%.

*Reprinted courtesy of Sports Illustrated: "Sports People: Don Calhoun" by Lisa Bessone, SI, April 26, 1993, Time Inc. All rights reserved.

Problem 5.1

A. Which of the following do you think is most likely to happen?

- Nicky will score 0 points. That is, she will miss the first shot.
- Nicky will score 1 point. That is, she will make the first shot and miss the second shot.
- Nicky will score 2 points. That is, she will make two shots.

Record what you think before you analyze the situation.

B. Plan a way to simulate this situation. Describe your plan.

C. Use your plan from part B to simulate Nicky's one-and-one situation 20 times. Record the result of each trial.

D. Based on your results, what is the experimental probability that Nicky will score 0 points? That she will score 1 point? That she will score 2 points?

E. Make an area model for this situation, using a 10 by 10 grid. What is the theoretical probability that Nicky will score 0 points? 1 point? 2 points?

F. How do the three theoretical probabilities compare with the three experimental probabilities?

◼ Problem 5.1 Follow-Up

1. Suppose Nicky is in a two-shot free-throw situation. This means that she will get a second shot even if she misses the first shot. What is the theoretical probability that Nicky will score 0 points? That she will score 1 point? That she will score 2 points? Explain your reasoning.

2. How do the theoretical probabilities for the one-and-one situation compare to the theoretical probabilities for the two-shot situation?

5.2 Finding Expected Value

In the last problem, you looked at the probabilities of different outcomes of Nicky's one-and-one free-throw situation. You might have been surprised about which outcome is most likely. In this problem, you will look at the number of points Nicky can expect to make each time she is in a one-and-one free-throw situation.

Problem 5.2

Suppose Nicky has a 60% free-throw average and is in a one-and-one free-throw situation 100 times during the season.

A. What total number of points would you expect Nicky to score in these 100 trips to the free-throw line?

B. What would Nicky's average number of points per trip be? This is the **expected value** for this situation.

■ Problem 5.2 Follow-Up

Use Labsheet 5.2 to investigate what is likely to happen in one-and-one situations involving players whose free-throw averages are different from Nicky's. When you have finished the labsheet, use it to help you answer the following questions.

1. How do the probabilities of scoring exactly 1 point in a one-and-one situation compare for 20%, 40%, 60%, and 80% shooters? Describe any pattern you see in the table.

2. In a one-and-one situation, what is the most likely outcome for a 20% shooter? For a 40% shooter? For a 60% shooter? For an 80% shooter? How do these outcomes compare?

3. a. Make a graph that shows the average numbers of points a 20% shooter, a 40% shooter, a 60% shooter, and an 80% shooter can expect to make in a one-and-one situation. Use your graph to answer parts b–d.

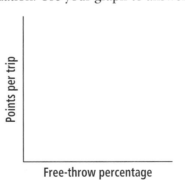

b. How do the expected values compare for a 20% shooter, a 40% shooter, a 60% shooter, and an 80% shooter?

c. Nicky's father noticed that he makes an average of about 1 point whenever he is in a one-and-one free-throw situation. What do you think his shooting percentage is?

d. If Nicky's twin sister Michelle is a 70% shooter, what is her expected value in a one-and-one situation? Check your answer by making an area model.

As you work on these ACE questions, use your calculator whenever you need it.

Applications

1. a. Brian is a 50% free-throw shooter. In a one-and-one free-throw situation, is he most likely to score 0 points, 1 point, or 2 points? Explain your reasoning.

b. Over the long run, what is the average number of points Brian can expect to score per one-and-one situation? That is, what is his expected value?

2. Nicky, a 60% free-throw shooter, is in a two-shot free-throw situation. Remember, this means that she will attempt the second shot no matter what happens on the first shot.

a. Is Nicky most likely to score 0 points, 1 point, or 2 points? Explain your answer.

b. Nicky plans to keep track of her score on two-shot free-throw situations. What average number of points can she expect to score per two-shot situation?

3. Fred and Josephina are experimenting with a new game. They figure out that the probability Fred will win a round is $\frac{1}{3}$, and the probability Josephina will win a round is $\frac{2}{3}$. They decided that to make the game fair Fred should score 3 points when he wins a round, and Josephina should score 2 points when she wins a round.

a. If they play 12 rounds of the game, how many points can Fred expect to score? How many points can Josephina expect to score?

b. How many points per round can each player expect to score? That is, what is the expected value for each player?

c. Is this a fair game? Why or why not?

In 4–6, use the information in this table, which shows free-throw statistics for some of the players on Mr. Luft's basketball team.

Name	Free throws attempted	Free throws made
Gerrit	54	27
David	49	39
Ken	73	45
Alex	60	42

4. Which of the boys listed has the best chance of making his next free throw? Explain your reasoning.

5. **a.** Alex has just been fouled and is in a one-and-one free-throw situation. What is the probability of each of the following outcomes?

    i. Alex will score 0 points. That is, he will miss the first shot.
    ii. Alex will score 1 point. That is, he will make the first shot and miss the second shot.
    iii. Alex will score 2 points.

    b. If Alex is in a one-and-one situation 100 times, how many times would you expect each of the outcomes listed in part a to occur?

    c. What is the average number of points you could expect Alex to make per one-and-one situation?

6. a. Suppose Gerrit is in a one-and-one free-throw situation. What is the probability of each of the following outcomes?

   i. Gerrit will score 0 points.
   ii. Gerrit will score 1 point.
   iii. Gerrit will score 2 points.

b. Suppose Gerrit is in a two-shot free-throw situation. What is the probability of each of the following outcomes?

   i. Gerrit will score 0 points.
   ii. Gerrit will score 1 point.
   iii. Gerrit will score 2 points.

c. Compare your answers to parts a and b. Explain why the answers to these two questions are not exactly the same.

Connections

7. The Wheel of Fortune® game show uses a large spinner with many sections. At least one section is labeled "bankrupt." If a player spins "bankrupt," she loses her turn and all her money. Luisa created her own version of the Wheel of Fortune spinner so she could play the game with her friends. Her spinner is shown here.

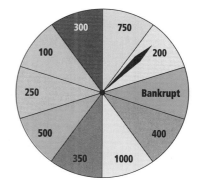

a. What is the probability that a player who spins this wheel one time will land on bankrupt?

b. What is the probability that a player who spins this wheel one time will get $500 or more?

c. Sam just spun the wheel and landed on $350. What is the probability he will land on $350 on his next spin? Explain your reasoning.

8. Wanda, the new Channel 1 weather reporter, said there was a 30% chance of rain on Saturday and a 30% chance of rain on Sunday. It rained both days, and Wanda's station manager is wondering if Wanda really knows how to predict weather.

a. Suppose Wanda had done all the calculations correctly, and according to her data there really was a 30% chance of rain each day. What was the probability that there would be rain on *both* days?

b. Do you think this incident means that Wanda doesn't know very much about predicting weather? Why or why not?

c. Wanda is working on her predictions for the next few days. She uses information from the weather satellite to calculate that there is a 20% chance of rain on Monday and a 20% chance of rain on Tuesday. If she is correct, what is the probability that it will rain on at least one of these days?

9. a. If you roll one number cube two times, what is the probability of getting a factor of 5 both times?

b. If you roll two different number cubes, what is the probability of getting a factor of 5 on both cubes?

c. How do your answers to parts a and b compare? Explain why the answers have this relationship.

10. Mr. Maldonado brought his dog Scout to the vet for a pregnancy test. Since the test gives an accurate prediction only 80% of the time, the vet decides to test Scout twice.

   a. If Scout is pregnant, what is the probability that both tests will say she is *not* pregnant? (It may help to use a 10 by 10 grid to make an area model of this situation.)

   b. If Scout is pregnant, what is the probability that at least one of the tests will indicate that she *is* pregnant?

Extensions

In 11 and 12, use the data about Mr. Luft's basketball team from questions 4–6.

11. What is the probability that Alex will make his next three free throws? Explain your reasoning.

12. David is in a one-and-one free-throw situation. What is the probability that he will make both shots?

13. Regina has worked hard all season and has increased her shooting percentage to 50%. She tells her coach that she would like to be a starter for the rest of the games this season. The coach makes a deal with Regina. At tomorrow's practice, Regina can attempt either to make three shots in a row or to make at least four out of five shots. If Regina is successful, she will start every game for the rest of the season. Which option should Regina choose? Explain your reasoning.

Mathematical Reflections

In this investigation, you learned how to find the average number of points a basketball player could expect to make per trip to the free-throw line. This average is the expected value for the situation. These questions will help you summarize what you have learned:

1 How would you calculate the probability of an outcome that has more than one step? Illustrate your answer by finding the probabilities of the possible outcomes for a 70% free-throw shooter in a one-and-one situation.

2 How would you calculate the expected value for a situation? Illustrate your answer by finding the average number of points per one-and-one situation for a 70% free-throw shooter.

Think about your answers to these questions, discuss your ideas with other students and your teacher, and then write a summary of your findings in your journal.

INVESTIGATION 6

Carnival Games

Next month, Martin Luther King School is having a carnival to raise money for new computer equipment. The students are planning to have a talent show, food stands, and games.

6.1 Drawing Marbles

A committee has been assigned to design and evaluate games for the carnival. The committee will test the games and decide which ones will help the school raise the most money. Julie and Li Fong have designed games that are quite similar.

Julie's idea
A bucket contains four blue marbles and one orange marble. Without looking, a player draws one marble from the bucket, replaces it, and then draws a second marble. If the marble is orange on either draw, the player wins.

Li Fong's idea
A bucket contains four blue marbles and one orange marble. Without looking, a player draws two marbles, one at a time, from the bucket. The player does not replace the first marble before drawing a second marble. If either marble is orange, the player wins.

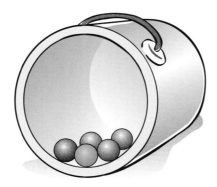

Problem 6.1

A. Play each game 20 times. Record your results on the board so everyone has access to the class data.

B. Based on the class data, if 100 people play Julie's game, how many people would you expect to win?

C. If 100 people play Li Fong's game, how many people would you expect to win?

■ Problem 6.1 Follow-Up

The carnival committee has decided to charge players four 50¢ tickets to play the game. Prizes awarded to the winners will cost the school $5 each.

1. If 100 people play Julie's game, how much money will the school collect? How much money can they expect to pay out in prizes?

2. If 100 people play Li Fong's game, how much money will the school collect? How much money can they expect to pay out in prizes?

3. The committee has decided that it needs only one of the games for the carnival. Which game do you think the carnival committee should use? Explain your choice.

6.2 Choosing the Best Game

Fergus and Judi think they have some interesting ideas for carnival games.

Fergus's idea

Fergus's game is played on a computer. When a player presses the *shift* key, the computer randomly throws two darts, one at a time, at the board shown below. If both darts hit a bonus space, the player wins.

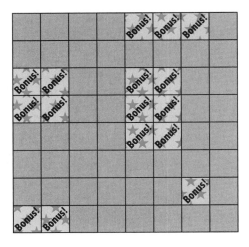

Judi's idea

A player tosses a coin four times. If the player gets three or four heads, he or she wins.

Problem 6.2

A. What is the theoretical probability of winning Fergus's game? Explain how you got your answer.

B. What is the theoretical probability of winning Judi's game? Explain how you got your answer.

■ Problem 6.2 Follow-Up

1. The carnival committee decides that Fergus's and Judi's games should cost two 50¢ tickets to play, but they are having a hard time deciding how much to spend on prizes. They want to award the same prize for each game. They want to make a profit, but they want the prize to be enticing. How much money do you think the school should spend for each prize? Explain your reasoning.

2. The committee decides it needs only one of the two games for the carnival. Which game do you think the committee should choose? Explain your reasoning.

3. Jovan suggests a slightly different version of Judi's game. As in Judi's game, a player pays two 50¢ tickets and tosses a coin four times. If the coin lands heads up all four times, the player wins a prize worth $5. If the coin lands heads up exactly three times, the player wins a prize worth $2. How much could the school expect to make if 100 students play Jovan's game?

6.3 Taking a Computer Safari

Scott and Regina designed two versions of a computer game called Safari Outrun for the school carnival. The hero of the game, Illinois Bones, drives on jungle roads. At each intersection, the computer randomly selects the path Illinois will travel. At the end of the journey, Illinois will be in city A or city B.

For each version of the game, Scott and Regina have developed a set of jungle roads and a set of prices and prizes.

Version 1

A player pays six 50¢ tickets to play the game. When the player presses the *shift* key, Illinois's journey begins. If Illinois ends in city A, the player receives a prize worth $2. If Illinois ends in city B, the player receives a prize worth $5.

Map for Version 1

Version 2

A player pays ten 50¢ tickets to play the game. When the player presses the *shift* key, Illinois's journey begins. If Illinois ends in city A, the player does not receive a prize. If Illinois ends in city B, the player receives a prize worth $10.

Map for Version 2

Problem 6.3

The carnival committee is trying to decide which version of the game to use for the carnival. For each version, answer parts A–D.

A. How much money will the school take in if the game is played 100 times?

B. How much money can the school expect to pay out in prizes if the game is played 100 times?

C. What is the average amount the school will pay out each time the game is played?

D. If the game is played 100 times, will the school make money or lose money?

▪ Problem 6.3 Follow-Up

Which version of the game do you think the committee should select for the carnival? Explain your answer.

As you work on these ACE questions, use your calculator whenever you need it.

Applications

1. In the Doubles Game, students can win carnival tickets to spend on games and food. A player pays one ticket to roll two number cubes. If the numbers match, the player wins five tickets. If a player plays this game 20 times, about how many tickets can he or she expect to win or lose? Show how you determined your answer.

2. Rashid's grandmother offers him a weekly allowance for helping her with chores around her home. She decides to make a game of it and offers him two options:

Option 1: Rashid's grandmother will give him $10 a week.

Option 2: Each week Rashid's grandmother will put four $1 bills, one $5 bill, and one $10 bill in a bag. Rashid gets to reach in and draw out two bills. This will be his allowance for the week.

The option Rashid chooses will be the method his grandmother uses to pay him for an entire year. Which plan should Rashid choose? Give mathematical reasons to support your answer.

3. Mr. Fujita hires Tasa to mow his lawn for the summer. When Tasa asks him how much he will pay her, he offers her two options:

Option 1: Mr. Fujita will pay Tasa $10 each time she mows his lawn.

Option 2: Each time Tasa mows Mr. Fujita's lawn, she will roll a pair of number cubes. If the sum on the cubes is 7, Mr. Fujita will pay her $30. If the sum is not 7, he will pay her only $3.

Which option should Tasa choose? Give mathematical reasons to support your answer.

Connections

4. a. Design a circular spinner that has six sections with the specified colors and central-angle measurements.

Section color	Central angle	Point value
yellow	20°	6
white	80°	2
black	95°	1
green	50°	4
red	35°	5
blue	80°	3

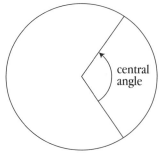

central angle

b. What is the probability that the spinner will land in each section?

c. If you spin this spinner 100 times, how many points can you expect to get per spin?

5. a. Create a circular spinner with four sections such that the probability of landing in each section is as follows:

red: 10%   yellow: 30%   blue: 45%   white: 15%

b. If you spin this spinner 500 times, how many times can you expect it to land in each section?

6. In the Funny Money game, players spin the spinner shown at right and win the indicated amount in play money. The play money can be used to purchase small prizes at the game store.

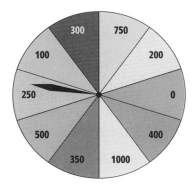

a. If this game is played 100 times, how much play money can the school expect to pay out?

b. What is the average payoff per spin?

Extensions

7. In the Rolling for Tickets game, players bet carnival tickets to try to win more tickets to spend on food and games. A player chooses an integer from 1 to 6 and bets as many tickets as he chooses on that number. The player then rolls three number cubes. If the player's number appears on exactly one cube, the player gets his tickets back. If the number appears on exactly two cubes, the player gets twice the number of tickets he bet. If the number appears on all three cubes, the player gets three times the number of tickets he bet.

a. How many outcomes are there when three number cubes are rolled?

b. How many ways are there to roll a specific double (such as two 1s or two 2s)? Do not count triples, or getting three of a kind.

c. What is the probability that exactly two cubes will match? That three cubes will match?

d. If a player repeatedly bets two tickets on the number 6, what will be the average payoff per roll? Explain how you found this average and what it means in this problem.

8. Della is chosen as a contestant on the Gee Whiz Everyone Wins! game show. The host gives her two red marbles, two green marbles, and two yellow marbles. He tells Della that she may put the marbles into two identical cans in any arrangement she chooses. While Della is blindfolded, the host may change the position of the cans, but he may not change the arrangement of the marbles in the cans. Della will then select a can at random and draw out a marble. If she draws a red marble, she will win a prize. How should Della arrange the marbles so she has the best chance of drawing a red marble?

9. Natasha designed a spinner game for the carnival. The spinner has 38 congruent sections, 18 orange, 18 blue, and 2 white. A player bets play money on orange or blue. If the spinner stops on the color the player has bet on, the player wins double the money bet. If the spinner lands on any other color, the player loses.

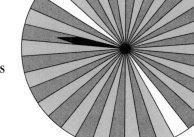

    a. What is the probability that a player will lose on one spin of the wheel?

    b. If a player bets $10 in play money on each spin, what is the average amount of money the player can expect to win or lose per spin of the wheel?

10. a. Curt has been practicing free throws. He has made 60% of his free throws during his practice sessions. The coach says that if Curt makes three free throws in a row, he can start Saturday's game. What is the probability that Curt will make three free throws in a row and start Saturday's game?

    b. Curt has a difficult time making three free throws in a row. The coach tells him to instead try making three out of four shots. What is the probability that Curt will make at least three out of four shots?

Mathematical Reflections

In this investigation, you evaluated potential carnival games. You were interested in the amount of money the school could expect to pay out if the games were played many times. These questions will help you summarize what you have learned:

1 Suppose the principal wants to make sure the school won't lose money at the carnival. How would you explain to the principal how the long-term average of each game, or the expected value, can be computed? Use an example to clarify your explanation.

2 How can expected value help you make decisions in situations involving probabilities and payoffs? Use an example if it helps you to explain your thinking.

Think about your answers to these questions, discuss your ideas with other students and your teacher, and then write a summary of your findings in your journal.

Analyzing Sequences of Outcomes

There are many actions that have exactly two equally likely outcomes. For example, when you toss a coin you may get a head or a tail. When a baby is born, it may be a boy or a girl. In this investigation, you will explore probabilities in situations involving a sequence of actions, each with two equally likely outcomes. For example, if you toss a coin twice, you may get head/head, head/tail, tail/head, or tail/tail. If a woman has two children, she may have two boys, two girls, a girl and then a boy, or a boy and then a girl.

7.1 Counting Puppies

Scout, Mr. Maldonado's Labrador retriever, is about to have puppies. Mr. Maldonado plans to sell the puppies.

Did you know?

Labrador retrievers are the second most popular dog in the world after cocker spaniels. Labrador retrievers make especially good guide dogs for blind people because they are smart and hardworking. In fact, the guide dog who holds the record for length of service to the blind—14 years, 8 months—is Cindy-Cleo, a Labrador retriever from Tel Aviv, Israel.

Source: *The Guinness Book of Records 1994.* Ed. Peter Matthews. New York: Facts on File, 1993.

Problem 7.1

The vet thinks Scout will have four puppies.

A. List all the possible combinations of female and male puppies Scout might have. Assume that for each puppy, a male and a female are equally likely.

B. Is Scout more likely to have four male puppies, or two male puppies and two female puppies? Explain your reasoning.

C. Is Scout more likely to have four male puppies, or a female puppy, a male puppy, a female puppy, and a male puppy, in that order? Explain your reasoning.

■ Problem 7.1 Follow-Up

Since female dogs can be bred to produce puppies, female puppies generally sell for more money than male puppies. Mr. Maldonado plans to sell Scout's female puppies for $250 each and her male puppies for $200 each. How much money can he expect to make for a litter of four puppies?

7.2 Guessing Answers

Have you ever forgotten to study for a quiz and had to guess at the answers? If you take a true-false test and guess on every question, what are your chances of getting every question right?

The following is a true-false quiz about animals. It is written in a secret code.

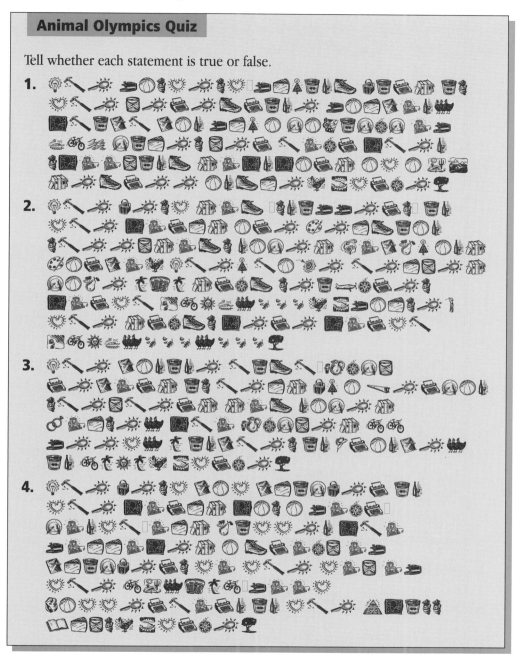

Animal Olympics Quiz

Tell whether each statement is true or false.

1.

2.

3.

4.

Take the Animal Olympics true-false quiz. How did you decide whether to answer true or false on each item?

Below are the results from two classes who took the test. Everyone guessed on every question.

TTFT	TFTF	TTTT	FTFF	FFTF	TFTF
FFTT	TTFF	TFTT	TTTF	FFTT	FFTF
TFFT	FFTT	TFTF	FTFT	TFFF	FTFF
FFFF	FTTF	FTTT	TFFF	FFFT	FFTF
TFFF	FTTT	FTTF	FFFT	TFTF	TTTF
TFTT	FTTF	TFFF	TTFF	FFTT	TFTF
TTFF	FTFT	TFFF	FTFT	TTTF	FTTT
TTFT	FFFT	TFFT	TFFF	FTTF	TFTT
TTTF	FFFF	FFTT	FFTF	TFTF	TFFT
TTTT	FFFT	FTFF	TTTT	TFFT	FFFF

Problem 7.2

Your teacher will give you the correct answers for the quiz.

A. Using the data above, what is the experimental probability that someone who guesses every answer will get all four answers right?

B. What is the experimental probability that someone who guesses every answer will get exactly three answers right?

C. What is the experimental probability that someone who guesses every answer will get exactly two answers right?

D. What is the experimental probability that someone who guesses every answer will get exactly one answer right?

E. What is the experimental probability that someone who guesses every answer will get no answers right?

■ Problem 7.2 Follow-Up

To figure out the theoretical probability of guessing the correct answer to zero, one, two, three, or all four questions, you need to figure out how many ways you can guess right or wrong on a four-question true-false quiz.

1. Use a counting tree to find all the combinations of right and wrong answers for a four-question true-false quiz. Use R to mean "right" and W to mean "wrong." For example, RRRR means all the answers are right, and RRRW means that the first three answers are right and the last answer is wrong.

2. How many right-wrong combinations are there on a four-question true-false quiz?

3. If you guess every answer to a four-question true-false quiz, are you more likely to get exactly two answers right or exactly three answers right? Explain your reasoning.

4. If you guess every answer to a four-question true-false quiz, are you more likely to get the first answer wrong and the last three answers right or to get the first two answers wrong and the last two answers right? Explain your reasoning.

5. Jim says that the probability of getting three answers right is the same as the probability of getting the first answer wrong and the last three answers right. Is he correct? Explain your reasoning.

6. When your class took the quiz, what was the average number of correct answers?

7. Will's teacher gives weekly four-question true-false quizzes. The questions on the quizzes are worth 25 points each. If Will guesses on every question of every quiz he takes, what average score can he expect on his quizzes?

8. a. How does the probability of answering four questions correctly on the quiz compare to the probability that Scout will have four female puppies?

b. How does the probability of answering two questions correctly on the quiz compare to the probability that Scout will have two female puppies?

c. Explain your answers to parts a and b.

As you work on these ACE questions, use your calculator whenever you need it.

Applications

1. It costs six tickets to play the Toss-a-Coin game at the school carnival. For each turn, a player tosses a coin three times. If the coin lands heads up two or more times in a turn, the player wins ten tickets to spend on food and games.

   a. If Ben plays the game 80 times, how many tickets can he expect to win or lose?

   b. What is the average number of tickets Ben can expect to win or lose per turn?

2. a. If you toss three coins at the same time, would the probability of getting three heads be the same as or different from the probability of getting three heads when you toss one coin three times in a row? Explain your reasoning.

   b. If you toss three coins and get three tails, what is the probability you will get three tails the next time you toss the three coins? Explain your reasoning.

3. Suppose the vet thinks Scout (from Problem 7.1) will have a litter of five puppies. How much money can Mr. Maldonado expect to make from selling the puppies?

4. a. If there were five questions on the Animal Olympics quiz instead of four, what would be the probability of guessing the correct answer to all five questions? Explain your reasoning.

   b. Suppose there were ten questions on the quiz. What do you think the probability of guessing the correct answer to all ten questions would be? Explain your reasoning.

5. How is finding the probability of getting different combinations of heads and tails the same as, or different from, finding the probability of different combinations of male and female puppies in a litter or right and wrong answers on a true-false test?

Connections

6. If you studied the *How Likely Is It?* unit, you learned about the genetics involved in tongue-curling ability. Recall that every person has a combination of two tongue-curling alleles—TT, Tt, or tt—where T is the dominant tongue-curling allele, and t is the recessive non-tongue-curling allele. A person with at least one T allele will be able to curl his or her tongue.

Ken figured out that his tongue-curling alleles are tt and his wife Diane's alleles are Tt. He made this table to help him determine the possible outcomes for their children.

	Ken	
	t	t
T	Tt	Tt
t	tt	tt

Diane (labels T and t rows)

The table shows that the possible combinations are Tt, Tt, tt, and tt. This means that each of Ken and Diane's children has a 50% chance of being able to curl his or her tongue.

a. If Ken and Diane have two children, what is the probability that both of the children will be able to curl their tongues? Make a counting tree to help you answer this question.

b. If Ken and Diane have four children, what is the probability that *none* of the children will be able to curl their tongues?

c. If Ken and Diane have four children, what is the probability that only the *oldest* child will be able to curl his or her tongue?

7. On Thursday, Waldo, the weather reporter for Channel 6 News, said there was a 50% chance of rain on Friday, a 50% chance of rain on Saturday, and a 50% chance of rain on Sunday. The station manager is upset because it rained all three days!

    a. Based on Waldo's predictions, what was the probability that it would rain all three days?

    b. Do you think Waldo's predictions might have been right even though it rained all three days? Explain your reasoning.

    c. If the chances of rain were actually 40% for Saturday and Sunday, what was the probability that it would rain both days? Explain your answer.

Extensions

8. Fill-in-the-Blanks is a two-person game. Each player rolls a number cube three times. After each roll, the player must write the resulting number in one of the three blanks below. The player who makes the highest three-digit number wins.

___ ___ ___

    a. What is the greatest possible three-digit number a player can get?

    b. What strategies would you use to play the game? Explain your reasoning.

    c. If the blank in which each number is written is chosen randomly, what is the probability that the greatest possible number will be obtained?

9. Brett invented a game that is played on the number line. At the start of a turn, a player places a marker on 0. The player tosses a penny and moves his marker one unit to the right if the penny lands heads up and one unit to the left if it lands tails up. The player's score for a turn is the number the marker is on after three tosses.

a. What scores are possible after one turn (three tosses)?

b. If Brett changes his game so that a turn consists of four tosses, what scores would be possible after one turn?

10. The largest hamster litter on record consisted of 26 babies. Suppose a hamster has 26 babies. Assume that for each baby, a female and a male are equally likely. What is the theoretical probability that all 26 babies will be male? Explain your reasoning.

11. Mindy is taking a ten-question true-false test. She forgot to study, so she is guessing at the answers.

a. What is the probability that Mindy will get all the answers correct?

b. What is the probability that Mindy will get at least nine answers correct?

12. a. If you toss six pennies, what is the probability that you will get two heads and four tails?

b. If you toss six pennies, what is the probability that you will get four heads and two tails?

Mathematical Reflections

In this investigation, you looked at probabilities for situations involving a sequence of actions, each with two equally likely outcomes. These questions will help you summarize what you have learned:

1 Describe five different situations in which there are two equally likely outcomes.

2 Tossing a coin three times is an example of a situation involving a sequence of three actions, each with two equally likely outcomes.

    a. Think of another situation that involves a series of three actions, each with two equally likely outcomes. Make a counting tree to find every possible combination of outcomes.

    b. Write a question about your situations that can be answered by using your tree.

3 As you increase the number of questions on a true-false test, what happens to the total number of possible outcomes? Use a specific example, such as the difference between a three-question test and a four-question test, to show what you mean.

Think about your answers to these questions, discuss your ideas with other students and your teacher, and then write a summary of your findings in your journal.

The Carnival Game

This project requires you to use the mathematics you have studied in several units, including this one. In this design project, you will work with a group to create a game for a school carnival and to test your game. Then, you will write a report to the carnival committee about your game.

Step 1: Design a Carnival Game

You can design a new game or redesign one of the games you analyzed in this unit. When you design your game, keep these guidelines in mind:

- The game should make a profit for the school running the carnival.
- The game should be easy to set up and use at a school carnival. It should not require expensive equipment to make or maintain.
- The game should take a relatively short time to play.
- The rules for the game should be easily understood by people your age.

Step 2: Test Your Game

After your group has drafted a game design, you need to decide whether the game you have designed is reasonable for a school carnival and will make a profit. Then, you will need to try out your game. Your group should play the game several times until you feel confident that you can predict what will happen in the long run. Keep track of your trials, and include that information in your report.

Step 3: Submit Your Game Design to the Carnival Committee

Once you are satisfied that your carnival game is reasonable, prepare to submit your game design. Your submission to the committee should include two things: a model or a scale model of the game, and a written report.

Create a Model or a Scale Model

With your group, prepare a model or a scale model of the game. If your group builds a scale model instead of an actual model, give the scale factor from the scale model to the actual game.

You can either construct the model out of similar material that you would use for the actual game, or you can prepare scale drawings of the game. If your group makes drawings, be sure to include enough views of your game so that anyone could look at the drawings and construct the game.

With your model, include a set of rules that explains how the game is played, how much it costs to play, how a player wins, and how much a player wins. Explain how the game would make a profit.

Write a Report

Write a report about your game to the carnival committee. Assume that the carnival committee is composed of teachers in the building (not just mathematics teachers), parents, and other students. Your report should include the following:

- *The probability of winning the game.* Give the experimental probability of winning the game that you found from playing the game several times. If possible, give the theoretical probability as well. For some games, such as tossing coins or drawing blocks from a container, finding the theoretical probability of winning is easy. For others, finding the theoretical probability may be too difficult. If you don't give the theoretical probability of winning for your game, explain why you did not.

- *The amount collected and expected payout per game.* Tell how much money the school will collect and how much they could expect to pay out if the game is played many times. Show how you determined these amounts.

- *An explanation of why your game should be chosen.* Explain why the game is worth having in the carnival and why you think people would want to play it.

Looking Back and Looking Ahead

Unit Reflections

The problems in this unit extended your knowledge of probability to several strategies for finding and interpreting *experimental* and *theoretical probabilities*. You used simulations to gather experimental data, *counting trees* and other listing techniques to find all of the possible outcomes in a problem situation, and *area models* in which probabilities are shown as parts of a whole rectangle or circle.

Using Your Probability Reasoning—To test your understanding and skill with probability ideas and strategies, consider the following problem situations.

1. *Sydney has a homework problem asking for designs of two dartboards that match these conditions:*

   - *The probability of landing in region A is 30%.*
   - *The probability of landing in region B is 25%.*
   - *The probability of landing in region C is 20%.*
   - *The remaining space on the dartboard is region D.*

   a. Draw a square dartboard that meets the given conditions.

   b. Draw a circular dartboard that meets the given conditions.

   c. For each dartboard, what is the probability that a dart will

   i. land in region D?

   ii. land in a region other than D?

   iii. *not* land in Region A?

2 *Glenda and Jim are playing the Match/No Match game. On each turn, the players spin the two spinners shown below. Player A scores 1 point if the spins match, and Player B scores 1 point if they do not match.*

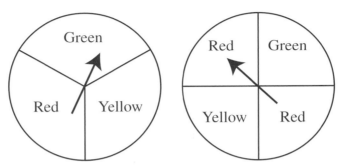

a. Use a counting tree to show all the possible outcomes for this game.

b. What is the theoretical probability of getting a match?

c. What is the theoretical probability of getting a non-match?

d. Is this a fair game? If you think the game is fair, explain why. If you think the game is not fair, explain how you could change the rules to make it fair.

3 *Kali and Tony designed a new computer game. They programmed the game so the probability that a player will win is $\frac{1}{4}$ on each turn. If the player wins, the score increases by four points. If the player loses, two points are deducted from the score.*

a. If Monte plans to play 12 rounds of the game, how many points can he expect to score?

b. How many points per round can Monte expect to win or lose?

c. Is this a fair game? If not, how would you change the points won or lost so that it would be a fair game?

Explaining Your Reasoning—When you use mathematical calculations or diagrams to solve a problem or make a decision, it is important to justify your reasoning. Answer these questions about your work.

1. What does it mean to say that the probability of some event is $\frac{1}{2}$ or $\frac{2}{3}$ or $\frac{5}{8}$?

2. How are experimental and theoretical probabilities for an event related to each other?

3. Explain and illustrate with a specific example how you could use each of these strategies to analyze probabilities.

   a. Counting trees   **b.** Area models

4. What does it mean to find the expected value of a chance activity with numerical outcomes? Give three examples of problems in this unit for which you had to compute expected value.

You will almost certainly meet this unit's ideas about probability in future study and problem solving in mathematics, science, and games of chance. These are the basis of statistical reasoning that will be developed in the *Connected Mathematics* unit *Samples and Populations* and in areas as diverse as the biology of genetics and the payoffs in state lotteries and local fund-raisers.

Glossary

counting tree A diagram used to determine the number of possible outcomes in a probability situation. The number of final branches is equal to the number of possible outcomes. The counting tree below shows all the possible outcomes for randomly choosing a yellow or red rose and then a white or pink ribbon. The four possible outcomes are listed in the last column.

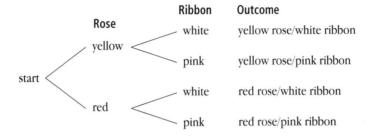

equally likely events Two or more events that have the same probability of occurring. For example, when you toss a fair coin, heads and tails are equally likely; each has a 50% chance of happening.

event A set of outcomes. For example, when two coins are tossed, getting two matching coins is an event consisting of the outcomes HH and TT.

expected value, long-term average The average payoff over many trials. For example, suppose you are playing a game with two number cubes in which you score 2 points when a sum of 6 is rolled, 1 point for a sum of 3, and 0 points for anything else. If you were to roll the cubes 36 times, you could expect to roll a sum of 6 about five times and a sum of 3 about twice. This means that you could expect to score $(5 \times 2) + (2 \times 1) = 12$ points for 36 rolls, an average of $\frac{12}{36} = \frac{1}{3}$ point per roll. This is the expected value of a roll.

experimental probability A probability that is determined through experimentation. For example, you could find the experimental probability of getting a head when you toss a coin by tossing a coin many times and keeping track of the outcomes. The experimental probability would be the ratio of the number of heads to the total number of tosses, or trials. Experimental probabilities are used to predict behavior over the long run.

fair game A game in which each player has the same chance of winning. The probability of winning a two-person fair game is $\frac{1}{2}$. An unfair game can be made fair by adjusting the scoring system, or the payoffs. For example, suppose you play a game in which two fair coins are tossed. You score when both coins land heads up; otherwise, your opponent scores. The probability that you will score is $\frac{1}{4}$, and the probability that your opponent will score is $\frac{3}{4}$. To make the game fair, you might adjust the scoring system so that you receive 3 points each time you score and your opponent receives 1 point when he or she scores.

outcome A possible result of an action. For example, when a number cube is rolled, the possible outcomes are 1, 2, 3, 4, 5, and 6.

probability A number between 0 and 1 that describes the likelihood that an event will occur. For example, a fair number cube is rolled. There is one way out of six possibilities that a 2 can be rolled, so the probability of rolling a 2 is $\frac{1}{6}$. The probability of a certain event is 1, while the probability of an event that cannot occur is 0.

random events Events whose outcomes are uncertain when viewed individually, but which may exhibit a predictable pattern when observed over many trials. For example, when you roll a fair number cube, you have no way of knowing what the next roll will be, but you do know that, over the long run, you will roll each number on the cube about the same number of times.

theoretical probability A probability obtained by analyzing a situation. If all the outcomes are equally likely, you can find a theoretical probability of an event by listing all the possible outcomes and then finding the ratio of the number of outcomes in which you are interested to the total number of outcomes. For example, there are 36 possible equally likely outcomes (number pairs) when two fair number cubes are rolled. Of these, six have a sum of 7, so the probability of rolling a sum of 7 is $\frac{6}{36}$, or $\frac{1}{6}$.

Index

Area, probability and, 4, 32–35, 41–44
  ACE, 18–29, 36–39, 45–48
Area model, 32–35, 42–44
Arrangements, probability and, 43–44

Certain event, probability of, 14
Counting tree, 4, 10–12
  ACE, 16–20, 28–29, 74–77

Dependent events, 41–44, 50–52

Equally likely events, 6
  ACE, 13–20, 74–77
  sequence of outcomes and, 69–73
Expected value, 4, 50–52
  ACE, 53–57, 64–67
  game design and, 59–63
Experimental probability, 4, 6–9,
  22–23
  ACE, 15, 19, 20, 26
  expected value and, 59–60, 70–73
  sequence of outcomes and, 69–73

Fair and unfair games, 4, 7, 22–23
  ACE, 13–20, 24–30

Games
  analyzing, 4
  area and, 32–35, 41–44
  arrangements and, 43–44
  evaluating, 5–12
  expected value and, 50–52, 59–63

fair and unfair, 4, 7, 22–23
two-stage, 41–44, 50–52

Impossible event, probability of, 14
Investigation
  Analyzing Number-Cube Games, 22–31
  Analyzing Sequences of Outcomes,
  69–78
  Analyzing Two-Stage Games, 41–49
  Carnival Games, 59–68
  Evaluating Games of Chance, 5–21
  Expected Value, 50–58
  Probability and Area, 32–40

Journal, 21, 31, 40, 49, 58, 68, 78

Long-term average, *See* **Expected value**
Looking Back and Looking Ahead:
  Unit Reflections, 81–83

Mathematical Highlights, 4
Mathematical Reflections, 21, 31, 40,
  49, 58, 68, 78
Multi-stage outcomes, 6–12, 41–44,
  50–52
  ACE, 13, 16–20, 45–48, 53–57,
  74–78
  sequence and, 69–73

Number-cube game
  addition, 22–23
  multiplication, 23

Organized list, of outcomes, 5–9, 22–23

Outcomes, 7
area models for, 32–35, 42–44
certain, 14
dependent, 41–44, 50–52
equally likely, 6
impossible, 14
multi-stage, 6–12, 41–44, 50–52
random, 33, 41
sequence and, 69–73
two-stage, 41–44, 50–52
using an organized list to find, 5–9, 22–23
using a counting tree to find, 10–12

Probability, 4, 5
area and, 4, 18–19, 32–35, 41–43
arrangements and, 43–44
certain event, 14
dependent events, 41–44, 50–52

equally likely events, 6
experimental, 6–9, 22–23
impossible event, 14
sequence of outcomes and, 69–73
theoretical, 4, 6–9, 22–23, 32–35

Random event, 33, 41

Sequence, of outcomes, 69–73
Simulation, 42, 51

Theoretical probability, 4, 6–9, 22–23
ACE, 13–20, 24–30, 36–39, 45–48
area and, 32–35, 41–44
sequence of outcomes, 69–73
Treasure Hunt, computer game, 32–35
Tree diagram, 10–12
ACE, 16–20, 28–29
Two-stage outcomes, 6–12, 41–44, 50–52
ACE, 16–20, 45–48, 53–57
sequence and, 69–73

Connected  Mathematics®

Data Around Us

Number Sense

Student Edition

Glenda Lappan
James T. Fey
William M. Fitzgerald
Susan N. Friel
Elizabeth Difanis Phillips

Prentice
Hall

Glenview, Illinois
Needham, Massachusetts
Upper Saddle River, New Jersey

Data Around Us

Connected Mathematics® was developed at Michigan State University with the support of National Science Foundation Grant No. MDR 9150217.

This project was supported, in part, by the
National Science Foundation
Opinions expressed are those of the authors and not necessarily those of the Foundation

The Michigan State University authors and administration have agreed that all MSU royalties arising from this publication will be devoted to purposes supported by the Department of Mathematics and the MSU Mathematics Education Enrichment Fund.

Contents

Mathematical Highlights   4

Investigation 1: Interpreting Disaster Reports   5
    1.1 Comparing Disasters   5
    1.2 Aiding Hurricane Victims   7
    Applications—Connections—Extensions   9
    Mathematical Reflections   11

Investigation 2: Measuring Oil Spills   12
    2.1 Describing an Oil Spill   12
    2.2 Finding Benchmarks for Units of Measure   14
    2.3 Developing a Sense of Large Numbers   16
    Applications—Connections—Extensions   19
    Mathematical Reflections   22

Investigation 3: Comparing Large Numbers   23
    3.1 Playing Dialing Digits   24
    3.2 Getting Things in Order   25
    3.3 Rounding Numbers   28
    3.4 Comparing Hog Populations   29
    Applications—Connections—Extensions   31
    Mathematical Reflections   37

Investigation 4: How Many Is a Million?   38
    4.1 Thinking Big   38
    4.2 Thinking Even Bigger   39
    4.3 Using Scientific Notation   41
    Applications—Connections—Extensions   44
    Mathematical Reflections   50

Investigation 5: Every Litter Bit Hurts   51
    5.1 Going Hog Wild   51
    5.2 Recycling Cans   52
    5.3 Going Down the Drain   53
    5.4 Making Mountains out of Molehills   54
    Applications—Connections—Extensions   55
    Mathematical Reflections   60

Investigation 6: On an Average Day   61
    6.1 Recycling Cans   61
    6.2 Making Comparisons in Two Ways   62
    6.3 Comparing by Using Rates   63
    Applications—Connections—Extensions   64
    Mathematical Reflections   69

Looking Back and Looking Ahead: Unit Reflections   70

Glossary   73

Index   74

Data Around Us

A typical human heart beats about 70 times a minute. How long does it take a heart to beat 1,000,000 times? How long does it take a heart to beat 1,000,000,000 times?

Suppose you were in charge of a relief effort to help 250,000 people who lost their homes in a hurricane. How would you calculate the number of tents and the amount of food and water needed for these people each day?

A news report stated, "Saturday's $43 million lottery Jackpot equals a trail of $1 bills that would stretch 4100 miles, from New York City to San Francisco and back to Glacier National Park in Montana." A dollar bill is about 6 inches long. How many dollar bills are needed to make a trail 1 mile long? How many dollar bills are needed to make a trail 4100 miles long?

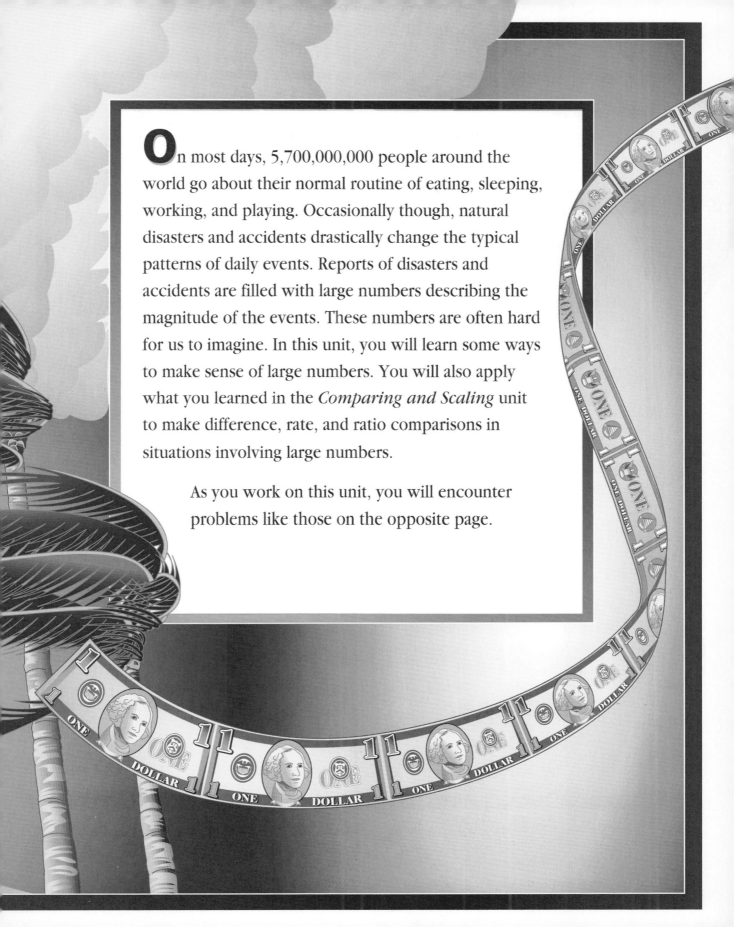

On most days, 5,700,000,000 people around the world go about their normal routine of eating, sleeping, working, and playing. Occasionally though, natural disasters and accidents drastically change the typical patterns of daily events. Reports of disasters and accidents are filled with large numbers describing the magnitude of the events. These numbers are often hard for us to imagine. In this unit, you will learn some ways to make sense of large numbers. You will also apply what you learned in the *Comparing and Scaling* unit to make difference, rate, and ratio comparisons in situations involving large numbers.

As you work on this unit, you will encounter problems like those on the opposite page.

Mathematical Highlights

In *Data Around Us,* you will explore ways to reason with quantities in order to build number sense. This unit will help you to

● Choose sensible units for measuring;

● Understand that measurement has two components, a unit of measure and a count;

● Build a repertoire of benchmarks to relate the measures of unfamiliar objects or events to the measures of objects or events that are personally meaningful;

● Review the concept of place value as it relates to reading, writing, and using large numbers;

● Read, write, and interpret large numbers that occur in everyday measurements using standard, scientific, and calculator notation;

● Choose sensible ways of comparing counts and measurements, including using differences, rates, and ratios; and

● Use estimates and rounded numbers for describing and comparing quantities.

As you work on the problems in this unit, make it a habit to ask questions about situations that involve number sense: *What quantities or measures are used or needed? How can benchmarks help make my understanding of the measurements clearer? What is the degree of accuracy that I need to use in working with these measurements? If I am making a comparison, do I want to use a simple difference or would using a percent or a ratio be a better choice?*

Interpreting Disaster Reports

When a natural disaster or major accident occurs, news reports are filled with numbers describing the magnitude of the event. In this investigation, you will learn some ways of making sense of such numbers.

1.1 Comparing Disasters

To make sense of the numbers in a disaster report, you may want to ask yourself two questions:

How accurate are the data in this report?

How do the data from this disaster compare with data from other disasters or with things I am familiar with?

Read the following reports, which describe four well-known disasters.

On October 17, 1989, as baseball's World Series was starting in San Francisco, a tremendous earthquake struck the Bay Area, leaving 67 people dead, 3000 people injured, and $10,000,000,000 in property damage. As a result of the earthquake, many major roads and bridges were closed for weeks, paralyzing traffic.

In the early morning of August 24, 1992, Hurricane Andrew roared across the state of Florida from Miami to the Gulf of Mexico. With a top wind speed of 164 miles per hour, it destroyed thousands of homes and businesses, caused $20 billion in property damage, and left 15 people dead and 250,000 homeless before it moved on to Louisiana.

On June 9, 1991, the top of 4795-foot Mount Pinatubo in the Philippine Islands exploded in a volcanic eruption that sent clouds of steam and ash into the atmosphere as high as 80,000 feet. The eruption poured lava as hot as 2000°F down the sides of the mountain. Pinatubo's volcanic ash fell to earth in a 60-mile radius around the mountain. The eruption caused the deaths of 700 people and destroyed 100,000 homes and a U.S. air base.

On April 29, 1986, equipment in several Scandinavian countries detected dangerous levels of radioactivity in the air. The radiation was from a nuclear power plant accident near Chernobyl in the Ukraine. The accident killed at least 34 people, contaminated land for miles around, and left millions of people deeply concerned about their health.

Problem 1.1

Use the information from the reports above to answer parts A–C.

A. Which numbers in the reports are probably very accurate, and which are probably only rough estimates?

B. Imagine that you are a journalist writing a story about these four disasters. Write several statements you could use to compare the disasters. For example, you might write, "The 67 deaths caused by the San Francisco Bay Area earthquake of 1989 were more than four times the number of deaths caused by Hurricane Andrew in Florida in 1992."

C. Describe the ways you found to compare the disasters.

■ Problem 1.1 Follow-Up

How do you think scientists, government officials, and journalists arrive at the numbers in their disaster reports?

Aiding Hurricane Victims

When a natural disaster or tragic accident occurs, people from around the world react quickly, sending clothing, food, medicine, and money. Many people offer their own time and effort to help the injured and homeless and to repair the damage.

When Hurricane Andrew struck south Florida, over 250,000 people were left homeless and without food or water. Relief poured into Florida from all over the United States. Making sure that food and supplies arrived where they were needed was a serious logistical problem.

Think about this!

Suppose you were in charge of a relief effort to help 250,000 people who lost their homes in a hurricane. How would you calculate the number of tents, the amount of food, and the amount of water needed for these people each day?

The United States Marine Corps and the American Red Cross sent relief supplies for families left homeless by the hurricane.

A. The U.S. Marines offered tents. Suppose each tent held 18 sleeping cots and covered 500 square feet of ground. Answer parts 1–4, and tell what assumptions you make to answer each question.

  1. How many tents would have been needed to take care of all the homeless?

  2. How much ground area would have been needed for all these tents?

  3. How does the area of one tent compare with the area of your classroom?

  4. How many people do you think could sleep in your classroom if a disaster struck your town? How many people do you think could sleep in your school?

B. The Red Cross provided cots, blankets, food, and water for the tent city and other shelters. They set up 126 feeding stations and 230 shelters. Answer parts 1–4, and tell what assumptions you make to answer each question.

  1. If each person received at least one meal a day, about how many meals did each feeding station have to provide each day?

  2. About how many students are served in your school's cafeteria each day?

  3. How many cafeterias like your school's would be needed to serve 250,000 people?

  4. The shelters housed a total of 85,154 people. What was the average number of people per shelter?

■ **Problem 1.2 Follow-Up**

The Red Cross reported serving 4,779,161 meals during the relief effort in Florida. How do you think this number was determined?

As you work on these ACE questions, use your calculator whenever you need it.

Applications

In 1–5, use the information from these reports of well-known American disasters.

The Blizzard of 1888   From March 11 through March 14 of 1888, a huge blizzard covered the eastern United States with as much as 5 feet of snow. The storm caused 400 deaths and $20 million in damage.

The Tropical Storm of 1972   In June of 1972, Tropical Storm Agnes moved up the East Coast of the United States, causing flash floods that killed 129 people, left 115,000 people homeless, and caused $3.5 billion of damage.

The Floods of 1993   From June through August of 1993, heavy rains in the midwestern United States led to flooding that caused 50 deaths, left 70,000 people homeless, and damaged $12 billion worth of crops and buildings.

1. Which numbers in these reports are probably very accurate, and which are probably only rough estimates?

2. Which disaster caused the greatest financial loss? How did you decide?

3. Compare the loss of life from the Blizzard of 1888 with the loss of life from Tropical Storm Agnes.

4. Compare the loss of life from Tropical Storm Agnes with the loss of life from the Midwest floods of 1993.

5. Compare the loss of life from the Blizzard of 1888 with the loss of life from the Midwest floods of 1993.

Connections

6. If the floor of a Marine hurricane-relief tent is a rectangle with an area of 500 square feet, what might the dimensions of the tent be?

7. On October 8, 1871, a wildfire destroyed the town of Peshtigo, Wisconsin, and much of the surrounding forest. More than 1200 people were killed, and 2 billion trees were burned.

  a. What method might have been used to estimate the number of trees burned?

  b. What similar estimation problems have you encountered in other Connected Mathematics units?

Extensions

8. Below are scale drawings of a cot and the floor of a Marine tent.

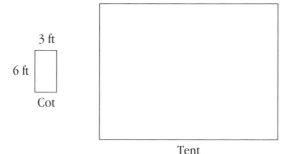

3 ft

6 ft

Cot

Tent

  a. How many cots could fit in a tent?

  b. If you were in charge of setting up the cots, how many cots would you put in each tent? How would you arrange the cots? Draw a diagram to illustrate your answer.

9. Read about great disasters in a world almanac.

  a. Which disaster do you believe was the worst of all time? Explain your choice.

  b. Make up a math problem about the disaster you chose for part a.

Mathematical Reflections

In this investigation, you looked at reports of natural disasters and accidents. You thought about how accurate the numbers in these reports might be and considered how the numbers might have been obtained. You also looked for ways to compare one disaster with another. These questions will help you summarize what you have learned:

1 What clues can help you decide whether a number is accurate or only a rough estimate?

2 In what ways can you compare data describing damage for one disaster with data describing damage for another disaster?

Think about your answers to these questions, discuss your ideas with other students and your teacher, and then write a summary of your findings in your journal.

Measuring Oil Spills

Our modern world depends on crude oil for energy and other products. As a result, huge tankers travel the world's oceans carrying oil from where it is found to where it is used. Unfortunately, some of these tankers have accidents and spill their sticky cargo on waters, beaches, and sea animals.

News reports of oil spills usually try to communicate the amount of oil spilled. Such reports may tell how many barrels were spilled, or they may give the surface area or volume of the spill. What do you think would be the best way to describe the size of an oil spill?

2.1 Describing an Oil Spill

Numbers are essential in reporting the size and effects of oil spills and in preparing for cleanup actions. To see how important numbers are, try reading this "censored" story about a famous oil spill.

Shortly after __A__ on __B__ a giant oil tanker left Valdez, Alaska, with a load of __C__ of crude oil from the Alaskan pipeline. To avoid icebergs, the ship took a course about __D__ out of the normal shipping channel. Unfortunately, less than __E__ later the ship ran aground on the underwater Bligh Reef. The rocks of the reef tore a __F__ gash in the tanker's hull, and __G__ of crude oil spilled onto the surface of Prince William Sound. For weeks, the world watched closely as the *Exxon Valdez* oil spill became an environmental disaster, despite extensive efforts to contain and clean up the oil. The spill gradually spread to form an oil slick, covering __H__ of water and killing __I__ sea otters and __J__ birds. The cleanup engaged __K__ of boats and workers, who struggled against the cold of __L__ water and air temperatures. The cleanup cost was over __M__, including __N__ for wildlife rescue alone.

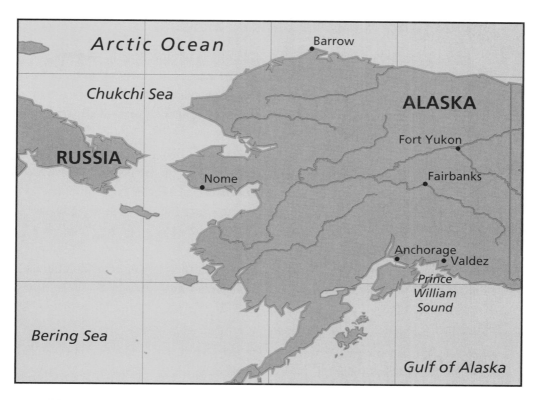

Problem 2.1

Match each lettered blank in the story with the correct measurement or range of numbers from the list below. Be prepared to explain your reasons for each choice.

800 square miles	10,080,000 gallons	$41 million
2000 to 3000	600-foot	2 miles
40° Fahrenheit	150 centimeters	90,000 to 300,000
$2 billion	March 24, 1989	52,000,000 gallons
thousands	3 hours	9:00 P.M.

■ Problem 2.1 Follow-Up

The numbers and measurements in Problem 2.1 describe attributes such as area, volume, and time. For example, "800 square miles" describes the area of the oil slick. You can tell that 800 square miles is an area measurement by looking at the units. Square miles are units of area. For parts A–N, describe what is being measured—for example, area, length, volume, weight, or time.

Finding Benchmarks for Units of Measure

The news report in Problem 2.1 gives measurements of time, length, area, volume, temperature, money, population, and so on. These measurements are given in two parts: a *count* and a *unit of measure.* The count tells how many units of measure are being considered. For example, 10,080,000 gallons is the volume of oil spilled. The unit of measure is gallons, and the count is 10,080,000.

To understand disaster reports in which large numbers are used, you need a sense of the size of different units of measure. You also need a sense of what large numbers "look like." For example, to imagine 10,080,000 gallons, you need a sense of "how big" a gallon is and of "how many" 10,080,000 is.

In this problem, you will develop some *benchmarks* to help you think about units of measure. In the United States, we use two systems of measurement. The *customary system* includes inches, gallons, and pounds. The *metric system* includes meters, liters, and grams.

Problem 2.2

This problem will help to refresh your memory of customary and metric units.

A. In your group, think of as many units of length, area, volume, weight or mass, temperature, and time as you can. Record each unit on a stick-on note. Be sure to think of both customary and metric units.

B. Group the units by the attributes they measure. Put all the units of length together, all the units of area together, and so on.

C. For each unit, try to think of something familiar that is about the size of 1 unit. For example, a sheet of notebook paper is about 1 foot long. A single-serving container of yogurt holds about 1 cup. Add each example to the stick-on note with the unit name. You can use these examples as *benchmarks* to help you imagine the size of something when a measurement is given.

■ Problem 2.2 Follow-Up

Sometimes it is convenient to know the relationship between customary and metric units of measure. The following are some common *conversions:*

$$1 \text{ inch} = 2.54 \text{ centimeters} \qquad 1 \text{ gallon} \approx 3.785 \text{ liters} \qquad 1 \text{ pound} \approx 0.454 \text{ kilogram}$$

1. a. Find or think of an object whose length is commonly measured in customary units. Give the length of the object in customary units, and then convert the length to metric units.

b. Find or think of an object whose length is commonly measured in metric units. Give the length of the object in metric units, and then convert the length to customary units.

2. a. Find or think of an object whose volume is commonly measured in customary units. Give the volume of the object in customary units, and then convert the volume to metric units.

b. Find or think of an object whose volume is commonly measured in metric units. Give the volume of the object in metric units, and then convert the volume to customary units.

Did you know?

Ounces and pounds are measures of weight. *Weight* is the force with which an object is attracted toward Earth (or some other body). Grams and kilograms are measures of mass. *Mass* is a measure of the amount of material an object contains. If you stood on the Moon, you would have the same mass that you have on Earth. However, since the gravitational pull of the Moon is weaker than that of Earth, you would weigh less on the Moon than you do on Earth. For measurements made on Earth, the distinction between mass and weight is not critical, and the terms are often used interchangeably.

---

3. a. Find or think of an object whose weight is commonly measured in customary units. Give the weight of the object in customary units, and then convert this measurement to metric units.

b. Find or think of an object whose mass is commonly measured in metric units. Give the mass of the object in metric units, and then convert this measurement to customary units.

4. Find three items in your home or school that are labeled with both customary and metric units.

2.3 Developing a Sense of Large Numbers

You can imagine what a gallon of oil looks like, but can you imagine 10,080,000 gallons spread over 800 square miles of Prince William Sound? You have a sense of how long a foot is, but can you picture a 600-foot gash in the hull of an oil tanker? You know the value of $1, but can you imagine the value of the $41 million spent rescuing wildlife from the *Exxon Valdez* oil spill?

One way to understand measurements with large numbers is to find something familiar that is the same size. For example, Los Angeles and New York City have a combined land area of just about 800 square miles. The *Exxon Valdez* oil slick would have nearly covered those two cities.

Another way to make sense of measurements with large numbers is to think about copies of something familiar. For example, an American football field is 300 feet long (without the end zones). The gash in the *Exxon Valdez* was as long as two football fields. Operating America's public schools costs an average of $4500 per student each year. The money spent on the *Exxon Valdez* wildlife rescue is equal to the cost of school for more than 9000 students—or all the seventh graders in Alaska!

Did you know?

The immediate impact of the *Exxon Valdez* oil spill on the marine wildlife in coastal Alaska was tremendous. Within two months of the disaster, cleanup crews had retrieved over 35,000 dead birds from the state's oily shorelines. Biologists estimate that a total of about 250,000 birds were killed by the spill. One species, the marbled murrelet, lost an amazing 30 percent of its native population. Fortunately, as the Alaskan ecosystem slowly heals, seabird colonies have been returning to their earlier population levels.

Problem 2.3

In parts A–G, facts about the *Exxon Valdez* disaster are given. Imagine you are a newspaper reporter assigned to the story. Use your own ideas or the hints given to write statements communicating each fact in a way that would be easy for your readers to understand.

A. *The* Exxon Valdez *spilled 10,080,000 gallons of crude oil.*
Hint: An Olympic-size swimming pool holds about 500,000 gallons of water. How many such pools could be filled with the 10,080,000 gallons of oil?

B. *The tanker strayed about 2 miles out of the usual shipping channel.*
Hint: What places in your area are about 2 miles apart?

C. *The water and air temperatures during the oil spill cleanup were about 40° Fahrenheit.*
Hint: When, if ever, do the water and air temperatures in your area reach these temperatures? Do you go swimming then?

D. *The tanker ran aground on Bligh Reef less than 3 hours after it left port.*
Hint: What familiar events last about 3 hours?

E. *The oil spill killed 90,000 to 300,000 seabirds.*
Hint: Consult an almanac or atlas to find cities or towns in your state with human populations about this size.

F. *The entire cleanup operation cost $2,000,000,000.*
Hint: In the United States, the mean annual pay for workers is about $25,000. How many annual salaries could be paid from the cleanup cost of the oil spill?

G. *The oil slick eventually covered 800 square miles of the ocean's surface.*
Hint: 1 mile is 5280 feet, so 1 square mile is $5280 \times 5280 = 27,878,400$ square feet. Estimate the area of your classroom floor. Then, figure out how many such classroom floors it would take to cover 1 square mile and to cover the 800-square-mile oil slick.

The *Exxon Valdez* oil tanker was 987 feet long. You can get a sense of this length by imagining a "human chain."

1. Make an estimate of the arm span, in feet, of a typical seventh grader. Figure out how many seventh graders it would take to stretch out in a line as long as the *Exxon Valdez*.

2. Would the chain require more students than are in your class? Would it require more students than are in your school?

3. Would this chain fit in the hall of your school? Would it fit across the football field or soccer field?

As you work on these ACE questions, use your calculator whenever you need it.

Applications

In 1–6, use the following information: On May 18, 1980, Mount St. Helens, a volcano in southwestern Washington, erupted with a blast of hot gas and rock that devastated more than **150,000 acres** of prime timberland and sent a mushroom cloud of ash **90,000 feet** into the atmosphere and then around the world. The blast triggered the largest landslide in recorded history—**4 billion cubic yards** of shattered rock poured down the mountainside at a speed of **17,600 feet per minute.** The Mount St. Helens eruption killed **60 people** and caused an estimated **$970 million** in damage. When the main eruption was over, the mountain had lost **1313 feet** from its original height of **9677 feet.**

1. Tell which of the boldface measurements are measures of the given attribute.

    a. length   **b.** area   **c.** volume   **d.** weight or mass

    e. money   **f.** speed   **g.** temperature   **h.** population

2. The Washington Monument is 550 feet tall. How many such monuments would be needed to make a tower reaching to the top of the Mount St. Helens ash cloud?

3. Glenn Robinson, the Milwaukee Bucks basketball star, earns about $6 million per year. How many years of his salary would be needed to pay for the damage from the Mount St. Helens eruption?

4. The median annual salary per worker in the United States in 1983 was about $16,300. About how many such salaries would it take to pay for the damage from the Mount St. Helens eruption?

5. The playing field in a major league baseball park covers about 2 acres of land. How many such fields would it take to cover the timberland destroyed by the Mount St. Helens eruption?

6. Use the given facts as benchmark data to write statements for a news report describing the size and effects of the Mount St. Helens eruption.

   a. The Louisiana Superdome is the largest sports arena in the world. It covers 13 acres and reaches a height of about 350 feet.

   b. A car traveling 65 miles per hour moves 5720 feet per minute.

   c. Sixty-seven deaths were caused by the San Francisco earthquake of October 17, 1989.

7. An offshore oil platform, Hibernia, is being built 200 miles off the coast of Newfoundland. It will weigh 600,000 tons, making it the heaviest such platform in the world. Develop a benchmark to help you make sense of the weight of this platform.

Connections

8. Tell what customary and metric units you could use to measure the following things. For example, for a television set, you could measure the length, width, or diagonal of the screen in inches or centimeters; you could measure the weight or mass in pounds or kilograms; and you could measure the area of the screen in square inches or square centimeters.

   a. a car

   b. a contact lens

   c. a trip from Boston to Seattle

   d. a house or an apartment

   e. the water used in your school each day

9. When oil began leaking from the *Exxon Valdez,* cleanup teams tried to contain the spill by surrounding it with floating booms. Before the slick could be contained, the oil spread too far for the supply of boom sections.

   a. Suppose you have 20,000 meters of boom sections to arrange in the shape of a rectangle. Of all the rectangles you could make from the boom sections, which rectangle would have the greatest area? Give the dimensions and the area of the rectangle.

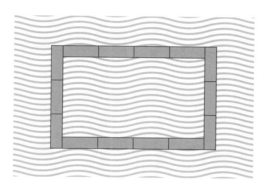

   b. Suppose you can arrange 20,000 meters of flexible boom sections in any shape you choose. Which shape could contain the greatest oil slick area?

Extensions

In 10 and 11, use the following information: In terms of gallons of oil spilled, there have been spills larger than the *Exxon Valdez* disaster. On July 19, 1979, two tankers collided near the islands of Trinidad and Tobago, releasing 88,200,000 gallons of crude oil into the Caribbean Sea. On June 3, 1979, an oil well in the Gulf of Mexico exploded and spilled 180,000,000 gallons of crude oil before it was capped.

10. Compare the *Exxon Valdez* disaster with these two spills.

11. If you were writing a news report on these spills, what other measures of damage would you want to include?

Mathematical Reflections

In this investigation, you reviewed customary and metric units of measure. You also practiced some useful strategies for making sense of disaster reports that include large numbers and many different units. These questions will help you summarize what you have learned:

1. What are some common units for measuring length, area, volume, weight or mass, temperature, and time?

2. What familiar things could you use as benchmarks to explain to someone the sizes of the units you listed in question 1? Select one or two units of measure for each type of measurement (length, area, volume, and so on), and give an example of a benchmark for each.

3. What are some strategies you can use to better understand the size of something that is expressed by a measurement with a very large number?

Think about your answers to these questions, discuss your ideas with other students and your teacher, and then write a summary of your findings in your journal.

Comparing Large Numbers

You have seen that the numbers used to report the size of natural disasters and accidents are often very large. Hurricane Andrew caused $20 billion in property damage; the *Exxon Valdez* oil slick covered about 22,300,000,000 square feet of ocean surface; and the Mount St. Helens eruption blasted 4 billion cubic yards of rock off the top of the mountain. To solve problems about situations like these and to discuss your results with others, you need to know how to write and read large numbers.

The standard notation for writing numbers involves ten digits—0, 1, 2, 3, 4, 5, 6, 7, 8, and 9—and a *place-value system.* To write and read numbers greater than 999, we group the places into clusters of three.

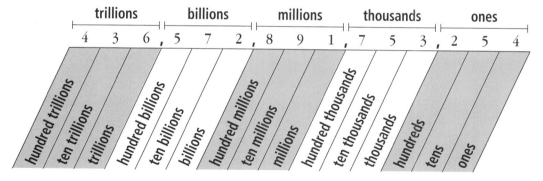

The number 436,572,891,753,254 is read "four hundred thirty-six *trillion,* five hundred seventy-two *billion,* eight hundred ninety-one *million,* seven hundred fifty-three *thousand,* two hundred fifty-four." Notice that in this number the digit 2 appears in two places. In one place, it stands for two billion; in the other place, it stands for two hundred.

Playing Dialing Digits

You can test your skill in reading, writing, and comparing numbers by playing the Dialing Digits game.

Rules for Dialing Digits

Dialing Digits is played by two or more players or teams.

Materials
- Pencils
- Dialing Digits spinner
- Dialing Digits game cards (1 per player)

On the Dialing Digits game card, the blanks for each game represent place values for a nine-digit number.

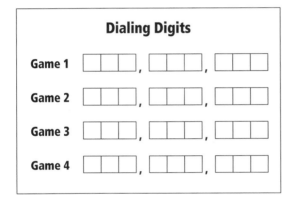

Directions
- Players take turns spinning the spinner. After each spin, each player must write the digit spun in one of the empty blanks for that game. Players should keep their game cards hidden from each other until the end of the game.
- The game proceeds until all the blanks have been filled. The player that has placed the digits to make the greatest number wins. However, before earning the win, the player must correctly read the number that has been produced.

Problem 3.1

Play Dialing Digits several times with different opponents. Record any strategies you find that help you win.

■ Problem 3.1 Follow-Up

You can vary Dialing Digits to make it more challenging. Here are two variations:

- Play two rounds of the game, and have each player add his or her numbers for the two rounds. The player with the greatest sum wins.
- Play two rounds of the game, and have each player subtract the number for round 2 from the number for round 1. The team with the greatest difference wins.

Play Dialing Digits again, using one of these variations. Describe a strategy for winning.

3.2 Getting Things in Order

You have seen that reports of natural disasters often involve large numbers. Large numbers also occur frequently in population data. The table below shows 1992 populations of the 20 largest metropolitan areas in the United States. A *metropolitan area* consists of a central city and smaller surrounding communities.

Metropolitan area	Population
Atlanta	2,959,950
Boston	5,455,403
Chicago	8,239,820
Cleveland	2,859,644
Dallas	4,037,282
Detroit	5,187,171
Houston	3,731,131
Los Angeles	14,531,529
Miami	3,192,582
Minneapolis	2,538,834
New York City	19,549,649
Philadelphia	5,892,937
Phoenix	2,238,480
Pittsburgh	2,394,811
St. Louis	2,492,525
San Diego	2,498,016
San Francisco	6,253,311
Seattle	2,970,328
Tampa	2,067,959
Washington, D.C.	6,727,050

Source: U.S. Bureau of the Census, as reported in
The World Almanac and Book of Facts 1996. Ed.
Robert Famighetti. Mahwa, New Jersey: Funk and
Wagnalls, 1995.

Problem 3.2

The census data are given in alphabetical order, but it is often interesting and important to look at *ranking* by size. An increase in population can bring greater political and economic power to an area.

A. Order the 20 metropolitan areas from most populated to least populated.

B. Describe some ways you could compare the populations of these metropolitan areas.

C. Locate each of the 20 metropolitan areas on the U.S. map on Labsheet 3.2. Look for interesting patterns in the locations of these areas.

1. What geographic factors seem to lead to large population centers?

2. How do you think the locations of these large metropolitan areas affect national and state government and business decisions?

■ **Problem 3.2 Follow-Up**

1. The table on the next page shows the population of the major city in each metropolitan area. List the cities in order from most populated to least populated.

2. Compare the ranking for the cities to the ranking for the metropolitan areas. Give some possible reasons for any differences you find.

Metropolitan area	Population of metropolitan area	Population of city
Atlanta	2,959,950	393,929
Boston	5,455,403	574,283
Chicago	8,239,820	2,783,726
Cleveland	2,859,644	505,616
Dallas	4,037,282	1,007,618
Detroit	5,187,171	1,027,974
Houston	3,731,131	1,629,902
Los Angeles	14,531,529	3,485,557
Miami	3,192,582	358,648
Minneapolis	2,538,834	368,383
New York City	19,549,649	7,322,564
Philadelphia	5,892,937	1,585,577
Phoenix	2,238,480	983,403
Pittsburgh	2,394,811	369,879
St. Louis	2,492,525	396,685
San Diego	2,498,016	1,110,554
San Francisco	6,253,311	723,959
Seattle	2,970,328	516,259
Tampa	2,067,959	280,015
Washington, D.C.	6,727,050	606,900

Source: U.S. Bureau of the Census, as reported in *The World Almanac and Book of Facts 1996.* Ed. Robert Famighetti. Mahwa, New Jersey: Funk and Wagnalls, 1995.

Did you know?

With more than half the state's automobile and human populations, New York City has its share of cleaning to do. While people may complain about how dirty the city is, the streets today are spotless compared to 150 years ago. Before the first sewer systems were built during the nineteenth century, New York City streets were so filthy that herds of abandoned farm hogs roamed the city, eating the trash that piled up along the roadside. During his visit to the city in 1842, British author Charles Dickens joked that New Yorkers ought to "take care of the pigs, for they are the city scavengers." Today, structural engineers face the difficult task of renovating old-fashioned sewer systems without disturbing the bustling businesses of America's largest city.

Rounding Numbers

The census data in Problem 3.2 are given as exact counts, but since exact populations are difficult to calculate and change daily, populations are often given as rounded figures. For example, the population of the Los Angeles metropolitan area might be rounded as shown:

Actual count (1992)	14,531,529
Rounded to the nearest ten million	10,000,000
Rounded to the nearest million	15,000,000
Rounded to the nearest hundred thousand	14,500,000

By using rounded numbers, you can give a general idea of size without claiming exactness. And, most people find it easier to think about and compare numbers with fewer non-zero digits. When you round a number, you need to consider the situation in order to decide how accurate the rounded number should be.

Problem 3.3

In 1990, the population of the United States was reported to be 248,709,873. Here are four possible roundings of this number:

200,000,000   250,000,000   249,000,000   248,700,000

A. The population of the world is about 5.7 billion. Which of the above roundings would you use if you wanted to compare the population of the United States with the population of the world? Give reasons for your choice.

B. The population of India is about 1 billion. Which rounding would you use if you wanted to compare the population of the United States with the population of India? Give reasons for your choice.

C. In 1980, the population of the United States was about 226,000,000. Which rounding would you use if you wanted to compare the 1990 U.S. population with this 1980 population figure? Give reasons for your choice.

■ **Problem 3.3 Follow-Up**

Look again at the list of the 20 largest metropolitan areas. Round these population figures in a way that makes sense to you. Explain your reasoning. Do your roundings preserve the original ranking? Why or why not?

3.4 **Comparing Hog Populations**

In areas with large populations of people or animals, finding ways to dispose of waste can be a problem. Any area must deal with the storage, treatment, and disposal of garbage and hazardous chemical wastes. Areas with industries involving great numbers of animals must also deal with the treatment and disposal of animal wastes.

Did you know?

In 1995, at a hog farm in northern Onslow County, North Carolina, the walls of an 8-acre wastewater lagoon collapsed. Within an hour, 25 million gallons of raw hog waste had poured through a 25-foot-wide breech in the 12-foot wall into a nearby river. Over the next few days, the wastewater swirled downstream, smothering and suffocating more than 3500 fish.

Hog farming is an important business in North Carolina. In fact, one area of the state, shown in dark orange on the map below, is known as the "hog belt."

The table below gives data for the 15 North Carolina counties with the greatest 1993 hog populations. For each county, the table gives the 1993 hog population, the percent growth from 1983 to 1993, and the number of hogs per square mile.

County	1993 hog population	Growth from 1983	Hogs per square mile
Sampson	1,152,000	363%	1218
Duplin	1,041,000	349%	1273
Wayne	333,000	265%	603
Bladen	271,000	1178%	310
Greene	231,000	82%	870
Pitt	193,000	128%	297
Lenoir	159,000	312%	399
Johnston	129,000	61%	163
Robeson	124,000	81%	131
Onslow	115,000	261%	150
Jones	105,000	999%	223
Beaufort	103,000	51%	125
Pender	97,000	588%	111
Halifax	82,000	18%	113
Northampton	81,000	53%	151

Source: U.S. Department of Agriculture, as reported in the *Raleigh News and Observer,* 19–26 February 1995.

Problem 3.4

A. Write at least three statements comparing the hog data for Johnston County with the hog data for Bladen County.

B. Choose two different pairs of counties from the table. For each pair, write at least three statements comparing the hog data for the two counties.

■ Problem 3.4 Follow-Up

Find the mean and median of the 1993 hog populations for the 15 counties. How do the mean and median compare? If they are different, explain why. How do the mean and median help in describing the hog populations of these counties?

As you work on these ACE questions, use your calculator whenever you need it.

Applications

In 1–7, use the following table, which gives data regarding U.S. casualties in major wars from the Revolutionary War to the Persian Gulf War. A dash (—) indicates that the information is not available.

War	People serving	Battle deaths	Other deaths	Battle injuries	Total casualties
Revolutionary War	184,000 to 250,000	6824	18,500	8445	33,769
War of 1812	286,730	2260	—	4505	6765
Mexican War	78,718	1733	11,550	4152	17,435
Civil War (Union)	2,213,363	140,414	224,097	281,881	646,392
Civil War (Confederate)	600,000 to 1,500,000	74,524	59,297	—	133,821
Spanish-American War	306,760	385	2061	1662	4108
World War I	4,743,826	53,513	63,195	204,002	320,710
World War II	16,353,659	292,131	115,185	670,846	1,078,162
Korean War	5,764,143	33,651	—	103,284	136,939
Vietnam War	8,744,000	47,369	10,799	153,303	211,471
Persian Gulf War	467,539	148	145	467	760

Source: Revolutionary War: *The Toll of Independence,* Ed. Howard H. Peckham, Chicago: University of Chicago Press, 1974. All other wars: U.S. Department of Defense, as reported in *The World Almanac and Book of Facts 1996.* Ed. Robert Famighetti. Mahwa, New Jersey: Funk and Wagnalls, 1995.

1. In World War II, 16,353,659 Americans served in the fighting forces. Write this number in words.

2. In the Civil War, 2,213,363 people served in the Union army. Write this number in words.

3. Rank the ten wars from greatest to least in terms of the number of people serving. (Combine Union and Confederate data for the Civil War.)

4. Rank the wars from greatest to least in terms of the total number of casualties. (Combine Union and Confederate data for the Civil War.)

5. a. For each war, what percent of the number of people serving were casualties? (Combine Union and Confederate data for the Civil War.)

b. Using the percents you found in part a, rank the wars from the greatest percent of casualties to the least percent of casualties.

c. How does this ranking compare with the rankings you made in questions 3 and 4? Give possible reasons for any differences in the rankings.

6. a. For each war, find the total number of deaths.

b. Round your answers from part a to the nearest thousand.

7. Find the five greatest numbers in the table, and round each to the nearest hundred thousand.

Connections

8. Suppose you play a two-digit version of Dialing Digits (from Problem 3.1).

a. What is the greatest number you could create?

b. What is the probability of getting this number on two spins?

c. If the result of the first spin is recorded in the first blank, what is the probability of getting a two-digit number in the forties?

9. Most of the war data used in questions 1–7 appear to be given as exact counts.

a. Which numbers do you think are probably most accurate?

b. If you wanted to round the data so you could make quick comparisons of size, what rounding would you use in each column? Why?

10. To make sense of the war data used in questions 1–7, you may find it helpful to compare the numbers with more familiar data.

   a. Find the three wars in which the greatest number of people served. Use the table on page 27 to find metropolitan areas and cities with populations approximately equal to the number of people serving in these wars.

   b. Armies are usually made up of young people. Find out the number of students in the senior class of your community high school. Then, find the number of senior classes of that size needed to equal the 8,744,000 people who served in the Vietnam War.

11. A news report about lottery winnings stated, "Saturday's $43 million Lotto Jackpot equals a trail of $1 bills that would stretch 4100 miles, from New York City to San Francisco and back to Glacier National Park in Montana."

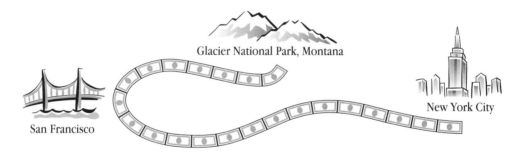

Glacier National Park, Montana

San Francisco

New York City

   a. A $1 bill is about 6 inches long. How many $1 bills are needed to make a trail 1 mile long?

   b. How many $1 bills are needed to make a trail 4100 miles long?

12. Look at the "Other deaths" column in the table of war data for questions 1–7.

   a. What might cause "other deaths" during a war?

   b. What might explain the changing proportion of "other deaths" to "battle deaths" from the Revolutionary War through the Persian Gulf War?

13. This table shows 1987 data for ten countries. For each country, the table gives the number of people serving in the military and the total population. Notice that the numbers of people in the military are given in thousands. For example, the number of people in the military in China is 3530 × 1000 = 3,530,000. The populations are given in millions. For example, the population of China is 1070 × 1,000,000 = 1,070,000,000.

Country	Number in military (thousands)	Population (millions)
People's Republic of China	3530	1070
Cuba	297	10
India	1502	790
Iraq	900	17
Israel	180	4
North Korea	838	21
Soviet Union	4400	284
Syria	400	11
United States	2279	245
Vietnam	1300	64

Source: *The World Almanac and Book of Facts 1992.* New York: Pharos Books, 1991.

a. Which of the countries listed have the greatest and least populations, and what are those populations? Write your answers in *standard notation.* That is, show all the places of each number. For example, the population of Cuba in standard notation is 10,000,000.

b. Which of the countries listed have the largest and smallest military forces, and what are the sizes of those military forces? Write your answers in standard notation.

c. Which of the countries listed have the greatest and least percents of their population serving in the military, and what are those percents?

14. In Problem 3.4, you looked at the 15 North Carolina counties with the largest 1993 hog populations. The bar graph below compares the total hog population of these counties with the total human population of these counties for every even year from 1984 through 1994. How do you think the 1995 hog population compared with the 1995 human population?

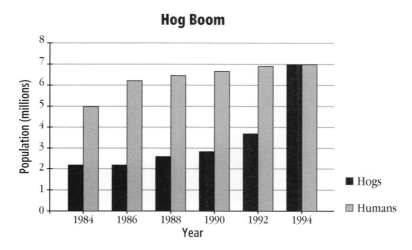

Hog Boom

15. The table below shows the change in the "hog inventory" from 1993 to 1994 for the five North Carolina counties with the highest 1994 hog populations.

a. If the percent change for each county was the same from 1994 to 1995 as it was from 1993 to 1994, how many hogs were in each county in 1995?

b. Use the information in the table to figure out what the hog inventory for Bladen County was in 1993. How does this number compare with the total 1993 hog population of Bladen County given in the table in Problem 3.4?

County	1994 hog inventory (millions)	Growth from 1993
Duplin	1.47	41%
Sampson	1.45	26%
Wayne	0.41	23%
Bladen	0.41	50%
Greene	0.28	22%

Note: The hog inventory is the number of hogs and pigs on farms as of December 1, 1994.
Source: North Carolina Department of Agriculture.

Extensions

In 16–19, a number in the given statement has been rounded from its actual value. Give the greatest and least possible actual values for the number.

16. The longest traffic jam of all time was 110 miles long (rounded to the nearest 10 miles).

17. The longest bridge in the United States is the Second Lake Pontchartrain Causeway in Louisiana. It is 125,000 feet long (rounded to the nearest 5000 feet).

18. In 1991, there were 50 million (rounded to the nearest 10 million) pet dogs in the United States.

19. As of 1989, the United States had the greatest number of telephones of any country in the world, 120,000,000 (rounded to the nearest 10,000,000).

Mathematical Reflections

In this investigation, you compared, ordered, and rounded large numbers. These questions will help you summarize what you have learned:

1 Describe several ways you can compare large numbers. Be sure to discuss percents, differences, and ordering.

2 Tokyo-Yokohama, Japan, is the most populous city in the world with 28,477,000 residents (as of 1995). How would you round this population to the nearest ten million? To the nearest million? To the nearest hundred thousand? Choose one of these three roundings, and describe a situation in which it would make sense to use this rounding. Explain your reasoning.

3 Describe some ways you could compare the population of Tokyo-Yokohama with the population of the largest metropolitan area in the United States.

Think about your answers to these questions, discuss your ideas with other students and your teacher, and then write a summary of your findings in your journal.

How Many Is a Million?

You have seen that it is sometimes difficult to get a sense of just how big a large number really is. In previous investigations, you developed some benchmarks to help you imagine large numbers. In this investigation, you will develop a sense of how many a million is. You will also learn a shorthand notation for writing large numbers.

4.1 Thinking Big

Large numbers appear in newspaper, radio, and television reports every day.

The Daily Gazette

| VOL. CXXXIV NO. 24 | FRIDAY, MAY 23, 1997 | ★ ★ ★ ★ |

Hog Lagoon Spills a Million Gallons of Waste in Creek!
Fish Kill Expected to Run into Millions!

How many is a million? This problem will give you a sense of what a million "looks like."

Problem 4.1

For each part of this problem, explain how you arrived at your answer.

A. How long does it take your heart to beat 1,000,000 times?

B. Advertisements for a popular brand of chocolate chip cookie claim that there are 1000 chips in each bag of cookies. How many bags would you need to have 1,000,000 chips? If one bag measures 20 centimeters by 12 centimeters by 6 centimeters, would all of these bags fit in your classroom?

C. If someone is 1,000,000 hours old, what is his or her age in years?

D. How many students can stand inside a square with an area of 1,000,000 square centimeters?

■ **Problem 4.1 Follow-Up**

Write another question you could ask to help someone get a sense of how many a million is.

4.2 Thinking Even Bigger

The questions in Problem 4.1 helped you get a sense of how many a million is. But what about a billion or a trillion? How can you make sense of newspaper headlines like these?

The Daily Gazette

VOL. CXXI NO. 7   THURSDAY, OCTOBER 2, 1995   ★ ★ ★ ★

U.S. Debt Nears $5 Trillion

Population of India Passes 1 Billion

Did you know?

The words *billion* and *trillion* do not mean the same thing in Great Britain as they do in the United States. In the United States, when we say "a million," "a billion," and "a trillion," we mean these numbers:

1 million = 1,000,000
1 billion = 1,000,000,000
1 trillion = 1,000,000,000,000

In Great Britain, a million is 1,000,000, as it is in the United States, but a billion is 1,000,000,000,000—the number we call a trillion. And a trillion is 1,000,000,000,000,000,000.

In this problem, you will try to imagine a million, a billion, and a trillion as collections of unit cubes. To start, you can line up ten unit cubes to form a *long*. You can then put ten longs together to make a *flat*.

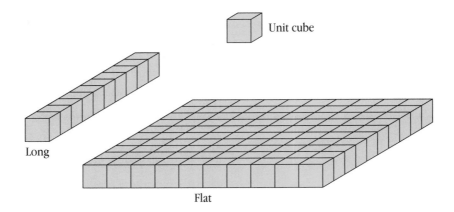

Problem 4.2

A. How many unit cubes are needed to make one *flat*?

B. You can stack ten flats to make a *super cube*. How many unit cubes are needed to make a super cube?

C. You can line up ten super cubes to make a *super long*. How many unit cubes are needed to make a super long?

D. You can put together ten super longs to make a *super flat*. How many unit cubes are needed to make a super flat?

E. You can put together ten super flats to make a *super-duper cube*. How many unit cubes are needed to make a super-duper cube?

■ Problem 4.2 Follow-Up

1. How many unit cubes would it take to build a *super-duper long* (made of ten super-duper cubes)? What are the dimensions of a super-duper long?

2. How many unit cubes would it take to build a *super-duper flat* (made of ten super-duper longs)? What are the dimensions of a super-duper flat?

3. How many unit cubes would it take to build an *extra-super-duper cube* (made of ten super-duper flats)? What are the dimensions of an extra-super-duper cube?

4. Which of the super, super-duper, or extra-super-duper arrangements contain more than a million unit cubes? More than a billion unit cubes? More than a trillion unit cubes?

4.3 Using Scientific Notation

Numbers used in scientific work are
often very large. For example, there are
about 33,400,000,000,000,000,000,000
molecules in 1 gram of water. There
are about 25,000,000,000,000 red
blood cells in a human body. According
to the big bang theory in astronomy,
our universe began with an explosion
18,000,000,000 years ago, generating
temperatures of 100,000,000,000° Celsius.

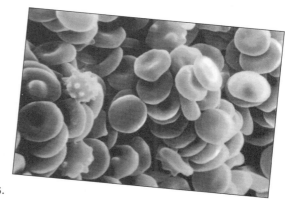

A calculator is a useful tool for working with large numbers. However, to use your
calculator effectively, you need to understand the special way it handles large numbers.

Think about this!

- Try entering 25,000,000,000,000 on your calculator. Does your calculator
  allow you to enter all the digits? If you are using a graphing calculator, press
  ENTER after you enter the number. What do you think the resulting
  display means?

- Use your calculator to find 500,000 × 500,000. What do you think the
  resulting display means?

- What does the $\boxed{\wedge}$ or $\boxed{y^x}$ key tell your calculator to do?

- Enter 10 $\boxed{\wedge}$ 5, 10 $\boxed{\wedge}$ 8, and 10 $\boxed{\wedge}$ 12 on your calculator (if you are
  using a nongraphing calculator, you will need to press 10 $\boxed{y^x}$ 5, 10 $\boxed{y^x}$ 8,
  and 10 $\boxed{y^x}$ 12). What do you think the resulting displays mean?

The product of 500,000 × 500,000 is 250,000,000,000. However, when you tried to
compute this product on your calculator, the display probably showed one of these
results:

$$\boxed{2.5\text{E}11} \qquad \text{or} \qquad \boxed{2.5 \quad 11}$$

Your calculator did not make a mistake. It was using a special notation.

To understand your calculator's notation, let's start by looking at a short way to write 100,000,000,000:

$$100{,}000{,}000{,}000 = 10 \times 10 \times 10 \times 10 \times 10 \times 10 \times 10 \times 10 \times 10 \times 10 \times 10$$
$$= 10^{11}$$

In the notation 10^{11}, 10 is the *base* and 11 is the *exponent.* The exponent tells you how many times the base is used as a factor.

We can use this short way of writing 100,000,000,000 to find a short way to write 250,000,000,000:

$$250{,}000{,}000{,}000 = 2.5 \times 100{,}000{,}000{,}000$$
$$= 2.5 \times 10^{11}$$

The number 2.5×10^{11} is written in scientific notation. A number is written in **scientific notation** if it is expressed in the following form:

a number greater than or equal to 1, but less than 10 $\times$ 10 raised to an exponent

Scientific notation looks a little different on a calculator. Your calculator was using scientific notation when it displayed

| 2.5E11 | or | 2.5   11 |

Both of these displays mean 2.5×10^{11}.

This example shows how you would use scientific notation to write 4,000,000:

$$4{,}000{,}000 = 4.0 \times 1{,}000{,}000$$
$$= 4.0 \times 10 \times 10 \times 10 \times 10 \times 10 \times 10$$
$$= 4.0 \times 10^{6}$$

How would your calculator display this number?

Problem 4.3

A. Write each number in standard notation.

1. 10^{22} **2.** 10^{13} **3.** 10^{11} **4.** 10^{10}

B. Write each number in a shorter form by using an exponent.

1. $10 \times 10 \times 10 \times 10 \times 10 \times 10 \times 10 \times 10 \times 10 \times 10 \times 10 \times 10$

2. 1,000,000

C. Write each number in standard notation.

1. 3.0×10^9 **2.** 2.5×10^{13} **3.** 1.75×10^{10}

D. Write each number in scientific notation.

1. 5,000,000   **2.** 18,000,000   **3.** 17,900,000,000

E. Experiment with your calculator to figure out how to get these displays. Then, write each number in both scientific and standard notation.

1. $\boxed{1.7E12}$ or $\boxed{1.7 \qquad 12}$

2. $\boxed{1.7E15}$ or $\boxed{1.7 \qquad 15}$

3. $\boxed{2.35E12}$ or $\boxed{2.35 \qquad 12}$

4. $\boxed{3.698E16}$ or $\boxed{3.698 \qquad 16}$

▪ Problem 4.3 Follow-Up

1. Look back at your answers for parts C and D of Problem 4.3. Compare the scientific notation for each number with the standard notation. What connections do you see between the two notations?

2. Write each of the following as a product of the base, without using an exponent.

a. 10^4 **b.** 10^7 **c.** 7^3

3. Describe how you would translate a number written in scientific notation, such as 4×10^{13} or 3.5×10^7, into standard notation.

4. Describe how you would translate a number written in standard notation, such as 32,000,000, into scientific notation.

5. Write 45,671,234,142 in scientific notation.

As you work on these ACE questions, use your calculator whenever you need it.

Applications

1. a. Is it possible for someone to be 1,000,000 minutes old? Explain.

   b. Is it possible for someone to be 1,000,000,000 minutes old? Explain.

2. How old would someone be if they were born 1,000,000 days ago?

3. A typical human heart beats about 70 times a minute.

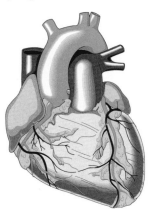

   a. How long does it take a heart to beat 1,000,000 times?

   b. How long does it take a heart to beat 1,000,000,000 times?

   c. How can you use your answers from parts a and b to figure out how long it takes a heart to beat 1000 times or 1,000,000,000,000 times?

4. a. How many times a million is a billion?

   b. How many times a million is a trillion?

   c. How many times a billion is a trillion?

5. The diameter of a penny is about 2 centimeters.

   a. How many pennies, laid side by side, would you need to make a line 1000 kilometers long? (Recall that 1 kilometer = 1000 meters and 1 meter = 100 centimeters.)

   b. The distance across the United States at its widest point is 3000 miles. How many pennies, laid side by side, would you need to span this distance? (Recall that 1 mile ≈ 1.6 kilometers.)

6. The population of the world is about 5,700,000,000. Write this number in scientific notation.

7. There are about 10,000,000,000 cells in the human brain. Write this number in scientific notation.

In 8–10, use the following table, which shows the monetary cost to the United States of four twentieth-century wars. The figures include the cost to fight the wars and the cost of veterans' benefits paid after the wars.

War	Cost (dollars)
World War I	6.3×10^{10}
World War II	4.48×10^{11}
Korean War	6.7×10^{10}
Vietnam War	1.67×10^{10}

Source: *The World Almanac and Book of Facts 1992*. New York: Pharos Books, 1991, p. 699.

8. Write the costs in standard notation.

9. Calculate the total cost of the four wars, and write the result in both scientific and standard notation.

10. Which war cost the most? Why do you think this war was the most expensive?

Connections

11. Recall that the *prime factorization* of a number is the factor string made up entirely of primes. One way to find the prime factorization of a number is to make a factor tree. The factor tree at right shows that the prime factorization of 20 is $2 \times 2 \times 5$, or $2^2 \times 5$.

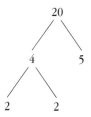

In a–f, write the prime factorization of the number using exponents.

a. 100 **b.** 1000 **c.** 10,000

d. 100,000 **e.** 1,000,000 **f.** 1,000,000,000

g. Look over the prime factorizations you found in parts a–f. What do you notice? Why do you think this happens?

12. In a–d, use what you discovered in question 11 to help you find the prime factorization of each number. Write the factorization using exponents.

    a. 900   **b.** 27,000

    c. 150,000   **d.** 24,000,000

13. In a–e, use what you discovered in questions 11 and 12 to find each product.

    a. $2^2 \times 3 \times 5^2$ **b.** $2^2 \times 5^3$ **c.** $2^4 \times 3^2 \times 5^3$

    d. $2^3 \times 5^4 \times 7$ **e.** $2^4 \times 3 \times 5^4 \times 7$

In 14–16, use the following table, which shows trends in the value of records, tapes, compact discs (CDs), and music videos sold from 1975 through 1990.

Music medium	Value (millions of dollars)			
	1975	1980	1985	1990
Albums	1485.0	2290.3	1280.5	86.5
Singles	211.5	269.3	281.0	94.4
Eight-track tapes	583.0	526.4	25.3	0
Cassettes	98.8	776.4	2411.5	3472.4
Cassette singles	0	0	0	257.9
Compact discs	0	0	389.5	3451.6
Music videos	0	0	0	172.3

Source: Recording Industry Association of America, as found in the *Statistical Abstract of the United States 1993.* Published by the Bureau of the Census, Washington, D.C., p. 250.

14. **a.** Find the total value of music sold in all media in 1975, and write the result in both scientific and standard notation.

    b. Find the total value of music sold in all media in 1990, and write the result in both scientific and standard notation.

    c. In a way that makes sense to you, compare the value of music sold in all media in 1990 with that sold in 1975.

15. Describe sales trends of various music media that would have helped an owner of a music store predict sales for 1995.

16. For each year, combine the data for albums and singles to get the value for all records, and combine the data for eight-track tapes, cassettes, and cassette singles to get the value for all audiotapes. Graph the data for records, audiotapes, and CDs on the same coordinate grid. Describe how the value of each medium changed from 1975 through 1990.

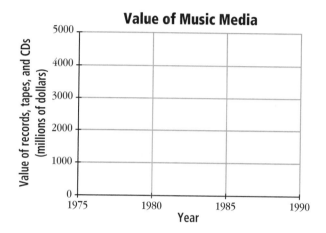

Extensions

17. a. Compute each product mentally.

i. 2000×300

ii. $2000 \times 30{,}000$

iii. 2500×3000

iv. $15{,}000 \times 50{,}000$

b. Describe the strategies you used to compute the products in part a. Can rewriting the factors in scientific notation help you do the mental calculations? If so, explain how.

In 18 and 19, consider the following information*: In the Northwest, some salmon species migrate up to 900 miles from the Pacific Ocean up rivers in the Columbia River basin to spawning streams to lay their eggs. During the 1950s, about 125,000 adult Snake River chinook salmon returned to their spawning streams in the spring and summer of each year. Because of factors such as dam and reservoir construction, the number of salmon that hatch in the spawning grounds, migrate to the ocean, and return to lay eggs has decreased significantly since the 1950s. During the 1980s, an average of 9600 adult Snake River chinook salmon returned to their spawning streams in the spring and summer of each year.

18. The table below gives the numbers of adult salmon that returned to their spawning streams each year from 1991 through 1994.

Year	Number of salmon
1991	3400
1992	3400
1993	7900
1994	1800

a. What is the mean number of adult salmon that returned each year from 1991 through 1994?

b. What is the average decrease in salmon per year from 1991 through 1994?

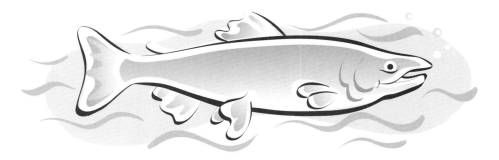

*Source: National Marine Fisheries Service

19. a. Two adult salmon produce about 4000 eggs, from which about 800 fry, or baby salmon, hatch. Of these 800 fry, about 200 smolts, or young salmon, survive to migrate to the ocean. What is the survival rate of salmon from eggs to young salmon that migrate to the ocean?

b. How many eggs must be laid to produce a migration of 1 million salmon to the ocean?

20. The table below gives population estimates for major regions of the world. Notice that the estimates are in millions.

Region	Population in 1995 (millions)
Africa	721
Asia	3403
North America	292
Latin America	481
Europe	807
Oceania	29

a. For each population estimate, tell what your calculator display would look like if you entered the number and pressed ENTER.

b. Find the difference between the population of Asia and the population of Africa in two ways: by using the numbers as shown in this table and by first writing the number in standard notation. Explain your results.

Mathematical Reflections

In this investigation, you developed a sense of how many a million, a billion, and a trillion are, and you learned how to use scientific notation to write large numbers. These questions will help you summarize what you have learned:

1. As you built or imagined larger and larger collections of unit cubes in Problem 4.2, you probably noticed some important connections between numbers.

    a. How many tens are in a hundred?

    b. How many hundreds are in a thousand?

    c. How many thousands are in a million?

    d. How many millions are in a billion?

    e. How many billions are in a trillion?

2. Describe how you can make sense of how many a million, a billion, or a trillion is.

3. When does your calculator display a number in scientific notation?

4. Describe a situation in which scientific notation may be useful.

Think about your answers to these questions, discuss your ideas with other students and your teacher, and then write a summary of your findings in your journal.

INVESTIGATION

Every Litter Bit Hurts

Sometimes data are reported as *totals*. In Investigation 3, you looked at the total number of people in 20 major metropolitan areas. At other times, data are given as *rates*. In Problem 3.4, you looked at the number of hogs per square mile. In this investigation, you will continue work with data given in both forms, and you will see how you can scale rate data to find useful information.

5.1 Going Hog Wild

In Problem 3.4, you looked at data for the 15 North Carolina counties that had the greatest 1993 hog populations. In this problem, you will work with the data from the top 5 counties.

County	1993 hog population	Growth from 1983	Hogs per square mile
Sampson	1,152,000	363%	1218
Duplin	1,041,000	349%	1273
Wayne	333,000	265%	603
Bladen	271,000	1178%	310
Greene	231,000	82%	870

Source: U.S. Department of Agriculture, as reported in the *Raleigh News and Observer,* 19–26 February 1995.

Did you know?

- Hogs are one of the most intelligent domesticated animals.
- Hogs have no sweat glands and wallow in the mud to keep cool.
- Hogs weigh about 2.5 pounds at birth. When fully grown, boars (male hogs) may weigh more than 500 pounds.
- Hogs have very poor eyesight but a very keen sense of smell.
- Scientists believe that people began domesticating hogs about 8000 years ago.

Problem 5.1

Assume the growth of the hog populations continues at the rates given in the table for the ten years from 1993 to 2003.

A. Predict the number of hogs in each county at the end of the year 2003. Which counties will have over a million hogs?

B. Will the ranking of these five counties be the same in 2003 as it was in 1993? Explain your answer.

■ Problem 5.1 Follow-Up

A square mile is about 640 acres. Find the number of hogs per acre for each county in 1993.

5.2 Recycling Cans

Do you recycle your aluminum soft drink cans? You might think that recycling the small number of cans you use won't make a difference. But what if everyone reasoned this way?

Problem 5.2

A. Take a class survey, asking each student to estimate the number of soft drink cans he or she uses in a typical week. Make a line plot of the data, and find the mean and the median.

B. Estimate the number of cans used by all the students in your class in one day, one week, one month, and one year.

C. Estimate the number of cans used by all the students in your school in one day, one week, one month, and one year.

D. Estimate the number of cans used by all 260,000,000 Americans in one day, one week, one month, and one year.

■ Problem 5.2 Follow-Up

1. It takes about 20 soft drink cans to make 1 pound of recycled aluminum. There are 2000 pounds in a ton. Based on your estimates from Problem 5.2, how many tons of recycled aluminum would be produced each year if Americans recycled all their soft drink cans?

2. Every ton of recycled aluminum saves 4 tons of *bauxite,* the ore from which aluminum is made. Based on your estimates from Problem 5.2, how much bauxite would be saved each year if Americans recycled all their soft drink cans?

5.3 Going Down the Drain

In some countries, droughts make water very precious. In the Middle East and North Africa, water is always in short supply.

Do you leave the water running while you brush your teeth? It may seem that this would not waste much water. In this problem you will investigate how these small amounts of water can add up.

Problem 5.3

A. Time yourself as you brush your teeth, and record the total brushing time. Then, let the water run from the faucet into a large pan for 10 seconds. Use a measuring cup to find the amount of water collected. Use these data to figure out how much water you would use if you let the water run while you brushed your teeth.

B. Collect the data for the entire class on the board, and then find the average amount of water used per student.

C. Suppose everyone let the water run while brushing their teeth. Estimate the amount of water used by your class for toothbrushing in a typical year. Assume each student brushes twice a day. Extend your estimate to find the amount of water that would be used yearly by all 260,000,000 Americans just for toothbrushing.

■ **Problem 5.3 Follow-Up**

Estimate the amount of water you would save if you used only enough water to wet and rinse your toothbrush and to rinse your mouth after brushing. Compare this figure with the "let it run" estimate you made in part A.

5.4 Making Mountains out of Molehills

Soft drink cans are only part of the American trash-disposal problem. Families, businesses, and factories produce many other waste materials. In 1988, the U.S. government estimated that the waste from American households and small businesses or industries, called *municipal waste,* amounts to about 4 pounds per person per day.* This may not seem like much, but remember, there are about 260 million Americans!

Problem 5.4

Suppose municipal waste could be compacted into cubes measuring 1 foot on each edge. Each such cube would be composed of about 50 pounds of waste.

If all the municipal waste collected from American homes, businesses, and industries were pressed into 1-foot waste cubes, how many cubes would be produced in just one day?

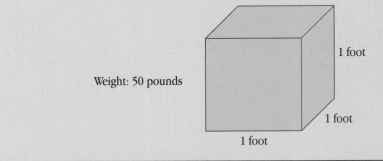

Weight: 50 pounds

1 foot
1 foot
1 foot

■ **Problem 5.4 Follow-Up**

Would the waste cubes produced by Americans in one day fit in your classroom? In your school?

*Source: *Facing America's Trash: What's Next for Municipal Solid Waste?* U.S. Congress OTA. Washington, D.C.: U.S. Government Printing Office, 1989.

As you work on these ACE questions, use your calculator whenever you need it.

Applications

In 1–4, use the following facts about recycling.*

- People in the United States use about 50 million tons of paper, made from 850 million trees, every year.

- The average household throws away 13,000 pieces of paper each year. Most is packaging and junk mail.

- The Sunday papers published in the United States each week use pulp from 500,000 trees. The *New York Times* alone requires paper from 75,000 trees per week to meet the demands of its Sunday publication.

1. a. How many pounds of paper are used in the United States every year? (Recall that 1 ton = 2000 pounds.)

    b. What is the average number of pounds of paper used per American each year? (Remember, there are about 260 million Americans.)

    c. On average, how many pounds of paper are made from one tree?

    d. How many trees does it take to make the paper used per American in a year?

2. The 260 million Americans live in 97 million households.

    a. What is the average number of people in an American household?

    b. How many pieces of paper are thrown away per American in a year?

3. a. How many trees are used in one year to make the newsprint for all American Sunday papers?

    b. How many trees are used in one year to make the newsprint for just the Sunday *New York Times*?

*Source: Rebecca Stefoff. *Recycling.* New York: Chelsea House, 1991.

Connections

4. Below is a table of data from a middle school class showing the water used by each student in one week.

Students' Water Use

Student initials	Gallons per student
RE	380
TW	420
HW	299
WE	334
GK	266
DJ	218
MJ	246
WD	246
MA	241
LR	206
FP	247
HA	197
TB	313
CH	188
ME	231
JW	228
PR	211
NP	273
BH	202
EB	189
PJ	182
HJ	160
HM	185
JZ	247

a. What is the median number of gallons of water used in a week by each student? Use this information to estimate the total number of gallons of water used by all 260,000,000 Americans in a week.

b. What is the mean number of gallons of water used in a week by each student? Use this information to estimate the total number of gallons of water used by all 260,000,000 Americans in a week.

c. How do the mean and median number of gallons used per student compare? Why do you think this is so? How did the difference between the mean and the median affect the estimates you made of the weekly use of water by all 260,000,000 Americans?

5. Rabies is a dangerous disease that can infect people and animals. Since 1990, rabies has been found in large numbers of raccoons in the eastern United States. In two counties in New Jersey, the cost of rabies prevention rose from $768,488 in 1988 to $1,952,014 in 1990. In New York State, the number of suspected rabies cases in animals rose from 3000 in 1989 to 12,000 in 1993.

In Europe, rabies in foxes has been controlled by mixing vaccine with bait and leaving the bait for the foxes to eat. In Europe, about 75 million vaccine doses were distributed from 1978 through 1994. Because this method was so successful, it is now being tried with raccoons in the United States.*

a. What was the percent change in the cost of rabies prevention from 1988 to 1990 for the two New Jersey counties mentioned above?

b. On average, how many vaccine doses were distributed per year in Europe from 1978 through 1994?

c. It takes 260 vaccine doses per square mile of land for the vaccine to be effective. If these guidelines were followed in Europe, about how many square miles of land were dosed per year?

*Source: C. E. Ruprecht, et al., "The Ascension of Wildlife Rabies: A Cause for Public Health Concern or Intervention?" *Emerging Infectious Diseases* 1, no. 4 (1995).

In 6–8, use the following table, which gives information about municipal solid waste produced in six U.S. cities.

Municipal Solid Waste in U.S. Cities, 1989

City	Kilograms per day	Kilograms per day per person
Austin, Texas	4.4×10^5	0.9
Chicago, Illinois	5.5×10^6	1.8
Chattanooga, Tennessee	7.1×10^5	4.3
Hamburg, New York	9.9×10^3	0.9
San Jose, California	1.6×10^6	2.2
Yakima, Washington	4.1×10^4	0.9

Source: *Facing America's Trash: What's Next for Municipal Solid Waste?* U.S. Congress OTA. Washington, D.C.: U.S. Government Printing Office, 1989.

6. a. Rank the cities according to the number of kilograms of solid waste produced each day.

b. Rank the cities according to the amount of solid waste produced per person each day.

c. Which measure of solid waste produced seems better for comparing the cities? Explain your choice.

7. Write each amount from the "Kilograms per day" column in standard notation and in words.

8. Estimate the population of each city.

Extensions

In 9 and 10, use the following information: Some of the natural resources we depend on, such as trees and water, are renewable or naturally recycled. Others, such as oil, coal, and gas, are not renewable. Some scientists are urging countries that use natural resources heavily to begin programs of conservation. The table on the following page shows 1989 oil consumption in seven major industrial countries.

1989 Oil Consumption

Country	Oil consumed (barrels)
Britain (England, Scotland, Wales)	6.34×10^8
Canada	6.431×10^8
France	6.774×10^8
West Germany	8.315×10^8
Italy	7.081×10^8
Japan	1.818×10^9
United States	6.324×10^9

9. What do you think is the best way to compare the oil consumption of the United States with the oil consumption of the other countries? Explain your choice.

10. a. A barrel of oil holds 42 gallons. For each country listed, calculate the oil consumption in gallons.

b. Find the 1989 populations of the listed countries in an atlas or almanac. Use this information to find the number of gallons of oil consumed per person in 1989 for each country.

c. Using your answer to part b, find the daily oil consumption per person for each country in 1989.

d. Compare the rate of oil consumption in the United States to the rates in the other countries. Explain any differences you find.

Mathematical Reflections

In this investigation, you explored data given both as totals and as rates. For example, in Problem 5.1, you worked with the total hog population and with the number of hogs per square mile. These questions will help you summarize what you have learned:

1 Look back over the problems in this and other investigations.

   a. Find examples of data that are expressed as totals and examples of data that are expressed as rates.

   b. When you rank a set of data, does it make a difference whether you use the totals or the rates? Explain.

2 a. If you are given a total for some group of people or time period, how do you calculate a rate per person or per shorter time period?

   b. If you are given a per-person rate or per-time-period rate, how do you calculate the total for a whole group or for a longer time period?

Think about your answers to these questions, discuss your ideas with other students and your teacher, and then write a summary of your findings in your journal.

INVESTIGATION 6

On an Average Day

Natural disasters and human catastrophes make the headlines in newspapers and on television and radio news broadcasts. But for a majority of people most days are "average" days. In this investigation, you will look at some interesting facts about average days.

The book *On an Average Day in Japan** compares life in the United States with life in Japan. The book contains lots of data about life in the two countries, and you can discover even more information by doing a little arithmetic. Note that this information was collected when the population of the United States was 250,000,000.

6.1 Recycling Cans

On an average day in Japan, about 52,055,000 aluminum cans are used. Japan's population of 123 million people recycles 34,356,000 of those cans. In the United States, which has a population of 250 million people, about 93,310,000 aluminum cans are used on an average day, and about half of them are recycled.

Problem 6.1

A. How many aluminum cans are *not* recycled in Japan on an average day?

B. How many aluminum cans are *not* recycled in the United States on an average day?

C. In an average week, how many aluminum cans are used in each country? How many cans are recycled?

■ Problem 6.1 Follow-Up

A standard aluminum can is about 12 centimeters tall. If all the cans used in Japan on an average day were stacked in a tower, how tall would the tower be in centimeters? In meters? In kilometers?

*Tom Heyman. *On an Average Day in Japan.* New York: Fawcett Columbine, 1992.

6.2 Making Comparisons in Two Ways

There are 250 million people in the United States and 123 million people in Japan. The population of the United States is clearly greater than the population of Japan, but how can you describe how much greater?

You could compare the populations by finding a difference. Since $250 - 123 = 127$, the population of the United States is about 127 million greater than the population of Japan.

You could also compare the populations by figuring out how many times greater the population of the United States is. Since the population of Japan is close to 125 million, and since $250 = 2 \times 125$ (or, equivalently, $250 \div 125 = 2$), the population of the United States is about two times the population of Japan.

Problem 6.2

The following statements give information about life in Japan and the United States. In each case, compare the data for the countries in the two ways described above, and decide which comparison better explains the similarities or differences.

A. The average Japanese child spends 275 hours each year playing sports and games. The average American child spends 550 hours each year in these activities.

B. The average American has $10,000 in savings accounts. The average Japanese has about $40,000 saved.

C. On an average day, Japanese children spend 7 hours in school, and American children spend 5 hours 25 minutes in school.

D. The average American makes 200 telephone calls each month. The average Japanese makes 45 calls each month.

E. On an average day, 40% of Japanese use public transportation, while fewer than 4% of Americans do.

■ Problem 6.2 Follow-Up

What are some reasons people in the United States and Japan might differ in the ways described in the problem?

6.3 **Comparing by Using Rates**

What is the message in the following statement about photography in Japan and the United States?

> Japanese take 714,500,000 pictures every month, and Americans take 1,250,200,000 pictures every month.

You might conclude that Americans take many more pictures than do Japanese, but remember that the population of the United States is about twice that of Japan.

One way to make a fair comparison in this kind of situation is to calculate a *rate*. In this case, you could find the number of pictures taken per person. In Japan, this rate is as follows:

> 714,500,000 pictures ÷ 123,000,000 people ≈ 6 pictures per person

In the United States, this rate is as follows:

> 1,250,200,000 pictures ÷ 250,000,000 people ≈ 5 pictures per person

This comparison tells a different story than does the total number of pictures. Although the number of pictures taken in the United States is greater than the number of pictures taken in Japan, Japanese take more pictures per person.

Problem 6.3

The table below gives some data about smoking in the United States and Japan.

Country	Population	Smokers	Total cigarettes smoked each day
United States	250,000,000	55,000,000	1,437,315,000
Japan	123,000,000	33,000,000	849,315,000

A. Compare the number of smokers in the two countries in as many ways as you can. Which comparison do you believe is best?

B. Compare the number of cigarettes smoked each day in the two countries in as many ways as you can. Which comparison do you believe is best?

■ **Problem 6.3 Follow-Up**

Would you say that smoking is more widespread in the United States or in Japan? Explain your reasoning.

As you work on these ACE questions, use your calculator whenever you need it.

Applications

In 1–4, compare the given measurements in two ways, and tell which of the two comparisons you think is better.*

1. The tallest man in medical history is Robert Wadlow, who was measured at 8 feet 11 inches (272 centimeters) shortly before his death in 1940. The shortest adult in history is Gul Mohammed of Delhi, India. In 1990, he was measured at $22\frac{1}{2}$ inches (57 centimeters).

2. The heaviest person in medical history is Jon Minnoch, who reached a weight of 1387 pounds (630 kilograms). Minnoch's wife weighed 110 pounds (50 kilograms).

3. In 1960, the U.S. navy submarine *Triton* traveled around the world in 84 days 19 hours. In 1986, Richard Rutan and Jeana Yeager became the first aviators to fly around the world without refueling, taking 9 days 3 minutes 44 seconds.

4. The largest hamburger on record was made at a county fair in Wisconsin in 1989. It weighed 5520 pounds (2509 kilograms) and had a diameter of 21 feet (6.4 meters). The largest pizza was baked at a market in South Africa in 1990. It had a diameter of 122 feet 8 inches (37.4 meters) and an area of 11,818 square feet (1098 square meters).

5. A NASA space shuttle travels about 30,000 kilometers per hour.

    a. How far will the shuttle travel in one day?

    b. How long would it take the shuttle to travel to the moon and back, a distance of about 400,000 kilometers each way?

*Source: *Guinness Book of Records 1994.* Ed. Peter Matthews. New York: Bantam Books, 1994.

6. A typical human heart beats about 70 times per minute.

    a. How many times does a typical heart beat in an hour?

    b. How many times does a typical heart beat in a day?

    c. How many times does a typical heart beat in a year?

7. There are about 3,225,000 12-year-olds in the United States.

    a. About how many Americans will celebrate their thirteenth birthday each day of the coming year?

    b. How many candles will be needed for all Americans who celebrate their thirteenth birthdays this year if each person has a cake with 13 candles?

    c. If there are 24 candles per box, how many boxes of candles will be needed for all the thirteenth-birthday cakes this year?

8. On an average day, Americans spend $945,111,233 for food.

    a. How much is this per person per day?

    b. How much is this per person per year?

Connections

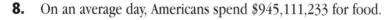

9. Reports from the Soviet Union, just before it broke into smaller countries in 1991, claimed that on an average day about 70 million Soviet citizens smoked cigarettes at a rate of three cigarettes per smoker.* How many cigarettes were smoked on an average day in the former Soviet Union?

*Source: Tom Heymann. *On an Average Day in the Soviet Union.* New York: Fawcett Columbine, 1990.

10. Health researchers estimate that 3 million Americans under age 18 smoke on a daily basis, averaging about 18 cigarettes per smoker per day. How many cigarettes are smoked by Americans under the age of 18 each day in the United States?

11. The table below gives the population and land area in 1992 for nine countries.

Country	Estimated population	Land area (km^2)
Brazil	150,800,000	8,511,957
Canada	27,400,000	9,976,136
France	56,900,000	547,033
Haiti	6,400,000	27,739
India	882,600,000	3,287,591
Nigeria	90,100,000	923,775
People's Republic of China	1,165,800,000	9,596,960
Russia	149,300,000	17,075,352
United States	255,600,000	9,363,109

Source: *1992 World Population Data Sheet* of the Population Reference Bureau, Inc.

a. Write each number in the table in scientific notation.

b. Write the numbers for the least and greatest populations in words.

c. Write the numbers for the least and greatest land areas in words.

d. When comparing two numbers, is it most useful to write the numbers in standard notation, scientific notation, or words? Explain your answer.

e. Divide each population by the corresponding land area to get the population per square kilometer. Then, order the countries by these population densities.

Extensions

12. Try to guess which state in the United States has the greatest population density and which state has the least population density. Then, look up population and land area data in an atlas or other source to check your guesses.

13. If you know the population density and land area for a country, state, or city, how can you calculate the population?

In 14–16, tell why the given conclusion is misleading, and explain how you could arrive at a better conclusion.

14. On an average day, about 300 Japanese students and about 900 American students drop out of school. *Misleading conclusion:* American students are three times more likely to drop out of school than Japanese students are.

15. On an average day, Japanese people make 200 million telephone calls, and Americans make 1800 million calls. *Misleading conclusion:* Americans make about nine times more phone calls each day than do Japanese.

16. On an average day, 10,726,000 Japanese travel by subway, and 6,323,000 Americans travel by subway. *Misleading conclusion:* About 1.7 times more Japanese travel by subway than do Americans.

17. Use the following newspaper article to answer a–d.

PROBE REACHES JUPITER FOR FIRST CLOSE-UP CONTACT WITH PLANET

After traveling over six years and more than 2,300,000,000,000 miles through space on a data-gathering mission, the *Galileo* spacecraft finally arrived at the planet Jupiter on December 7, 1995. The craft was released from the space shuttle *Atlantis* on October 18, 1989.

A space probe released from *Galileo* on July 13, 1995, slowed from its speed of 106,000 miles per hour as it entered Jupiter's atmosphere, beaming data to the waiting *Galileo* orbiting 133,000 miles above. The spacecraft relayed this infor-mation back to Earth, where scientists received the transmissions roughly 50 minutes after they were sent—the amount of time it takes radio signals to travel the 400,000,000 miles between Jupiter and our planet.

The largest planet in our solar system, Jupiter has a diameter of 88,000 miles, roughly 11 times that of Earth. An average distance of a half a billion miles from the sun, Jupiter takes almost 12 Earth years to make one complete circuit around the sun.

The mass of Earth is 600,588,000,000, 000,000,000,000 short tons. This mass is read as 600 sextillion, 588 quintillion short tons. One short ton is 2000 pounds. ■

a. Find the average number of miles per day traveled by the *Galileo* spacecraft. How many miles per hour is this?

b. At what rate do radio signals travel between Jupiter and Earth? At this rate, how long would it take to send a signal to a spacecraft 1.9×10^{15} miles away?

c. Write some statements comparing Earth to Jupiter using information from this article.

d. Do you think that Jupiter's mass is 11 times Earth's mass? Why?

Mathematical Reflections

In this investigation, you continued to study data given as totals and as rates. You used ideas from *Comparing and Scaling* to make meaningful comparisons between the United States and Japan. These questions will help you summarize what you have learned:

1 Look back at your work from this and other investigations. Describe the methods you used to compare two or more numbers.

2 In a school fund-raiser, students at Hilltop Middle School sold calendars to their friends and families.

    a. Sales for the sixth grade were $500, sales for the seventh grade were $625, and sales for the eighth grade were $1000. If you were to write a story about the sale for the school paper, what comparison statements could you make on the basis of these data?

    b. At Hilltop, there are 100 sixth graders, 125 seventh graders, and 100 eighth graders. How would you adjust your statements from part a on the basis of this information?

3 How do you decide which method for comparing data is best in a given situation?

Think about your answers to these questions, discuss your ideas with other students and your teacher, and then write a summary of your findings in your journal.

Unit Reflections

The problems of this unit extended your understanding and skills in practical use of numbers and operations. You learned ways to *compare counts* and *measurements* in a variety of situations and how to work with very large and very small numbers. You developed skill in use of *place value* and *exponents* for *standard, scientific,* and *calculator number notation.*

Using Your Number Sense—To test your number sense, consider several important problem situations that require the ideas and strategies of numerical literacy.

1 *Here is a short newspaper report about flooding that occurred in parts of the midwestern United States in March of 1997. These eight numbers are missing:* 25; 60,000; 12; 26; 900; 38.8; 6; and 250,000,000.

> Record flooding has chased residents from their homes and killed ___(1)___ people. Ninety-nine counties in ___(2)___ states have been declared disaster areas following fierce weather that swept through the region. The Ohio River crested about ___(3)___ feet above normal levels in Louisville, Kentucky. Normal river levels at this time of year are about ___(4)___ feet, but Friday's high point was ___(5)___ feet. Guardsmen built ___(6)___-foot-long dikes using about ___(7)___ sandbags. Officials estimate the waters have caused $___(8)___ in damage in Kentucky alone.

a. Match the missing numbers with the blanks in the story where you think they fit best.

b. Which numbers in the story do you think were estimates and which were probably determined from actual counts or measurements?

2 *According to the National Hurricane Center, from 1990–1996 there were 158 hurricanes. Hurricanes are categorized using the Saffir-Simpson Hurricane Scale, which gives a 1–5 rating based on the hurricane's intensity. Of the 158 storms,*

- *57 were category 1 (winds 74–95 mph with storm surge 3–5 feet above normal);*
- *37 were category 2 (winds 96–110 mph with storm surge 6–8 feet above normal);*

- *47 were category 3 (winds 111–130 mph with storm surge 9–12 feet above normal);*
- *15 were category 4 (winds 131–155 mph with storm surge 13–18 feet above normal);*
- *2 were category 5 (winds greater than 155 mph with storm surge greater than 18 feet above normal).*

a. One equivalent measure is 1 mile ≈ 1.61 kilometers. For each of the five hurricane categories, write the ranges for wind speeds in km/h (kilometers per hour).

b. Another equivalent measure is 1 inch = 2.54 centimeters. For each of the five hurricane categories, write the ranges for storm surges in meters.

3 *Three of the most destructive hurricanes and the cost of damages each caused are listed.*

- *Andrew: 1992, category 4; $26,500,000,000*
- *Hugo: 1989, category 4; $7,000,000,000*
- *Fran: 1998, category 3; $3,200,000,000*

a. Write the cost of damages for each of the storms in scientific notation.

b. Compare the costs of the damages for the three storms in two ways and explain your choice for the better of the two comparison strategies.

   i. by calculating the difference in costs for each pair

   ii. by calculating the ratio of costs for each pair

c. Several numbers are used to measure the severity of hurricanes. Which numbers do you think are estimates and which are determined by actual measurements?

   i. ranges of wind speeds

   ii. ranges of storm surges

   iii. costs for repair of storm damage

4 *The population in the United States includes people who are immigrants from many countries. The table on page 72 gives information about immigration by decade from 1901 to 1997.*

U.S. Immigration: 1901–1997		
Period in Years	Number in thousands	Rate per 1000 U.S. Population
1901–1910	8795	10.4
1911–1920	5736	5.7
1921–1930	4107	3.5
1931–1940	528	0.4
1941–1950	1035	0.7
1951–1960	2515	1.5
1961–1970	3322	1.7
1971–1980	4493	2.1
1981–1990	7338	3.1
1991–1997	6945	3.8

Source: Statistical Abstract of the United States 1999 (page 10)

a. Write the number of people who immigrated during each period in standard notation.

b. Write each number of immigrants in scientific notation.

c. Which data would you suggest for ordering the decades for which immigration records are available from greatest to least: (1) the number in thousands; or (2) the rate per 1000 U.S. population?

Explaining Your Reasoning—Making sense of the numbers that occur in real-life problems requires careful reasoning. You need to be able to justify the use of estimates and exact counts or measurements, notation for large and small numbers, and strategies for comparing numbers.

1. How do you decide when a number reported in a story is an estimate and when it must be an exact count or measurement?

2. What is the value of using scientific notation? Explain, with illustrative examples, the procedures for using scientific notation to write very large numbers.

3. Very large numbers are often rounded in order to make them easier to read. Explain, with illustrative examples, general procedures for rounding

    a. numbers that are greater than a million to the nearest thousand.

    b. numbers that are greater than a billion to the nearest million.

4. Give examples that illustrate situations when it makes sense to compare two measurements or counts by finding

    a. the difference of the two numbers.

    b. the ratio of the two numbers.

Glossary

benchmark A handy reference point to help in understanding the magnitude of other numbers. When working with decimals or fractions, we sometimes use whole numbers and halves as benchmarks, rounding the decimals or fractions to the nearest half. Benchmarks can help us to make sense of the magnitude of a very large number. If the *Exxon Valdez* disaster cost $20,000,000,000 to clean up and the average annual pay for a U.S. worker is $25,000, looking at the number of annual salaries required to pay the cleanup bill can help us to understand the magnitude of this cost. In this example, $25,000 is used as a benchmark.

customary system A complex measurement system that originated primarily in the British empire and includes the units of measure inch, yard, pound, and gallon. The system was in use in the United States from the nation's beginnings and is still used today in many situations. In commercial and scientific applications, the metric system is becoming more and more common.

metric system, international system of measurement, SI system A measurement system used throughout the world that is based on the powers of 10. The basic units of length, volume, and mass are the meter, liter, and gram, respectively.

million, billion, trillion The numbers 1,000,000 (or 10^6), 1,000,000,000 (or 10^9), and 1,000,000,000,000 (or 10^{12}), respectively.

scientific notation A short way to write very large or very small numbers. A number written in scientific notation is expressed in this form:

a number greater than or equal to 1 but less than 10 $\times$ 10 raised to an exponent

standard notation The most common form of written numbers. For example, 254 is the standard notation for 2 hundreds, 5 tens, and 4 ones.

Index

Accuracy
  ACE, 9–11
  of reported numbers, 5–8
  of rounded numbers, 28

Base, in scientific notation, 42
Benchmarks, for measurement, 4,
  14–15
Billion, 23, 39–40

Calculator, scientific notation on,
  41–43
Comparing data, 4, 5–8, 12–18, 61–63
  ACE, 9–11, 19–21, 64–68
Comparing large numbers, 4, 23–30,
  61–63
  ACE, 31–36, 64–68
Comparing rates, 29–30, 63
Conversion, between customary and
  metric units, 15
Customary system, 14
  conversion to metric system, 15

Dialing Digits game, 24–25

Estimate
  ACE, 9–11
  identifying, 5–8
  methods of determining, 5–8
Estimation
  ACE, 19–21, 55–59, 64–68

  using benchmarks, 16–18
  using rates, 51–54, 63
  using totals, 51–54, 61–63
Exponent, in scientific notation, 42
Exxon Valdez, 12–18

Growth, rate of, 51–54
Hog facts, 27, 29, 51

Investigation
  Comparing Large Numbers, 23–37
  Every Litter Bit Hurts, 51–60
  How Many is a Million?, 38–50
  Interpreting Disaster Reports, 5–11
  Measuring Oil Spills, 12–22
  On an Average Day, 61–69

Journal, 11, 22, 37, 50, 60, 69

Large numbers
  billion, 23, 39–40
  comparing, 23–30
  million, 23, 38–43
  modeling, 39–40
  operations with, 5–8, 51–54, 61–63
  ordering, 25–27
  scientific notation and, 41–43
  sense of, 16–18
  trillion, 23, 39–40
  writing, 23
Looking Back and Looking Ahead:
  Unit Reflections, 70–72

Mass, 15

Mathematical Highlights, 4

Mathematical Reflections, 11, 22, 37, 50, 60, 69

Measurement systems, 14

Metric system, 14
conversion to customary system, 15

Million, 23, 38–43

Operations
ACE, 9–10, 55–59, 64–68
with large numbers, 5–8, 51–54, 61–63

Ordering, large numbers, 25–27

Place-value, 23–30

Prediction
ACE, 55–59, 64–68
using rates, 51–54, 63
using totals, 51–54, 61–63

Prime factorization, 45

Ranking, by size, 26–27

Rates
ACE, 35–36, 55–59, 64–68
comparing, 4, 29–30, 63
data expressed as, 29–30, 51–54, 61–63
of growth, 51–54

Rounding, 4, 28

Scientific notation, 41–43
ACE, 40–49

Standard notation, 23
scientific notation and, 41–43

Totals
ACE, 31–36, 55–59, 64–68
data expressed as, 23–30, 51–54, 61–63

Trillion, 23, 39–40

Units of measure, 14
benchmarks for, 14–15
types of, 12–18

Weight, 15